Nelson's Annual

Preacher's Sourcebook

2007 EDITION

Nelson's Annual Preacher's Sourcebook

2007 EDITION

ROBERT J. MORGAN, EDITOR

NELSON REFERENCE & ELECTRONIC
A Division of Thomas Nelson Publishers
Since 1798

www.thomasnelson.com

Published in Nashville, Tennessee, by Thomas Nelson, Inc.

Published in association with the literary agency of Alive Communica-tions, 7680 Goddard Street, Suite 200, Colorado Springs, CO 80920.

Unless otherwise indicated, Scripture quotations are from the New King James Version of the Bible, © 1979, 1980, 1982, 1990, Thomas Nelson, Inc., Publishers.

Verses marked "NIV" are taken from the Holy Bible: New International Version, copyright © 1973, 1978, 1984 by the International Bible Soci-ety. Used by permission of Zondervan Publishing House. All rights reserved.

Typesetting by ProtoType Graphics, Inc., Nashville, Tennessee.

Morgan, Robert J. (ed.)
    Nelson's annual preacher's sourcebook, 2007 edition.

ISBN 1-4185-0134-4

Printed in the United States of America

1 2 3 4 5 6 7 — 10 09 08 07 06

Contents

Introduction and Acknowledgments   *xi*

Editor's Preface   *xiii*

Create a Sermon Series!   *xix*

Contributors   *xxi*

2007 Calendar   *xxvii*

Sermons and Worship Suggestions for 52 Weeks   1

January 7   *Spiritual Exercise in the New Year*   2
Hebrews 12:1–3

January 14   *Who Is on My Side?*   8
Job 19:1–29

January 21   *Anger*   16
Ephesians 4:26–27

January 28   *The Fear of the Lord*   25
Proverbs 1:1–7; 3:1–8

February 4   *Father Forgive Them*   34
Luke 23:34

February 11   *Searching for a Spouse*   44
Genesis 24:1–27

February 18   *Someone's Here to Help You*   53
Hebrews 2:17—3:1

February 25   *How to Treat Your Neighbor*   64
Proverbs 3:27–30

March 4   *When a Husband Loves His Wife*   72
Ephesians 5:25–29; Colossians 3:19; 1 Peter 3:7

March 11   *The State of Joyful Living*   78
Psalm 84

March 18   *More Than a Song: A Fresh Vision for Worship*   86
John 4:19–24

March 25   *The Devil's Devices*   92
2 Corinthians 11:14

April 1   *The Great Betrayal*   100
Matthew 26:17–25

April 8   *How Jesus Gives Us a Peace of His Mind*   106
Luke 24:36–49

April 15   *Living in Christ, with Christ, through Christ*   112
John 15:1–11

April 22   *The Power of the Cross*   120
1 Corinthians 1:18—2:5

April 29   *Stones of Adversity*   126
Deuteronomy 4:27–31

May 6   *Dealing with Deception*   134
1 John 2:21

May 13   *The Importance of Mothers and Grandmothers*   144
2 Timothy 1:1–7

May 20   *All Things Work Together for Good*   153
Romans 8:28

May 27   *Spirit Filled*   163
Ephesians 5:15–20

June 3   *What Authentic Conversion Looks Like*   169
Luke 19:1–10

June 10   *Bring the Joy Back!*   179
John 15:11; Galatians 5:22–23

June 17   *Walking with Christ: A Fresh Vision*
for Discipleship   187
Colossians 2:6–7; Ephesians 4:11–13

June 24   *The Mysteries of His Love and the*
Testing of Our Faith   196
John 11:1–27

July 1   *Divine Direction*   205
Genesis 24:26–67

July 8   *The Seriousness of Sin*   212
Romans 6:23

July 15   *Down a Mine Shaft*   218
Exodus 40:43—Leviticus 1:1

July 22   *Husbands and Wives*   227
I Peter 3:1–7

July 29   *Ripe for Judgment*   233
Amos 8:1–14

August 5   *Speech*   240
Ephesians 4:29

August 12   *Partnership*   251
I John 1:1–8

August 19   *The Spectrum of Salvation*   262
Romans 1:16

August 26   *Life Lessons from a Flawed Hero*   269
I Kings 3:1–3, 11:1–6

September 2   *How to Survive a Lion's Attack*   277
I Peter 5:8–10

September 9   *Who's to Blame When Towers Fall?*   283
Luke 13:1–8

September 16   *The Appeal of Wisdom*   289
Proverbs 8:1–11; 32–33

September 23   *I Need Help with My Finances*   297
I Timothy 6:3–19

September 30   *Training Yourself for Life*   305
I Timothy 4:6–10

October 7   *Dealing with Dishonesty*   311
2 Corinthians 4:2

October 14   *Work*   317
Ephesians 4:28

October 21   *When Life Doesn't Seem Fair*   326
Psalm 73:1–28

October 28   *The Word of Life Revealed*   333
I John 1:1–4

November 4   *I Believe in Jesus*   339
John 1:1–16

November 11   *Cultivating Spiritual Hunger*   347
Matthew 5:6

November 18   *Wisdom's Protection Plan*   *354*
Proverbs 2:11–22

November 25   *A Fresh Look at John 3:16*   *363*
John 3:16

December 2   *A Greater Than Solomon*   *370*
Luke 11:31

December 9   *He's My Son Too!*   *376*
Matthew 1:18–25

December 16   *You CAN Miss It!*   *382*
Luke 2:4–7; Matthew 2:1–12

December 23   *Prepare the Way . . . with Receptivity!*   *388*
Luke 2:8–20

December 31   *The Danger of Finishing Badly*   *394*
1 Kings 3, 10:23—11:13

Wedding Messages
Garden Enclosed, A   *400*
Promise-Anchored Home, A   *404*

Funeral Messages
Appropriate for an Unexpectedly Tragic Situation   *415*
Departures and Arrivals   *408*
Mercy of God, The   *412*
Suitable for the Death of a Child, Baby,
    or Pre-born Infant   *410*

Subject Index   *443*

Scripture Index   *445*

SPECIAL FEATURES:

Special Occasion Sermons
Communion Sermon: Remember the Old Way:
    A Communion Meditation   *70*
Missions Sermon: The Missions Mandate   *118*
Patriotic Sermon: Do You Remember?   *160*
Sanctity of Life Sermon: Jesus Loves Me, This I Know!   *22*
Thanksgiving Sermon: How to Have a Great Attitude!   *360*
Youth Sermon: Sexual Purity   *150*

Classics for the Pastor's Library
Alleine's Alarm ... 295
Foxe's Book of Martyrs ... 132
Samuel Logan Brengle: Portrait of a Prophet ... 224
Scripture Promises ... 40

Conversations in the Pastor's Study
Keeping the Sound of Music in the Pastor's Soul ... 246
Pastoring When You Aren't Well ... 83
Pastor's Morning Devotions, The ... 303
Preaching that Connects ... 175

Helps for the Pastor's Family
Hit the Road, Jack: The Pastor's Family Vacation ... 193
When You're Worried about a Child ... 323

Heroes for the Pastor's Heart
Bowles, Rev. Charles ... 98
Lull, Raymond ... 353
Newton, John ... 185
Prudentius, Aurelius Clemens ... 14
Veitch, William and Marion and
    the Providence of God ... 275

Prayer for the Pastor's Closet
God's Word ... 159
Jesus, Thou Divine Companion ... 268
Patience for the Wayward ... 183

Quotes for the Pastor's Wall
Aaron, Hank ... 67
Bounds, Rev. E. M. ... 190
Brengle, Samuel Logan ... 60
Havner, Vance ... 215
Keller, Helen ... 95
Larson, David L. ... 129
Morgan, G. Campbell ... 43
Olford, Stephen ... 272
Scroggie, W. Graham ... 19
Shaw, George Bernard ... 137
Slade, Mary B. ... 300
Ward, William A. ... 103
Warner, Anna B. ... 379

Whitefield, George 115
Whyte, Alexander 89
Wiersbe, Warren W. 5

Special Services Registry
Baby Dedication Registration 434
Baptisms/Confirmations 432
Funeral Registration 438
Funerals Log 430
Marriages Log 428
Sermons Preached 421
Wedding Registration 436

Techniques for the Pastor's Delivery
Deep Breathing 345
Finding New Words for Old Truths:
    From Humdrum to Hallelujah 202
Impromptu Remarks 258
In the First Place . . . 50

Thoughts for the Pastor's Soul
Good Book for Worried Pastors, A 31
Holiness and Worry 61
Reading the Classics 141

Introduction and Acknowledgments

I can't preach a lick, but I keep trying my darned'est.

I don't typically use minced oaths, but I jotted those words in my Journal one Sunday after feeling I'd botched another sermon. Well, maybe not *botched;* but I left church with an all-too-familiar sinking feeling that despite my best efforts I wasn't a very good preacher.

Later, in my study, I turned at random to 2 Corinthians 10, and Paul's words stared up at me: "Some say (of me), 'His letters are weighty and forceful, but in person he is unimpressive and his speaking amounts to nothing.' "

Not your usual verse-for-the-day, but for me it was a needed dose. If we sometimes feel our preaching amounts to nothing—well, Paul had the same thoughts whispered in his ear. It isn't our ability, but God's blessing that makes the difference. Not our delivery, but His dynamic. Not our skill, but His Spirit. We're doing more good than we know, and the Lord has promised that our work—and His Word—would not be invested in vain.

Sometimes we just need some help and a little encouragement.

Enter *The Preacher's Sourcebook*—a one-volume stockpile of outlines, stories, quotes, weddings, funerals, encouragements, and inspirations designed to be your personal research assistant. It's a toolbox, a warehouse, a strongbox, a stockroom, a lumberyard, a . . . well, a sourcebook, designed with you in mind.

A couple of kudos are in order to two very gifted young men. My editor, Michael Stephens, is the best in the business; and my assistant, Joshua Rowe, is phenomenal. Both of them are so much smarter than I am, and the quality of this book is entirely due to their efforts.

I also want to thank my closest associate, Jeff Nichols, who has worked beside me for over ten years and is the Executive Pastor (and virtual co-pastor) of the Donelson Fellowship in Nashville, Tennessee. It's to him that I gratefully dedicate this book.

Editor's Preface

Waterproofing the Preacher's Soul
2 Corinthians 4:16–18

A few months ago I came across the journal of a faithful pastor who is now with the Lord, and I was amazed at how honestly he described his difficulties in ministry. I related with his struggles; and as I read his words I underlined some significant phrases: *All our troubles . . . Great distress, anguish of heart, many tears . . . Grieved . . . Distressed . . . No peace of mind . . . The hardships we suffer . . . Great pressure beyond endurance . . . Not equal to the task . . . Not competent . . . Deadly peril . . . Hard pressed on every side . . . Harassed at every turn . . . Struck down . . . Perplexed . . . Downcast . . . Beaten . . . Weak . . . Sorrowful . . . Poor . . . Sleepless nights . . . Made a fool of myself . . . I am afraid . . . I fear . . . We may seem to have failed . . . my deep concern for all the churches.*

Those words came from the Apostle Paul, of course, in his journal called 2 Corinthians. It's the most autobiographical of all Paul's letters, and when you read it with a red pencil underlining the verses about his own struggles, it highlights the human-ness of Paul's ministry.

Yet when you finish reading 2 Corinthians, you come away with the impression that Paul was anything but discouraged. This is a book of victory, optimism, and success in which Paul articulates various secrets for waterproofing the soul.

If you're feeling emotionally waterlogged, adrift, or sinking now, let me remind you of that wonderful little paragraph at the end of chapter 4:

> *Therefore we do not lose heart. Even though our outward man is perishing, yet the inward man is being renewed day by day. For our light affliction, which is but for a moment, is working for us a far more exceeding and eternal weight of glory, while we do not look at the things which are seen, but at the things which are not seen. For the things which are seen are temporary, but the things which are not seen are eternal.*

The Onward Dimension

This passage describes a four-dimensional ministry. Verse 16 begins with an onward dimension—*therefore we do not lose heart*. Paul actually opens chapter 4 by saying: *Therefore, since we have this ministry, we do not lose heart*. And now in verse 16 he repeats it: *Therefore do not lose heart*.

He may lose sleep, friends, fame and prestige, worldly wealth and comfort, skin off his back and years off his life, but Paul was determined to sustain his enthusiasm. He wasn't going to lose the morale and motivation of ministry. As long as he had the promises of God in his hand and the Spirit of God in his heart, he was bound to press on.

The Greek word for *lose heart* means to lose motivation, to become weary and discouraged, to give up. We can't let that attitude seep into our souls. We need onward-facing determination, which is commended in the Bible. There may be times to make a strategic withdrawal or to change pastures; there are times to take a step back and to compromise; but there's never a time to quit.

The greatest leaders in both politics and athletics have one thing in common—they refuse to give up when things turn downward.

> ᴥ Winston Churchill said, *Never give in! Never, never, never!*

> ᴥ *Harriet Beecher Stowe said: When you get into a tight place and everything goes against you, till it seems as though you could not hang on a minute longer, never give up then, for that is just the place and time that the tide will turn.*

> ᴥ Thomas Carey, the brother of William Carey, the father of modern missions, said, *I recollect that (William) was, from a boy . . . always resolutely determined never to give up any point or particle of anything on which his mind was set.*

> ᴥ John Eliot, early missionary to the American Indians, said: *I can do little; yet I am resolved through the grace of Christ, I will never give over the work, so long as I have legs to go.*

> ᴥ Alabama coach Bear Bryant said: *Don't give up at halftime. Concentrate on winning the second half.*

> ᴥ Michael Jordan said: *If you run into a wall, don't turn around and give up. Figure out how to climb it, go through it, or work around it.*

❧ Golfer Tony Lema said: *If I had to cram all m
experience into one sentence, I would say, "Don't
don't let up!"*

The old apostle would have agreed, for twice he sai   ... his
difficulties: "Therefore we do not lose heart." We've got to press onward.

The Outward Dimension

There's also an outward dimension to ministry, and at first it doesn't
sound too encouraging: *We do not lose heart. Even though our outward
man is perishing . . . .* In other words, physically we aren't getting any
younger, and sooner or later we start deteriorating.

A senior citizen, driving down the freeway, heard his cell phone
ring. It was his wife, urgently warning him, "Herman, I just heard on
the news that there's a car going the wrong way on the interstate.
Please be careful!" "You wouldn't believe it!" said Herman, "It's not
just one car going the wrong way. It's hundreds of them!"

Well, funny things happen to us as we get older, and Paul describes it in frank and plain-spoken terms—our outward man is perishing; it is wasting away. In chapter 4, Paul described his body as an
earthen vessel. In chapter 5, he said it was a tattered tent. In chapter
12, he complained about his poor health. But he also told the Corinthians that the body is the temple of the Holy Spirit, to be honored and
guarded.

That means we have to take care of ourselves physically, especially
guarding against prolonged fatigue one of our greatest enemies. When
my children were young, I noticed how they fell into tantrums and lost
control of themselves when they were exhausted. Now I notice that
same thing happening to me.

I've been studying this subject for thirty years, and I've come to a
conclusion. There's a remarkable answer for the problem of prolonged
fatigue. It's called REST, and there are two kinds of it. Jesus prescribed
a cure for both kinds using the word COME.

Regarding physical rest, Jesus said to His weary disciples, "Come
apart and rest awhile." Regarding mental and spiritual rest, Jesus said,
"Come unto me, all you who are weary and heavily laden, and I will
give you rest."

It's important for pastors to rest strategically. We have to give some thought to caring for ourselves and develop some tricks that work for us. One of my newly discovered secrets is signing up for a pastors' conference somewhere. I'll check into the hotel, put a do not disturb sign on the door, rest, sleep, pray, read my Bible, work out in the exercise room, sleep some more, pray some more—and by the end of the conference I'm a new man. I've gotten more out of the conference than some who went to every session!

The Inward Dimension

We must care for ourselves outwardly, though at the very best we are outwardly perishing. What we really need is the inner dimension of ministry: *Though our outward man is perishing, yet the inward man is being renewed day by day.*

Recently a friend shared with me Richard Wentz's story of a church named St. George by the Vineyard in the foothills of the Alleghenies. It holds the deed to a vineyard which produces luscious grapes and exceptional wine. No one knew the secret of the vineyard until Jeremy, the old sexton, died. His family had tended the vineyard for generations, but Jeremy was the last of the line. He left a note saying, "The key to everything is under the altar."

The parish priest, going to the altar to investigate, found a stone slab opening into the crypt. To his surprise, he heard the gurgling of water. There were rich underground streams feeding the vineyard, hidden from the eyes of all on the surface.

The psalmist said, "All my springs are in You" (Ps. 87:7); and the prophet Isaiah said, "A vineyard of red wine! I, the LORD, keep it, I water it every moment" (Is. 27:2–3). When we learn to renew ourselves daily, we're like trees planted by underground streams of water whose leaves stay green in drought times.

For me, the leisurely contemplation of Scripture—good old-fashioned Bible meditation and prayer—is the key to the hidden springs. It's not just a matter of routine or ritual, but of relationship; for in meditation and prayer I draw near to the Fount of every blessing.

Here in 2 Corinthians 4, Paul wants us to meditate on a very precise biblical truth. Our light affliction, he says, which is but for a moment, is working for us a far more exceeding and eternal weight of glory.

This is a profound sentence which is stated in similar terms in Romans 8:18. To stay inwardly renewed, we must keep reminding ourselves that our current sufferings are not worth comparing with our coming glory.

Here in 2 Corinthians 4:17, the apostle is using the analogy of weights. Inside of us is a set of scales. One side represents our temporary problems which may appear heavy at the time. The other side, however, is our glorious eternal future in Christ which is so heavy in the scales that the balances are tipped totally to one side. It's like comparing a flea with an elephant.

We remain inwardly fresh when we remind ourselves of God's perspective on the equations of time/eternity and suffering/glory.

Suppose you dropped your business card in a fishbowl and won a first-class, all-expense-paid tour of the world. You'd be traveling on private jets and yachts, staying in spas and villas, and seeing the most remarkable sights on this planet.

An envelope arrived in the mail with your tickets, but while opening the envelope, you got a little paper cut. "This is terrible!" you might say. "This is a disaster. I wish I had never won that cursed trip! Now look at what's happened to me! Look at my finger. Look at this terrible paper cut! Look at that drop of blood!"

Of course, you'd say no such thing. You'd say, "This little cut is nothing compared to the glorious trip we're about to take." That is Paul's point. The paper cuts of life—our light and momentary afflictions—are not worth comparing to the joys to be revealed or to our exceeding and eternal weight of glory.

The Upward Dimension

That naturally leads to the upward dimension: "Our light affliction . . . is working for us a far more exceeding and eternal weight of glory, while we do not look at the things which are seen, but at the things which are not seen. For the things which are seen are temporary, but the things which are not seen are eternal."

What "eternal things" was Paul referring to? He could have been referring to the results of our ministry, because most of that is invisible. It can't be calculated till the end of time because of the ripple effect and the pass-along events that will keep going until Christ returns. We never know the long-term consequences of a single word we speak for Christ; and while we frequently overestimate the immediate results of our ministry we virtually always underestimate the eventual results.

Or Paul might have been referring to our invisible Lord. Hebrews

11:27 says, "By faith (Moses) . . . endured as seeing Him who is invisible." Think of the theological irony of those words—seeing Him who is invisible. That's what Moses did, and the writer of Hebrews commends the same practice to us, telling us to look to Jesus, the Author and Finisher of our faith.

Here in 2 Corinthians 4, however, when Paul tells us to keep our eyes on the unseen, he is thinking about our everlasting life. The chapter divisions were not in the original, and the next verse, 2 Corinthians 5:1, says: "For we know that if our earthly house, this tent, is destroyed, we have a building from God, a house not made with hands, eternal in the heavens." That's a reference to the resurrection body, a subject about which the Bible has more to say than we think. The Lord wants us to anticipate the future, and to use that knowledge as a waterproofing against the heavy rains of current difficulties.

So I recommend a four-fold ministry—onward going, outwardly prudent, inwardly renewing, and upwardly looking. And when, in coming eras, someone picks up your journal and reads of all your problems, make sure the victory of Christ is shining through.

> *Found in Christ, I will not falter,*
> *Faint, or fail to do His will.*
> *Outwardly I'm growing weaker;*
> *Inward, stronger still!*
> *Day by day His Word renews me*
> *With the Spirit's inner flow*
> *As I look at things eternal,*
> *Not at things below*
> *Inward, outward, onward, upward*
> *As I ask Him to impart*
> *Daily strength and hope eternal*
> *To my trusting heart.*

Create a Sermon Series!

If you would like to publicize and preach a series of messages, you can assemble your own by mixing and matching various sermons and sermon outlines in this *Sourcebook*. Here are some suggestions:

Love and Marriage

- Searching for a Spouse (February 11)
- To Marry or Not to Marry (February 11)
- An Unhealthy Marriage (February 18)
- When a Husband Loves His Wife (March 4)
- Commitment in Marriage (June 3)

Missing the Mark

- Why Do People Stray? (January 21)
- Life Lessons from a Flawed Hero (August 26)
- The Peril of Disbelief (September 9)
- The Peril of Defiance (September 30)
- The Peril of Defection (November 25)

Pit-Stop Christianity: The Basics of Getting Around Life's Track

- Abiding in the Name (January 14)
- Anger (January 21)
- Battle Gear 101 (February 4)
- Faith: The Spiritual Tool We Can't Live Without (April 29)
- The Bible: God's Instruction Manual (July 22)
- Christian Certainties (July 29)
- Speech (August 5)
- Work (October 14)

Ready to Run: Spiritual Disciplines

- Spiritual Exercise in the New Year (January 7)
- Renew Your Resolutions (January 7)
- Training Yourself for Life (September 30)
- Cultivating Spiritual Hunger (November 11)
- Focus on Finishing (December 31)

Talking with God: Practical Insights on Prayer

- Power Prayers: The Relationship Factor (March 18)
- Jabez Times Four (June 3)
- Serious Business (July 22)
- Paul's Prison Prayers (August 5)
- A Pattern for Prayer (August 26)
- The Process of Love's Perfection (October 14)
- How Should We Pray? (November 11)

A Word to the Wise

- The Appeal of Wisdom (September 16)
- Wisdom's Protection Plan (November 18)
- A Greater Than Solomon (December 2)

"What Think Ye of Christ"?

- Redeemer, Savior, Lord (January 21)
- Someone's Here to Help You (February 18)
- The Supremacy of Christ—Parts 1 and 2 (March 25)
- The Unveiling of God (October 7)
- The Word of Life Revealed (October 28)
- The Ultimate Priest (November 4)
- A Special Name (December 2)
- You CAN Miss It! (December 16)
- And the Word Was God (December 23)

Contributors

Dr. Timothy K. Beougher
Billy Graham Professor of Evangelism and Associate Dean of the Billy Graham School of Missions, Evangelism and Church Growth, The Southern Baptist Theological Seminary, Louisville, Kentucky

Spiritual Exercise in the New Year (January 7)
The Great Cloud of Witnesses (January 7)
To Marry or Not to Marry (February 11)
The Message of the Cross (February 25)
More Than a Song: A Fresh Vision for Worship (March 18)
Living Beyond Fear (April 8)
Right Wrongs in the Right Way (May 6)
Commitment in Marriage (June 3)
Walking with Christ: A Fresh Vision for Discipleship (June 17)
What Is the Gospel? (July 1)
A Pattern for Prayer (August 26)
When Life Doesn't Seem Fair (October 21)
You CAN Miss It! (December 16)
Do You Remember? (Patriotic Sermon)

Rev. E. M. Bounds (1835–1913)
Methodist Minister and Writer

The Cultivation of Faith (April 1)

Samuel Clarke (1675–1729)
English Theologian, Philosopher, Physicist

Great and Precious Promises (July 1)

Dr. Al Detter
Senior Pastor, Grace Baptist Church, Erie, Pennsylvania

How to Treat Your Neighbor (February 25)
What Authentic Conversion Looks Like (June 3)
The Appeal of Wisdom (September 16)
Wisdom's Protection Plan (November 18)

Dr. Ed Dobson
Pastor, Calvary Church in Grand Rapids, Michigan, and Moody Bible Institute's 1993 Pastor of the Year

Father Forgive Them (February 4)
All Things Work Together for Good (May 20)
Who's to Blame When Towers Fall? (September 9)
Cultivating Spiritual Hunger (November 11)

Rev. W. H. Finney
Minister and Keswick Theologian

Cleansing the Leper (March 4)

Rev. Billie Friel
Pastor, First Baptist Church, Mt. Juliet, Tennessee

Why Do People Stray? (January 21)
An Unhealthy Marriage (February 18)
The Christian and Trouble: Part 1 (March 18)
The Christian and Trouble: Part 2 (April 15)
The Practice of Hospitality (May 20)

Rosalind Goforth (1864–1942)
British Writer and Missionary to China and Manchuria

Prevailing Prayer (September 2)
The Holy Spirit: God's Great Provision (December 31)

Rev. Peter Grainger
Pastor, Charlotte Baptist Chapel, Edinburgh, Scotland

The Fear of the Lord (January 28)
The Power of the Cross (April 22)
Ripe for Judgment (July 29)
Earthquake, Eclipse, Famine (July 29)
The Danger of Finishing Badly (December 31)

Rev. Mark Hollis
Former minister of 15 years and current freelance writer in Nashville, Tennessee. Master of Arts in Pastoral Counseling.

I Have Seen the Lord (September 9)
God Our Creator (September 23)
The Unveiling of God (October 7)
The Ultimate Priest (November 4)

Rev. E. H. Hopkins (1837–1918)
British Minister (born in South America) and a Founding Keswick Theologian

Abiding in the Name (January 14)
He Who Has Come Is Now Present to Fill (February 4)
Holiness in Relation to the Holy Spirit (May 27)

Dr. David Jeremiah
Senior Pastor of Shadow Mountain Community Church, El Cajon, California, and chancellor of Christian Heritage College

When a Husband Loves His Wife (March 4)
Bring the Joy Back! (June 10)
Trust and Obey (July 8)
The Joy and Music of Christmas (December 23)

Rev. Todd M. Kinde
Pastor of Grace Bible Church, Grandville, Michigan. Former pastor of North View Alliance Church, Grand Rapids Michigan.

Searching for a Spouse (February 11)
Divine Direction (July 1)
The Word of Life Revealed (October 28)
Prepare the Way . . . with Receptivity! (December 23)
Remember the Old Way (Communion Sermon)

Rev. Larry Kirk
Christ Community Church, Daytona Beach, Florida

I Believe (March 4)
Living in Christ, with Christ, through Christ (April 15)
The Results of Remaining in Christ (April 15)
The Mysteries of His Love and the Testing of Our Faith (June 24)
A Glimpse of History (July 15)
The Mark of the Christian (August 12)
Training Yourself for Life (September 30)
I Believe in Jesus (November 4)
How Should We Pray? (November 11)

Dr. Woodrow Kroll
President and Senior Bible Teacher of Back to the Bible Broadcast

Stones of Adversity (April 29)
Life Lessons from a Flawed Hero (August 26)

Rev. C. G. Moore
Pastor and Keswick Theologian

The God of Jacob (June 10)

Dr. Robert Norris
Senior pastor of Fourth Presbyterian Church in the Washington suburb of Bethesda, Maryland

Who Is on My Side? (January 14)
The Great Betrayal (April 1)
Husbands and Wives (July 22)
He's My Son Too! (December 9)

Dr. Larry Osborne
Senior Pastor, North Coast Church, Vista, California

Anger (January 21)
Battle Gear 101 (February 4)
Making Good Decisions (February 25)
Power Prayers: The Relationship Factor (March 18)
Faith: The Spiritual Tool We Can't Live Without (April 29)
Spirit Filled (May 27)
Dreams and Goals (June 10)
The Bible: God's Instruction Manual (July 22)
Speech (August 5)
Dream Big, Work Hard, Leave It to God (August 26)
Upside-Down Living: Part 1 (September 16)
Upside-Down Living: Part 2 (September 16)
Work (October 14)
Deep Roots (October 28)
Esther's Surprise Assignment (November 11)
Mary's Blessing in Bethlehem (December 9)
Life Lessons for Your Own Journey (December 9)
Sexual Purity (Youth Sermon)

Joshua D. Rowe
Assistant Editor to Robert J. Morgan and Graduate of Columbia International University, degrees in Bible and Biblical Languages

The Supremacy of Christ: Part 1 (March 25)
The Supremacy of Christ: Part 2 (March 25)

Palm Sunday Confessions (April 1)
Comfort for a Tough Mother's Day (May 13)
Put on Love (August 19)
How to Survive a Lion's Attack (September 2)
A Bird's-Eye View of 1 Peter (September 2)
Heavenly Minded (September 30)
Thankful Living (November 18)
A Fresh Look at John 3:16 (November 25)

Dr. W. Graham Scroggie (1877–1959)
Scottish minister and writer

Redeemer, Savior, Lord (January 21)
Come—Learn—Take (April 22)
The Lordship of Christ (May 6)
The Flesh or the Spirit? (June 24)
Paul's Prison Prayers (August 5)
The Process of Love's Perfection (October 14)

Rev. Richard S. Sharpe, Jr.
Director of Small Church Ministries and President of Christian Home Crusade

The State of Joyful Living (March 11)
The Importance of Mothers and Grandmothers (May 13)
Partnership (August 12)

Rev. Charles Haddon Spurgeon (1834–1892)
Pastor, Metropolitan Tabernacle, London

A Greater Than Solomon (December 2)

R. A. Torrey (1856–1928)
American evangelist, pastor, educator, and writer

The Wind of God (February 11)
Names of the Holy Spirit (May 27)

Dr. Melvin Worthington
Pastor, Former Executive Secretary, National Association of Free Will Baptists

Renew Your Resolutions (January 7)
The Model Man (January 28)

Cursed Cain (February 18)
When We Worship (March 11)
The Devil's Devices (March 25)
Thoughts from the Tomb (April 8)
Allegiant Abel (April 22)
Dealing with Deception (May 6)
Feed the Flock (May 20)
Moses My Man (June 17)
The Seriousness of Sin (July 8)
Ranking Responsibilities (July 15)
Christian Certainties (July 29)
The Peril of Drifting (August 12)
The Spectrum of Salvation (August 19)
The Peril of Disbelief (September 9)
The Peril of Defiance (September 30)
Dealing with Dishonesty (October 7)
The Master's Mandate (October 21)
The Mother of Mankind (November 4)
The Peril of Defection (November 25)
The Master's Men (December 2)
Christ Is Christmas (December 16)
Focus on Finishing (December 31)
The Missions Mandate (Missions Sermon)

(Note: Bold Print indicates main outlines)

All other outlines are from the pulpit ministry of the general editor, Rev. Robert J. Morgan, of The Donelson Fellowship in Nashville, Tennessee. Special appreciation goes to Corey Hawkins, music minister of the Donelson Fellowship, for his invaluable assistance.

2007 Calendar

January 1	New Year's Day
January 6	Epiphany
January 7	
January 14	
January 15	Martin Luther King, Jr. Day
January 21	**Sanctity of Human Life Sunday**
January 26	Australia Day
January 28	
February 1–28	Black History Month
February 4	**Superbowl Sunday**
February 5	Lincoln's Birthday
February 11	
February 14	Valentine's Day
February 18	
February 19	Presidents' Day
February 21	Ash Wednesday
February 22	Washington's Birthday
February 25	**First Sunday of Lent**
March 4	**Second Sunday of Lent; Purim**
March 11	**Third Sunday of Lent**
March 17	St. Patrick's Day
March 18	**Fourth Sunday of Lent**
March 21	Spring Begins
March 25	**Fifth Sunday of Lent**
April 1	**Palm Sunday; Daylight Saving Time Begins**
April 3	Passover

April 5	Holy Thursday
April 6	Good Friday
April 8	**Easter Sunday**
April 13	Jefferson's Birthday
April 15	**Holocaust Remembrance Day**
April 22	**Earth Day**
April 25	Administrative Professionals Day
April 29	
May 3	National Day of Prayer
May 6	
May 13	**Mother's Day**
May 17	Ascension Day
May 19	Armed Forces Day
May 20	
May 27	**Pentecost**
May 28	Memorial Day
June 3	**Trinity Sunday**
June 10	
June 14	Flag Day
June 17	**Father's Day**
July 21	Summer Begins
June 24	
July 1	**Canada Day**
July 4	Independence Day
July 8	
July 15	
July 22	**Parents' Day**
July 29	

August 5	**Friendship Day**
August 6	Transfiguration Day
August 12	
August 19	
August 26	
September 2	
September 3	Labor Day
September 9	**Grandparents' Day**
September 12	Rosh Hashanah Begins
September 16	
September 21	Yom Kippur Begins
September 23	**Autumn Begins**
September 28	Native American Day
September 30	
October 1–31	Pastor Appreciation Month
October 7	
October 8	Columbus Day
October 14	**Clergy Appreciation Day**
October 16	National Boss's Day
October 21	
October 28	**Reformation Day; Daylight Saving Time Ends; Mother-in-Law Day**
October 31	Halloween
November 1	All Saints Day
November 4	
November 11	**International Day of Prayer for the Persecuted Church; Veterans' Day**
November 18	

November 22	Thanksgiving Day
November 25	
December 2	**First Sunday of Advent**
December 4	Hanukkah Begins
December 7	Pearl Harbor Remembrance Day
December 9	**Second Sunday of Advent**
December 16	**Third Sunday of Advent**
December 22	Winter Begins
December 23	**Fourth Sunday of Advent**
December 24	Christmas Eve
December 25	Christmas Day
December 26	Kwanzaa Begins
December 30	
December 31	New Year's Eve

Boldface dates are Sundays

SERMONS AND
WORSHIP SUGGESTIONS
FOR 52 WEEKS

JANUARY 7, 2007

Spiritual Exercise in the New Year

By Dr. Timothy Beougher   *Date preached:*

Scripture: Hebrews 12:1–3, especially 1b–2a
. . . let us lay aside every weight, and the sin which so easily ensnares us, and let us run with endurance the race that is set before us, looking unto Jesus, the author and finisher of our faith . . .

Introduction: How are you doing on your New Year's Resolutions? Newspapers and magazines are flooding us with challenges to make resolutions; most focus on exercise. Paul teaches us that physical exercise is useful but temporary, while spiritual exercise is vital and eternal (1 Tim. 4:8). The author of Hebrews uses athletic imagery to drive home the importance of spiritual exercise. In Hebrews 12:1–3, we find four crucial spiritual exercises, resolutions we should adopt for 2007:

1. **Remember Forerunners of the Faith (v. 1a).** The word "therefore" in this verse points us back to chapter 11, the great "Hall of Faith" where Bible characters from the Old Testament and great martyrs are exemplified. Chapter 12 calls them a "cloud of witnesses." How should we interpret this phrase? First, they are certainly witnesses *to* us. Men and women who have run the race well serve as examples for us. However, it also *could* mean that they are witnesses *of* us, that they are spectators. The author of Hebrews seems to be alluding to the ancient Greek and Roman games. A great number of spectators would gather in the stands to watch those running on the track below. Commentators caution us, however, that we must not press this imagery too far. Whether or not people in heaven actually watch is not specifically revealed in Scripture, but this passage teaches us that we should run as if they were in the stands, cheering us on in our race of faith.

2. **Remove Hindrances to Your Faith (v. 1b).** Notice the contrast between the first phrase "let us lay aside every weight" and the second part, "the sin which so easily ensnares." This first phrase refers to things that aren't necessarily sinful, but get in the way of running

our spiritual race with excellence. Good things hinder our spiritual vitality when we focus on them—our career, our possessions, our hobbies, our relationships, etc. While all are good, if they become our preoccupation, we're in trouble! The verse continues to address "the sin which so easily ensnares." If we must remove hindrances that might be innocent in themselves, how much more do we need to remove sin from our life! Sin "ensnares" us as we seek to run the race; it trips us up!

3. **Run the Race of Faith (v. 1c).** Get in the race! Every believer should be racing, not sitting on the sidelines! The passage mandates persistence. The Christian life isn't a sprint, it's a marathon. The root of the word translated *race* is the word *agon,* from which we get our word *agony.* It signifies an athletic endeavor in which we will face the desire to quit, to throw in the towel. We face difficulty as we strive to glorify God in the midst of a fallen world. We are always either advancing or back-sliding. The Christian race is not running in place! How do we run the race of faith with such persistence? The fourth spiritual exercise brings it all together for us.

4. **Recover the Focus of Faith (vv. 2–3).** Jesus is to be our daily focus in life. We are to *glance* at others (like those in Hebrews 11), but we are to *gaze* at the Lord Jesus Christ. Above all others in that great cloud of witnesses is the Lord Jesus Christ. The word for fixing our eyes suggests a concentrated focus. It literally means "looking away from all else and zeroing in completely on Him." The tense of the original word suggests it's a continual action; we could interpret this as "keep fixing your eyes upon Jesus." Remember that He ". . . endured the cross, despising the shame." The application for us is in verse 3, ". . . consider Him who endured such hostility from sinners against Himself, lest you become weary and discouraged in your souls." Running the race of faith requires laying aside certain things and keeping our focus on Jesus. In order to do both, the Word of God must be prominent in our lives.

Conclusion: Where is your focus this morning? For those who don't know Jesus as your personal Lord and Savior, there's no better way to start this year. For those who are weary in your walk, abandon wasteful preoccupations and rid yourselves of sin! Gaze upon Jesus, considering all He endured; He will give you a second wind!

STATS, STORIES, AND MORE

Running the Race
A couple years back, one of my daughters began to run track, the open 400 meter race and the 4 x 400 meter relay. Many people believe that the 400 meters is the hardest race to run; it's between an all out sprint and a distance race. During her races, I would position myself at a point on the home stretch about 75 meters from the finish line, the point where the race is the hardest, when your body is telling you to slow down and not push so hard. Why? Because I knew that was the point in the race when she needed encouragement. I would stand there to cheer her on, to encourage her to keep going in spite of the temptation to slow down or give up. I believe that is a major idea conveyed in Hebrews 12:1: the saints from Hebrews 11 are to exercise a similar influence on us. We are to envision them cheering us on as we run the race of faith! These men and women faced obstacles just like we do, but they placed their faith in God and through Him achieved victory. They are encouraging us that what they have done, we can do! God's strength and grace will see us through just as it did them!   —Dr. Timothy Beougher

Back Trouble
I heard about a man who went to the doctor with back trouble. The doctor examined him and said, "You are not having back trouble. You are having front trouble!" The doctor was saying that the source of his back problem was the excess weight up front. Hebrews 12:1 reminds us that there are weights we must shed if we are going to finish the race well. They may be innocent in themselves, but if they are hindering our spiritual race we need to get rid of them.

APPROPRIATE HYMNS AND SONGS

"Runner," Starla Paris/Twila Paris, 1985 Straightway Music (EMI Christian Music Publishing).

"When the Night Is Falling," Dennis Jernigan, 1990 Shepherds Heart Music (Word Music Group).

"Little Is Much When God Is in It," Kittie Louise Suffield, 1969 Brentwood (Benson Music Publishing).

"Faith Is the Victory," John H. Yates/Ira D. Sankey, Public Domain.

"Trust and Obey," John H. Sammis/Daniel B. Towner, Public Domain.

FOR THE BULLETIN

John Hooper, born in Sommersetshire, England, in 1495, discovered the truth of the Book of Romans while studying at Oxford. He embraced Reformation theology, but when "Bloody" Queen Mary ascended the throne, Hooper was thrown into Fleet. He described conditions in a letter on January 7, 1554: "On the one side is the sink and filth of the house, and on the other side the town-ditch, so that the stench hath infected me with sundry diseases—during which time I have been sick; and the doors, bars, and chains being closed, and made fast upon me, I have mourned and cried for help . . . But I commit my cause to God, whose will be done, whether it be by life or death." Soon afterward, Hooper was burned at the stake. ● Robert Morrison, Protestant's first missionary to China, was ordained on this day in 1807. During his nearly thirty years in China, he saw only three or four people converted to Christ; yet he opened the door for all the missionaries who followed him. ● Today is the birthday, in 1828, of Frederick Whitfield, author of the hymn "Oh, How I Love Jesus." It's also the birthday, in 1832, of the American Presbyterian giant, Thomas DeWitt Talmage. ● Today is the wedding anniversary of Rev. Charles Haddon Spurgeon and his wife, Susannah, who were married in 1856. ● The prolific American hymn composer, William Bradbury, died on January 7, 1868. He wrote the music for such popular hymns as "Jesus Loves Me," "Savior, Like a Shepherd Lead Me," "Take My Life and Let It Be," and "He Leadeth Me."

Quote for the Pastor's Wall

Preaching is a divinely appointed way to transmit God's truth. This does not minimize teaching, personal witnessing, or any other valid means of sharing the Word; but it does emphasize the importance of preaching. God had one Son and he was a preacher.

—WARREN W. WIERSBE[1]

[1]Wiersbe, W. W., & Wiersbe, D., *The Elements of Preaching: The Art of Biblical Preaching Clearly and Simply Presented* (Wheaton, Ill.: Tyndale House Publishers, 1986), electronic edition.

WORSHIP HELPS

Call to Worship
But as for me, I will come into Your house in the multitude of Your mercy; In fear of You I will worship toward Your holy temple (Ps. 5:7).

Word of Welcome
We welcome you here to our church today to share the Lord's Day with us. This is the first day of the week, and it's the day in seven when we weekly commemorate our Lord's resurrection from the dead. There's an old writing, attributed to the fifteenth-century devotional writer, Thomas à Kempis, that says about Sunday:

> Again the Lord's own day is here,
> The day to Christian people dear,
> As week by week, it bids them tell
> How Jesus rose from death and hell.
>
> And therefore unto Thee we sing,
> O Lord of peace, eternal King;
> Thy love we praise, Thy Name adore,
> Both on this day and evermore.

Offertory Comments
A missionary in Africa spent a Sunday's sermon talking about open-handed giving, and in the process he described the habit of tithing. The next day there was a knock at the door of his house. A local boy was there, holding in his hands a large fish. "Here it is," said the boy. "I've brought my tithe." As the missionary took the fish, he asked the youngster, "If this is your tithe, where are the other nine fish?" The boy replied, "Oh, they're still in the river. I'm going back now to catch them."

Additional Sermons and Lesson Ideas

The Great Cloud of Witnesses

Date preached:

By Dr. Timothy Beougher

SCRIPTURE: Hebrews 11

INTRODUCTION: Have you considered the testimony of men and women from Hebrews 11?

1. Noah (v. 7). When we are anxious, Noah's life speaks to us: "Patience! I had to wait 120 years to see God's plan fulfilled in my life; a few more weeks of waiting will do you good!"
2. Sarah (vv. 11–12). She had the faith to believe God for the impossible. When we run the race and begin to doubt, Sarah shouts, "Keep going! God is able to do the impossible!"
3. Joseph (v. 22). One hardship after another faced Joseph: sold into slavery by his brothers, imprisoned on false charges, forgotten by those he helped. His life testifies to us, "Trust God in spite of your circumstances!"

CONCLUSION: Many others are mentioned in Hebrews 11, whose lives testify to us today. With one voice they cry out to us today, "God is faithful! Trust Him and don't give up! He will see you through!"

Renew Your Resolutions

Date preached:

By Dr. Melvin Worthington

SCRIPTURE: Various Scriptures

INTRODUCTION: This time each year should be a season to reflect, remember, and resolve for Christians. Have you thought to renew your resolutions in the following areas?

1. To Study the Scriptures (2 Tim. 2:15). Is it your goal to read the Bible through at least once this year? Read God's Word regularly, reverently, and reflectively.
2. To Share the Savior (Acts 1; 2 Cor. 5; Matt. 28). Christians are visual, verbal, and vital witnesses for Christ.
3. To Support the Servants (2 Cor. 8—9). Resolve to give systematically, scripturally, and sacrificially. Biblical giving radiates adoration, appreciation, affection, and acknowledgment of God's blessings in one's life.
4. To Stand for Scriptural Separation (2 Cor. 6; John 17; Eph. 5; 1 John 2).
5. To Make Supplication in the Spirit (1 Thess. 5; Eph. 2; 1 Tim. 2).

CONCLUSION: Set high and noble resolution goals. It is better to miss "high and noble" by a fraction, than to hit dead center on "I can't change and who cares anyway!"

JANUARY 14, 2007

SUGGESTED SERMON

Who Is on My Side?

Date preached:

By Dr. Robert Norris

Scripture: Job 19:1–29, especially verses 25–26
For I know that my Redeemer lives, and He shall stand at last on the earth; and after my skin is destroyed, this I know, that in my flesh I shall see God.

Introduction: Have you ever felt yourself trapped by life, believing it cannot get any worse? Job was there! His wealth was demolished, his children were struck dead, and even his own body was afflicted with disease and unbearable pain. He believed that the only thing left for him was to die (19:8–9). With life, his friends, and (seemingly) God against him, Job was questioning, "Who is on my side?" We often ask the same thing. The answer is found in God's redemptive work in Job's life, and ultimately in Jesus Christ.

1. **Job Sunk into the Pit of Humiliation (19:1–22).** Job's friends attributed Job's suffering to his sin, even accusing him of not knowing God (18:21)! As Job argued, he constantly proved himself righteous. However, neither logic, nor scoring debating points against his human opposition brought any comfort to Job while God remained "silent" in the face of his suffering. We can feel the intensity of his pain as he vividly describes his feelings of being entangled by a net, walled in by a fence, set on a dark path, stripped of his crown, broken into rubble, uprooted like a tree, counted as an enemy and under siege by armies (19:9–22). Job plummeted to the depths. As low as he had thought he could fall, now Job found that he had fallen even lower!

2. **Job Ascended to the Pinnacle of Faith (19:23–29).** When Job hit the bottom, he slowly and painfully looked up. Perhaps for the first time he had to deal with the shock that he may not live to see himself cleared of all the charges of his friends. Thus he looked ahead. He reached the very depths of despair, and then he cried: "For I know that my Redeemer lives, and He shall stand at last on the earth; and after my skin is destroyed, this I know, that in my flesh I shall see God" (19:25–26). In these words we see:

A. **Conviction.** Despite all his troubles, Job said, "I know . . ." In that moment, Job joined with Isaiah in seeing the Lord sitting on a throne (Is. 6:1). In his most depressed moments he had questioned if there was any life after death (14:1–2). But here, when he was even more depressed, he was convicted and convinced of the truth!

B. **Salvation.** Job saw his Savior. The word "redeemer" is the Hebrew word *goel* meaning "vindicator." This was the nearest next of kin whose duty it was to undertake the cause of his kinsman and defend him. Job saw in heaven that there was One who would acquit him of all charges. Earlier Job has looked for an "arbiter" or "mediator" who would plead his case. Now he knows he cannot stand before God in his own righteousness. His blameless behavior is not enough to redeem him. A brother is his only hope. There is a brother who is willing to shed his blood in order to vindicate Job in the future. Dimly but surely he looks to and sees the atoning work of Christ. But his eyes of faith remain open, and he sees yet more. "He shall stand at last on the earth"—His vindicator, his hope, will come in flesh and blood. He will accomplish what Job's friends have failed to do; he will bring comfort and peace. Here the incarnate Christ will come and work that work of grace living and dying to redeem His people.

C. **Eternity.** "In my flesh I shall see God." Job knew that he would live beyond the grave. Job saw his future linked to a mediator, between God and man. He saw, however dimly, Jesus, incarnate, atoning, and resurrected.

Conclusion: In Jesus we find the complete fulfillment of what dawned upon Job in the midst of his darkness, and which shone as a light of hope and confidence. The One who ever lives came into our earthly life, stood upon the dust for us, and argued our case on the earth by taking our place, fulfilling our roles (see Heb. 7:1–25). He even died our death and was raised from the dead and argues now our case in the courts of heaven. Are you in despair today? Do you feel like you've hit rock bottom? Jesus Christ, the Redeemer, lives! Won't you turn to Him and entrust your life to Him?

STATS, STORIES, AND MORE

More from Dr. Norris

G. F. Handel composed the Messiah in 24 days. A servant came in as Handel was writing the Hallelujah Chorus and found the composer weeping; and when he could speak, he explained, "I think I did see all heaven before me and the Great God Himself." The great chorus is immediately preceded by the soprano aria, "I know that My Redeemer Liveth." Not as clearly as Handel, but as surely, Job, too, saw "all heaven and the great God Himself" and knew that He had a redeemer!

Missionary Rosalind Goforth remembered hearing her grandfather tell about the time he was lost in the woods. He and his cousins, when small, were out playing when they became hopelessly lost. After trying vainly to find their way out, the oldest child, crying, gathered the others around and said, "When Mother died she told us to always tell Jesus if we were in any trouble. Let us kneel down and ask Him to take us home." They knelt and prayed together, then noticed a bird lingering close by. When a child reached out to it, it hopped away, but not too far. Soon all the children were chasing the bird, which flew and hopped before them. Then suddenly it flew into the air and away. The children looked up to find themselves on the edge of the woods and in sight of home.[1]

APPROPRIATE HYMNS AND SONGS

"My Redeemer Lives," Reuben Morgan, 1998 Hillsong Publishing.

"I Know that My Redeemer Liveth," Jessie B. Pounds/James H. Fillmore, Public Domain.

"Count Your Blessings," Johnson Oatman Jr./Edwin O. Excell, Public Domain.

"My Faith Looks Up to Thee," Ray Palmer, Lowell Mason, Public Domain.

"Jesus, Lover of My Soul," John Ezzy/Daniel Grul/Stephen McPherson, 1992 Hillsong Publishing.

---

[1]Related by Rosalind Goforth in *How I Know God Answers Prayer*, published in 1921.

FOR THE BULLETIN

The Spanish theologian Juan de Valdes published "Dialogue on Christian Doctrine" on January 14, 1529. ● The famous Hampton Court Conference convened on January 14, 1604, at Hampton Court outside of London, called by King James I to discuss differences between the English Bishops and the Puritan leaders. In almost all the decisions, the king sided with the bishops. The most lasting contribution of the conference, however, was the king's authorization of a new translation of the Bible, which is today known as the Authorized (King James) Version, published in 1611. ● Today is the birthday, in 1811, of Rowland H. Prichard, who, when he was a teenager, composed one of Christianity's best-loved melodies, HYFRDOL ("Jesus! What a Friend of Sinners!"). Today is also the birthday, in 1875, of Albert Schweitzer, popular medical missionary and musician who won the Nobel Peace Prize in 1952. Martin Niemoller was also born on this day in 1892. He became a prominent Lutheran pastor who personally confronted Hitler, an act of courage that led to his imprisonment in Sachsenhausen and Dachau concentration camps. ● On January 14, 1892, young Amy Carmichael, later to become a world-renowned missionary and author, wrote a letter to her mother, announcing her plans for overseas service. She wrote in part: "My Precious Mother, Have you given your child unreservedly to the Lord for whatever He wills . . . Oh, may He strengthen you to say 'Yes' to Him . . . Darling Mother, for a long time, as you know, the thought of those dying in the dark—50,000 of them every day while we at home live in the midst of blazing light—has been present with me, and the longing to go to them and tell them of Jesus has been strong upon me . . . ."

WORSHIP HELPS

Call to Worship

It is good to give thanks to the LORD, and to sing praises to Your name, O Most High; to declare Your lovingkindness in the morning, and Your faithfulness every night (Ps. 92:1–2).

Reader's Theater (or Responsive Reading)

Reader 1: Great is the LORD, and greatly to be praised; and His greatness is unsearchable. One generation shall praise Your works to another, and shall declare Your mighty acts.

Reader 2: The works of the LORD are great, studied by all who have pleasure in them. Oh, how great is Your goodness, which You have laid up for those who fear You, which You have prepared for those who trust in You. Your righteousness is like the great mountains; Your judgments are a great (ocean).

Reader 1: Great is the glory of the LORD. Great is Your faithfulness. Great is Your mercy toward me.

Reader 2: How shall we escape if we neglect so great a salvation? Among the gods there is none like You, O Lord; nor are there any works like Your works. All nations whom You have made shall come and worship before You, O Lord, and shall glorify Your name.

Reader 1: For You are great, and do wondrous things; You alone are God (Ps. 145:3–4; 111:2; 31:19; 36:6; 138:5; Lam. 3:23; Ps. 86:13; Heb. 2:3; Ps. 86:8–10).

Additional Sermons and Lesson Ideas

The Gospel in One Verse

SCRIPTURE: John 3:16

INTRODUCTION: This verse gives us the gospel in a nutshell, and we can even find the word gospel hidden inside the verse itself:

> G—God
> O—Only Begotten
> S—Son
> P—Perish
> E—Everlasting
> L—Life

CONCLUSION: This isn't just good news, it's the best news in all the world. Have you heard? Have you received? Are you passing it on?

Abiding in the Name

Based on an Outline by Rev. E. H. Hopkins

SCRIPTURE: Various, especially Colossians 3:17

INTRODUCTION: Colossians 3:17 tells us, whatever we do in word or deed, to do it all in the name of the Lord Jesus. Abiding in the Name of Christ, we find:

1. Our Righteous Standing Before God (Acts 2:38; 1 Pet. 3:18).
2. A Prevailing Argument in Prayer (John 14:13–14).
3. An Authority for Service (Acts 4:10).
4. An Armor for Conflict (Rom. 13:15; Eph. 6:11).

CONCLUSION: God has given Jesus the name which is above every name (Phil. 3:5–11), and Scripture demands a lifestyle carried out in the name of the Lord Jesus. Are you abiding in His Name?

Aurelius Clemens Prudentius

Last year a college student sauntered into my office to tell me about a new song he'd discovered, one with haunting melody and pensive words; and pulling out a CD, he played it for me. I smiled when I realized his "new" song was one of our oldest hymns, "Of the Father's Love Begotten."

This ancient Latin hymn is by Aurilius Clemens Prudentius, who was born in northern Spain in A.D. 348, not long after Christianity was legalized in the Roman Empire following three centuries of persecution. It's speculated that Prudentius was born into a Christian family because he never later speaks of his conversion.

Prudentius became a lawyer and provincial governor in Spain where his leadership skills attracted the attention of Emperor Theodosius I who appointed him to an imperial military post.

In time, Prudentius became more deeply devoted in his commitment to Christ, for at age fifty-seven, he retired from government service and entered a monastery where he devoted himself exclusively to worship and writing.

Today we have nearly four hundred poems from his hand, and he is sometimes called "the prince of early Christian poets." Though he and Ambrose were both writing hymns about the same time, the ones by Prudentius are more reflective, displaying greater warmth and glow. Perhaps it was his warm Spanish blood. His major works are:

- The *Cathemerinon,* comprising twelve lyric poems on various times of the day and on church festivals.

- The *Peristephanon,* with 14 lyric poems about the early Spanish and Roman martyrs.

- The *Apotheosis,* in which Prudentius addresses the doctrines of the Trinity and the Deity of Christ.

- The *Hamartigenia,* an anti-Gnostic address.

- The *Psychomachia*, ("The Contest of the Soul") was the first completely allegorical poem in European literature and cast a long shadow over medieval times. "Of the Father's Love Begotten" is taken from this work.

- Two *Contra Symmachum* (Books Against Symmachus), written in response to Roman Senator Symmachus' requests that a pagan altar be restored to the Senate house.

"Of the Father's Love Begotten" is among the greatest Christian hymns and Christmas carols in western history, and thankfully its popularity is on the increase, partly owing to the tender beauty of its probing score, *Divinum Mysterium*, composed nearly a thousand years ago.

> *Of the Father's love begotten, ere the worlds began to be,*
> *He is Alpha and Omega, He the source, the ending He,*
> *Of the things that are, that have been, and that future years shall see,*
> *Evermore and evermore!*
>
> *O that birth for ever blessed! When the virgin, full of grace,*
> *By the Holy Ghost conceiving, bare the Savior of our race,*
> *And the babe, the world's redeemer, first revealed his sacred face,*
> *Evermore and evermore!*[2]

---

[2]Adapted from the editor's book, *Come, Let Us Adore Him* (Nashville: J. Countryman Publishers, 2005).

JANUARY 21, 2007

SUGGESTED SERMON

Anger

Date preached:

By Dr. Larry Osborne

Scripture: Ephesians 4:26–27
"Be angry, and do not sin": do not let the sun go down on your wrath, nor give place to the devil.

Introduction: Ephesians 4:26–27 is a very simple and straightforward passage, but presents an incredible challenge to us. Today we will look at what Scripture says of anger, so that we might learn to deal with anger in a way in which we do not sin. We must first understand two things about anger if we are to take a Scriptural and healthy lifestyle of dealing with it:

1. **It's Not a Sin to Be Angry.** A misconception exists even in Christian circles about anger which holds that a true Christian doesn't get angry about anything. Nothing could be further from the truth! Anger is often attributed to God Himself. For example: God gave Moses the assignment to be His representative to deliver the Israelites from Egypt, but Moses objected despite God's promises. The Lord's anger burned against Moses (Ex. 4:14). The Spirit of God came upon Saul in power and made him angry (1 Sam. 11:6). Jesus was often angry at the Pharisees or other religious leaders (Mark 3:1–6; cf. Matt. 23:13, Luke 11:46, John 2:14–17). So, we have God the Father who gets angry, God the Spirit who can produce anger in God's servants, and God the Son who also gets angry. Anger is often appropriate in our lives as Christians.

2. **We Can't Control Feelings of Anger—We Can Control How We Respond (Eph. 4:26).** The truth about anger is that it just shows up. We don't often consider whether or not we should get angry. It's useless to tell an angry person not to be angry, but it's not useless to help them know what to do as a result. While we don't have control of that emotion, we have full control of our actions. We often justify our actions, saying "I was so angry, I couldn't help it." This simply isn't ever the case.

Application:

1. **Lengthen Your Fuse.** Even if we can't control the feelings of anger in a particular moment, we can learn from it so that next time it takes longer to get there. There's one thing about God's anger we must not forget. Exodus 34:6 tells us that the Lord "passed in front of Moses, proclaiming, 'The LORD, the LORD, the compassionate and gracious God, slow to anger, abounding in love and faithfulness" (NIV). Aren't you thankful God's fuse is long? We are commanded to be the same way (James 1:19–20). This means we must change the way we think. It also means we might need to change our friends and environment (Prov. 22:24–25). We also have to get rid of our excuses and self-justification (Prov. 28:13).

2. **Let God Even the Score.** Scripture teaches us to overcome evil with good and never to repay evil with more evil (Rom. 12:17–21). When we take things into our own hands this way, we do several things: we usurp God's authority, we do evil just like the person that made us mad, and our witness is hurt.

3. **Keep Your Mouth Shut.** Angry words are seldom appropriate words. Often when we're angry, we use more words to get our point across, making us more likely to sin (Prov. 10:19). Our words are powerful and can easily be hurtful, which doesn't give us the right to "mouth off" but the responsibility to keep quiet (see Prov. 15:28; 29:11; Col. 3:8; Rev. 12:10; Eph. 4:29).

4. **If You Can, Let Go—If You Can't, Deal with It Now.** It's a sign of maturity to be able to look over things that could make us angry (Prov. 12:16; 19:11; 20:3). When anger turns to bitterness, it kills us spiritually, physically, and relationally. This is why Scripture tells us not to sin in our anger and not to let the sun go down on our anger (Eph. 4:26, 31–32).

5. **Keep a Good Mirror Handy and Use It.** When we look at our own faults, we begin to realize that we have no right to be angry in many cases. At the very least it helps to lengthen our fuse (see Matt. 7:1–2; Rom. 2:1).

Conclusion: Does the devil have a "guest room?" Are we leaving space for the enemy in our hearts with our bitterness (Eph. 4:27; 2 Cor. 2:10–11)? This week, look over these five applications and find which ones most apply to you. Ask the Lord to teach you to treat anger appropriately.

STATS, STORIES, AND MORE

Seeking Out and Rooting Out Our Short Fuses

Many of us who hear Scriptures or sermons about anger find it easy to think of other hot-heads we know and justify ourselves, but everyone has particular fuses that are too short. It's not really my personality to get easily or quickly angered. When my children were little, there was one child in particular that really could push my buttons. My wife and I would be sitting in the same room, see the same rebellious behavior and I would react much more abrasively than she. I finally realized that I was so concerned with my child growing up to be godly, that I was too harsh when I saw any form of rebellion. I went to my child and said "next time daddy yells, you have the right to say 'time out'." Sure enough, a couple weeks later that child did something that really upset me. The reaction to my discipline wasn't "yes dad, you're right," but it was argumentative. I automatically began to yell louder. My child said, "time out!" I almost wept. It never happened again. Even for people who aren't usually angered, it is imperative that we recognize and do something about our short fuses!

—Dr. Larry Osborne

Losing Logic to Anger

I remember a classic example of how sinful anger makes you lose your logical thinking. My wife and I were eating at a restaurant in Florida, when all of the sudden a fight broke out over at the bar area of the restaurant. We found out that someone just got angry and punched another man in his rage without good reason and his buddy even joined in to make things worse. The men were chased out of the restaurant and almost detained by restaurant staff, but got away at the last minute. As my wife and I walked out to get our car, I said to the woman running the valet booth, "It's too bad they got away." She said, "Oh, no, we got them." I asked her how and, with a smile, she said, "They valet parked their car."   —Dr. Larry Osborne

APPROPRIATE HYMNS AND SONGS

"Choose to Forgive," Rick Riso/Mark Levang, 1994 Integrity's Hosanna! Music (c/o Integrity Music Inc.).

"Deeper and Deeper," Morris Chapman/Claire Cloninger, 1990 Maranatha Music (Word Music Inc.).

"Lay It Down," Cheri Keaggy, 1996 SparrowSong (div. of EMI Music Publishing).

"Search Me, O God," J. Edwin Orr/"Maori" melody, 1936.

"Spirit of the Living God," Daniel Iverson, 1935. Renewed 1963 Birdwing Music (div. of EMI Christian Music Publishing).

FOR THE BULLETIN

In the eleventh century, Pope Gregory VII insisted that he, not secular kings, had the right to appoint church leaders in the various nations of Europe. Germany's Emperor Henry IV resisted and tried to replace Gregory. The Pope excommunicated Henry, and after much intrigue, the king finally realized the only way to save his crown was by seeking Gregory's forgiveness. He traveled to the palace housing the pope in Canossa, Italy, on January 21, 1077, and stood for three days in the snow. Gregory finally forgave him. ● On January 21, 1189, Philip II, Henry II, and Richard the Lion-Hearted launched the Third Crusade. ● The Anabaptist Movement was launched in church history on January 21, 1525, in Zurich, when Conrad Grebel (re-)baptized George Blaurock, a former monk. ● On January 21, 1549, the English Parliament passed the first of four British Acts of Uniformity, this first requiring the exclusive use of the Book of Common Prayer in all public services of the Anglican Church. ● On January 21, 1672, John Bunyan was elected pastor of the Bedford Baptist Church. Bunyan was a mender of pots and pans who, following his conversion, had been imprisoned for preaching without receiving permission from the Established Church. He remained in jail for over twelve years, but the Act of Pardon freed him in 1672, and he was immediately installed as the pastor of the church in Bedford, a position he maintained the rest of his life. ● Today is the birthday, in 1797, of Edward Mote, a British cabinetmaker who wrote the hymn, "My Hope Is Built on Nothing Less," also known as "The Solid Rock." Julia Johnston was born on this day in 1849. She wrote the hymn, "Marvelous Grace of Our Loving Lord."

Quote for the Pastor's Wall

Let me relate it as my deliberate conviction that, unless the Church of God returns to the preaching of the gospel as that is set forth in the New Testament, her power to bless the world is gone.

—W. GRAHAM SCROGGIE,
in *Facets of the Faith*

WORSHIP HELPS

Call to Worship
The LORD, the LORD God, merciful and gracious, longsuffering, and abounding in goodness and truth (Ex. 34:6).

Pastoral Prayer
Father, speak to our hearts as to when, where, and why today's scriptural principles apply to our hearts as individuals. Speak to us about ourselves and not others, that our fuses might be lengthened and that our anger would be handled appropriately according to Your agenda, for Your glory, Amen.

Related Proverbs
- 14:16–17; 18:6–8, 13, 20–23
- 19:1
- 20:15
- 21:23
- 22:11
- 22:17–18
- 23:9
- 24:7, 26
- 25:1–5
- 27:2
- 28:23
- 29:20

Benediction

> Part in peace: is day before us?
> Praise His Name for life and light;
> Are the shadows lengthening o'er us?
> Bless His care Who guards the night.
>
> —"Part in Peace: Is Day Before Us,"
> SARAH F. ADAMS, 1841

Additional Sermons and Lesson Ideas

Redeemer, Savior, Lord

Date preached:

Based on a Sermon by Dr. W. Graham Scroggie

SCRIPTURE: Isaiah 60:16

INTRODUCTION: Those who follow Christ must not only believe in Him mentally, but we must accept Him as:

1. Redeemer (Is. 60:16; Luke 24:20–21). Redemption is a market-place term carrying the idea of being bought with a price. The Lord, through Jesus Christ's blood, bought us (redeemed us) out of slavery to sin.
2. Savior (Is. 60:16; Luke 2:11). He who redeemed us also saved us. Redemption is through faith, but salvation is by grace through faith (Eph. 2:8). Our responsibility is to daily act out our faith in Christ.
3. Lord (Is. 60:16; Matt. 25:37–46). Jesus cannot be our Redeemer and Savior unless He is our Lord. True salvation is marked by obedience to Jesus as the Lord, the Master, the King of our lives.

CONCLUSION: Is the Redeemer your personal Savior? Is the Savior your Lord?

Why Do People Stray?

Date preached:

By Rev. Billie Friel

SCRIPTURE: James 5:19–20

INTRODUCTION: The hardest person to reach, according to surveys, is the person who has drifted away from the Lord and is out of fellowship with God's people.

1. The Reality of Straying People (v. 19). Christians can stumble in many ways (James 3:2). Christians can stray or wander from the truth. We are not perfect.
2. The Reasons People Stray (v. 19). People stray because of sin (1:14–15), bitterness towards others, falling out of good habits, doubts, or trials that cause them to think God has failed them.
3. The Response of Christians (vv. 19–20). A healthy Christian is used by God to turn the straying person back to the truth. In so doing, a person may be saved from premature death and the committing of needless sins.

CONCLUSION: We participate with God in a noble work with eternal dividends when we are used to bring the straying Christian back to Christ and His people.

SANCTITY OF LIFE SERMON

Jesus Loves Me, This I Know! *Date preached:*

Scripture: Psalm 139:14
I will praise You, for I am fearfully and wonderfully made; marvelous are Your works, and that my soul knows very well.

Introduction: When we talk about the "culture of death" and the "sanctity of life," we are entering the realms of both theology and politics. This is an area in which Christians should voice their convictions; and there is a place and a time for the church to speak to the moral issues of our day. But today I'd like to present the sanctity of life—not in terms of public debate—but in terms of private praise. God's love for us before, during, and after birth is a cause for earnest and sustained thanksgiving on the part of His people. The psalmist said, "I will praise You, for I am fearfully and wonderfully made."

1. **God Loves Us After Birth.** The word "sanctity" means "sacred" or "holy," and Christians view God as the Author and Giver of life. As it relates to the children, we can say with full Scripture authority that God loves them very much. Children are never viewed as second-class citizens in the Bible, but as precious souls to be raised in the nurture and admonition of the Lord. See Deuteronomy 6:4–9 and Ephesians 6:4. He loves the newborn infant, the temper-prone toddler, the precocious preschooler, and the quickly growing elementary child. "Jesus loves the little children, all the children of the world." The very words *child* and *children* occur 94 times in the Gospels alone, telling us that they are as important as any other element in the story of the Gospels. Some of our favorite stories involve children, such as the lad who brought his five loaves and two fish for Christ, and in so doing occasioned one of our Lord's greatest miracles. Jesus rebuked His disciples for keeping the children at a distance from Him, and He said, "Let the little children come to Me, . . . for of such is the kingdom of heaven" (Matt. 19:14).

2. **God Loves Us Before Birth.** According to Scripture, life begins from the moment of conception, and God knows and loves the unborn baby even in the womb. See Psalm 139:13–16 and Jeremiah 1:4. The psalmist said in Psalm 22:9–10: "Yet you brought me out of the

womb; you made me trust in you even at my mother's breast. From birth I was cast upon you; from my mother's womb you have been my God" (NIV). In fact, the Lord knows and loves children even *before* we are conceived in the womb. Ephesians 1:4 says, "He chose us in Him before the foundation of the world." Have you praised God for loving you when no one else could see you, when you were carried in the warm darkness beneath your mother's heart?

3. **God Loves the Holiness of Conception.** Dr. Hilary Jones wrote (not in a Christian publication, but in a medical one): "So complex are the biological mechanisms through which pregnancy takes place that conception really is a miracle of life." The Lord created Adam and Eve as full and mature adults; but He built into their physical and emotional systems the capacity of a loving touch whereby another human being would be created from a tiny sperm and a tiny egg, and done so in a moment of joy. Out of that miracle comes you and me. When you look at modern medical pictures showing the development of the baby inside the womb, it is an engineering marvel, a brilliant stroke of creation that defies description. At that remarkable moment of conception, all the characteristics of each person—sex, eye color, shoe size, intelligence, etc.—are determined by the baby's genetic code in the 46 human chromosomes. Every person begins as a separate single cell; nothing new is added but oxygen and nutrition. At three weeks, the baby's heart begins to beat and pump blood. At six weeks, the baby has brain waves that can be measured with an electroencephalogram. What creative genius on God's part, to so design and build such wondrous complexity into the human body.

Conclusion: I know the sanctity of life is a political issue today, but apart from political morality and public policy, it's a matter of praise and thanksgiving for believers. The psalmist praised God for the marvel of his life before birth and after birth. God loves you and He loves your children. We are precious in His sight. He loves the little ones kicking in the womb and the big ones kicking their soccer balls. We can all say, "Jesus loves me, this I know; for the Bible tells me so." Have you ever praised and thanked Him that you are so fearfully and wonderfully made? Before we can enter the realm of politics with our ideas, we must enter the realm of praise with our wonder and awe at His loving genius.

O Lord, life is sacred, a gift from above;
Each person is worthy of honor and love.
Your works are so marvelous, we're wonderfully made;
We each bear Your image, conception to grave.

Your hands shaped and formed us before we took breath;
You knit us together and clothed us with flesh.
You give us our life and ordain all our days;
Your works, Lord, are wonderful; we lift our hearts in praise.

Upheld since conception and carried since birth,
To old age and hair of gray, we're still of great worth.
We still bear Your likeness, the stamp of Your hand;
You made us in Jesus for all the works you planned.

And so, may we honor each person we meet;
The kindness You've shown us, we wish to repeat
From children to agèd—we'll serve them in Your Name;
As You honor us, O Lord, we pledge to do the same.
—Susan H. Peterson, 1998[1]

---

[1] This hymn, "O Lord, Life Is Sacred," by Susan H. Peterson has been released into the public domain and may be freely used. It's found at www.cyberhymnal.org, and may be sung to the tune of "My Jesus, I Love Thee."

JANUARY 28, 2007

SUGGESTED SERMON

The Fear of the Lord

Date preached:

By Rev. Peter Grainger

Scripture: Proverbs 1:1–7; 3:1–8, especially 1:7
The fear of the LORD is the beginning of knowledge, but fools despise wisdom and instruction.

Introduction: The opening paragraph of the Book of Proverbs summarizes the message of the whole book: "The fear of the LORD is the beginning of knowledge, but fools despise wisdom and instruction" (Prov. 1:7). There are two contrasting ways to live:

I. **The Way of the Wise.** The wise person, the one who is really in the know, lives his or her life in relationship with God. We should note that we can believe in God yet still be a fool.

A. **We Should Fear the Lord in a Relational Sense (Prov. 1:1–7).** Both the word "fear" and the special name for God, "the LORD," demonstrate that living wisely means living your life in relationship with God. The word "fear" has both negative and positive aspects. Negatively it means "dread" or "terror"; positively it means "awe" or "reverence." So the wise person lives in the fear of the Lord—drawn by the beauty of the radiance of the Lord's presence yet not overstepping the bounds into a familiarity in which the same light can also damage or even destroy a mere mortal.

B. **We Should Fear the Lord in a Universal Sense (Prov. 3:19–20).** This fear of the Lord extends to every part of life, not just to some religious dimension or activity. Why? Because the Lord is the Creator and Governor of all things which reflect and display His purpose and design. So Proverbs 3 tells us, "The LORD by wisdom founded the earth; by understanding He established the heavens; by His knowledge the depths were broken up, and clouds drop down the dew" (vv. 19–20). So the wise person who lives in the fear of the Lord lives in harmony with the world God has created. Our very lives belong to God; we must live in obedience to God and in dependence on God.

2. **The Way of the Fool (Prov. 3:1–8).** The way of the fool is already obvious for it is diametrically opposed to the way of the wise. It is to live in rebellion or opposition to God: passively, by trying to ignore Him, and actively, by directly disobeying Him. We must recognize two things:

A. **Humans Have All Chosen the Fool's Way (Ps. 14:1–3).** Human history is full of foolish rebellion against God, beginning with our first parents who chose to disobey the Creator's instructions and eat the forbidden fruit. They believed the serpent, that in eating it they would become all *wise* like God (Gen. 3). The promise was a lie, and the harmony of God's perfect creation was disrupted as sin and death entered the world. The relationship with God for which human beings were made was broken. Despite this, ever since then all human beings have followed the same path for by nature we are rebels against God's authority.

B. **Humans Are Without Excuse for Choosing the Fool's Way (Rom. 1:18–23).** From this passage, we see that being religious does not make us wise; we can be religious fools. We were created to be worshipers. The problem is that we want a religion where we are in control, a god who will legitimatize how we want to live, and a god who we can manipulate to do what we want. So we make and worship idols and dethrone the true God from His rightful place in our lives and in our societies.

Conclusion: So, there are only these two ways to live: the way of the wise and the way of the fool. We have all chosen the wrong option resulting in the tragic consequences of pain and death; this is the bad news. The New Testament gives us the good news, the "gospel" which means "good news." Rather than leaving us to suffer the consequences of our foolish rebellion which we fully deserve, God stepped into our fallen world in human flesh in the person of His Son, Jesus. For the first time in human history since Adam fell, a human being (Jesus) perfectly lived the way of the wise, in perfect harmony with the Creator's design, in perfect obedience to the Father's will. Now, beyond the evidence of God's character seen in creation and in His will as revealed to Israel, God spoke finally and decisively through His Son, Jesus: His last and best Word. When Jesus died on the Cross, He paid the price for our rebellion and made a way by which we can be reconciled to God— providing that we lay down our arms and submit to His authority. I beg you to make this decision today, the wisest decision you will ever make.

STATS, STORIES, AND MORE

Cleverer than Ever!
The headlines of a leading article in the Daily Express announced:

Daily Express, Monday January 7 2002
Why We Brits are Cleverer than Ever

The article was based on a survey undertaken by James Flynn, professor at the University of Otago in New Zealand. Professor Flynn, a leading expert in IQ—intelligence quotient—says that data from thousands of tests show that the IQs of Brits have improved by an average of 27 points since the Second World War. In America, by comparison, average IQ has risen by just 24 points since 1918—and no other major competitor matches this boost in British cleverness.

Whether this is to be believed is a matter for debate. As a Brit, I must say I warm to the professor's findings; as an older Brit I find it very hard to believe that today's generation of young people are smarter than mine.

But whatever the case, of one thing I am sure: though we may be cleverer than ever, we are not necessarily any wiser. There is a world of difference between being clever and being wise. It is possible to be a clever fool.

The premise behind the subtitle of the article demonstrates this failure to distinguish between being clever and being wise:

The Future Looks Bright as Research Shows
Our IQ Outstrips World Competitors

In other words, if we Brits are cleverer than the rest, then our national prospects are better than those of the rest of the world. Or, on a personal level, the cleverer you are, the better your prospects in life. But in fact it is not only possible to be a clever fool; it is also possible to be a prosperous fool. You can even be a religious fool. Even in Britain, polls regularly demonstrate that around two-thirds or three-quarters of the population say that they believe in God.   —Rev. Peter Grainger

APPROPRIATE HYMNS AND SONGS

"Be Thou My Vision," Eleanor Hull/Mary E. Byrne, Public Domain.

"I Stand in Awe," Mark Altrogge, 1987 People of Destiny International (Admin. PDI Ministries).

"I Exalt Thee," Pete Sanchez, Jr., 1977 Pete Sanchez, Jr. (Admin. Gabriel Music Inc.).

"My Savior's Love," Charles H. Gabriel, Public Domain.

"Awesome God," Rich Mullins, 1988 BMG Songs Inc. (Admin. BMG Music Publishing).

FOR THE BULLETIN

Charles the Great (Charlemagne, King of the Franks) died on this day, January 28, in 814. His great ambition in life was to unite under his rule all the Teutonic and Latin peoples and bring them under the authority of the Pope. He is highly respected for his efforts to further education during the Middle Ages. ● Emperor Charles V convened an Imperial Congress in Worms, a German city on the Rhine, on January 28, 1521, to investigate the teachings of Martin Luther. Luther's arrival in Worms was heralded by city watchmen blowing horns, and thousands gathered to watch him step from his wagon and enter the congress. It was at this assembly that Luther reportedly uttered the famous words, "Here I stand. I can do no other. God help me! Amen." ● On January 28, 1548, King Henry VIII, died at age fifty-five, with Archbishop Thomas Cramner by his side. Cramner was then left to guide the nation and the new king, young Edward VI, toward Protestantism. ● Today is the birthday, in 1814, of the great Roman Catholic clergyman, Frederick W. Faber, whose hymns are loved by Protestants and Catholics alike. They include "My God How Wonderful Thou Art," "Faith of Our Fathers," and "There's a Wideness in God's Mercy." This is also the birthday of the eccentric British preacher, author, educator, and hymnist, Sabine Baring-Gould, who wrote the hymns "Onward Christian Soldiers," and "Now the Day Is Over." ● R. A. Torrey was born on January 28, 1856. And missionary John Paton passed away on this day in 1907. His biography is stranger than fiction as he invested a lifetime of adventurous ministry among the cannibals of the New Hebrides Islands.

Call to Worship

If anyone thirsts, let him come to Me and drink. He who believes in Me, as the Scripture has said, out of his heart will flow rivers of living water (John 7:37–38).

Offertory Comments

I read about a panhandler who asked a woman for a dollar. She paused, dug into her purse, and handed him a dollar bill, saying, "I'm giving you this dollar, not because you deserve it but because it pleases me to do so." He took the dollar and said, "Thank you ma'am; but while you're at it, why not make it ten and really enjoy yourself!"

We should enjoy being able to give generously to the Lord's work, for the Bible says, "So let each one give as he purposes in his heart, not grudgingly or of necessity; for God loves a cheerful giver. And God is able to make all grace abound toward you, that you, always having all sufficiency in all things, may have an abundance for every good work" (2 Cor. 9:7–8).

Scripture Reading

Then some of the scribes and Pharisees answered, saying, "Teacher, we want to see a sign from You." But He answered and said to them, "An evil and adulterous generation seeks after a sign, and no sign will be given to it except the sign of the prophet Jonah. For as Jonah was three days and three nights in the belly of the great fish, so will the Son of Man be three days and three nights in the heart of the earth. The men of Nineveh will rise up in the judgment with this generation and condemn it, because they repented at the preaching of Jonah; and indeed a greater than Jonah is here. The queen of the South will rise up in the judgment with this generation and condemn it, for she came from the ends of the earth to hear the wisdom of Solomon; and indeed a greater than Solomon is here (Matt. 12:38–42).

Additional Sermons and Lesson Ideas

The Model Man
By Dr. Melvin Worthington

Date preached:

SCRIPTURE: Various, especially Genesis 1—3

INTRODUCTION: The crown of God's creation was man. The creation record is found in Genesis 1—3. Adam was the first created man and the father of the human race.

1. Adam's Creation: The Sovereign Molded Him (Gen. 1:26–28). *The treatise on the Creation* (Gen. 1; 2; Heb. 11; 2 Pet. 3), *the testimony of the Creator* (Gen. 1:26–28), and *the truth of creation* (Gen. 1; 2) are addressed.
2. Adam's Corruption: The Sin that Marred Him (Gen. 3, Rom. 5). Adam's fall can be summarized by *disobedience* (Gen. 3:6; 2:16–17; 1 Tim. 2:13–14), by *depravity* (Gen. 3:7–11), *by death* (Gen. 3:19; Rom. 5), and *by dismissal* (Gen. 3:22–24).
3. Adam's Covering: The Salvation that Mended Him (Gen. 3:21). We see in Adam's covering *a provision, a picture,* and *a punishment.*
4. Adam's Children: The Siblings that Marked Him (Gen. 1; Gen. 4; 5; 6; Rom. 5).

CONCLUSION: Jesus Christ came as the "second Adam" to reconcile God's created people to Himself (Rom. 5)!

At All Times

Date preached:

SCRIPTURE: Psalm 62

INTRODUCTION: There is a sermon in each of the three lines of this verse, and the key to each sermon is found in the first word of each line (NKJV).

1. TRUST. In Psalm 62, David was distressed by certain difficult people (vv. 3–4 and 9–10). My own reaction to troubling people swings from anxiety to anger, but the psalmist advised trusting our Lord at all times. The phrase "at all times" occurs four times in the Psalms. We should bless the Lord at all times (Ps. 34:1); trust Him at all times (Ps. 62:8); live righteously at all times (Ps. 106:3), and desire His Word at all times (Ps. 119:20).
2. POUR. Three times in the Psalms, prayer is likened to pouring our hearts out to God (Ps. 42:4; 62:8; 142:2).
3. GOD. Here in Psalm 68, God is our Rock, our Salvation, our Defense, our Expectation, our Glory, the Rock of our Strength, and our Refuge.

CONCLUSION: Visualize Him enclosing you within the boundaries of His grace, for there's no safer place to be. He's your Mighty Fortress, a Bulwark never failing.

A Good Book for Worried Pastors

A pastor from Tanzania recently told me he had planted a church of about five hundred people, but the Muslims came and burned it down, scattering the people. My friend continued the services in a hotel, but the Muslims broke into his house and beat his wife and children. Now he has moved his family out of the area, and he's going back to minister to his beleaguered people, about 200 of which still meet out-of-doors under a tree. I asked how he was dealing with the stress, and he said, "I cry some, then I pray some, then I put it in the Lord's hands."

A lot of us pastors do the same thing with our own burdens. Not even the apostle Paul could avoid the stress of pastoring and preaching. To me, one of the most amazing admissions in Paul's life occurred in 2 Corinthians 2:12, when he said, "Furthermore, when I came to Troas to preach Christ's gospel, and a door was opened to me by the Lord, I had no rest in my spirit, because I did not find Titus my brother; but taking my leave of them, I departed for Macedonia."

That's a truly remarkable confession. Troas was a port city on the Aegean, closer to Europe than any other Asian harbor. Here a great door opened for Paul to establish a church. We don't know the exact nature of the opportunity, but Paul specifically says it was opened by the Lord Himself.

But Paul was too paralyzed with anxiety to function. He couldn't seize the opportunity because he was worried about Titus and the Corinthians. Titus was to have rendezvoused with him in Troas, bringing news about the unsettled church in Corinth and perhaps transporting a sizable offering. But Titus didn't show up, and Paul was thrown off balance. He admitted, in effect: "I lost my inner peace. I had no rest. I couldn't focus on my work. I finally had to leave Troas and go on to Macedonia in agitation."

His mental state in Macedonia was no better. "For indeed, when we came to Macedonia, our bodies had no rest, but we were

Continued on the next page

THOUGHTS FOR THE PASTOR'S SOUL—*Continued*

troubled on every side. Outside were conflicts, inside were fears" (2 Cor. 7:5).

We know how he felt, don't we? When my teenage youngster, for example, strayed away from the Lord, we encountered a series of crises that almost paralyzed me. Perhaps you're going through something similar now, for the enemy often attacks our families in an effort to hinder our work.

A man told me the other day he worked for years to lead his church into a building program. At last the congregation moved into a beautiful new sanctuary, and their first Sunday in the building was a day of great joy. "But," he said, "not for me. I could hardly concentrate. In the wee hours of the morning, my teenage son had come home drunk and belligerent and ruined our night and broke our hearts. And though I tried to hide it that day, I felt only pain and grief."

The devil looks for every opportunity, and Paul often blamed Satan with the stresses and distresses that occurred in his ministry.

But here's the thing with Paul. He didn't stay down. He didn't lose heart or falter in the ultimate power of his enthusiasm. He knew how to encourage himself in the Lord; and in 2 Corinthians he tells us his secrets with verses like:

> *Furthermore, when I came to Troas to preach Christ's gospel, and a door was opened to me by the Lord, I had no rest in my spirit, because I did not find Titus my brother; but taking my leave of them, I departed for Macedonia. Now thanks be to God who always leads us in triumph in Christ.*

> *Not that we are sufficient of ourselves, to think of anything as being from ourselves, but our sufficiency is from God.*

> *Now the Lord is the Spirit; and where the Spirit of the Lord is, there is liberty. But we all, with unveiled face, beholding as in a mirror the glory of the Lord, are being transformed into the same image from glory to glory, just as by the Spirit of the Lord.*

🐚 *For though we walk in the flesh, we do not war according to the flesh. For the weapons of our warfare are not carnal but mighty in God for pulling down strongholds. . . .*

🐚 *We are hard-pressed on every side, yet not crushed; we are perplexed, but not in despair. . . .*

🐚 *A thorn in the flesh was given to me, a messenger of Satan to buffet me, lest I be exalted above measure. Concerning this thing I pleaded with the Lord three times that it might depart from me. And He said to me, "My grace is sufficient for you, for My strength is made perfect in weakness."*

🐚 *Be of good comfort. . . . And the God of love and peace will be with you.*

I believe 2 Corinthians is God's special book for worried pastors. If you're anxious or troubled, you might try camping out there for awhile. It's like an extended counseling session with the apostle Paul; or even better—with the Lord Jesus Himself. I did this in Chicago at a little coffee shop on the plaza of the Hancock Building. My wife and I took a few days for rest and relaxation, and while she readied herself for the day, I'd go sit in the sunshine, drink a cup of strong coffee, and work my way through 2 Corinthians.

A lakeside picnic table would have done just as well, or a tent in the woods, or a kitchen table in the country. Take a pen, paper, some markers, whatever works for you. Let the Lord speak to you personally about your pressures. Let Him renew you in this amazing little book of thirteen lucky chapters. And . . .

. . . *do not lose heart. Even though out outward man is perishing, yet the inward man is being renewed day by day. For our light and momentary affliction, which is but for a moment, is working for us a far more exceeding and eternal weight of glory, while we do not look at the things that are seen, but at the things which are not seen. For the things which are seen are temporary, but the things which are not seen are eternal.*

FEBRUARY 4, 2007

SUGGESTED SERMON

Father Forgive Them

Date preached:

By Dr. Ed Dobson

Scripture: Luke 23:34
Father, forgive them, for they do not know what they do.

Introduction: Someone once said that you can truly know a man's heart by his last words. If you knew today was your last, what words would come out of your mouth? If you were being led away to execution, what would you say? The perfection of Christ is magnificently displayed by His last words, seven phrases He said from the Cross. Today, we will look at the first phrase: "Father, forgive them, for they do not know what they do."

1. **The Definition of Forgiveness.** To forgive is to release another person from a debt that they owe me as a result of a wrong they have done against me. There are three elements to forgiveness. First, I am wronged. Second, there is a sense of debt, that person owes me something. Finally, forgiveness is releasing that person, canceling the debt. It is to say, "You hurt me, and there is a sense of debt and obligation that accompanies that hurt, but I release you, I forgive you, I cancel the debt."

2. **The Essence of Forgiveness.** The essence of forgiveness is found in the first three words of this statement: Father, forgive them.

   A. **The Source of Forgiveness.** The source of all forgiveness is God. Human beings cannot forgive the debt of sin that we owe to God. The church cannot forgive the debt of sin we owe to God. Religious ceremonies and liturgies cannot forgive the debt of sin we owe to God. Only one person can forgive sin.

   B. **The Means of Forgiveness.** Who is making this request? Jesus. God is the source of forgiveness, God cancels the debt, we owe the debt to God, but the means of that forgiveness is through Jesus Christ. In fact, the name Jesus means savior. He came to this earth to suffer and to die and to rise again so that through Jesus the Savior we could be forgiven by a holy God.

C. **The Benefactors of Forgiveness.** Father, forgive *them*. It's God forgiving human beings, you and me. Father, forgive them. So you have the essence of forgiveness.

3. **Questions About the Forgiveness of Christ from the Cross.** This statement raises some difficult theological and moral issues; issues like, who is Jesus forgiving? Of what are they forgiven? Does God forgive people without people asking forgiveness? If these people are forgiven, does that then mean that they are "off the hook with God"? Let's look at these questions.

A. **Who Is Jesus Forgiving?** In this passage, Jesus has a specific group in mind. Is He speaking of religious leaders or the crowds? The context actually makes it very clear. Verse 32 tells us that when they arrived at Golgotha, *they* crucified Him, that is, the Roman soldiers. That group of soldiers was assigned the military duty to crucify all of these criminals. They were doing their duty.

B. **Of What Did Jesus Forgive Them?** The Father certainly would have unbelievable wrath towards those who crucify the image of His glory! Jesus forgave them of their crucifixion, their execution of Himself.

C. **Does God Forgive People Without Their Asking?** The answer is no. The Bible makes it clear that we must confess our sins to God to be forgiven (1 John 1:9). The principle of both Old and New Testament is that forgiveness is premised on confession and repentance with one historical exemption: at the foot of the cross where Jesus, on the cross, asks the Father not to hold this sin of crucifixion against the soldiers who nailed Him to the cross.

D. **Were the Soldiers Off the Hook with God?** Were they forgiven of all of their sins? No. It only means that Jesus asked that this one sin of crucifixion not be held against them. They were, like we are, fully responsible and accountable to God for all of the sins that they had committed.

E. **Why Did Jesus Specifically Forgive This Sin?** First, Jesus was simply practicing what He had preached. This was entirely consistent with His teaching (see Matt. 5:43–48). Second, Christ was offering a model, an example for all believers. When we are misrepresented, rejected, persecuted, and unjustly treated, our response must be like that of our Savior.

Conclusion: So I ask you a question: what about the people who have wronged me, or oppose me, or harass me? What is my response to them? If we will practice the forgiveness of Christ, people will begin to ask us the reason of the hope which lies within us.

STATS, STORIES, AND MORE

How to Treat Others

➤ "Beginning today, treat everyone you meet as if they were going to be dead by midnight. Extend to them all the care, kindness, and understanding you can muster, and do it with no thought of any reward. Your life will never be the same again." —*Og Mandino*

Clogged Pipes

Suppose you went into a restroom to find a commode had been used again and again without anyone having bothered to flush it. Suppose, being a brave (or desperate) soul, you edged close enough to flush it. But the drain was so clogged that the water backed up, spilling the entire mess across the floor. That's a picture of a human heart that refuses to flush away its anger, resentment, and bitterness. The unhealthy debris builds up and backs up until the person's life becomes toxic and repulsive. It spills into other people's lives. That's why Ephesians 4:32 tells us to be kind and compassionate to one another, forgiving each other just as in Christ God forgave each of us. Colossians 3 tells us to rid ourselves of all such things as these: anger, rage, malice . . . Bear with each other and forgive whatever grievances you may have against one another. Forgive as the Lord forgave you." I wonder if someone here needs a spiritual plumber. Your heart is clogged by anger, bitterness, hurt feelings, or an unforgiving spirit. God has forgiven you of your sins against Him through Jesus Christ. But you haven't extended His grace toward others. The grace of God demonstrated in Jesus Christ is a plunger that can unclog the heart and clear the pipes. Discover the power of forgiveness.

APPROPRIATE HYMNS AND SONGS

"Amazing Grace How Can It Be," Baynard L. Fox, 1967 Fox Music Publications (Admin. Fred Brock Music Co.).

"Choose to Forgive," Rick Riso/Mark Levang, 1994 Integrity's Hosanna! Music (Integrity Music, Inc.).

"Forgive One Another," Lenny LeBlanc/Kelly Willard/Rita Baloche, 1990 Maranatha Music/Doulos Publishing.

"He Set Me Free," Albert E. Brumley 1939. Renewed 1967 Stamps-Baxter Music (Brentwood-Benson Music Publishing, Inc.).

"Sweet Forgiveness," Brent Helming, 1998 Mercy/Vineyard Publishing (Admin. Mercy/Vineyard Publishing).

FOR THE BULLETIN

In A.D. 776, Rabanus Maurus was born in Germany. His parents sent him to the best schools, and he was eventually mentored by the great Alcuin. He went on to become principal of the school in Fulda, and under his leadership German youth, both poor and rich, were afforded an education. His graduates were in demand across Europe. At the heart of Rabanus' educational genius was a passion for God's Word, and he worked faithfully for Christ until February 4, 856, when, at age 80, the Lord transferred him home. ● On February 4, 1555, John Rogers became the first of many Protestant martyrs to be burned alive at Smithfield under Queen Mary. He left a wife and eleven children. ● Aboard the *Simmonds,* John and Charles Wesley spot the colony of Georgia for the first time. "I saw land," John wrote in his journal. "A great door and effectual is opened unto us. O let no man shut it." Nevertheless, the brothers' time in America was difficult, and they returned to England with a sense of failure. Shortly afterward, the two men, first Charles and then John, experienced Christ in a new way and went on to become history-altering evangelists. ● On February 4, 1810, the Cumberland Presbyterian Church was organized in Middle Tennessee as an outgrowth of the Great Revival of 1800. ● The Codex Sinaiticus was discovered by Konstantin von Tischendorf in St. Catherine's Monastery on Mount Sinai, on this day in 1859. ● February 4, 1873, marks the birth of George Bennard, American Methodist preacher, who wrote over three hundred gospel songs including "The Old Rugged Cross." On this day in 1874, hymnist Frances Ridley Havergal wrote her testimony song, "Take My Life and Let It Be." ● Today is the birthday, in 1906, of the German martyr Dietrich Bonhoeffer.

Kid's Talk

Ask the children, "When you do something really bad, does it make you afraid of your mom or dad?" Allow a few to answer. Then say, "Let me ask a different question: who do you think loves you more than anyone in this world?" Again, allow responses. When one or more answers "my mom" or "my dad," tell them: "You know, the Bible tells us to fear God. We are supposed to fear Him because He will discipline us like our parents do when we do wrong. But, just like our parents, we still know that He loves us more than anyone ever could and only disciplines us because of His love."

WORSHIP HELPS

Call to Worship
With gladness and rejoicing they shall be brought; they shall enter the King's palace (Ps. 45:15).

Pastoral Prayer
Our God, we confess how far we fall short of the example and the model of Jesus. Grant us the inner attitudes and outward actions, the gentleness and kindness and patience and love and compassion of Jesus Christ. I pray for those who are struggling with this issue of forgiveness. May we through the grace and forgiveness that You have given us extend that grace and forgiveness to those who have wronged us. Dismiss us now with Your blessing and in Jesus' name, Amen.

Reader's Theater (or Responsive Reading)

Reader 1: The fear of the LORD is the beginning of knowledge, but fools despise wisdom and instruction (Prov. 1:7).

Reader 2: Do not be wise in your own eyes; fear the LORD and depart from evil (Prov. 3:7).

Reader 1: The fear of the LORD is to hate evil; pride and arrogance and the evil way and the perverse mouth I hate (Prov. 8:13).

Reader 2: The fear of the LORD prolongs days, but the years of the wicked will be shortened (Prov. 10:27).

Reader 1: In mercy and truth atonement is provided for iniquity; and by the fear of the LORD one departs from evil (Prov. 16:6).

Reader 2: Do not let your heart envy sinners, but be zealous for the fear of the LORD all the day; for surely there is a hereafter, and your hope will not be cut off (Prov. 23:17–18).

Additional Sermons and Lesson Ideas

He Who Has Come Is Now Present to Fill
Date preached:
Based on an Outline by Rev. E. H. Hopkins

SCRIPTURE: Various

INTRODUCTION: Our message today is for believers who long to be filled with the Holy Spirit. Let me suggest three steps:

1. Recognize You Have the Spirit (1 Cor. 3:16). We must recognize the Spirit's presence in our lives despite our shortcomings; the Corinthians to whom this verse was written were called "carnal" a few verses before (3:1)!
2. Put Away Every Evil Thing (Eph. 4:25–31). Bitterness, evil, anger, lying, and all the sins listed in this passage are but a few of those that grieve the Holy Spirit.
3. Don't Expect the Spirit's Power to Replace Faith (Acts 4:23–31). The apostles' prayer was recorded in these verses after Pentecost, yet they were humble, full of faith, and asking God for His enabling and empowering.

CONCLUSION: Believers, we are indwelled by the Spirit. Let's live a Spirit-filled life; reject sinful behavior and continue in humility and complete dependence upon the Spirit!

Battle Gear 101
Date preached:
By Dr. Larry Osborne

SCRIPTURE: Various

INTRODUCTION: What soldier goes into battle with no gun, no helmet, and no camouflage? Our soldiers are always well equipped. We must be just as prepared for spiritual war as the Bible describes it. We must:

1. Identify Our Enemy. Our enemy is not Christians whom we have problems with (Eph. 4:2–6; 1 Cor. 3:1–9; Col. 3:13; Rom. 14—15), nor is it "bad" people (John 3:15; 2 Tim. 2:24–26). Our enemy is Satan and his demonic forces (Eph. 6:12–13; 1 Pet. 5:8; 1 John 5:19; Rev. 12:9–10).
2. Recognize Our Vulnerability. Scripture reminds us both that we have power and victory over the enemy, but we must not become careless or haughty (Eph. 6:10–11, 13; Jude 9–10; 1 Cor. 10:12; Phil. 4:13).
3. Prepare for Satan's Strategy. He desires to knock us off track with attacks that make us question God's goodness and dependability; we must be prepared (Eph. 6:11, 13, 16; John 8:44; Gen. 3:1–5; Job 1:8–11; Ps. 73).
4. Carry Out Our Assignment. Put on the full armor of God (Eph. 6:11, 13) and persevere, doing right no matter what (1 Pet. 4:19, 5:8–11; Matt. 4:1–11).

CONCLUSION: Put on your battle gear!

Scripture Promises
By Samuel Clarke

It's funny how a book can endure for several generations, make a gigantic impact on the world, then fade away like the ghost of Christmas past. Such is the way with classics, but only because the human race is as short-sighted as the individuals who comprise it. Italian novelist Italo Calvino put it well when he reminded us, "A classic is a book that has never finished saying what it has to say."

Here's a classic that should be rediscovered: *A Collection of Scripture Promises Under the Proper Headings.* Commonly called *Scripture Promises,* it was edited and compiled by Samuel Clarke, who lived from 1684 to 1750 (not to be confused with the British philosopher and theologian by the same name who lived 1675–1725). Clarke, who came from a long line of Puritan ministers, was ordained in 1712, and the closing exhortation at his ordination service was given by none less than Matthew Henry, the famous Bible commentator.

Clarke's ministry was marked by a love and concern for young people. He taught a weekly Bible class for young people, and he launched a charity school for the children of Protestant Dissenters. It was Clarke who rescued and discipled a boy named Philip Doddridge who arrived destitute on his doorstep at age thirteen and who later became a famous pastor and the author of the hymn "O Happy Day!" Doddridge later preached Clarke's funeral, saying, "To him under God I owe even myself and all my opportunities of public usefulness in the church."

It was while working with young people that Clarke decided to compile a small list of promises for them to study and memorize. The more he searched the Scriptures and jotted down references, the more he was overwhelmed by the sheer number and practicality of promises he found. As he imported these verses onto his private lists, he began to categorize and organize them under various headings, and thus was born Clarke's *Scripture Promises.*

The best and older editions of this book contain Clarke's original introduction which is a priceless commentary on the power and efficacy of God's precious promises. In his quaint Puritan style, he wrote:

> A fixed, constant attention to the promises, and a firm belief in them, would prevent solicitude and anxiety about the concerns of this life. It would keep the mind quiet and composed in every change, and support and keep up our sinking spiritus under the several troubles of life. "In the multitude of my thoughts within me, thy comforts delight my soul." Christians deprive themselves of their most solid comforts by their unbelief and forgetfulness of God's promises. For there is no extremity so great but there are promises suitable to it, and abundantly sufficient for our relief in it.
>
> A thorough acquaintance with the promises would be of the greatest advantage in prayer. With what comfort may the Christian address himself to God in Christ when he considers the repeated assurances that his prayers shall be heard! With how much satisfaction may he offer up the several desires of his heart when he reflects upon the texts wherein those very mercies are promised! And with what fervour of spirit and strength of faith may he enforce his prayers by pleading the several gracious promises which are expressly to his case!

The year of Clarke's death, a new edition of his *Scripture Promises* was published with his friend, Isaac Watts, writing a new introduction. I love the way Watts described the promises of Scripture:

> These are the most powerful motives of duty; these are the constant food of a living Christian, as well as his highest cordials in a fainting hour. And in such a world as this, where duties perpetually demand our practice, and difficulties and trials are ever surrounding us, what can we do better than to treasure up the promises in our hearts, which are the most effectual persuasives to fulfill the one and sustain

Continued on the next page

CLASSICS FOR THE PASTOR'S LIBRARY—*Continued*

the other? Here are laid up the true riches of a Christian, and his highest hopes on this side of heaven.

A hundred years later, the English General Charles Gordon introduced this book to a new generation of readers by advocating it as one of the most powerful books ever compiled and giving a copy to every member of the Cabinet of Prime Minister William Gladstone.

In the twentieth century, missionary/author Rosalind Goforth told her readers how this book had virtually saved her life during the Boxer Rebellion. She and her husband, Jonathan, and their four children were trapped in the city of Hsintein. Multitudes of Christians and scores of missionaries were being slaughtered throughout China by the Boxers, and a bloodthirsty mob gathered around the inn where the Goforths were resting. The whole family knew their survival was unlikely. Rosalind later wrote in her 1921 book, *How I Know God Answers Prayer:*

> Suddenly, without the slightest warning, I was seized with an overwhelming fear of what might be awaiting us. It was not the fear of after death, but of probable torture, that took such awful hold of me. I thought, "Can this be the Christian courage I have looked for?" I went by myself and prayed for victory, but no help came. Just then someone called us to a room for prayer before getting into the carts. Scarcely able to walk for trembling, and utterly ashamed that others should see my state of panic . . . I managed to reach a bench beside which my husband stood. He drew from his pocket a little book, Clarke's *Scripture Promises,* and read the verses his eyes first fell on . . . . The effect of these words at such a time was remarkable. All realized that God was speaking to us. Never was there a message more directly given to mortal man from his God than that message to us. From almost the first verse my whole soul seemed flooded with a great peace; all trace of panic vanished; and I felt God's

presence was with us. Indeed, His presence was so real it could scarcely have been more so had we seen a visible form.

I found a small, green, hardbound copy of Clarke's *Scripture Promises* from a used book seller, and I cherish it as one of my favorite classics. Except for Clarke's introduction, it is totally comprised of Scripture verses, but what Scriptures they are! Reading them with a contemplative heart makes us aware of the very presence of the Lord, for His promises reflect His presence and reveal His power. As the apostle Peter reminds us, His divine power has given us all things that pertain to life and godliness, through the knowledge of Him who called us by glory and virtue, by which have been given us to exceedingly great and precious promises.

Quote for the Pastor's Wall

For years I have made it a very careful and studied rule never to look at a commentary on a text, until I have spent time on the text alone. Get down and sweat over the text yourself. That is my method.

—G. Campbell Morgan in *Preaching*[1]

---

[1]G. Campbell Morgan, *Preaching* (Fleming H. Revell, 1937), p. 61.

FEBRUARY 11, 2007

SUGGESTED SERMON

Searching for a Spouse

Date preached:

By Rev. Todd M. Kinde

Scripture: Genesis 24:1–27, especially verses 3 and 4

. . . and I will make you swear by the LORD, the God of heaven and the God of the earth, that you will not take a wife for my son from the daughters of the Canaanites, among whom I dwell; but you shall go to my country and to my family, and take a wife for my son Isaac.

Introduction: One of the great ironies of our culture is how desperately people long for the love of their life but the divorce rate certainly doesn't reflect a lifetime of love. As God's people, how are we to be different in searching for a spouse? If you think your search is serious business, consider Isaac. He needed a wife not merely for his own comfort (Gen. 24:67), but so that the Messiah could come through his line some two thousand years yet in the future! Let's look at applications we can draw from his search.

1. **We Are to Marry Within the Family of God (24:1–9).** Verse 3 is quite clear: do not get a wife from among the Canaanites. The concern is that the line would be pure. We should not read ethnic purity into this text. The concern is spiritual purity. The Canaanites were a cursed people group because of their wickedness and rebellion against God (Gen. 9:24). Abraham was called away from the pagan idol worship of his own family. So to geographically return would have its dangers of wickedness too. The servant asks what he should do if the woman will not come back with him. Is Isaac then to go back to the old country and the old way of life? The answer is a resounding, "No!" The same principle applies to us (1 Cor. 7:39; 2 Cor. 6:14–15; cf. 1 Cor. 7:12–14; 1 Pet. 3:1–7).

2. **We Are to Pray for the Lord's Leading in Seeking Marriage (24:10–14).** The servant has managed the journey to the city of Nahor and now is faced with the task of finding the right family in the city. How will he accomplish that? He prays. He asks the Lord to lead

him to the right woman. He not only asks the Lord for guidance and direction, he also places himself in a very good spot to see all the women of the city—at the well. This is where most of the young women will be to get water for their households. So, we are to pray and to trust the Lord to direct us, but there's nothing wrong with joining a church singles group for an outing or purposely keeping our eyes out for other Christian single people—in fact, it's advisable.

3. **We Are to Reserve Sexual Intimacy for Marriage (24:15–21).** Before the servant has even finished praying God is providing the answer (v. 15). Rebekah comes from the right family. And not only is she from the right family but she is beautiful and she is sexually pure. She is a maiden and a virgin. We learn that we are to remain sexually pure in anticipation of marriage. This is the standard of God's holiness for us today. Sexual activity outside the bonds of covenant marriage is sin (1 Cor. 6:17–20; 1 Thess. 4:3–8).

4. **We Worship the Lord for His Love and Faithfulness to Us in Marriage (24:22–27).** The servant, discerning that he may have been successful in his mission, responds not with pride but with humility. He bows his head and worships the Lord who has been faithful. The servant has been "on the way" and the Lord directed his paths to the very point of fulfillment (Prov. 3:5–6). When we stand at the wedding ceremony and we see the bride coming down the aisle we don't say to ourselves, "What a great catch I made." No, we say, "Look who God has brought me to! God has been faithful to me!" Women, looking at that groom, you don't say "I sure got him where I want him," but, "Thank You Lord for giving me such a committed man of God."

Conclusion: There is yet another picture in this chapter that we must see. The work of Jesus Christ in His living and dying for sinners involves the promise of a Bride for Him. Jesus lived and died for His Bride. The Father gives to Christ the church as His Bride. God is faithful to His Son. Dear ones, we who are repentant of our sins, trusting Christ, and living a new life are the Bride of Christ. If you are not, we invite you to put your faith in Christ today.

STATS, STORIES, AND MORE

James Gilmour sailed for China in 1870, and plunged into re-opening the London Missionary Society's work in Mongolia. But he was lonely and badly in need of a wife. "Companions I can scarcely hope to meet," he wrote, "and the feeling of being alone comes over me." As labors increased, so did loneliness.

The pain deepened when his proposal to a Scotch girl was rejected. "I then put myself and the direction of this affair—I mean the finding of a wife—into God's hands, asking Him to look me out one, a good one, too."

In 1873, Gilmore visited friends in Peking, a Mr. and Mrs. Meech. Seeing a picture of Mrs. Meech's sister, Emily Prankard, James asked about her. As his hostess described Emily, James found himself falling in love. He gazed at her picture, saw some of her letters, and asked more and more questions.

Early next year, James wrote to Emily, proposing marriage in his first letter. By the same mail he informed his parents in Scotland: "I have written and proposed to a girl in England. It is true I have never seen her, and I know very little about her; but I have put the whole matter into the hands of God, asking Him, if it be best, to bring her, if it be not best, to keep her away, and He can manage the whole thing well."

Receiving Gilmore's letter, Emily took it at once to the throne of grace. Later Gilmore recalled, "The first letter I wrote her was to propose, and the first letter she wrote me was to accept." By autumn, Emily was in China, arriving on this day, November 29, 1874. A week later, they were married. Gilmore acquired both wife and colleague, and they labored faithfully side by side for years, reaching northern China for Christ (from *On This Day* by Robert J. Morgan).

APPROPRIATE HYMNS AND SONGS

"Household of Faith," Brent Lamb/John Rosasco, 1983 Straightway Music (EMI Christian Music Publishing).

"O Perfect Love," Dorothy Gurney/Joseph Barnby, Public Domain.

"I Will Be Here," Steven Curtis Chapman, 1989, 1990 Greg Nelson Music (EMI Christian Music Publishing).

"In This Very Room," Ron Harris/Carol Harris, 1979 Ron Harris Music (The Ron Harris Publishing Companies).

"Seekers of Your Heart," Melodie Tunney/Dick Tunney/Beverly Darnall, 1985 BMG Songs, Inc./Pamela K. Music (EMI Christian Music Publishing).

FOR THE BULLETIN

Today, February 11, is the birthday of William Williams (1717), Welch evangelist and hymnist, the author of "Guide Me, O Thou Great Jehovah" and nine hundred hymns. On this day in 1757, Anne Steele wrote her surprisingly vivid hymn, "Come, Let Our Souls Adore the Lord," the first lines of which read "Come, let our souls adore / the Lord whose judgments yet delay; / Who yet suspends the lifted sword, / And gives us time to pray." ● Today is also the birthday, in 1826, of Alexander Maclaren, the Scottish expository preacher. His set of expositional sermons through the Scripture is ranked next to Spurgeon's as the most widely read sermons of their day. ● Today is also the birthday, in 1836, of Washington Gladden, best known as the author of the hymn "O Master, Let Me Walk with Thee." Gladden, however, was liberal in his theology and is sometimes called the father of the American Social Gospel. ● On February 11, 1917, a nervous William Sangster preached his first sermon. Born in London in 1900, Sangster became a Christian at age thirteen and went on to become pastor of Westminster Central Hall, a Methodist church near London's Westminster Abbey. During his first worship service he announced to his stunned congregation that Britain and Germany were officially at war. He converted the church basement into an air raid shelter, and for 1,688 nights Sangster ministered to the various needs of all kinds of people. He became known as Wesley's successor in London and was esteemed as the most beloved British preacher of his era. ● On February 11, 1929, Vatican City was created as an independent sovereign state by the Lateran Treaty, signed by Mussolini, giving sovereignty to the Holy See for 109 acres. It is commonly called the smallest nation in the world.

WORSHIP HELPS

Call to Worship

Though you have not seen him, you love him; and even though you do not see him now, you believe in him and are filled with an inexpressible and glorious joy, for you are receiving the goal of your faith, the salvation of your souls (1 Pet. 1:8–9 NIV).

Offertory Prayer

For today's offertory prayer, try offering this verse, written by Samuel Longfellow (1819–1892). You could also sing it as a congregational hymn following the offering. It can be sung to the tune of the hymns "Lord, Speak to Me that I May Speak," "O Master, Let Me Walk with Thee," or even to the tune of the Doxology. (There is also a Twila Paris version of this hymn using her composition Lamb of God.)

> Bless Thou the gifts our hands have brought;
> Bless Thou the work our hearts have planned.
> Ours is the faith, the will, the thought:
> The rest, O God, is in Thy hand.

Benediction

I wait for your salvation, O LORD, and I follow your commands. I obey your statutes, for I love them greatly (Ps. 119:166–167 NIV).

Additional Sermons and Lesson Ideas

To Marry or Not to Marry
Date preached:

By Dr. Timothy K. Beougher

SCRIPTURE: 1 Corinthians 7:1–9

INTRODUCTION: While this message may be of particular help to those of you who are still single, Paul's words are very important to understand for all of us, as we have single children, friends, coworkers, etc., who may ask us for wisdom. Scripture is our source of wisdom, so let us study this topic together:

1. Consider the Context of this Passage (v. 1a)
2. Realize that Singleness is not Second Class (v. 1b)
3. Understand that Marriage is the Common Course (v. 2)
4. Recognize the Obligations of Marriage (vv. 2–5)
   A. Mutual Monogamy (v. 2)
   B. Mutual Responsibility (v. 3)
   C. Mutual Respect (vv. 4–5)
5. Follow God's Gifting and Direction (vv. 6–9)

CONCLUSION: Marriage is the norm, but God has called certain special people to a fuller devotion to His ministry, and has enabled them to carry out this calling.

The Wind of God
Date preached:

Based on an Outline by R. A. Torrey

SCRIPTURE: John 3:5–8

INTRODUCTION: The Holy Spirit is the "wind of God." Although we cannot see the wind, we can perceive and study its laws. Likewise, the Holy Spirit is invisible, but through Scripture we may learn the laws that govern the Holy Spirit.

1. The Holy Spirit Is Sovereign: "The wind blows where it wishes . . ." (v. 8).
2. The Holy Spirit Is Perceivable: "you hear the sound of it . . ." (v. 8).
3. The Holy Spirit Is Inscrutable: "but (you) cannot tell where it comes from or where it goes . . ." (v. 8).

CONCLUSION: The Holy Spirit Is Indispensable: "unless one is born of water and of the Spirit, he cannot enter the kingdom of God" (v. 5). Jesus Christ died on the Cross to pay for our sins, but rose to life and sent us His Spirit so we might be reborn. Have you been born again?

In the First Place . . .

One day in college, my buddy asked me to make a list of twenty-five objects without letting him know what they were. I grabbed a notepad and made my list: car, lamp, Bible, ball, puppy, heart, pizza, firecracker . . . .

"Now," he said, "read me the list."

I slowly did so while he listened with eyes closed. Then to my astonishment he opened his eyes and instantly quoted the list back to me item-for-item. Then he gave it to me backward, then he gave it to me skipping every other item.

"How did you do that?" I asked incredulously.

"Oh," he said, "it was nothing. It's a memory technique going back to the ancient Greek orators. It's called 'In the first place, in the second place.'"

He then explained that he had previously walked through his own house, selecting twenty-five sites. The first was his front porch, then the table in the entry hall, then the rug in the entry hall, then the sofa in the parlor, then the fireplace, etc. He memorized those twenty-five spots. "If you ask me for number fifteen," he said, "that's the kitchen stove. It took a little work to memorize the twenty-five spots, but once it's done, it's done."

"So when you read your list to me, you said your first item was a car. I simply visualized a car sitting on my front porch. Your second item, a lamp. I 'saw' that sitting smartly on the table in the entry hall. For the third item, I imagined an open Bible thrown down on the entry rug. A ball was rolling across the sofa, and the puppy was playing in the fireplace chasing sparks."

Since then, I've watched memory experts wow crowds at conventions with similar tricks, instantly learning and repeating long series of words—but I know how they do it. In fact, I occasionally do it myself while preaching.

Here's how it works for me. I've gone through my house and selected twelve spots, which is about all I need for my purposes. My first spot is the front yard, the second is the front porch, the third is the living room, the fourth is the back porch, the fifth is the kitchen table, the sixth is the stove island in the middle of the kitchen, the seventh is the . . . well, you get the picture. It's just a matter of walking into and through my house.

Having learned that grid, there are several ways I might put it to use. Suppose I have a message with these five points: (1) Our hope is in Christ. (2) Our peace is in Christ. (3) Our destiny is in Christ. (4) Our purpose is in Christ. (5) Our life is in Christ. Those five nouns are not objects like puppies or automobiles, so I have to do a little converting. For the first point I might visualize the Hope Diamond arranged for display on my front yard. Second, I might imagine a peace treaty being signed on my front porch. With destiny, I might visualize a huge European-style train board listing all the destinations for the trains leaving the station. Purpose might become porpoise, and I'll visualize one splashing in a tub on my back porch. And for life? I might see a box of Life Cereal sitting on my kitchen table.

It's not too hard once you get the hang of it.

It's also possible to insert sub-points or illustrations into this paradigm. For example, if my first point is Our Hope in Christ, and I have an illustration about a mother in West Virginia who keeps hope alive for her missing child, I might have the Hope Diamond in the first of my mental categories, and place the mother on the front porch; then my second point would go in the third place, but instead of worrying about aligning points to places, my message would simply amount to my walking into and through my house, dealing with every truth as I came to it.

I find this memory technique especially helpful when preaching topically. My expositional messages don't generally need this kind of technique, for they flow right out of the passage in my Bible in front of me. Expositional sermons should unfold naturally from the text, and it's not hard to sustain the outline.

But when I preach on "Ten Reasons Children Need Discipline"—well, that's another matter. It seems to amaze my congregation that I can get up without a pulpit, read the text, and launch

Continued on the next page

into all ten reasons, clicking them off one-by-one, without referring to any notes before me. I had one visitor call me up later to see if I was using a teleprompter. No, I said, just my old buddy's memory system.

Last year I was asked to address a Bible College class on the subject, "A Dozen Ways to Increase Missions Involvement in the Local Church." I prepared the entire lecture the night before, went to sleep reviewing my points, and delivered the talk without using a single note the next morning.

The purpose, of course, isn't to amaze or impress the audience. If it's a stunt to draw attention to myself, then I'm better off discarding it. But if it can help me maintain better eye-content, keep a better grasp of my material, and communicate God's truth more effectively, then it's a method worth learning.

Why?

Well, in the first place . . .

FEBRUARY 18, 2007

SUGGESTED SERMON

Someone's Here to Help You

Date preached:

Scripture: Hebrews 2:17—3:1, especially 3:1
Consider the . . . High Priest of our confession, Christ Jesus.

Introduction: The word "priest" dredges up many different images today, some good and some bad; and the Old Testament priesthood in the Bible is a subject about which most Christians have little interest. We don't often read Leviticus, and we find many of the Levitical rituals distasteful or confusing. But one of the great themes of Hebrews is the high priestly ministry of Jesus Christ. Hebrews 3:1 commands us to think about this subject, to consider it carefully. So today, let's devote our attention to it.

1. **What Our Great High Priest Is to Us**

    A. **He Is Merciful.** Verse 17 says: . . . that He might be a merciful . . . High Priest in things pertaining to God. The Greek word *éleos* conveys the idea of looking at someone, seeing their need, and having compassion and sympathy for them. I want to quote you three times when this work occurs in the New Testament. Luke 1:58 talks about God's great mercy. Luke 1:78 speaks of His tender mercy. And 1 Peter 1:3 describes His abundant mercy. Someone told me the other day about a new term that's becoming popular in the United States. It's called "Dumpster Driving." People go from Dumpster to Dumpster, pulling out things that other people have thrown away and restoring them to use. Sometimes we feel like we've been thrown into the dumpster of life. We feel worthless. We feel tossed aside. We feel dirty and broken. But we have a merciful High Priest who recovers, reclaims, and restores.

    B. **The Second Adjective Used to Describe Him Is Faithful: . . . a Merciful and Faithful High Priest.** The word faithful means that He is going to keep every single promise and obligation He has made. Joshua 21:45 says, "Not a word failed of any good thing which the LORD had spoken to the house of Israel. All came to pass." Two chapters later, Joshua said, "You know in all your hearts and in all your souls that not one thing has failed of all the good things which the LORD your God spoke concerning you. All have come to pass for you; not one word of them has failed" (Josh. 23:14). Centuries later, Solomon said, "There has not failed one word of all His good promise, which He promised through His servant Moses" (1 Kin. 8:56). I was reading the other day what hymnwriter Frances Havergal said on her deathbed: "Splendid to be so near the gates of heaven! I am lost in amazement! There has not failed one word of all His good promises!" He is faithful.

2. **What Our High Priest Does for Us**

A. **Just as There Are Two Adjectives in the First Part of this Passage, There Are Two Activities in the Last Part.** Verse 17 goes on to say that Jesus Christ had to be a merciful and faithful priest to make propitiation for the sins of the people. A propitiation is a sacrifice that turns away the wrath of God. There is only one substance in the universe that will avert the judicial wrath of God, and that is the blood of the Lamb of God, the crimson blood of our Lord Jesus Christ.

B. **Verse 18 Gives Us the Second Great Activity of Our High Priest:** For in that He Himself has suffered, being tempted, He is able to aid those who are tempted. He helps us in our times of trials and temptations. He comes alongside as a Pastor, as a Priest, as a Comforter and counselor and Friend. He knows and He understands and He helps. When the doctor told Bill Bright, founder of Campus Crusade for Christ, that he had only a short time to live, Bill's response was, "Thank You, Lord." The doctor said, "You don't seem to realize what's happening to you. You're dying . . . . You are going to die a miserable death. Bill's response was, "Well, praise the Lord. I'll see the Lord sooner than I had planned."[1] His great High Priest strengthened him in a terrible moment of testing, and amid the trials and temptations of life we have a High Priest who aids us. He Himself has suffered, so He is able to aid those who are tested, tried, and tempted.

Conclusion: That's Jesus, our High Priest. He is our Propitiation and He is our Preoccupation. He is merciful and faithful. He atones for sin and aids us in our trials and temptations. He wants to be our Great High Priest today, and His service to us in that role is worth considering all the time.

---

[1]Bill Bright, *The Journey Home* (Nashville: Thomas Nelson Publishers, 2003), pp. xvi and 7.

Jesus, my great High Priest,
Offered His blood, and died;
My guilty conscience seeks
No sacrifice beside:
His powerful blood did once atone,
And now it pleads before the throne.
—ISAAC WATTS

STATS, STORIES, AND MORE

I think the best thing I've ever read about the mercy of our Great High Priest is a hymn, a poem, written by Charles Wesley. Even though this is a very old hymn, it still conveys the mercy of God with such vivid imagery:

Depth of mercy! Can there be
Mercy still reserved for me?
Can my God His wrath forbear,
Me, the chief of sinners, spare?

I have long withstood His grace,
Long provoked Him to His face,
Would not hearken to His calls,
Grieved Him by a thousand falls.

There for me the Savior stands,
Shows His wounds and spreads His hands.
God is love! I know, I feel;
Jesus weeps and loves me still.

Now incline me to repent,
Let me now my sins lament,
Now my foul revolt deplore,
Weep, believe, and sin no more.

Averting the Wrath of God

I'm so glad that God is a God of wrath, because there would be something very insufficient about a God who could look at the evils that torment this world and be passionless about it. There is an exhibit in a museum in Baghdad, sponsored in part by the International Olympic Committee. It is made up of certain instruments of torture that Saddam Hussein used on Iraq's Olympic athletes who didn't win any medals. They were taken to a prison outside of Baghdad and tortured, along with their coaches and managers. To hear of that, to see that, to be aware of that, and to have no emotion, no anger would be wrong. The problem, of course, is that some of that evil is inside of you and me. There is none righteous, no not one. And so we all face the holy and pure and perfect wrath of an Almighty God. And the Bible says that it is a fearful thing to fall into the hands of an angry God.

APPROPRIATE HYMNS AND SONGS

"He Ransomed Me," Julia H. Johnston/J. W. Henderson, Public Domain.

"Be Exalted," Doug Holck, 1984 Pilot Point Music (Admin. The Copyright Co.).

"Day by Day," Carolina Sandell Berg/Oscar Ahnfelt/A. L. Skoog, Public Domain.

"Faithful and True," Dennis Jernigan, 1988 Shepherd's Heart Music, Inc. (Word Music Group).

"Great Is Thy Faithfulness," Thomas O. Chisholm/William M. Runyan, 1923. Renewed 1951, Hope Publishing Co. (Admin. Hope Publishing Co.).

FOR THE BULLETIN

February 18, 999, marks the death of the first Germany Pope, Gregory V. It was also on this day that the great Reformer Martin Luther died in Eisleben, Germany. On this deathbed he quoted John 3:16 and Psalm 31:5 in Latin and prayed the prayer of Simeon from Luke 2: "Lord, now let your servant depart in peace." Luther then said, "Yet I know as a certainty that I shall live with you eternally and that no one shall be able to pluck me out of your hands." A few moments later, responding to a question as to whether he was ready to die steadfast in Christ, he answered, "Yes," and fell silent. ● Michelangelo Buonarroti, the Italian Renaissance artist and one of the greatest artists of Western history, died on this day in 1564. ● *Pilgrim's Progress,* history's greatest best-seller, was published on February 18, 1678. In it, John Bunyan tells the story of a pilgrim named Christian who encounters many trials, toils, and triumphs while traveling from the City of Destruction to the Celestial City. Princeton's Dr. Emile Gaillet, who read this book fifty times, said, "Next to the Bible, *The Pilgrim's Progress* rates highest among the classics . . . the reason is that as I proceed along the appointed course, I need not only an authoritative book of instruction; I need a map. Bunyan's masterpiece has provided us with the most excellent map found anywhere."[2] ● Today is the birthday, in 1781, of Anglican missionary Henry Martyn, who translated the New Testament both into Hindustani and Arabic, before his premature death at 31. Today marks the death of Emma Bounds, 30, wife of E. M. Bounds, in 1886. It was on this same day in 1892 that Bounds began publishing his popular writings about prayer.

---

[2]Quoted in "From the Publisher," *Christian History,* Volume V, No. 3, p. 3.

Call to Worship

I will hear what God the LORD will speak, for He will speak peace to His people and to His saints; but let them not turn back to folly. Surely His salvation *is* near to those who fear Him, that glory may dwell in our land (Ps. 85:8–9).

Scripture Medley

Jesus told His disciples . . . that they should always pray and not give up. He taught them, saying . . . When you pray, go into your room, and when you have shut your door, pray to your Father who is in the secret place; and your Father who sees in secret will reward you openly. This is the confidence that we have in Him, that if we ask anything according to His will, He hears us. And if we know that He hears us, whatever we ask, we know that we have the petitions that we have asked of Him.

He . . . is able to do exceedingly abundantly above all that we ask or think . . . great and mighty things, which you do not know.

Moreover, as for me, far be it from me that I should sin against the LORD in ceasing to pray for you.

Now when Daniel knew that the writing was signed, he went home. And in his upper room, with his windows open toward Jerusalem, he knelt down on his knees three times a day, and prayed and gave thanks before his God, as was his custom since early days.

Now in the morning, having risen a long while before daylight, He went out and departed to a solitary place; and there he prayed.

As for me, I will call upon God . . . Evening and morning and at noon I will pray, and cry aloud, and He shall hear my voice . . . Cast your burden on the LORD, and He shall sustain you; He shall never permit the righteous to be moved. Be

Continued on the next page

WORSHIP HELPS—*Continued*

anxious for nothing, but in everything by prayer and supplication, with thanksgiving, let your requests be made known to God.

. . . come boldly to the throne of grace, that (you) may obtain mercy and find grace to help in time of need. Be joyful in hope, patient in affliction, faithful in prayer. Pray in the Spirit on all occasions with all kinds of prayers and requests. Pray without ceasing, in everything give thanks; for this is the will of God in Christ Jesus for you. Watch and pray, lest you enter into temptation.

The Lord is far from the wicked, but He hears the prayer of the righteous. If you abide in Me, and My words abide in you, you will ask what you desire, and it shall be done for you. The prayer of a righteous man is powerful and effective (Luke 18:1 NIV; Matt. 5:2 and 6:6; 1 John 5:14–15; Eph. 3:20, Jer. 33:3; 1 Sam. 12:23; Dan. 6:10; Mark 1:35; Ps. 55:16–17, 22; Phil. 4:6; Heb. 4:16; Rom. 12:12 NIV; Eph. 6:18 NIV; 1 Thess. 5:17–18; Matt. 26:41; Prov. 15:29; John 15:7; James 5:16 NIV).

Additional Sermons and Lesson Ideas

An Unhealthy Marriage
Date preached:
By Rev. Billie Friel

SCRIPTURE: 1 Samuel 25

INTRODUCTION: Marriage is a quiet hell for over 50 percent of couples. These loveless relationships exist solely because of children, finances, and fear of society's impressions.

Our passage describes an unhealthy marriage.

1. The Characters in an Unhealthy Marriage. Nabal was the husband in these verses. He had *posterity* (v. 3), *prosperity* (v. 2), and a *partner* in life, Abigail (v. 3), yet he was wicked. Abigail, Nabal's wife, she was physically attractive (v. 3), wise (v. 3), trusted (v. 14), decisive (v. 18), and a believer in God (vv. 23–31).
2. The Characteristics of an Unhealthy Marriage. Nabal was responsible for the failure of this marriage. Notice his:
   A. Materialism (v. 2).
   B. Harshness (vv. 3, 14).
   C. Lack of Communication (vv. 17, 19).
   D. Ingratitude (vv. 15–16).
   E. Drunkenness (v. 36).
   F. Contempt for Spiritual Things (v. 10).

CONCLUSION: No problem marriage is hopeless. God can heal and help your marriage (Ps. 127:1), but we should search ourselves to root out any characteristics we share with Nabal.

Cursed Cain
Date preached:
By Dr. Melvin Worthington

SCRIPTURE: Genesis 4:1–24

INTRODUCTION: The devastating consequences of sin are manifested in the first child born following the Fall of man.

1. Cain's Conception (Gen. 4:1). Cain's conception includes *the declaration, the delivery,* and *the delight.*
2. Cain's Crime (Gen. 4:2–8). Cain's *occupation, offering, obstinacy, offence,* and *opportunity* are addressed.
3. Cain's Curse (Gen. 4:9–15). God pronounced a curse on Cain for his murderous offence. We note *the brother's death, the banishment decreed,* and *the boundaries disclosed.*

4. Cain's Children (Gen. 4:16–24). We note their *names, number, and nature.*
5. Cain's Contribution (Gen. 4). Cain serves as a warning regarding one's disposition, devotion, deeds, defiance, disobedience, and disregard for God's will, God's way, and God's worship.

CONCLUSION: Cain serves as a reminder of the danger of disregarding the way God has established to approach and address Him. He also reminds us to avoid the pride and jealousy that cause us to harm others.

> **" Quote for the Pastor's Wall**
>
> *Many make the mistake of giving more time to the preparation of their addresses than to the preparation of their own hearts, affections, emotions, and faith; the result often is beautiful, brilliant words that have the same effect as holding up glittering icicles before a freezing man. To warm others— and is not that your purpose in preaching?—a man must keep the fire burning hot in his own soul.*
>
> —SAMUEL LOGAN BRENGLE[3] **"**

---

[3]Samuel Logan Brengle, in *Clarence W. Hall: Samuel Logan Brengle: Portrait of a Prophet* (Atlanta, GA: The Salvation Army Supplies and Purchasing Dept., 1933), p. 114.

Holiness and Worry

From Samuel Logan Brengle's classic,
The Way of Holiness, published in 1902

Worry is a great foe to holiness, and perfect trust puts an end to worry. "I would as soon swear as fret," said John Wesley. The murmuring and complaining of His children has ever been a great sin in the sight of God, and has led to untold suffering on their part.

Most people do not see this to be a sin, but it is. It dishonors God, blinds the eyes to His will, and deafens the ears to His voice. It is the ditch on one side of the pathway of trust. Lazy or heartless indifference is the ditch on the other side. Happy is the Christian who keeps out of either ditch, and walks securely on the pathway. Though it may be often narrow and difficult, it is safe. Praise the Lord!

Worrying prevents quiet thought and earnest believing prayer, and it is, therefore, always bad. If circumstances are against us, we need quietness of mind, clearness of thought, decision of will, and strength of purpose with which to face these circumstances and overcome them. But all this is prevented or hindered by fret or worry.

First, we should not worry over things that we can help, but set to work manfully to put them right. Sir Isaac Newton, one of the greatest of men, labored for eight years preparing the manuscript of one of his great works when one day he came into his study, and found that his little dog, Diamond, had knocked over a candle and burned all his papers. Without a sign of anger or impatience, the great, good man quietly remarked, "Ah, Diamond, little do you know the labor and trouble to which you have put your master!" and without worrying sat down to do that vast work over again.

Second, we should not worry over the things we cannot help, but quietly and confidently look to the Lord for such help as He sees best to give. There is no possible evil that may befall us from

Continued on the next page

which God cannot deliver us, if He sees that that is best for us, or give us grace to bear, if that is best. Holiness of heart enables us to see this. An accident befell a little child I heard of, which for twenty-four hours endangered its life. The sanctified mother did all she could, then committed her darling to the Lord, and peacefully awaited the issue. Within twenty-four hours the danger was passed, and the child was safe. An old colored auntie who had witnessed the calm trust of the mother said, "You certain is de queeres' woman I ever see! Here dis chile been in danger ob its life for twenty-four hours, and you not worried a bit!"

"Well, auntie," said the mother, "I couldn't trust the Lord and worry too; so I did what I could, and trusted, and you see that all is well. And I have had the peace of God in my heart for twenty-four hours."

Paul says, "Be careful for nothing; but in everything by prayer and supplication with thanksgiving let your requests be made known unto God. And the peace of God, which passeth all understanding, shall keep your hearts and minds through Christ Jesus." Again, Isaiah says: "Thou wilt keep him in perfect peace whose mind is stayed on Thee; because he trusteth in Thee."

Our business is, then, always to pray, give thanks for such blessings as we have, and keep our minds stayed on God, and worry about nothing.

Holiness makes a man so sure of the presence and love and care of God, that, while doing with his might what his hands find to do, he refuses to worry, and sings from his heart: "I will trust Thee, I will trust Thee, All my life Thou shalt control"; and he is certain that while he trusts and obeys, neither devils nor men can do him real harm, nor defeat God's purpose for him.

The heart realization of heavenly help, of God's presence in time of trouble, of angels encamping round about them that fear Him, is the secret of a life of perfect peace, in which anxious care is not shunned, but joyously and constantly rolled on the Lord, who "careth for us," and who bids us cast our care on Him. Are you poor, and tempted to worry about your daily bread? God sent the ravens to feed Elijah, and later made him dependent upon a poor widow woman, with only enough flour and oil to make one meal for herself and her child. But through long months of famine God suffered not that flour to waste, nor that oil to fail.

The God of Elijah is the God of those who trust in Him forevermore. Now, mind, such trust is not a state of lazy indifference, but of the highest activity of heart and will, and it is both a privilege and a duty. Of course, only such a perfect trust can save from undue anxiety, but this trust is an unfailing fruit of the Holy Spirit dwelling in a clean heart. And we can only keep this trust by always obeying the Holy Spirit, strict attention to daily duty, watchfulness against temptation, much believing, persevering, unhurried prayer, and by nourishing our faith on God's Word daily. The promises are given us to believe, and so we may rest in God's love and care, and not worry and fret ourselves with useless anxiety.

Has someone talked unkindly or falsely about you? Don't worry, but pray, and go on loving them and doing your duty, and some day God will "bring forth thy righteousness as the light, and thy judgment as the noon-day" (Ps. 37:6).

Are you sick? Don't worry, but pray. The Lord can raise you up (James 5:15) or make the sickness work for good (Rom. 8:28), as He did for a sister I knew in Chicago, who for five years was helpless in bed with rheumatism, but had five big sons converted during that time, and was so happy that she said she would not have had those five years spent in any other way.

Have your own wrong-doings brought you into trouble? Don't worry, but repent to the very bottom of your heart, trust in Jesus, walk in your present light, and the Blood will cleanse you, and God will surely help you.

Are you troubled about the future? Don't worry. Walk with God today in obedient trust, and tomorrow He will be with you. He will never fail you, nor forsake you.

If our trust were but more simple, we should take Him at His word. And our lives would be all sunshine in the sweetness of our Lord.

FEBRUARY 25, 2007

How to Treat Your Neighbor

Date preached:

By Dr. Al Detter

Scripture: Proverbs 3:27–30

Do not withhold good from those to whom it is due, when it is in the power of your hand to do so. Do not say to your neighbor, "Go, and come back, and tomorrow I will give it," when you have it with you. Do not devise evil against your neighbor, for he dwells by you for safety's sake. Do not strive with a man without cause, if he has done you no harm.

Introduction: Many of you may be familiar with the second great commandment, ". . . love your neighbor as yourself" (Matt. 22:39). In Jesus' view, how we treat our neighbors is second only in importance to our love relationship with God. The word "neighbor" in Proverbs means anyone from our casual acquaintances to our very best friends. The word in Proverbs is used even for our enemies. So how should we treat others, our neighbors?

I. **Help Your Neighbors When They Have a Need (Prov. 3:27–28).** Did you ever stop to figure out how God meets needs? God doesn't send chariots from heaven with money and clothes and food. He meets the needs people have through other people. These two verses indicate two kinds of neighbors we should bless:

A. **Be Generous with the Neighbor Whose Need We Owe (v. 27).** This verse is talking about relationships in which we owe a debt of some kind, "Do not withhold good from those to whom it is due." The literal sense is the idea of paying a financial debt we owe, but this verse goes much deeper. By virtue of some relationships, you owe the other person something. If you are married, you *owe* good to each other. Children owe their parents obedience and honor; parents owe children time, love, and discipline. The list goes on. Are you paying your "debts" to others out of the gifts, time, resources, and talents God has equipped you with?

B. **Be Generous with the Neighbor Whose Need We Know (v. 28).** What do we do about the needs of people who aren't very close to us, even people we don't know at all? Once we know of a need and realize we have resources that can help, we become obligated. There's a flip side to the coin. Perhaps someone asks for help that you know, maybe someone in the church. In our individualistic mindset fed to us by our culture, we think they should have worked harder, that there's no reason for us to bail them out, so we either avoid them or flat out refuse. We are not to ignore or refuse the need when we have the resources to meet the need. We are to step up immediately and minister a blessing.

2. **Guard Against Mistreating Your Neighbors in Any Fashion (Prov. 3:29–30).** We live in a day of troubled relationships. There will be times that relationships will be strained. It happens in every marriage, in every friendship, in every partnership. Solomon gives us some good advice. Don't make unnecessary trouble with your neighbor.

   A. **Avoid Harmful Intentions and Actions against Other People (v. 29).** The most important part of this verse is the period. There are some people in life we just aren't naturally drawn to. There are some we may not like. There are some who have wounded and injured us. It doesn't matter. There is never a reason to plan harm against someone else. Period! God says, "Vengeance is Mine. I will repay" (Heb. 10:30).

   B. **Be Sure There Is an Offense before You Confront (v. 30).** There is a time and a place to confront someone. When you need to confront someone and don't, things will only get worse. But we are not to be contentious in our manner of life—confronting and challenging and faultfinding about everything that offends us. The word for "contend" in verse 30 is a strong word. It literally means, "to come to hard blows." It came to mean "to quarrel, to argue noisily, to fight because one is angry." It describes a reaction we have in response to an actual or perceived injustice against us.

Conclusion: Two great hindrances to our blessing others were in our text today—selfishness (vv. 27–28) and aggression (vv. 29–30). We need the wisdom of God if we are going to treat people right. Your neighbor is the person in your marriage. It's the parent or child at home. It's the person you know in this church. It's the ticket agent in the airport. It's the person who has wronged you. Are you willing to take an honest look at how you are treating your neighbors?

STATS, STORIES, AND MORE

My wife and I took a trip to Hilton Head a few years ago. We were delayed out of Erie. We ran for our flight connection in Pittsburgh. We got there with two minutes to spare. The plane was still at the gate, but they had shut the door. The lady wouldn't let us board. I got as nasty as I could without sinning in word or deed. She kept her composure and asked for my ticket. It said, "REV. Al Detter." She gave me a look. So did my wife. She got us on the next flight and as I sat in my seat, the Spirit of God said to me, "You didn't know that lady. But did you bless her? Did you bring Me glory?" I was smitten in my spirit. Every day for the entire week, I prayed an impossible prayer, "Lord, if you could arrange for me to see that lady again at the Pittsburgh airport, I'll make things right." On the way back, we are at the ticket counter seemingly miles from the gate of the incident. I'm standing in a long line. Perhaps nine agent windows are open. I'm praying when I spot the same lady behind one of the windows. Now I'm asking the Lord to get me to her window. Incredibly, He did. She took my ticket and I said to her, "Do you remember me?" Her head came up and the light dawned with the look, "Not you again." I had violated one of the principles we're going to talk about today. So I apologized to her. Her countenance brightened. I was blessing her. You could feel it. I felt so much better. God calls upon us to nurture and guard our relationships with neighbors. Failure to do so can lead to all kinds of strife and hurt. Solomon gives us some key advice in two areas that will go a long way to make life easier for all of us.
                                                                    —Dr. Al Detter

Making Your Own Baloney
Senate Chaplain Barry Black tells this story. Two construction workers took their lunch break. When they opened their lunch boxes, one of them said, "Not another baloney sandwich! Every day it's a baloney sandwich." The other guy said, "Tell your wife to fix you something else." He said, "I'm not married. I make my own sandwiches." The truth of the matter is this. *Much of the baloney in our lives we put there ourselves.*

APPROPRIATE HYMNS AND SONGS

"Tell the World," Marsha Skidmore, 1994 Doulos Publishing (Admin. Maranatha Music).

"You Shall Love the Lord," Frank Hernandez, 1990 Birdwing Music (EMI Christian Music Publishing).

"They'll Know We Are Christians by Our Love," Peter Scholtes, 1966 F.E.L. Publications (Admin. Lorenz Corporation).

"Brother's Keeper," Scott Wesley Brown/David Hampton, 1996 Maranatha Music (Admin. Maranatha Music).

"O the Deep, Deep Love of Jesus," Samuel Trevor Francis/Thomas J. Williams, Public Domain.

FOR THE BULLETIN

February 25, 1536, is the anniversary of the martyrdom of Anabaptist Jakob Hutter. An ancient writer described it like this: "They put him in ice-cold water and then took him into a warm room and had him beaten with rods. They lacerated his body, poured brandy into the wounds, and set it on fire." He was burned at the stake before a large crowd. ● On February 25, 1570, Pope Pius V excommunicates England's Protestant Queen Elizabeth I, declaring her to be a usurper to the throne. It was the last time a pope "deposed" a reigning monarch. ● A series of "firsts" occurred in American history on this day. The first performing monkey exhibited in the United States (1751), the first U.S. bank was chartered (1791), and the first cabinet meeting (1793 at George Washington's home). ● Today is the birthday, in 1824, of the Baptist General Tract Society. It first organized in Washington, D.C. before moving to Philadelphia. Today is also the birthday of the English preacher, pastor, and writer J. Sidlow Baxter, author of several insightful books including *Explore the Book*. ● Dr. Edward Riggs, son of missionary Elias Riggs, began his own missionary career in Turkey in 1869, and during the course of his ministry he was robbed, threatened, and endangered many times. He pursued his work with such courage that he became known as the "Bishop of the Black Sea Coast." He died on February 25, 1913, having served the area for forty-four years and leaving five of his seven children on the field.

Quote for the Pastor's Wall

My motto was always to keep swinging. Whether I was in a slump or feeling badly or having trouble off the field, the only thing to do was keep swinging.

—HANK AARON[1]

---

[1]http://www.indianchild.com/sports_quotes_quotations.htm, accessed March 10, 2006.

WORSHIP HELPS

Call to Worship

Even the sparrow has found a home, and the swallow a nest for herself, where she may lay her young—*even* Your altars, O Lord of hosts, my King and my God. Blessed *are* those who dwell in Your house; they will still be praising You (Ps. 84:3–4).

Offertory Comments

I read about a young man who was touring a locomotive factory in England. At the end of the tour, he reached out his hand to thank the guide and was surprised by the limp, unresponsive grip he received. The guide seemed like a strong young man, yet his handshake was almost nonexistent. A bit embarrassed, the host explained, "You must excuse my hand. When I was an apprentice, I met with an accident, and a nail was driven completely through it. Since then, I have never been able to close my hand." The visitor later pondered that saying. How like Christ, he thought. Two thousand years ago, the nails were driven completely through His palms, and since then He, too, has never closed His hands. They stretch open and outward toward a needy world. The Bible says there is a sense in which we have been crucified with Christ (Gal. 2:20), and one of the characteristics of His followers is generosity. Our hands are incapable of closing in tight-fisted greed. His people are open-handed givers, just like Him.

Suggested Scriptures

Genesis 12:1; Leviticus 19:13; Deuteronomy 24:14–15; Proverbs 3:27–30; Matthew 18:15–16, 22:39; Romans 4:16, 13:8; 1 Corinthians 7:3; Galatians 3:7, 6:10; Ephesians 6:5–9; Hebrews 10:30; James 2:15–16; 1 John 3:17

Additional Sermons and Lesson Ideas

Making Good Decisions

Date preached:

By Dr. Larry Osborne

SCRIPTURE: Various, especially Proverbs 2:6–11

INTRODUCTION: We can't overlook the importance of making good decisions, for decisions determine the course of our lives! There are four pillars you can build on as a good framework for making decisions:

1. God. We should always look to Scripture for wisdom to make the right decisions (Prov. 2:6–11; 1:7; 3:5–7; Rom. 12:1–2; James 1:5).
2. Facts. Our decisions should not be based on assumptions (Prov. 19:2–3; 14:15; 13:16; Josh. 9:1–27).
3. Advice. What do the experts say? We should look to other wise people to help us along with our decisions (Prov. 19:20; 14:7; 12:5, 16; 15:22; Eccl. 4:13).
4. Impact. What are the long term and hidden consequences of our decisions (Prov. 22:3; 27:12; Eccl. 2:26)?

CONCLUSION: Good decisions do not come from intellect or luck, but by using a scriptural framework as a lens through which we can see clearly and decide effectively.

The Message of the Cross

Date preached:

By Dr. Timothy Beougher

SCRIPTURE: 1 Corinthians 1:18–25

INTRODUCTION: The message of the Cross is the central message of Scripture. God's greatest gift, and what brings Him the most glory, is His work through Jesus Christ to redeem His people. The message of the Cross as described in 1 Corinthians 1:18–25 is:

1. A Saving Message (v. 18)
2. A Simple Message (vv. 19–21)
3. A Substitutionary Message (vv. 22–23)
4. A Solemn Message (vv. 18; 23–25)

CONCLUSION: This message is the best news you will ever hear. It's up to you to turn to Jesus Christ, turning from your sin, and committing all you are to Him in faith.

COMMUNION SERMON

Remember the Old Way: A Communion Meditation

Date preached:

By Rev. Todd M. Kinde

Scripture: Isaiah 46:8–13, especially verses 8–10 (ESV)
Remember this and stand firm, recall it to mind, you transgressors, remember the former things of old; for I am God, and there is no other; I am God, and there is none like me, declaring the end from the beginning and from ancient times things not yet done, saying, "My counsel shall stand, and I will accomplish all my purpose."

1. **The Problem.** The setting of this passage is in Babylon, where God's people find themselves in captivity and at odds with the idol worship of the Babylonians. For Israel there is a twofold problem to their situation.

   A. **Is God the Only True God?** The first is that by all outer appearances the idol gods of Babylon seem to be mightier and stronger than the God of Abraham, Isaac, and Jacob. Israel is, in fact, destroyed as a national power and the best of the people have been deported to Babylon away from the temple where they might worship Yahweh. Is Yahweh the one true God or not?

   B. **Why Does God Allow Difficulty?** The second problem is that if, in fact, Israel acknowledges that Yahweh is the one true God, then why would God do this to them? God sent Cyrus, the king of Babylon to sack Jerusalem. Cyrus is the bird of prey from the east and the man of counsel in verse 11. If Yahweh is God, and the idols are nothing as the prophet has told, then why would He do this to His own people?

Application: Where are you today? We should learn to express our difficulties to each other as we come together. If your marriage is going down the tubes, your kids are rebellious, and your spiritual life is dragging, don't smile at others here and say, "Yes, we're doing great. Praise the Lord." That's not being spiritual, that's lying. Part of the sacrament of communion is a true community, with others who can help us through our suffering. Let's be honest and open when we come together for the Lord's Supper.

2. **The Promise.** The answer God gives to both problems is simply to remember who He is and what He has done. He also reminds the people that the reason they are in this place of discipline is because of their own transgression (v. 8) and their own stubborn heart (v. 12). They want to do things their own way and not in accord with the Law of God. The Lord reminds Israel of His promise to save, "I bring near my righteousness; it is not far off, and my salvation will not delay" (v. 13). On what basis to we trust His promise? Because He is the architect of history. "I am God, and there is no other; I am God, and there is none like me, declaring the end from the beginning and from ancient times things not yet done, saying, 'My counsel shall stand, and I will accomplish all my purpose . . .' (ESV).

Application: We can identify with the predicament, I think. We seem to be held in enemy territory. As we begin to identify our values for life and ministry together, we realize how hard hearted the church at large in our society has gotten in reference to the ways of the Lord. Perhaps we ourselves have forgotten our heritage. And even some of us have never even been told our heritage of faith in the first place. When we ponder on our situation of life—our work, marriage, friendships, and finances—we might wonder if the gods of this age have more to offer than the One True Living God. Or perhaps we begin to doubt because, "I do not understand why God would allow this to happen to me."

3. **The Provision:** The remedy for this spiritual despondency is the same as it was for Israel—remember the old way. In Isaiah, the Lord says, "Remember this . . . ." Jesus says, "Do this in remembrance of me . . . ." In Isaiah, the Lord says, "I will accomplish all my purpose." Jesus says, "It is finished."

Application: "And the life [we] now live in the flesh [we] live by faith in the Son of God, who loved [us] and gave himself for [us]" (Gal. 2:20 ESV). Come to the Table where Christ gives Himself in remembrance of the Cross that you might live by faith.

MARCH 4, 2007

SUGGESTED SERMON

When a Husband Loves His Wife

By Dr. David Jeremiah

Date preached:

Scripture: Ephesians 5:25–29, Colossians 3:19, and 1 Peter 3:7,
          especially Ephesians 5:25
Husbands, love your wives, just as Christ also loved the church . . .

Introduction: Three major passages in the New Testament speak of a husband's responsibility to his wife—Ephesians 5, Colossians 3 and 1 Peter 3. Whenever I preach on this, I get into trouble; so I'm going to be diplomatic, but I still hope to get the point across. What I'm teaching today can change a lot of things in our lives. When a husband loves his wife, what should she expect? How can we translate these biblical instructions into everyday life?

1. **When a Husband Loves His wife, He gives Her a Sense of Security (Eph. 5:25–29).** Husbands should have *authentic* love for their wives—we love them as they are, as Christ loved us as we are. We're to love with *sacrificial* love, for Christ gave Himself for us. We're to love with *deliberate* love, for Christ had a purpose in mind, to present us chaste and perfect before God. We're to love with *unconditional* love, just as we love our own bodies. When a wife knows she is cherished, treasured, and held in high regard by her husband, it gives her a secure, settled, and wonderful experience. I say pointedly to men: We are not asked to love if we feel like it; we are commanded to love. If we fail to do that, the joy of marriage will slowly erode and slip away.

2. **When a Husband Loves His Wife, He Gives Her a Sense of Intimacy (1 Pet. 3:7).** Peter tells husbands is to "dwell" with their wives. The word "dwell" in the Greek means "dwell with her at home." It's found only here in the Bible, and it's a special word having to do with living together as husband and wife. Many scholars believe it means living a shared, intimate, involved life. One translator put it: "Husbands, make a home for her at home." Our task is companionship, togetherness, and closeness. The home should be a retreat

center for the two of you, a place to come away from the pressures of the world and to share the things you have in common as a couple.

3. **When a Husband Loves His Wife, He Gives Her a Sense of Identity (1 Pet. 3:7).** What does it mean to dwell with your wife "with understanding" (1 Pet. 3:7)? When a husband loves his wife with understanding, she'll sense he is deeply interested in her as a person. Not as a lover, or homemaker, or mother for his children, or someone to balance the checkbook; but "according to knowledge," which means you have a tremendous desire to understand her as a person and to ever know her better.

4. **When a Husband Loves His Wife, He Gives Her a Sense of Spirituality (1 Pet. 3:7).** Husbands should honor their wives as the weaker vessel, heirs together of the grace of God, that their prayers be not hindered. Now, I don't plan to go too far with that "weaker vessel" comment. Every time I've mentioned that in my preaching, it's taken me three weeks to get out of trouble. (Yes, women, I know you are the ones who go through childbirth. I know that there is no man alive who could ever endure that. . . .) There are many ways to approach this text; but we know the husband is the leader in the home. In that respect, since the wife is in submission to her husband in a godly way and they are submitting to each other, you might consider her position relationship-wise as the weaker, not the stronger one. The point Peter is making is: When it comes to our relationship with Christ, it doesn't matter because we are heirs together. As husband and wife, we share the spiritual intimacies and realities we have in the Word of God, prayer and fellowship. So important is this that Peter warns us if we don't take it seriously, it will affect our prayer lives.

Conclusion: What powerful verses! It says to us, simply, men, that we have the power to build security, intimacy, identity, and spirituality into our homes. If we, over a long period of time, neglect this, the need is so great in the heart of the woman, she will find some way to get that need met. That doesn't excuse any act of infidelity or indiscretion. But while it is within our hands to meet the needs of those to whom we are married, let us go forth to be husbands to our wives and love one another as Christ loves His church.

STATS, STORIES, AND MORE

More from Dr. Jeremiah

I think what Peter was saying to his readers in this wonderful passage is he wants husband and wife to dwell together as one flesh. We're to share our lives, our hopes, our dreams, our aspirations, and yes, our fears and failures. Unfortunately, some men never do get that. I read about a husband and wife who had fussed and fought for fifty years. On their golden wedding anniversary, the kids got together and decided to present them with a lovely gift—a trip to the psychiatrist. Well, they argued about who was going to take them. Then they argued about who was going to sit where in the car when they went. And they finally got over to that psychiatrist and for fifteen minutes, they argued back and forth over who was going to tell the story of what was wrong with their marriage. Finally, the young psychiatrist who had only been in practice for a short time, after listening to them for about fifteen minutes, got up and walked over to the little old lady, pulled her right up out of the chair in his arms and planted a long Hollywood kiss right on her mouth. Then he turned her loose and said, "Now, Pops, she needs that at least three times a week." Her husband said, "I can bring her Monday, Wednesday and Friday, if that's alright."

APPROPRIATE HYMNS AND SONGS

"Bind Us Together," Bob Gillman, 1977 Kingsway's ThankYou Music (Admin. EMI Christian Music Publishing).

"When There's Love at Home," John Hugh McNaughton/Gloria Gaither, 1987 William J. Gaither, Inc. (ARR UBP of Gaither Copyright Management).

"Love Will Be Our Home," Steven Curtis Chapman, 1988 Careers—BMG Music Publishing, Inc./Sparrow Song (Admin. EMI Christian Music Publishing).

"Growing Together in Love," Bruce T. Ballinger, 1989 Sound III, Inc./ Universal—MCA Music.

"O Love That Will Not Let Me Go," George Matheson/Albert Lister Peace, Public Domain.

FOR THE BULLETIN

March 4, 1583, marks the death of Bernard Gilpin, English clergyman whose ministry to neglected sections of Northumberland and Yorkshire earned him the title "Apostle of the North." Gilpin's favorite verse was reportedly Romans 8:28, and he became famous for quoting it on all occasions. When Queen Mary ascended the throne Gilpin was summoned to London to be tried and executed, but along the way he broke his leg. Some mockingly asked him if he imagined that his accident would work out for his good. But it *did* work out for good. His journey was delayed while he recovered at an inn, and before he reached London, word came that Queen Mary had died. ● On March 4, 1681, England's King Charles II granted William Penn a contract for territory in North America, which eventually became the state of Pennsylvania. ● On Saturday, March 4, 1797, a group of missionaries aboard the missionary ship, *The Duff,* arrived from London in the South Pacific from London. ● The British and Foreign Bible Society was founded on March 4, 1804; and today is the birthday, in 1829, of Presbyterian missionary, John Livingston Nevius, who labored in China with great effect. ● On March 4, 1859, James A. Garfield, 18, was baptized upon his profession of faith in Christ. Thirty one years later to the day— March 4, 1881—Garfield was sworn into office as President of the United States. He was assassinated later that year. ● Alexander Campbell, founder of the Disciples of Christ, died on this day in 1866. The Bible commentator, Franz Delitzsch, also died on this day in 1890. Today marks the death of evangelist and hymnist, Daniel Whittle, in 1901. Hymnist Gloria Gaither was born on this day in 1942.

Kid's Talk

Explain to the children that the Book of Psalms is full of prayers and praises to God. Ask them to choose from three things: things they would like to say to God, things they are thankful for, or things they like about God. Have them (or with help from parents depending on age) write out a prayer to God about whatever they chose, and ask them to put the prayers in the offering plate the following week. You can then use these "psalms" written by children in many ways: print one per week in your bulletin, read one as a call to worship, use them as sermon illustrations, or make a collage to frame and put on a wall in the church.

WORSHIP HELPS

Call to Worship
Bless the LORD, O my soul! O LORD my God, You are very great: You are clothed with honor and majesty (Ps. 104:1).

Word of Welcome
I'd like to read to you from Luke 18:9–14: "Also He spoke this parable to some who trusted in themselves that they were righteous, and despised others: "Two men went up to the temple to pray, one a Pharisee and the other a tax collector. The Pharisee stood and prayed thus with himself, 'God, I thank You that I am not like other men—extortioners, unjust, adulterers, or even as this tax collector. I fast twice a week; I give tithes of all that I possess.' And the tax collector, standing afar off, would not so much as raise his eyes to heaven, but beat his breast, saying, 'God, be merciful to me a sinner!' I tell you, this man went down to his house justified rather than the other; for everyone who exalts himself will be humbled, and he who humbles himself will be exalted."

Unfortunately, church-goers sometimes have the reputation of being like this Pharisee, looking down on others they view as less righteous. If you're a visitor here, know that members of this church only find their righteousness in Jesus Christ. If you're a member here, heed these words and remember to humble yourself in prayer and worship before the Lord. It has been said that the ground is level at the foot of the Cross, and that applies in this church. None of us is more righteous than the other, for all of us are equal in Christ. As Paul said over a thousand years ago, "Here there is no Greek or Jew, circumcised or uncircumcised, barbarian, Scythian, slave or free, but Christ is all, and is in all" (Col. 3:11 NIV).

Benediction
I urge you in the sight of God who gives life to all things, and before Christ Jesus who witnessed the good confession before Pontius Pilate, that you keep this commandment without spot, blameless until our Lord Jesus Christ's appearing, which He will manifest in His own time, He who is the blessed and only Potentate, the King of kings and Lord of lords, who alone has immortality, dwelling in unapproachable light, whom no man has seen or can see, to whom be honor and everlasting power. Amen.

Additional Sermons and Lesson Ideas

Cleansing the Leper

Date preached:

Based on a Sermon by Rev. W. H. Finney

SCRIPTURE: Luke 17:14; Leviticus 14

INTRODUCTION: A group of leprous men met Jesus begging for cleansing. He commanded them to go to the priests (to follow Lev. 14). We can learn from their experience:

1. The Priest's Part. The lepers' offerings were brought to the priest, who then sacrificed them on their behalf, a symbol of what Christ would do for us.
2. The Lepers' Responsibility. The lepers were then to cleanse themselves externally, symbolizing their new spiritual and physical purity. Similarly, our baptism is an external symbol of our inward cleansing.
3. Identification with the Offering. Blood shed by offerings were visual representations of the sacrifice made on their behalf. How often do we remember the blood shed at Calvary for us?
4. The Anointing Oil. The priest placed anointing oil on certain spots of the lepers' bodies. The anointing oil is representative of the Holy Spirit, which is given to us when we are cleansed through Christ once and for all.

CONCLUSION: The lepers in this passage met Jesus knowing their need, trusting in Him to meet that need, and being determined to receive His help; they were cleansed as a result. Have you met Jesus in this way? Have you been cleansed?

I Believe

Date preached:

By Rev. Larry Kirk

SCRIPTURE: 2 Timothy 1:7–14

INTRODUCTION: God, through Paul, gives us solid doctrinal ideas to live by. Two major points stand out as we look at this passage:

1. A Strong Spiritual Life Requires a Set of Core Christian Convictions. A whole set of core beliefs exist in Scripture, and should apply to us (vv. 8–10, 13). We are instructed to "guard" or to "hold fast" the teachings of faith we find in Scripture (v. 14). The Apostle's Creed is a great guide to scriptural doctrines.
2. A Strong Spiritual Life Requires True Faith in God (v. 12). We must remember that true faith is personal (v. 12), we ourselves must believe, not just go to a believing church. Secondly, true faith is somewhat paradoxical, for faith is God's gift, but also our responsibility. Finally, true faith is powerful, making us bold, disciplined, loving, and not fearful (v. 7).

CONCLUSION: Have you taken time to nail down whether you hold to the core convictions of Scripture?

MARCH 11, 2007

SUGGESTED SERMON

The State of Joyful Living

Date preached:

By Rev. Richard S. Sharpe, Jr.

Scripture: Psalm 84, especially verse 10
For a day in Your courts is better than a thousand. I would rather be a doorkeeper in the house of my God than dwell in the tents of wickedness.

Introduction: Do you roll out of bed in the morning with barely enough time to shower, dress, and rush out the door? Are your days or evenings so packed with activities that you don't have time for the Lord? Does all this business make you feel overwhelmed instead of joyful? Few Christians take enough time out of their schedules for worshiping the Lord daily. The psalms are written to be sung in the daily life of the children of Israel. Kings, priests, and singers wrote the psalms over a thousand year time period; they took worship seriously. This psalm has the distinction of using the same Hebrew word three times: *'esher.* This word means happiness, blessed, good fortune, and state of joyful mind. In our study of this psalm we find four areas of our lives that are influenced by the promise of blessing.

1. **Home (vv. 1–4).** The psalmist looks at the place of worship as the only place he wanted to be. It was a place that the psalmist cried out for the living God. We all need a place to call home. We should be at home with the Lord. Our place to worship is first in our own hearts. In the New Testament we learn that the Holy Spirit takes up permanent residence in our hearts when we accept Christ as our personal Savior. The Bible also tells us that we need to make the fellowship of other believers a priority in our lives. Ours is not an individual faith, it is a faith that requires fellowship. Our fellowship is with the Lord and our fellow believers. With that fellowship, we are to manifest praise. Are we praising the Lord in our daily walk with the Him?

2. **Strength (vv. 5–7).** Each morning when we wake up, we need strength to face the day. Our strength has to have a source. As believers in Christ, He promises to give us daily strength to face our days full of trials. We all have to go through valleys in our lives

and sometimes they last a long time. The psalm tells us that we can make out well in our times of trial. The Lord will refill us with strength daily. Everyone who appears before God will receive strength through the Word and the leading of the Holy Spirit. Make time in your morning for the Lord!

3. **Prayer (vv. 8–9).** The psalmist makes three pleas to the Lord. First, he wants the Lord to hear his prayer. We know that the Lord doesn't hear the prayers of those who don't confess their sin on a regular basis. Second, he pleads with the Lord to give him His ear. Finally, he pleads for the Lord to look upon the face of His anointed. Each one of us is anointed of the Lord. This model can guide us in our prayers.

4. **Happiness (vv. 10–12).** The one word that is used three times is found in this section of the psalm. It means happiness to all those who trust in the Lord. Our goal is to learn to trust the Lord more and more. One of the ways that we can do this is to spend time in a place of worship. The psalmist said that he would rather be a doorkeeper in the house of the Lord than to be around the wicked. He realized that the Lord gives light and protects us on a daily basis. The Lord also gives us grace. Grace is unmerited favor. We are getting something we don't deserve. At the end of the lives of those who trust in the Lord we will receive glory. We will have a glorified body. We will be in the presence of the Lord forever. What a blessing! Let's not wait until that day to look back and see all the neglected opportunities we had to worship. We can begin the eternal task of worship now!

Conclusion: The psalmist helps us understand what he expected from a relationship with the Lord. He expected a place called home. He expected strength for each day. He expected the Lord to answer his prayer requests. Finally, he expected happiness. Do these expectations fill our lives? They should!

STATS, STORIES, AND MORE

Attitudes

🔖 In his book, *Today Matters,* John Maxwell tells about a woman who was out shopping with her daughter a few days before Christmas. The woman complained about everything in the mall—the crowds, the long lines, the quality of the merchandise, the prices, and her sore feet. Finally, after a tense exchange with a particular clerk, the woman left the store fuming and saying, "I'm never going back to that store again. Did you see the dirty look she gave me?" The daughter answered, "She didn't give it to you, Mom. You had it when you went in!"[1]

🔖 *When I met Christ, I felt that I had swallowed sunshine.*
—E. Stanley Jones

🔖 *Some cause happiness wherever they go; others whenever they go.*
—Oscar Wilde

🔖 *Your day goes the way the corners of your mouth turn.* —anonymous

🔖
I chanced to pass a window
While walking through a mall
With nothing much upon my mind,
Quite blank as I recall.
I noticed in that window
A cranky-faced old man,
And why he looked so cranky
I didn't understand.
Just why he looked at ME that way
Was more than I could see
Until I came to realize
That cranky man was ME!
—UNATTRIBUTED, on a "clean joke" Web site

APPROPRIATE HYMNS AND SONGS

"Joyful, Joyful We Adore Thee," Henry Van Dyke/Ludwig Van Beethoven, Public Domain.

"Joy Unspeakable," Barney E. Warren, Public Domain.

"Come Let Us Sing for Joy," John Rowe, 1985 Dayspring Music, Inc. (Admin. Word Music Group).

"The Joy of the Lord," Twila Paris, 1991 Ariose Music/Mountain Spring Music (Admin. EMI Christian Music Publishing).

"Trading My Sorrows," Darrell Evans, 1998 Integrity's Hosanna! Music (Admin. Integrity Music Inc.).

[1]John C. Maxwell, *Today Matters* (New York: Warner Faith, 2004), p. 42.

FOR THE BULLETIN

During Medieval times, Christians began worshiping and praying to saints, a practice that gradually led to the prominence of icons—flat pictures representing Christ, Mary, or some other saint. The Byzantine Emperor Leo III was repelled by the worship of icons, and in 726 he outlawed image worship and soon thereafter ordered the destruction of icons everywhere. But image worship had become so entrenched in the Byzantine church that his edicts were viewed as attacks on Christianity itself. A great uprising raged through his empire, and many died. On March 11, 843, icons were formally sanctioned and reintroduced in all Eastern Orthodox churches. This day, the so-called "Triumph of Orthodoxy," has been commemorated in Eastern congregations around the world for over a thousand years. ● On March 11, 1513, Leo X was elected pope. His eight years in office are primarily remembered by his excommunication in 1520 of Martin Luther. ● On this day in 1812, fire destroyed the printing shop of missionary William Carey in Serampore, India. Carey said, "The loss is heavy, but as traveling a road the second time is usually done with greater ease and certainty than the first time, so I trust the work will lose nothing of real value . . . We are cast down but not in despair." ● Today marks the death, in 1847, of Jonathan Chapman, better known as Johnny Appleseed. Henry Drummand died on this day in 1897. He was a close friend of evangelist D. L. Moody and the author of a popular meditation in 1 Corinthians 13 titled *The Greatest Thing in All the World.*

WORSHIP HELPS

Call to Worship
How lovely is Your tabernacle, O LORD of hosts! My soul longs, yes, even faints for the courts of the LORD; My heart and my flesh cry out for the living God (Ps. 84:1–2).

Benediction
God is our refuge and strength, a very present help in trouble. Therefore we will not fear, even though the earth be removed, and though the mountains be carried into the midst of the sea; though its waters roar and be troubled, though the mountains shake with its swelling (Ps. 46:1–3).

Additional Sermons and Lesson Ideas

When We Worship
By Dr. Melvin Worthington

Date preached:

SCRIPTURE: Various

INTRODUCTION: Often we substitute activity for adoration. We must recognize:

1. The Need for Worship. The Bible emphasizes the *day* of worship (Gen. 2; Ex. 20; 1 Cor. 16), the *duty* of worship (Ex. 20; John 4), and the *discipline* in worship (Heb. 10:25).
2. The Nature of Worship. The Old Testament concept of worship included a reverent attitude of mind and body combined with religious adoration, obedience, and service. Worship in the New Testament combines the reverent attitude of man and body and feelings of awe, veneration, and adoration (John 4:23–24; Acts 17:25; Phil. 3:3).
3. The Neglect of Worship. To neglect worship is to *disobey* God. The *disposition* of saints is affected by neglect of worship. The *degeneracy* of society (Rom. 1) can be traced to the neglect of worship.

CONCLUSION: Do you live a lifestyle of worship?

The Unflappability of Faith

Date preached:

SCRIPTURE: Psalm 46 (Based on the NIV)

INTRODUCTION: Have you ever seen a child in a tizzy—upset, crying, fretful? The dad or mom hugs him close, calms his fears, and he becomes quiet once again. That's the way the Lord deals with our alarms. He wants to work in us the unflappability of faith.

1. Be still and know that I am God (Ps. 46:10).
2. You need only to be still (Ex. 14:14).
3. Be still, for this is a sacred day (Neh. 8:11).
4. Be still before the Lord and wait patiently for Him (Ps. 37:7).
5. Be still before the Lord, all mankind (Zech. 2:13).
6. Peace! Be still (Mark 4:39).

CONCLUSION: When the German philosophy professor, Samuel Rodigast, heard his friend, Severus Gastorius, was ill and not expected to live, he wrote a hymn to cheer him. Gastorius not only recovered, but went on write the music to which this hymn is now sung in Lutheran churches. The words say: "Whate'er my God ordains is right: / His holy will abideth; / I will be still whate'er He doth; / And follow where He guideth; / He is my God; though dark my road, / He holds me that I shall not fall: / Wherefore to Him I leave it all."

Pastoring When You Aren't Well
An Interview with Dr. Ed Dobson

Briefly describe the challenge you've encountered physically in your ministry.

I was diagnosed with ALS or Lou Gehrig's disease and so, for the last four-and-a-half years I've continued to struggle with increasing disability and just recently announced my resignation as senior pastor after eighteen years.

How did the Lord enable you to continue your pastoral ministry for over four years as you battled this?

First of all, I chose not to ask the question "why" because I felt there wasn't a legitimate biblical or theological answer to that question, and so I wasn't going to waste my limited resources wrestling with the question for which I ultimately knew there was no answer. Second, I had to preach every Sunday, I had to do weddings, I had to do funerals. Had I been left on my own, I wouldn't have done any of that; but I had to get out of bed and minister to others.

Third, the prayers, love, support, and understanding of the community that I served sustained me so that when I couldn't pray, they were praying for me. There is something mystical about the power of prayer in the community that helps us.

What specific Bible passages have strengthened you?

The one text that really sustained me is found in Hebrews where God has said, "I will never leave you or forsake you. So we say with the confidence, the Lord is my helper. I will not be afraid." Struggling with a terminal disease is as much a struggle in the mind as it is a struggle in the body, and whenever I begin to think about the future, I sink into depression and darkness. So I learned early on, when I started to sink, to take a ten-minute timeout and simply repeat those verses over and over and over and over and over until I refocus my mind on God and His promise.

Continued on the next page

CONVERSATIONS IN THE PASTOR'S STUDY—*Continued*

Has it been awkward to minister without the total focus being on your health?

Yes. But I have tried very hard not to bring up my illness when I preach or teach. I would say maybe once or twice a year I've mentioned specifically my illness; I don't want my whole life to be judged by a disease and so I work hard at not making the disease the issue. But the church has been very helpful, very supportive, has adjusted my schedule, reduced my preaching load, and taken away some of my responsibilities so that I can continue.

We're conducting this interview in a coffee shop, and I've found you here with your legal pad, your Greek text, your Hebrew text, and your New Testament opened before you. Obviously, your appetite for the Word of God hasn't waned during this time.

No, not at all. In fact, this last year, I decided to re-learn Hebrew even though I had taken it thirty years ago. I decided I needed to retake it, so I took three semesters of Hebrew at a seminary, knowing that I may only have a limited number of years to use it, but nonetheless, I am very committed to wrestling with the Scriptures until the day I die.

Has this illness done anything in your heart to quicken your feelings or interest in heaven?

Actually, no, it's done the opposite. People often ask, "I'm sure you're thinking a lot about heaven." No. That's the last thing I'm thinking about. I'm attached to my ministry, to my family, to my kids, to my grandkids; and while I'm not afraid of being dead, I don't cherish the thought of getting dead. Maybe the time will come when I will think more about heaven, but right now, I'm pretty rooted in the here and now.

Has ALS enabled you to minister in ways that otherwise would not have been available to you?

Oh, absolutely. God has opened wonderful ministry to people who are terminally ill and, when I look them in the eyes, I see their soul, and when they look me in the eyes, they see my soul. So what I would say to them is much better received because I am a fellow pilgrim.

What would you say to a pastor who is reading this propped up in a hospital bed trying to recover from a heart attack or waiting in the doctor's waiting room for a chemotherapy treatment and who is discouraged?

I would first of all say, welcome to the club of the discouraged, broken, half-depressed, struggling people. I think the second thing I would say is, there is no verse and no prayer that will make it go away; that you are in for a long, long journey; but God will be faithful to you in the journey, and give you the grace when you need it, but generally not ahead of time.

Do you have specific plans for that day after your final Sunday in the pulpit at your church? Are you making plans for a post-pastorate life?

Not at this point. I am going to take a couple of months away from Grand Rapids with my wife just to pray, meditate, reflect, recover. But I really have no clue after Calvary—what I will do or what I should do or what I shouldn't do. I will discover the day after how much of my identity was wrapped up in being the senior pastor and how much is truly wrapped up in Jesus, and I am sort of afraid that it will be more of the former than the latter.

Any concluding thoughts?

If I could say one thing to pastors it would be: Teach the Word. The church today has been, in part, seduced by relevancy, by being contemporary, by being cool, and I happen to believe the great hunger of all generations is for the question, "What does the Bible say?" So, devote your life to what matters—the teaching of the Bible.

MARCH 18, 2007

More Than a Song: A Fresh Vision for Worship

Date preached:

By Dr. Timothy Beougher

Scripture: John 4:19–24, especially verse 24
God is Spirit, and those who worship Him must worship in spirit and truth.

Introduction: I'd like to begin this morning with a word association. The word is "worship"; what comes to mind first? For some of you, it is the word "church." For others of you, it is singing. For others it may be a particular style of worship. What came to your mind? If you thought about anything but God when I said the word worship, you need to refocus your vision of worship. Worship is all about Him! We tend to evaluate everything through our perspective. How did I like it? What did it do for ME? Was it the kind of music I like? What did I get out of the service? But it is so not about us!

1. **What Is Worship?** In attempting to define "worship," it is interesting to note that the word "worship" is nowhere defined in Scripture. Some selected definitions include: an encounter with the living God; declaring God's worth; when we put God first in our lives; communicating to God how much we love Him; when you see God and admire Him. The key to understanding genuine worship is that it's about giving to God, not getting from God. Genuine worship is about pleasing God, not having God please you.

2. **Why Should We Worship?**

   A. **Worship Changes Us (2 Cor. 3:18).** What you worship determines what you become. Worship is why we were created; as we worship we become that for which we were created! True worship changes us, but that is not the primary reason we worship.

   B. **God Desires Our Worship (John 4:23b).** ". . . for the Father is seeking such to worship Him." Worship pleases God. We bring pleasure to God by worshiping Him.

   C. **God Deserves Our Worship (Rev. 4:11).** "You are worthy, O Lord, to receive glory and honor and power; for You created all things, and by Your will they exist and were created." It is not wrong for someone to want what they truly deserve. God is worthy of our praise because He is our Creator and our Lord.

3. **How Should We Worship (John 4:19–24)?** The context of this passage is Jesus' conversation with the Samaritan woman at the well of Jacob. In the midst of the conversation, the subject of worship comes up. Jesus' statements help us understand how we should worship. The Samaritan woman thought worship was defined by a geographic location. We often do the same. We often think worship is only done at church. We also tend to define worship by a timeframe: 10:45 A.M. to 12:00 P.M. on Sunday mornings, for example. Some define worship as simply singing from a hymn book or worship chorus. Christ explained that worship is more than where you are, what time it is, and whether you sing.

A. **God Seeks Those Who Worship Him in Spirit.** Our spirit is our inner life, our emotions, our will, our heart. Genuine worship happens only when the very core of our being is involved in worshiping God. That means genuine worship is "heartfelt" and "honest" before God (1 Sam. 16:7). We can sing and not worship. Worshiping in spirit means our heart must be His. You can't worship God until your heart is changed. The only way you can draw near to God is to connect with Him through His Son. If God doesn't have your heart, then nothing else you do on Sunday morning matters.

B. **God Seeks Those Who Worship Him in Truth.** Some want to say, "I'll just worship God in my own way." No, we must worship God in His way. We must worship according to God's revelation. We need more than sincerity; we need truth, namely through the Scriptures. That is where the Samaritans got it wrong: they were sincere about their worship, but they had incomplete information about God to base it on. The Samaritans used only the first five books of the Bible, thus limiting God's complete revelation. Sincerity alone does not make for acceptable worship.

C. **God Seeks Those Who Worship Him Holistically (Mark 12:30).** Another definition: *"Worship is responding to all that God is, with all that we are."* Worship isn't passive but participatory. Giving is a part of worship. Not only this, but we are to dedicate our entire lives: our time and our talents.

Conclusion: Humans are all born as worshipers. Either we worship God, or we will worship or live our lives for created things rather than the Creator (Rom. 1:25). Let's dedicate ourselves to worshiping God in Spirit and in truth with everything we are.

STATS, STORIES, AND MORE

More Than a Song
Matt Redman, a worship leader in England, tells how his pastor helped teach his church the real meaning of worship. To show that worship is more than music, the pastor banned all singing in their services for a period of time while they learned to worship in other ways. Through that experience, Matt Redman wrote the classic song, "Heart of Worship."

The Heart of Worship
Consider what the Lord says through the prophet Isaiah: "Inasmuch as these people draw near with their mouths and honor Me with their lips, but have removed their hearts far from Me" (Is. 29:13). That is NOT what God wants. Rev. Charles Haddon Spurgeon once said, "God does not regard our voices, He hears our hearts, and if our hearts do not sing, we have not sung at all."

Worth-Ship
Our word "worship" comes from the old English word "worth-ship," which means worthiness. To worship is to declare God's worth. This shines through our lives, attitudes, and deeds—not just our Sunday morning songs. David Larson, in his book, *The Company of Preachers,* has this profound sentence: "All human activity is to be doxological in nature."

Praise the Lord!
An expressive woman wandered into a liturgical service. As the pastor preached, she became so caught up in his message that she exclaimed, "Praise the Lord!" A fellow worshiper leaned over and whispered, "Excuse me, but we don't praise the Lord in the Lutheran church." A man down the pew corrected him: "Yes we do; it's on page 19."

APPROPRIATE HYMNS AND SONGS

"Heart of Worship," Matt Redman, 1997 Kingsway's ThankYou Music (Admin. EMI Christian Music Publishing).

"I Worship You Almighty God," Sondra Corbett, 1983 Integrity's Hosanna! Music (Admin. Integrity Music Inc.).

"Brethren We have Met to Worship," George Atkins/William Moore, Public Domain.

"All Creatures of Our God and King," St. Francis of Assisi/William H. Draper, Public Domain.

"O Worship the King," William Kethe/Johann Michael Haydn/R. Grant, Public Domain.

FOR THE BULLETIN

Cyril, bishop of Jerusalem, died on March 18, A.D. 386. He was an early promoter for the veneration of relics and of the doctrine of Transubstantiation. ● Today is the birthday, in 1775, of British hymnist, John Cawood, and of the hymnist, Charlotte Elliott, in 1789. She is the author of the famous invitational hymn, "Just As I Am." The author of "Fairest Lord Jesus," the Moravian hymnist, Joseph August Seiss, was born on this day in 1823. ● The Metropolitan Tabernacle was opened in London on March 18, 1861. This was the sanctuary of the famous English Baptist preacher, Charles Haddon Spurgeon. The building as Spurgeon envisioned and designed it was enormous, and underneath were basement rooms filled with lecture halls, Sunday school classes, various offices and storerooms. In the main auditorium, there were 3,600 seats with side-flaps on the aisles capable of seating another 1,000; yet the room was often packed with 6,000 wanting to hear Spurgeon preach, many of them standing. After Spurgeon's death, the tabernacle burned down, leaving the outer walls intact. The interior was rebuilt but with smaller seating. The building was bombed during World War II and again rebuilt. ● The Cambridge Seven, young British aristocrats who decided to become missionaries to China, arrived in Shanghai on March 18, 1885. C. T. Studd, one of England's most famous cricket players and a convert of D. L. Moody, was among them. ● The Bible scholar and professor, Dr. Merrill C. Tenney, died on March 18, 1985.

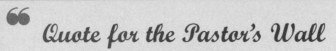

" Quote for the Pastor's Wall

Never think of giving up preaching!
The angels around the throne
envy your great work.
—ALEXANDER WHYTE[1]

"

---

[1]Quoted by Warren W. Wiersbe and Lloyd M. Perry in *The Wycliffe Handbook of Preaching and Preachers,* (Chicago: Moody Press, 1984), p. 257.

WORSHIP HELPS

Call to Worship
Oh, magnify the LORD with me, and let us exalt His name
together (Ps. 34:3).

Scripture Reading Medley
Be glad in the LORD and rejoice, you righteous; and shout for
joy, all you upright in heart! / Let the heavens rejoice, and let
the earth be glad; and let them say among the nations, "The
LORD reigns." / Let all those who seek You rejoice and be glad
in You; let such as love Your salvation say continually, "The
LORD be magnified." / Let all those rejoice who put their trust
in You; let them ever shout for joy, because You defend them;
let those also who love Your name be joyful in You. For You,
O LORD, will bless the righteous; with favor You will surround
him as with a shield. / . . . this day is holy to our Lord. Do not
sorrow, for the joy of the LORD is your strength. / Make a joyful
shout to the LORD, all you lands! Serve the LORD with
gladness. / Because you did not serve the LORD your God with
joy and gladness of heart, for the abundance of everything,
therefore you shall serve your enemies . . . / For the kingdom of
God is not eating and drinking, but righteousness and peace
and joy in the Holy Spirit. For he who serves Christ in these
things is acceptable to God and approved by men. / The fruit of
the Spirit is . . . joy (Ps. 32:11; 1 Chr. 16:31; Ps. 40:16; Ps. 5:11–
12; Neh. 8:10; Ps. 100:1–2; Deut. 28:47–48; Rom. 14:17–18; Gal.
5:22).

Benediction
But whoever keeps His word, truly the love of God is perfected
in him. By this we know that we are in Him. He who says he
abides in Him ought himself also to walk just as He walked
(1 John 2:5–6).

Additional Sermons and Lesson Ideas

Power Prayers: The Relationship Factor
Date preached:
By Dr. Larry Osborne

SCRIPTURE: Various, especially Luke 18:9–14

INTRODUCTION: Prayer is dependent upon our relationship with God. Consider:

1. The Kind of People God Listens to (Luke 18:9–14; Jer. 26:3; Ezek. 18:23).
2. The Kind of Prayer God Answers. Three key principles to keep in mind:
   A. When People Complain that God Didn't Help, It's Often Because He Didn't Hear (Prov. 1:23–28; Zech. 7:13; Prov. 15:29).
   B. Prayer Is a Family Privilege (John 14:6; 15:7–9; Matt. 6:9; 1 Pet. 3:12). It flows out of our relationship with God, not out of religious ritual (Prov. 15:8; Luke 18:9–14), positive thinking (Luke 17:5–6; Matt. 13:31–32; Acts 12:1–17), magic words or special formulas (John 14:13–14; Col. 3:17; Matt. 6:7–8).
3. A Good Relationship with God. Prayer depends on your relationship, which is based on humility toward God and others (Luke 18:9–14; 2 Chr. 7:14; Prov. 16:5; 21:4; 1 Pet. 3:7) and on obedience (Prov. 28:9; Ps. 66:18–20; Is. 59:1–2; Zech. 7:13; Prov. 15:29; Judg. 10:6–16; Rom. 7:21–25; 1 John 1:8–9).

CONCLUSION: The effective, fervent prayer of a righteous man avails much (James 5:16).

The Christian and Trouble (Part 1)
Date preached:
By Rev. Billie Friel

SCRIPTURE: Various

INTRODUCTION: Trouble is a part of life. As Christ said, "(God) makes His sun rise on the evil and on the good, and sends rain on the just and on the unjust" (Matt. 5:45). As Christians, we should understand both the promise that trouble will occur and the plan Scripture lays out to deal with it:

1. The Promise of Trouble (Job 5:7).
   A. We Are Born into a Sinful World (Rom. 5:12).
   B. We Are Born into a Sinful Body (Ps. 51:5).
   C. We Are Born into a Spiritual Warfare (1 Pet. 5:8).
2. The Plan for Trouble.
   A. Trouble Refines and Purifies Us (Is. 1:25).
   B. Trouble Drives Men to God in Prayer (Acts 4:23–24).
   C. Trouble Can Produce Spiritual Maturity (Ps. 71:19–21).
   D. Trouble Can Glorify God and Spread the Gospel (Phil. 1:12–18).

CONCLUSION: With Christ you can face the coming trouble.

MARCH 25, 2007

SUGGESTED SERMON

The Devil's Devices

Date preached:

By Dr. Melvin Worthington

Scripture: Various, especially 2 Corinthians 11:14
. . . For Satan himself transforms himself into an angel of light.

Introduction: Commanders in battle say one of the most important strategies is to know your enemy. The devil is alive and active in the world. He is *described* as an angel of light, an accuser of the loyal and an adversary like a lion seeking to devour his prey (Gen. 3; Matt.; 1 Pet. 5:8; Eph. 2; 6 and Rev. 20:1–3). He *desires* to distract, detour, deceive, and devour the saints. His *design* is to deny, dilute, and distort the Scriptures. His *devices* delude and damn sinners. Consider:

1. **The Personality of the Devil (Ezek. 28:11–19; Is. 14:12–14; Gen. 3; Job 1, Eph. 6:10–12).** Lewis Sperry Chafer notes, "The strategies and warfare of Satan against the children of God . . . are proof positive of the personality of Satan. There is no mention in the Scriptures of warfare by Satan against the unregenerate: they are his own, and therefore under his authority" (John 8:44; Eph. 2:2; 1 John 5:19 R.V.). The tragic record of the deception of Eve and the deliberate disobedience of Adam through the temptation by Satan further confirms the personality of Satan. The Bible sets forth clearly and convincingly that the devil is a real person with personality.

2. **The Presence of the Devil (Is. 14).** He tempted the Lord Jesus Christ (Luke 4:1–13). The apostle Peter declares, "Be sober, be vigilant; because your adversary the devil walks about like a roaring lion, seeking whom he may devour. Resist him, steadfast in the faith, knowing that the same sufferings are experienced by your brotherhood in the world" (1 Pet. 5:8–9). Paul notes, "For Satan himself transforms himself into an angel of light" (2 Cor. 11:14).

3. **The Power of the Devil.** Satan's position and power must not be underestimated. He is morally fallen and has been judged on the cross (John 12:31; 16:11; Col. 2:15) but his position and power over the kingdoms of this world remain. Christ acknowledged that Satan's power and authority always operate within the permissive will

of God. The devil desires to control the minds, morals, motives, manners, and materials available to mankind (2 Thess. 2:9–10; Job 1; Eph. 6:12; Matt. 4; John 14:30; 2 Cor. 4:4). The devil has personal power and he is also aided by myriads of demons that do his bidding. Lewis Sperry Chafer declares, "Though he is not omnipresent, omnipotent, not omniscient, through the wicked spirits he is in touch with the whole earth."

4. **The Program of the Devil.** The devil's program includes *the times, the seasons*. This remarkable truth is confirmed by Satan's temptation of Jesus (Matt. 4). Satan tempted David at the time or season when kings go to battle (2 Sam. 11). The devil knows just the right time and season to tempt mankind. He often comes with temptation following great victories or when we are in periods of discouragement and depression. Matthew says following the temptation of Christ, "Then the devil left Him, and behold, angels came and ministered to Him" (Matt. 4:11). The devil's program also includes the *tactics, the snares*. The devil attacks, allures, and accuses. He appeals to our *appetites* (Matt. 4; Gen. 3; 1 John 2:1); our *ambition* (1 John 2:15; Gen. 3; Matt. 4) and our *allegiance* (Matt. 4). The devil misleads, misinforms, and misrepresents the human race regarding God's revelation: His eternal Word. The devil's program includes the *tragedy, the successes*. The Scriptures record the tragic episodes regarding the devil's seduction and deception of Lot, David, Adam, Eve, Samson, and Peter. The devil's program is designed to entice, enslave, embitter, and embarrass. He blinds, binds, blames, beguiles, and belittles.

5. **The Perdition of the Devil.** Revelation 19:11; 20:1–10 records the final destiny of the devil. His defeat is revealed, recorded, and remains. The final doom of the devil is summed up by Lewis Sperry Chafer when he says, "Having promoted an open rebellion against God during the "little season," Satan is then cast into the lake of fire to be tormented day and night for ever and ever" (Rev. 2:10).

Conclusion: Satan by deception sows doubt and discouragement and by design he sows dissatisfaction and division. He deliberately discredits and distorts and by delusion he causes destruction and damnation. A biblical understanding of the person, presence, power, program, and perdition of the devil enables one to withstand his power and flee his presence.

STATS, STORIES, AND MORE

Beware the Snake in your Shirt

Many years ago, a strong young Indian decided to climb to the summit of a nearby, snow-capped peak. He donned his buffalo-hide shirt, wrapped his blanket around him, and set off. When he at last reached the summit and gazed over the endless panorama below, feeling the cold against him, he swelled with pride over his accomplishment.

Then he saw a motion at his feet. It was a snake, which promptly and pitifully spoke to him. "I'm about to die," said the snake. "It is too cold for me up here and I am freezing. There is no food, and I am starving. Please up me under your shirt and take me down to the valley."

"No," said the young man. "I know your kind. You are a rattlesnake, and if I pick you up you will bite and kill me."

"No," said the snake. "I will treat you differently. If you do this for me, you'll be special and I'll not harm you."

At last the youth gave in to the creature's pleading and tucked the snake under his shirt. Arriving down in the valley, he removed it and laid the snake on the ground. Whereupon the snake immediately coiled, rattled, struck, and planted his deadly fangs in the young man's leg.

"But you promised," said the young man, falling, feeling the deadly venom enter his bloodstream.

"You knew what I was when you picked me up," said the serpent, slithering away.

Paul wrote to the Corinthians, "I fear, lest somehow, as the serpent deceived Eve by his craftiness, so your minds may be corrupted from the simplicity that is in Christ (2 Cor. 11:3).[1]

APPROPRIATE HYMNS AND SONGS

"Onward Christian Soldiers," Sabine Baring-Gould/Arthur Seymour Sullivan, Public Domain.

"The Solid Rock," Edward Mote/William B. Bradbury, Public Domain.

"A Mighty Fortress Is Our God," Martin Luther, Public Domain.

"Greater Are You," Dennis Jernigan, 1990 Shepherd's Heart Music, Inc. (Admin. Word Music Group).

---

[1]Adapted from *The Preacher's Illustration Service*, Volume 3, Number 4, July/August, 1990, p. 5.

FOR THE BULLETIN

Today—exactly nine months before Christmas—is the traditional day of the Annunciation and of the conception of Jesus within the womb of Mary. This date can be traced back to the Roman Church historian Dionysius Exiguus in the 500s. ● According to Foxes' *Book of Martyrs,* three sisters named Agrape, Chionia, and Irene, were set afire and martyred on this day in A.D. 304. ● The First Council of Pisa was assembled on March 25, 1490, for the primary purpose of deposing two rival popes. ● King James I, the English monarch who authorized the "King James Version" of the Bible, died on this day in 1625. ● Evangelist George Whitefield was a zealous advocate of caring for orphans. On March 25, 1740, with Whitefield raising most of the funds, construction began on the Bethesda Orphanage in Savannah, Georgia, the oldest existing orphanage in America. ● Today is the birthday, in 1783, of Luther Rice, missionary to India. ● The great Scottish minister and revivalist, Robert Murray McCheyne, preached his last sermon on March 12, 1846, and shortly afterward was sickened with a fever, perhaps by visiting ill parishioners. On Saturday, March 25, attended by his physician, McCheyne lifted his hand toward heaven as if in an attitude of blessing, then sank down onto the bed. He passed away at just past nine in the morning, and that day the entire city of Dundee mourned, with people bursting into tears in meeting each other on the street. His influence remains to this day. He was only twenty-nine.

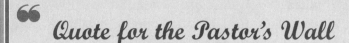

❝ *Quote for the Pastor's Wall*

*I long to accomplish a great and noble task;
but it is my chief duty and job to accomplish
humble tasks as though they were
great and noble.*

—HELEN KELLER[2] ❞

---

[2]Quoted by John Maxwell in *Success: One Day at a Time* (Nashville: J. Countryman, 2000), p. 124.

WORSHIP HELPS

Call to Worship
And we, who with unveiled faces all reflect the Lord's glory, are being transformed into His likeness with ever-increasing glory, which comes from the Lord, who is the Spirit (2 Cor. 3:18 NIV).

Scripture Reading
Blessed be the LORD my Rock, who trains my hands for war, and my fingers for battle—My lovingkindness and my fortress, my high tower and my deliverer, my shield and the One in whom I take refuge, who subdues my people under me. LORD, what is man, that You take knowledge of him? Or the son of man, that You are mindful of him? Man is like a breath; His days are like a passing shadow (Ps. 144:1–4).

Offertory Comments
Samuel Logan Brengle, a leader of the Salvation Army movement in America, was one of the most respected and powerful men in American church history, a dedicated evangelist who led multitudes to faith in Christ. In his biography, *Samuel Logan Brengle: Portrait of a Prophet,* Clarence W. Hall quotes Brengle as saying this about the practice of tithing: "I tithed every cent of my money even when I was getting my education, and was so poor and in debt that I wore celluloid collars and ate oatmeal almost exclusively. The money I tithed was borrowed. The devil said: 'Here, why do you do this? This is not your money; it belongs to your creditors.' I said: 'Devil, you're a liar. This is my Father's money; it's only passing through my hands, and He shall have His tenth.' And God prospered me, according to His Word. In a remarkably short time, I was able to pay back every cent I owed."[3]

---

[3]Clarence W. Hall, *Samuel Logan Brengle: Portrait of a Prophet* (Atlanta: The Salvation Army Supplies and Purchasing Dept., 1938), p. 186.

Additional Sermons and Lesson Ideas

The Supremacy of Christ (Part 1)

Date preached:

By Joshua D. Rowe

SCRIPTURE: Colossians 1:15–16

INTRODUCTION: I can think of few other passages in Scripture that send me straight to my knees in awe of Christ than these verses. Here, we see Christ as:

1. The Firstborn of All Things (v. 15): "He is the image of the invisible God, the firstborn over all creation." Before man and woman were created, the true and full image of God was present in the person of Jesus Christ!
2. The Creator of All Things (v. 16a): "For by Him all things were created that are in heaven and that are on earth, visible and invisible, whether thrones or dominions or principalities or powers." Ultimately, there is no ruler but Jesus over the earth, over spiritual powers, and over earthly leaders.
3. The Owner of All Things (v. 16b): "All things were created through Him and for Him." Do you think of your possessions as your own? Everything that exists is ultimately Jesus Christ's possession!

CONCLUSION: In Christ, we can be restored to the image of God that existed before the Fall of Genesis 3. He is not only the Savior, but the Creator and Owner of everything: won't you turn to Him in submission and complete trust today?

The Supremacy of Christ (Part 2)

Date preached:

By Joshua D. Rowe

SCRIPTURE: Colossians 1:17–20

INTRODUCTION: Jesus Christ is more than just the Savior of the world. He is also:

1. The Sustainer of All Things (v. 17). "He is before all things, and in him all things hold together" (NIV). Do you rely on yourself, your family, your organization, your company, your bank account, or anything else to hold things together in your life? If so, you're looking to the wrong "lord."
2. The Ruler of All Things (v. 18). "And he is the head of the body, the church; he is the beginning and the firstborn from among the dead,

so that in everything he might have the supremacy" (NIV). No one can claim the throne over all things but Christ Himself!

3. The Reconciler of All Things (vv. 19–20). "For it pleased the Father that in Him all the fullness should dwell, and by Him to reconcile all things to Himself, by Him, whether things on earth or things in heaven, having made peace through the blood of His cross." Have you been reconciled to the Savior through His death and resurrection?

CONCLUSION: No other response is suitable but to lay down our lives in complete trust, dependence, obedience, and submission to our incredible Lord, Creator, Owner, Sustainer, Ruler, and Reconciler.

HEROES FOR THE PASTOR'S HEART

Rev. Charles Bowles

Rev. Charles Bowles, an African-American, was born in Boston in 1761 and fought for the Colonies in the War of Independence, after which he settled down in New Hampshire where he became a Christian. When he felt God calling him to ministry, he initially fled to the sea like a modern Jonah, but eventually yielded and was ordained by the Freewill Baptists.

Bowles is indicative of the influence black evangelicals had on America in the Revolutionary era, and of the hardships they faced because of racial hatred. On one occasion as he preached, he was threatened by a mob that was determined to throw him in a nearby pond. He continued preaching with such power, however, that a number of people were converted, and Bowles ended up throwing them in that very pond—in Christian baptism.

On another occasion, Charles had an appointment to preach near a tavern in which a gentleman from New York put up for the night. In the evening the landlord informed the guest that a "colored man" was to preach near by, and invited him to attend; but he indignantly refused, alleging that the sermon was probably borrowed; but being urged again, consented on condition that the landlord give Charles the following text, and he would preach from it that evening.

They went to the house, laid the text on the desk, and took their seats. It was Proverbs, 30th chapter, 19th verse. At first Charles thought of declining; it was a new and difficult subject; one which he had never studied and upon which he was unprepared to preach. Elder Nathaniel Bowles, a white man who had labored much with him, was present with him, and they consulted for some time upon it. At last Charles determined that brother Nathaniel should read a long hymn to be sung, then make a long prayer, then read another long hymn, so as to give Elder Charles time to prepare his subject.

When the last hymn was being sung, the text appeared clear in his mind, and after speaking for a few moments upon the literal meaning, began to make a spiritual application of the subject. The gentleman who gave the text was cut to the heart, and soon after converted to God.

In his latter years, Charles Bowles suffered from blindness, but he nonetheless continued traveling, preaching pastoring, and soul-wining until his death on March 16, 1843, in Malone, New York.

APRIL 1, 2007

The Great Betrayal

Date preached:

By Dr. Robert Norris

Scripture: Matthew 26:17–25, especially verse 21
Now as they were eating, He said, "Assuredly, I say to you, one of you will betray Me."

Background: Palm Sunday is a day of celebration. We recall the coming of Christ to Jerusalem and His welcome by the crowds. Matthew captures that sense of welcome when he records; ". . . the whole city was moved . . ." (Matt. 26:10). It was the triumphal entry of a King in triumph, for Jesus is welcomed with the cry; "Hosanna to the Son of David" (v. 9). Yet Matthew also makes clear that the coming of Jesus was a solemn occasion, for directly preceding, he records the cleansing of the temple (21:12–22), the hostility of the Jewish religious leaders seeking to arrest Jesus (21:46), Jesus' lament over Jerusalem (23:38), the impending destruction of the temple itself (24:2), the revelation that Jesus knows He will be betrayed to His enemies to be killed (26:2) namely by Judas (26:14). We learn from this scene:

1. **God's Purposes Always Face Opposition by Evil.** What made Judas betray Jesus? Scripture makes clear that Judas, who was the treasurer of disciples, had in that position stolen from their treasury which had grown somewhat with the support of the wealthy wives of Chuza and Susanna (Luke 8:3). Earlier Matthew recorded Judas' seeking out the "chief priests" and his offer to betray Jesus (26:14). There, he agrees to betray his Master for thirty pieces of silver. Judas' love of money leads him to this dreadful action. We are warned here how the power of a single obsessive sin can enwrap, possess, enchain, and degrade the character of a man or a woman.

2. **Evil Never Takes God by Surprise.** Judas' actions are no surprise to Jesus. Not only did Jesus know that He was going to be betrayed, but He also knew who it was who would betray Him. Contrary to appearances He is not falling into the trap that Judas has laid.

Rather, Judas, by his actions in rejecting the Christ, has become an instrument of God's plan. Jesus says: "The Son of Man indeed goes just as it is written of him . . ." (26:24). God is not ever taken by surprise, even by the wickedness of His people. Evil is not outside of the knowledge of the Living God. We can take comfort from this great truth, for it reminds us that no matter what confronts us, no matter how seemingly evil are the circumstances of life, God knows them and they do not surprise Him.

3. **Evil Is Judged.** The arch-enemy of God from all eternity indwelt Judas Iscariot (John 13:27). Jesus was about to institute the sacrament of the Lord's Supper, and He wanted no evil thing present, saying: "What you do, do quickly" (John 13:27). While the disciples imagined that Judas had been sent out to buy things for the feast, he had in fact been sent from the presence of Jesus. It was a picture of his judgment and his damnation. Judas is also named "the son of perdition" (John 17:12) indicating Judas was the only "lost" disciple.

4. **Evil Cannot Ultimately Triumph.** God used even this terrible act of treachery to bring about His plan of redemption. Judas, even as he planned and executed his terrible deed, nonetheless became an instrument through which God would bring forth blessing. The dreadful act of betrayal was used to further the plan of redemption that had from the beginning been the will of God. An unholy man and his unholy actions were nevertheless used by the sovereign Lord to accomplish a holy purpose, your redemption and mine! God brought good out of evil. The "son of perdition" did not become a "son of righteousness" because he was used as an instrument in the hand of God. We can be comforted by the fact that the apparent triumph of evil is also mysteriously a work of God, and what man meant for evil God purposed for good.

Conclusion: The war with evil continues, and we are a part of it. Guard your hearts, and in the conflict we who are disciples can rest our hearts upon the truth that God Himself is the sovereign Lord. Even failure and evil itself can be used by God to work out His will. Rest your souls in this.

STATS, STORIES, AND MORE

A Strange Story from the *Times of London*
The *Times of London* recently carried an article headlined, "Judas the Misunderstood," written by Richard Owen in Rome. The subtitle said, "Vatican Moves to Clear Reviled Disciple's Name." According to the article, "Judas Iscariot, the disciple who betrayed Jesus with a kiss, is to be given a makeover by Vatican scholars.

The proposed 'rehabilitation' of the man who was paid 30 pieces of silver to identify Jesus to Roman soldiers in the Garden of Gethsemane, comes on the ground that he was not deliberately evil, but was just 'fulfilling his part in God's plan.'"

The article went on to say that while Luke's Gospel claims that Judas was possessed by Satan, modern scholars believe it's time to reconsider the Judas story in a way that resolves "the problem of an apparent lack of mercy by Jesus toward one of his closest collaborators."

Some Bible experts say Judas was "a victim of a theological libel which helped to create anti Semitism" and his rehabilitation could help the Pope's drive to improve Christian-Jewish relations, which he has made a priority of his pontificate.[1]

APPROPRIATE HYMNS AND SONGS

"Blessed Is He Who Comes," Carman, 1984 Lehshem Music, LLC dba (Leshem Songs; Admin. Lehshen Music).

"We Cry Hosanna Lord," Mimi Farra/Claire Cloninger, 1975, 1987 Celebration (Admin. Celebration).

"All Glory Laud and Honor," Theodulph of Orleans; translated by John M. Neale, Public Domain.

"Tell Me the Stories of Jesus," William H. Parker/Frederic A. Challinor, Public Domain.

---

[1] "Judas the Misunderstood" by Richard Owen in *The Times of London*, January 12, 2006, accessed on January 17, 2006.

FOR THE BULLETIN

When Philip II, King of Spain, sent the Duke of Alva against the Dutch in an effort to defeat the Protestant movement in the Lowlands, William Prince of Orange assumed leadership of the Dutch resistance. On April 1, 1572, William launched a successful offensive against Spanish forces in the north by breaking the dikes and flooding the plains around the city. ● On April 1, 1548, the British Parliament commissioned the first printing of the English *Book of Common Prayer.* Archbishop Thomas Cranmer, working with a committee of scholars, compiled this book which has been the gold standard for Anglican worship to this day. ● On April 1, 1745, Colonial missionary David Brainerd began his four-year work among the New England Indians in Massachusetts. His Journal is a classic in American Christian history, and Brainard's self-sacrificing example has moved generations of Christians to enter missionary service. ● Today is the birthday, in 1815, of revival preacher and Presbyterian missionary William Burns, who served in China and became a treasured friend of J. Hudson Taylor. Another missionary, John Coleridge Patteson was born on this day in 1827. He served in the South Pacific as a gifted missionary linguist. ● The composer, Arthur H. Messiter, was born on April 1, 1834. He served as organist at Trinity Church in New York City for 31 years. He is best known for writing the music for the hymn, "Rejoice, Ye Pure in Heart." ● On April 1, 1893, The *Salvation Army War Cry* published the words of a hymn by Nathan Atkinson Aldersley that became quite popular in its day: "Of all in earth or Heaven, the dearest name to me, / Is the matchless Name of Jesus, the Christ of Calvary."

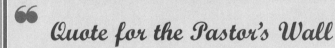

Quote for the Pastor's Wall

Adversity causes some men to break;
others to break records.

—WILLIAM A. WARD[2]

---

[2]http://www.indianchild.com/sports_quotes_quotations.htm, accessed March 10, 2006.

WORSHIP HELPS

Call to Worship

Then the multitudes who went before and those who followed cried out, saying: "Hosanna to the Son of David! 'Blessed is He who comes in the name of the LORD!' Hosanna in the highest!" And when He had come into Jerusalem, all the city was moved, saying, "Who is this?" So the multitudes said, "This is Jesus, the prophet from Nazareth of Galilee" (Matt. 21:9–11).

Pastoral Prayer

Jesus, we read that on Palm Sunday almost 2,000 years ago people worshiped You as You rode into Jerusalem as Scripture had prophesied. Lord we want to worship You, too, as You make Your triumphant presence known to us today. We do not wave palm branches, but we lift our hearts to You. You come, not on a colt, but by Your Spirit—not into our city, but into our hearts and lives. Jesus, we look forward to the day that You will return again, triumphant, with the shout of the archangel and the trumpet call of God, when not just a few will acknowledge You, but every knee will bow! We celebrate that You have made a way through Your suffering, death, and triumphant resurrection for us to be reconciled to You. Upon Your second triumphal entry, we will meet You in the clouds to be forever with You, Amen.

Benediction

Now by this we know that we know Him, if we keep His commandments. He who says, "I know Him," and does not keep His commandments, is a liar, and the truth is not in him. But whoever keeps His word, truly the love of God is perfected in him. By this we know that we are in Him. He who says he abides in Him ought himself also to walk just as He walked (1 John 2:3–6).

Additional Sermons and Lesson Ideas

The Cultivation of Faith

Date preached:

Adapted from the writings of Rev. E. M. Bounds

SCRIPTURE: 1 Peter 1:7

INTRODUCTION: Doubt and fear are the twin foes of faith. Sometimes they actually usurp the place of faith, and although we pray, it is a restless, disquieted prayer that we offer. Doubts should never be cherished nor fears harbored. We need to guard against unbelief as we would against an enemy. Faith needs to be cultivated. It is susceptible of increase. Paul's tribute to the Thessalonians was that their faith grew exceedingly.

1. Faith is increased by exercise, by being put to use. It is nourished by sore trials (1 Pet. 1:7).
2. Faith grows by reading and meditating on the Word of God (Rom. 10:17).
3. Faith thrives in an atmosphere of prayer (Phil. 4:6).

CONCLUSION: All of us need to mark well the caution given in Hebrews: "Take heed, brothers, lest there be in any of you an evil heart of unbelief."

Palm Sunday Confessions

Date preached:

By Joshua D. Rowe

SCRIPTURE: Matthew 21:1–11

INTRODUCTION: We cannot be sure if the crowd completely understood all of these things, but we see through them a glimpse of the Gospel and how we should react to Christ:

1. We Should Acknowledge Who Jesus Is (vv. 9, 11). As the crowds, we need to realize Jesus is the Son of David, the King who was to come (v. 9, v. 11, cf. Matt. 2:23). Whether through typology, foreshadowing, or outright predictive prophecy: Christ fulfills every prophecy of the Old Testament.
2. We Should Praise Him (v. 9). The crowds shouted the word "Hosanna." This word can be defined as an exclamation of praise that implies Lordship.
3. We Should Cry Out to Him for Salvation (v. 9). The same word "Hosanna" literally means, "Save us!" or "Save us please!" Christ alone is the Source of salvation. We must call out to Him to save us too.

CONCLUSION: Have you cried "Hosanna," save us, recognizing that only the Son of David, the King of kings, the One worthy of praise can deliver us from the punishment our sin deserves?

APRIL 8, 2007

How Jesus Gives Us a Peace of His Mind

Date preached:

Scripture: Luke 24:36–49, especially verse 36
Now as they said these things, Jesus Himself stood in the midst of them, and said to them, "Peace to you."

Introduction: Easter is Miracle Day. One of the reasons we enjoy getting up, getting dressed up, and coming to church is because in a world of worry and weariness, we need a miracle—and Easter is a miracle that out-miracles all the others. Rosalind Goforth, pioneer missionary to China, told of an Easter miracle that occurred when she was a child. In her book, published in 1921, *How I Know God Answers Prayer: The Personal Testimony of One Lifetime*, she said that one year it was unusually warm on Easter Sunday and everyone broke out their spring clothes. Rosalind's family was poor and had been unable to purchase new clothes. Rosalind decided she couldn't go to church in her old winter dress. Going to her room, she opened her Bible at random, and it opened to Matthew 6: "Why take ye thought of raiment? . . . Seek ye first the kingdom of God, and all these things shall be added to you." Those words spoke so directly to Rosalind that she determined to go to church even if she had to humiliate herself in her old winter dress. The service that morning was wonderful, and years later she could still remember the messages spoken. The whole morning was a sort of miracle to her. But then, another little miracle occurred. That afternoon, a box arrived from a distant aunt, containing not only new spring dresses but lots of other things as well. Rosalind later viewed this as one of the first tokens in her young experience of the prayers and provision that would characterize her entire life. The Lord wants to give you a miracle this Easter, and our text today contains four of them. When Jesus appeared to the disciples on the evening of Easter Sunday, He bore four presents.

1. **He Gives You His Peace (vv. 36–37).** When Jesus said, "Peace be to you," it wasn't just an ordinary salutation or polite sentiment.

The terrified disciples were at that moment in confusion and fear. Rumors and reports were rampant, and their lives were in jeopardy. Seeing the form of Jesus suddenly appear, they were terrified. Our Lord's first words were of peace. The peace that Jesus gives is not the absence of problems, but the freedom to deal with those problems without the stress and strain that come from worry and uncertainty. Notice His next words: "Why are you troubled? And why do doubts arise in your hearts?" Can't you hear His sturdy voice saying that to you right now, whatever your circumstances? "I have overcome even death itself. I have performed history's ultimate miracle. Why are you so worried and troubled? Why do doubts arise in your heart? Peace I give you."

2. **He Gives You His Presence (vv. 37–43).** Jesus went on to explain that His peace was available because His presence was accessible. "Behold My hands and My feet," He said, "It is I Myself." If we would practice the presence of Jesus today, it would make a world of difference in our actions and attitudes.

3. **He Gives You His Promises (vv. 44–45).** Jesus went on to explain that by His death and resurrection, He was fulfilling the prophecies and promises made about Him. In so doing, He was ratifying all the other promises in the Bible that sustain us in daily life. One man counted over 7,000 promises made by God to you and me in the Scriptures, and we need to learn to use them. R. A. Torrey said about the Christian leader, George Mueller: "When it was laid upon George Mueller's heart to pray for anything, he would search the Scriptures to find if there was some promise that covered the case. Sometimes he would search the Scriptures for days before he presented his petition to God. And then when he found the promise, with his open Bible before him and his finger upon that promise, he would plead that promise."

4. **He Gives You His Purpose (vv. 46–49).** Our Lord's final words here comprise His Great Commission, giving us the responsibility of reaching others with the news of the Easter Miracle.

Conclusion: Do you need a miracle in your life today? It's found in Christ! And in His peace, His presence, His promises, and His purpose. And it's yours for the taking.

STATS, STORIES, AND MORE

More from Rosalind Goforth
In her book, *How I Know God Answers Prayer,* Rosalind Goforth wrote about one of the first conversions she witnessed in China. The man's name was Wang Geng-ao, who was a bright Confucian scholar who despised missionaries and who beat his wife whenever she would listen to the gospel message. The Goforths prayed earnestly for his conversion. One night, Mr. Wang dreamed he was struggling in a deep, miry pit out of which he could find no way of escape. Just when he was about to give up in despair, he looked up and saw Jonathan Goforth on the bank above him reaching out his hand. Mr. Wang searched frantically for some other way of escape, but finding none, he allowed Goforth to draw him up. As a result of this dream, Mr. Wang became a Christian and for many years one of China's most valued evangelists.

Not Quite Right
A group of four-year-olds were gathered in a Sunday school class in Chattanooga. The teacher, looking at her class enthusiastically, asked, "Does anyone know what today is?" One little girl knew. "It's Palm Sunday!" she said.

"Very good," said the teacher. "And does anyone know what next Sunday is?" The same little girl lifted her hand again. "Yes, next Sunday is Easter," she announced. The teacher was very pleased with this little girl, and she complimented her effusively before asking a third question. "Now, does anyone know what makes Easter so special. It was the same little girl who again raised her hand and offered this answer: "Yes, next Sunday is Easter because Jesus rose from the dead . . ."

Before the teacher could compliment her, she kept on talking: ". . . but if He sees His shadow, He has to go back in for seven weeks."

APPROPRIATE HYMNS AND SONGS

"Christ the Lord Is Risen Today," Charles Wesley, Public Domain.

"My Redeemer Lives," Reuben Morgan, 1998 Reuben Morgan (Hillsong) (Admin. Integrity Music Inc.).

"End of the Beginning," David Phelps, 2001 Soulwriter Music Co. (Gaither Copyright Management).

"Via Dolorosa," Niles Borop/Billy Luz Sprague, 1983 Meadowgreen Music Co. (Admin. Word Music Group).

"Because He Lives," William J. Gaither/Gloria Gaither, 1971 William J. Gaither, Inc. (ARR UBP of Gaither Copyright Management).

FOR THE BULLETIN

On Holy Thursday, April 8, 1527, while Pope Clement was blessing the crowd of 10,000 people in St. Peter's Square, a fanatic dressed only in a leather apron climbed on the statue of St. Peter and shouted, "Thy bastard of Sodom! For thy sins Rome shall be destroyed. Repent and turn thee! If thou wilt not believe me, in fourteen days thou shalt see." Strangely, the prophecy was fulfilled in the sacking of Rome shortly afterward. ● On this day, April 8, in 1546, the Council of Trent adopted *Jerome's Latin Vulgate* as the official Bible for the Roman Catholic Church. ● Today marks the death, in 1586, of the "Second Martin," Martin Chemnitz, student of Philipp Melanchthon who became a leading Reformation theologian and leader in Germany in the latter 1500s. ● "Safe in the Arms of Jesus" by Fanny Crosby, later to be of widespread comfort to parents whose children had passed away, was played for the first time on April 8, 1885, at the funeral of U.S. President Ulysses S. Grant in Riverside Park in New York. ● On April 8, 1868, George Matheson was ordained as pastor of the Clydeside parish of Innellan in Argyllshire, Scotland, where he served for eighteen years before moving to Edinburgh. He was blind and is today best known as the writer of the hymn, "O Love That Will Not Let Me Go." ● On April 8, 1917, Billy Sunday began his New York campaign, which proved to be his greatest crusade ever with nearly 100,000 conversions in ten weeks and over 7,000 on the final day. ● On April 8, 1966, Child Evangelism Fellowship, Inc. was incorporated in Chicago, Illinois.

WORSHIP HELPS

Call to Worship
If then you were raised with Christ, seek those things which are above, where Christ is, sitting at the right hand of God (Col. 3:1).

Hymn Story: In the Garden
C. Austin Miles was a pharmacist who began writing gospel songs, eventually becoming an editor of hymnals and songbooks, and a popular music director at camp meetings, conventions, and churches. His hobby was photography, and he found his darkroom perfect for developing, not just his photographs, but his devotional life. In its privacy and strange blue glow, Miles could read his Bible in total privacy.

One day in March, 1912, while waiting for some film to develop, he opened to his favorite chapter, John 20, the story of the first Easter. Miles later said: "As I read it that day, I seemed to be part of the scene . . . . My hands were resting on the Bible while I stared at the light blue wall. As the light faded, I seemed to be standing at the entrance of a garden, looking down a gently winding path, shaded by olive branches. A woman in white, with head bowed, hand clasping her throat as if to choke back her sobs, walked slowly into the shadows. It was Mary. As she came to the tomb, upon which she placed her hand, she bent over to look in and hurried away. John, in flowing robe, appeared, looking at the tomb; then came Peter, who entered the tomb, followed slowly by John.

"As they departed, Mary reappeared, leaning her head upon her arm at the tomb. She wept. Turning herself, she saw Jesus standing; so did I. I knew it was He. She knelt before Him, with arms outstretched and looking into his face, cried, 'Rabboni!'

"I awakened in full light, gripping my Bible, with muscles tense and nerves vibrating. Under the inspiration of this vision I wrote as quickly as the words would be formed the poem exactly as it has since appeared. That same evening I wrote the music."[1]

---

[1] Adapted from the editor's book, *Then Sings My Soul* (Nashville: Thomas Nelson Publishers, 2003), p. 270.

Additional Sermons and Lesson Ideas

Thoughts from the Tomb
By Dr. Melvin Worthington

Date preached:

SCRIPTURE: Various

INTRODUCTION: While at a garden outside Jerusalem near the empty tomb where Jesus was buried, three truths worked their way into my consciousness and hung there as the guide moved through his speech.

1. The Father's Will. Jesus' birth, life, death, resurrection, and ascension fulfilled the Father's will (Heb. 10:7; Matt. 26:39, 42, 44; John 8:31).
2. The Finished Work. Jesus' final words on the Cross were, "It is finished." Then He bowed His head and died (John 19:30).
3. The Final Word. Following the resurrection Jesus appeared on numerous occasions. His final word includes winning, working, watching, and warning converts.

CONCLUSION: Standing before the open tomb, I realized the most important truth is its emptiness. Jesus is not there now, was there only one weekend, and He is never going back. It is finished. Before the empty tomb, my heart surrendered anew to the last orders of Jesus—Tell the World!

Living Beyond Fear
By Dr. Timothy Beougher

Date preached:

SCRIPTURE: Matthew 28:1–15

INTRODUCTION: The good news of Easter Sunday is that because of the Resurrection of Jesus Christ we can live beyond fear. In the passage we are looking at this morning, Matthew 28:1–15, we find the phrase "do not be afraid" repeated two distinct times.

1. We Can Live Without Fear because:
   A. The Savior Is Alive (vv. 1–10). He rose and He lives today!
   B. Our Sins Can Be Forgiven (v. 5). Jesus was crucified for our sins, to reconcile us to God (1 Cor. 15:3; 2 Cor. 5:21; Gal. 3:13; Is. 53:5).
   C. The Scriptures Can Be Trusted (v. 6). Notice the phrase "just as He said."
2. How to Live Without Fear:
   A. Come and See (vv. 6, 11).
   B. Believe (vv. 8–9; 12–15).
   C. Go and Tell (vv. 7, 10).

CONCLUSION: Because of the Resurrection we can live without fear.

APRIL 15, 2007

SUGGESTED SERMON

Living in Christ, with Christ, through Christ

Date preached:

By Rev. Larry Kirk

Scripture: John 15:1–11, especially verse 4a
Remain in me, and I will remain in you (NIV).

Introduction: Have any of you gone on a family camping trip? This tends to usually be dad's idea, to go out into the woods for a week with no electricity, no running water, and "rough it." After a day or two, we get awfully tired of not being plugged in. We can't function properly without the power source we depend on in daily life. Do you ever feel this way spiritually? Unplugged from the source? In our passage today, Jesus teaches us how to stay plugged in to the source, or as He puts it, how to remain in Him.

1. **To Remain in Christ We Must Draw on His Life (vv. 4–6).** In all of this Christ is telling you that you have to draw your life from Him. The branch doesn't have a source of life in itself. It has to find a source of life. To remain in Christ is to find your life in Him.

   A. **Two Great Invitations: Come to Me and Remain in Me.** To lost people in the world separated from God and trying to find life and a life Jesus says: "Come to Me." To people who come to Christ to find life in Him, Jesus says, "Remain in Me." It's easy to say that Christ is your life, but what are you really depending on? What motivates you? What do you get excited about? Whatever it is, that's where you are trying to find life and strength.

   B. **What You Live From Will Determine What You Live For.** If a man who tucks his Bible under his arm on Sunday says: "I believe in Christ, He's my Source of life," but in his life he neglects his relationship with Christ and gives his best energy and time to the work place—if he neglects his relationship with God and time with God and his wife, family, church, and God-given responsibilities to focus all his real energy and emotion on his work—is Christ really his Source of life?

C. **Jesus Christ Is the Only Truly Sufficient Source of Life.** Jesus Christ Himself gives us life, and all the things we need for fullness of life (2 Pet. 1:3). He gives us perfect love and forgiveness. He is a constant unfailing companion in life. Christ is the only perfect and sufficient Source of life and fullness and fruitfulness in life.

2. **To Remain in Christ We Must Delight in His Words (vv. 7–8).** What does it mean to have the words of Christ remain in you? One of the basic meanings of the Greek word translated "remain" is "to stay in a certain place and be at home there." Christ says: "If you are going to remain in me and draw life from me then my words are going to have to find a home in your heart."

A. **Remaining in His Word.** Christ Himself is speaking to you in and through His Word (see Col. 3:16).

B. **Responding to His Word.** What are the thoughts and ideas that are at home in your mind and heart? Unless our minds and hearts are filled with the thoughts and truths and words of Christ, all kinds of falsehood, foolishness, delusion, and deception will flood in.

3. **To Remain in Christ We Must Depend on His Love (v. 9).** Jesus reveals two things in the incredible measure of the love He has for us.

A. **The Measure of Christ's Love.** "As the Father has loved me, so have I loved you" (v. 9a NIV).

B. **The Means of Christ's Love.** "Now remain in my love" (v. 9b NIV). Don't let anything shake you, seduce you, chase you, or move you out of the love of Christ for you.

4. **To Remain in Christ We Must Do as He Says (vv. 10–11).**

A. **Your Obedience Displays Your Love.** The obedience that comes from love for Christ results in a deeper relationship with Christ (see John 14:21).

B. **Your Obedience Tests Your Faithfulness.** The bad fruit of disobedience does not come from roots that remain in Christ. Our disobedience is, at root, an unwillingness to remain in Christ and to find life in Him.

Conclusion: If you remain in Christ, you will draw on His life, delight in His words, depend on His love and do what He says. You will draw on the depth of His life, delight in the breadth of His words, depend on the heights of His love, and go the lengths of His commands. You will bear much fruit.

STATS, STORIES, AND MORE

Plugged In
Not long ago, after moving my computer, I tried to print a document and nothing happened. I wondered what was wrong and then suddenly a message popped up on my computer screen and said this: "Your printer is not responding, make sure your power cable is plugged in and your printer is connected." The truth is sometimes we feel that way about ourselves don't we? Sometimes there's no sense of being plugged in and properly connected to an adequate source of power for life. Today, we will look at a passage where Jesus tells us how to keep our lives properly connected to the Source of life and power. In John 15 He doesn't talk about computers and cables but He does talk about being connected. He uses an illustration from His own day. He says: "I am the vine; you are the branches" (v. 5a NIV).   —Rev. Larry Kirk

Competing with the Source of Life
There are so many things that compete with Christ and call out to us and say "let me be the vine for you, let me be the source of your life." Consider a teenage girl who discovers that she has the power to turn a boy's head. And it feels good. It's empowering and exciting and she feels alive when boys pay attention. So she draws her life from it and she gives her life to it. It motivates her, it influences the choices she makes, where she wants to go and what she wants to do and how she wants to dress. Too often that girl grows up and lives the same way as an adult. What about a middle-aged father who draws his energy from that younger woman at work who pays attention to him?
     What is it that has seduced you into thinking that it can be the vine of life for you? You don't find life in some identity or persona that you assume: You don't find your source of life in an identity; you don't say I'll find life in being a pastor, a biker, a punk rocker, a good mom, a pilot, everybody's helper or everybody's friend, somebody's hero. There's only one true and fruitful vine.   —Rev. Larry Kirk

APPROPRIATE HYMNS AND SONGS

"Abide with Me," Henry F. Lyte/William H. Monk, Public Domain.

"Be Strong in the Lord," Linda Lee Johnson/Tom Fettke, 1979 Hope
     Publishing Co.

"Draw Nigh to God," Colbert Croft/Joyce Croft, 1981 Dayspring Music Inc.

"I'll Lead You Home," Michael W. Smith/Wayne Kirkpatrick, 1996 Milene
     Music Inc./Deer Valley Music (BMG Music Publishing).

FOR THE BULLETIN

On April 15, 1415, Jerome of Prague, a supporter of the Bohemian reformer John Hus, was seized, put in chains, and imprisoned, for his reformation views. Under great pressure, Jerome temporarily wavered, reading a document on September 11, 1415, accepting the authority of the Pope. Hoping to gain as much publicity as possible, the church placed him on trial at the Cathedral of Constance. Jerome recomposed himself and defended his views with powerful eloquence. He renounced his recantation and proclaimed the innocence of Hus and his own adherence to the teachings of Wycliffe. The enraged authorities stuffed a paper cap on his head, painted with red devils, and led him to the very spot where Hus had been burned. The fire consumed him slowly, and his ashes were tossed into the Rhine. ● April 15, 1452, is the birthday of Leonardo da Vinci, Italian Renaissance artist and the painter of The Last Supper. ● On Good Friday, April 15, 1729, in Leipzig, Johann S. Bach conducted his first and only performance of his "Passion of Our Lord Jesus Christ According to St. Matthew." ● Today is the birthday of Lelia Naylor Morris, wife of an American Methodist and a blind hymnist who wrote such enduring classics as: "What If It Were Today?" "Let Jesus Come into Your Heart," "Sweeter As the Years Go By," and "Nearer, Still Nearer." ● On August 23, 1978, the Dutch Christian, Corrie ten Boom, suffered a serious stroke and lost her ability to speak. She died on April 15, 1983, without speaking again following her stroke. It was her 91st birthday.

Quote for the Pastor's Wall

"Lord, give me a warm heart!"

—GEORGE WHITEFIELD[1]

---

[1]Quoted by Clarence Edward Macartney in *Preaching Without Notes* (New York: Abingdon Press, 1946), p. 18.

WORSHIP HELPS

Call to Worship

Blessed be the LORD God, the God of Israel, who only does wondrous things! And blessed be His glorious name forever! And let the whole earth be filled with His glory. Amen and Amen (Ps. 72:18–19).

Offertory Comments

Someone once said, "By the way some people give, they must think the church is coin-operated." Someone else added, "It's remarkable how big a dollar looks when you take it to church, and how small it looks when you take it to the supermarket." Well, the Bible doesn't specify a dollar amount to our giving; it just tells us to give "as God has prospered us." May the Lord bless our gifts and our givers for His kingdom.

Benediction

I am the vine, you *are* the branches. He who abides in Me, and I in him, bears much fruit; for without Me you can do nothing (John 15:5).

Kid's Talk

Have the children gather around you near an electric outlet. Show them a CD player and tell them, "I've got an idea. Let's all listen to a song and sing together!" Press the play button, turn the switches and volume as if confused. Tell the children, "I'm pressing all the right buttons, I'm turning up the volume, but it's not doing what a CD player is supposed to do! What's wrong?" When the children tell you it's not plugged in, say: "You know that reminds me a lot of us. I was pushing the right buttons, but it wasn't receiving any power from a power source like an outlet. Lots of times, we do the right things like go to church, but we aren't really plugged in. Do you know how you can be plugged in? Not just by doing the right things, but also by having a friendship with Jesus and trusting Him for everything in your life!"

Additional Sermons and Lesson Ideas

The Results of Remaining in Christ

By Rev. Larry Kirk

Date preached:

SCRIPTURE: John 15:1–11

INTRODUCTION: Jesus said, "Abide in Me" and . . .

1. Your Prayers Will Be Empowered (v. 7).
2. Your Life Will Bear Much Fruit (v. 8).
3. Your Father Will Be Glorified (v. 8).
4. You Will Show Yourselves to Be Disciples of Jesus (v. 8).
5. Your Joy Will Be Full (v. 11).

CONCLUSION: We will see fruit in our lives when we stay connected to the Source of life, the Vine: Jesus Christ Himself.

The Christian and Trouble (Part 2)

By Rev. Billie Friel

Date preached:

SCRIPTURE: Various

INTRODUCTION: Sometimes troubles we face could have been prevented. As Christians, we often bring trouble upon ourselves due to our sin or our neglect of spiritual disciplines. Let's look at how to prevent trouble and how to deal with it when it comes.

1. The Prevention of Trouble.
   A. Knowing God's Word (Ps. 119:105; Hos. 4:6; Matt. 22:29).
   B. Fellowship with Believers (Prov. 11:14; 24:6).
   C. Honesty with God in Finances (Mal. 3:11).
   D. Keeping Short Accounts: Daily Confession (1 John 1:7, 9)
2. The Procedure When Trouble Comes.
   A. Spend Time with God, Casting Your Cares on Him (1 Pet. 5:7).
   B. Trust God's Promises (John 14:1; Rom. 8:28).
   C. Count Your Blessings (1 Thess. 5: 18).

CONCLUSION: Revive me, O Lord, for Your name's sake! For Your righteousness' sake bring my soul out of trouble (Ps. 143:11).

MISSIONS SERMON

The Missions Mandate

Date preached:

By Dr. Melvin Worthington

Scripture: Matthew 28:16–20, especially vv. 18–20

And Jesus came and spoke to them, saying, "All authority has been given to Me in heaven and on earth. Go therefore and make disciples of all the nations, baptizing them in the name of the Father and of the Son and of the Holy Spirit, teaching them to observe all things that I have commanded you; and lo, I am with you always, even to the end of the age." Amen.

Introduction: Missionary zeal is lagging in many churches. One might expect minimal missionary interest among groups who do not believe the Bible, but if those who call themselves Evangelicals downplay Christ's commission, we face a serious problem. Efforts to stimulate interest in missions have not been successful in the larger context of the church. Some churches have restated their mission statement in light of the felt needs of contemporary society. The mission statement of Christ's church is not often repealed or restated. Christ is building His church and the gates of hell will not prevail against it. Rather than restate Christ's mission statement for His church we need to respond obediently to it. The missionary enterprise is not elective but essential, not optional but an obligation.

1. **Christ's Assertion (v. 18).** Jesus left no doubt what He had in mind when He announced, "All power is given unto Me in heaven and in earth." Power means authority. The *Scope of Christ's Authority* encompasses all that is in heaven and in earth. His power is complete and His claim is universal. The *Source of Christ's Authority* is in the counsels of the eternal Trinity where Jesus, as Son of man, is appointed heir of all things—that He is the mediator between God and men, that the salvation of all who are saved is laid upon Him, and that He is the great fountain of mercy, grace, life, and peace. The *Sufficiency of Christ's Authority* to redeem His people, gather His church, and defend His chosen is the encouragement needed by those engaged in the missionary enterprise. We must remember that the missionary enterprise set forth in the Bible rests upon the authority of the One who gives the command—Jesus Christ. Vested with the authority of Jesus Christ the church can boldly embark on His command to go into the entire world and preach and teach the gospel to all nations.

2. **Christ's Assignment (vv. 19–20a).** Christ set forth the task in terms which could not be misunderstood. The church's mandate and mission has not changed. Christ's assignment commences with *Evangelism.* All men must hear the gospel. Bishop J. C. Ryle was correct when he thundered, "It may be well questioned whether a man knows the value of the gospel himself, if he does not desire to make it known to the entire world." Caution should be exercised lest we get distracted from our assigned responsibility—to evangelize the world. Our main business must be proclaiming the gospel, telling the world that there is a balm in Gilead. Few men have understood this truth more clearly than Joseph Parker, "Christianity starts with men upon no little errands. Christianity has no merely short journeys for its propagandists to undertake. Every journey is a long one. There is no stopping in place for Christian evangelists until the knowledge of the Lord spreads itself over the globe." Christ's assignment continues with *Education.* Those who have been evangelized must be instructed and taught to observe all the commandments of Christ. The Christian instructor has still fallen short of his task unless those he instructs learn what Christ's commandments are and learn to observe them. Christ's assignment concludes in *Edification.* Those who have been evangelized and educated must grow in the grace and knowledge of Christ.

3. **Christ's Assurance (v. 20b).** The missions mandate not only includes the power and the program, but also the presence of Christ. Having announced His power and assigned His personnel, Christ then assures them of His presence. He tenderly reminds them, "Lo I am with you always." There is no vagueness; it is a solid fact. By His spirit, His providence, His counsel and guidance, He would accompany them as they fulfilled the commission He assigned. He would strengthen, direct, and assist them in the work. Christ's assurance includes *The Promise—"I am with you."* This denotes certainty and is the speech of the One who is highly exalted. It covers all the dimensions of time from was, to is, to will be. *Christ's assurance includes His Presence—"I am with you."* More comforting words could not be given than, "I am with you." Though left alone like orphan children in a cold, unkind world, the disciples must not feel deserted, for their Master was with them. We must ever be mindful that Christ is with us.

Conclusion: We are unfaithful ambassadors if we fail to respond to Christ's mandate while allowing those around the world to perish. What will you do about the mission's mandate?

APRIL 22, 2007

SUGGESTED SERMON

The Power of the Cross

Date preached:

By Rev. Peter Grainger

Scripture: 1 Corinthians 1:18—2:5, especially 1:23–24
We preach Christ crucified, to the Jews a stumbling block and to the Greeks foolishness, but to those who are called, both Jews and Greeks, Christ the power of God and the wisdom of God.

Introduction: Don Carson, one of the foremost New Testament scholars in the world, once spoke on this passage at the Free Church College on the Mound in Edinburgh, Scotland. He gave a masterful exposition lasting an hour and described it as "a light exegesis of the text." How you would describe what I hope to do in half of that time, I do not know, but let me try and at least touch on the main themes that we find here.

1. **Two Ways to Live (vv. 18–25):**

   A. **The Way of the World (vv. 18–23).** The word "world" in these verses—as in "the wisdom of the world" (v. 20)—does not mean the created world or universe in which we live. Rather, it means the world or society of human beings and their thinking, characterized by two rebellious ideas: the search for (human) wisdom and the demand for power. Paul mentions two groups who devote themselves to the pursuit of one of these goals.

      (1) **The Greeks: the Search for Wisdom.** The Greeks were characterized by an insatiable thirst for knowledge. They worshiped a whole pantheon of gods who were described in all-too human terms because they were the product of human minds. We have these types in our society too. In pursuing wisdom, they have totally excluded God or any possibility that He may exist.

      (2) **The Jews: the Demand for Power.** In contrast to the Greeks, Paul says that "Jews demand miraculous signs" (v. 22 NIV). In this respect, the Jews were closer to the truth than the

Greeks, for the one true God had revealed Himself to His chosen people in history. They were ruled by the most powerful empire in existence: Rome. They weren't seeking or asking God to step in, but demanding miracles as if they deserved them by their own merit.

B. **The Way of God (vv. 23–25).** What kind of demonstration do you think the God who created the universe might put on to convince those who are demanding proof of His power? No human being would ever come up with the answer which God did. God chose to demonstrate His power and wisdom in and through a person "Christ the power of God and the wisdom of God" (v. 24 NIV). What was totally unexpected was not the birth of Jesus but the death of Jesus: nailed to a cross as a common criminal by the Roman authorities. To the Christian, the death of Jesus was not some unfortunate end to a promising career, but the very heart of the message that they preached. The Christian message is unequivocal: God displays His power and wisdom to their fullest extent in Christ, His Son, dying on a cross.

2. **Two Ways to Tell if a Church Is Cross-Centered or Off-Centered (1:26—2:5).**

   A. **The Composition of the Congregation (1:26–31).** Paul suggests they take a look at the social profile of the Christian congregation in Corinth. He says not many are wise, influential, or of noble birth. He teaches that this is part of God's plan so that no one can boast about themselves and how they earned their standing before God. Those who come to the Cross of Christ, empty-handed, find they receive from Him all they need: "righteousness" (a right standing before God), "holiness" (being set apart for God's service) and "redemption" (set free from the power of sin to live for Him; v. 30).

   B. **The Communication of the Message (2:1–5).** Paul reminds them that he did not preach to them from eloquence or superior wisdom: instead he simply proclaimed the message about Christ and His Cross. Paul was trembling with fear and a sense of his own weakness and was relying on the Holy Spirit's power. At the heart of all he preached was the Cross of Christ, which is the heart of the gospel. Sadly the same problem exists today where churches and Christian organizations are known for their leaders rather than Christ and Christ crucified.

Conclusion: Finally, we end where Paul does, by reminding ourselves that this has a crucial personal implication. If your faith is in a preacher and his gifts rather than Christ crucified, then it is based on very shaky foundations, for no preacher can save you and all preachers will ultimately disappoint you. So, on who or what is your faith relying? There is only one secure foundation: Christ and the power of His Cross.

STATS, STORIES, AND MORE

Contempt for the Cross
A piece of graffiti from around A.D. 225 was discovered on the Palatine Hill in Rome, on the wall of a house which was probably used as a training school for imperial pages. You can now see it in the Kircherian Museum in Rome. It's a crude drawing of a crucifixion with a human figure on a cross. What is unusual is that the human figure has the head of donkey. The caption scrawled beneath it says, ALEXAMENOS CEBETE THEON: "Alexamenos worships God." What the cartoon illustrates is the utter contempt and ridicule with which the Christian faith was viewed in the Roman Empire.

As for the Greeks, Herodotus, the Greek historian of the fourth century B.C., says of his people: "All Greeks were zealous for every kind of learning." They were absorbed in speculative philosophy. The names of their great thinkers are still known to us today and their writings still studied by today's intellectuals. From their ivory towers of learning they looked down and despised all others who failed to appreciate their wisdom, designating them by the term "barbarians." This included the Christians who thought Christ to be the wisdom of God.

Someone Once Said
- *All of my life, I have been looking for a pot of gold at the foot of a rainbow, and I found it at the foot of the cross.* —Dale Evans
- *Only one act of pure love, unsullied by any taint of ulterior motive, has ever been performed in the history of the world, namely the self-giving of God in Christ on the cross for undeserving sinners.* —John Stott
- *Christianity is a cross, and a cross is "I" crossed out.* —John Bisagno

APPROPRIATE HYMNS AND SONGS

"The Wonderful Cross," Isaac Watts/Chris Tomlin/Jesse Reeves/J. D. Walt, 2000 WorshipTogether.com Songs/Six Steps Music (EMI Christian Music Publishing).

"Calvary Covers It All," Mrs. Walter G. Taylor, 1934 Mrs. Walter G. Taylor (Renewed 1962 Word Music, Inc.).

"In the Cross of Christ I Glory," John Bowring/Ithamar Conkey, Public Domain.

"Near the Cross," Fanny Crosby/William H. Donne, Public Domain.

"It Was My Sin," Dennis Jernigan, 1992 Shepherds Heart Music, Inc. (Word Music Group).

FOR THE BULLETIN

The Council of Constance dissolved on April 22, 1418, having successfully ended the Great Schism within the Roman Catholic Church by deposing three rival popes. This council also condemned and executed the two Bohemian reformers, John Hus and Jerome of Prague. ● On April 22, 1530, reformer Martin Luther wrote a famously tender letter to his young son, Hans, which began: "To my dear son, Hans Luther: Grace and peace in Christ, my darling little son. I am very glad to hear that you are studying well and praying diligently. Go on doing so, my little son, and when I come home I will bring you a beautiful present." ● On April 22, 1538, the Council of Two Hundred met in Geneva, fired John Calvin and ordered him to leave town within three days. "Very well," said Calvin, "it is better to serve God than man." He fled to Strassburg, married his beloved Idelette, and pastored a group of French evangelicals until the tide again shifted in Geneva. By 1541, the time was ripe for Calvin and the Reformation to return, this time for good. ● The motto "In God We Trust" first appeared on U.S. coins on April 22, 1864. ● Today marks the birthday, in 1913, of Jack Wyrtzen, who became a popular band leader in the United States. Following his conversion he entered evangelism and became the founder of "Word of Life" ministries. ● Today marks the death, in 1987, of Dr. J. Edwin Orr, noted church historian who wrote extensively on the subject of revivals.

WORSHIP HELPS

Call to Worship

You are great, O Lord GOD. For there is none like You, nor is there any God besides You, according to all that we have heard with our ears (2 Sam. 7:22).

Word of Welcome

Today, our message reflects on the Cross of Jesus Christ. The Scripture for today's message teaches us that Christ called us not because we are wise, influential, or noble (1 Cor. 1:26–31). It also warns us that people often fall prey to the humanistic standards of their own race (1 Cor. 1:18–25). The truth is, despite our influence, nobility, wisdom, or race, all of us would be dead in our sins if not for Christ. Christ's work on the Cross has earned us the privilege of coming together in unity. You are welcome here regardless of your background, your paycheck, or the color of your skin. There's a great old hymn that says it well:

> *In Christ there is no East or West,*
> *In Him no South or North;*
> *But one great fellowship of love*
> *Throughout the whole wide earth.*

Offertory Scripture Reading

Honor the LORD with your possessions, and with the firstfruits of all your increase. "Bring all the tithes into the storehouse, that there may be food in My house, and try Me now in this," says the LORD of hosts. Give, and it will be given to you: good measure, pressed down, shaken together, and running over. So let each one give as he purposes in his heart, not grudgingly or of necessity; for God loves a cheerful giver (Prov. 3:9; Mal. 3:10; Luke 6:38; 2 Cor. 9:7).

Benediction

Grace and peace to you from God our Father and from the Lord Jesus Christ (Rom. 1:7 NIV).

Additional Sermons and Lesson Ideas

Come—Learn—Take

Date preached:

Based on a Sermon by Dr. W. Graham Scroggie

SCRIPTURE: Matthew 11:28–30

INTRODUCTION: Let's look at a simple but crucial lesson Jesus would have His followers learn:

1. The Rest of a New Life; *Come* (v. 28). The Lord calls those who labor and are heavy laden to His rest. The labor problem goes back to the Garden of Eden, when man was cursed with labor. He always had and always will have to work, but the curse included labor and toil. We can find rest from our labor in Christ.
2. The Rest of a True Life; *Learn* (v. 29). Jesus tells us to learn from Him. He is both the Teacher and the Lesson! His lessons: He is gentle and He is lowly in heart. The rest of a true life comes in our being meek and lowly.
3. The Rest of a Full Life; *Take* (vv. 29–30). The yoke of the Lord is the symbol of service. Some may say, "Serving the Lord isn't easy or light." But we must learn that our responsibility is obedience; the work belongs to the Lord. We can rest in that.

CONCLUSION: Are you living in reliance upon Jesus? Are you resting in His sufficiency?

Allegiant Abel

Date preached:

By Dr. Melvin Worthington

SCRIPTURE: Genesis 4:1–8; Hebrews 11:4

INTRODUCTION: Abel serves as a model for us to imitate. He believed God and approached Him in the right manner and with the right motive. We note the following truths regarding Abel:

1. The Family of Abel (Gen. 4:1–2). We learn of *his brother, his birth,* and *his business.*
2. The Faith of Abel (Gen. 4:4; Heb. 11:4). Abel's faith is demonstrated by *his offering, his obedience,* and *his obeisance.* He worshiped God's way.
3. The Favor of Abel (Gen. 4:4; Heb. 11:4). God's favor was extended to Abel as He respected and received his offering.
4. The Fate of Abel (Gen. 4:5–8; Heb. 11:4). In these passages we read of *Abel's menace, Abel's murder, Abel's martyrdom,* and *Abel's memorial.*

CONCLUSION: Abel is a perpetual reminder that God requires that we approach, address and give adoration to Him in the required way.

APRIL 29, 2007

SUGGESTED SERMON

Stones of Adversity

Date preached:

By Dr. Woodrow Kroll

Scripture: Deuteronomy 4:27–31, especially verse 30
When you are in distress . . .

Introduction: Difficulty and adversity come to all of us, in small ways that nag at us like a pebble in our shoes and in large ways that overwhelm us like a rockslide. None of us is exempt just because we're Christians. You can be going along and things seem fine, then you go to the doctor and get a report you didn't want to hear. Or a phone call you didn't want to receive. Moses knew all about adversity, and that's why I find Deuteronomy 4:27–31 so comforting. If you think about the life of Moses and the Children of Israel, their lives parallel our lives in many respects; and we can learn from their examples. Today there are three principles I'd like you to know.

1. **Whatever You're Going Through, It's Not Necessarily Because of Sin in Your Life.** Sometimes adversity *is* associated with sin. David numbered the people, a display of pride on his behalf that resulted in significant trouble for him. Jonah ran from God, and his disobedience brought adversity. Does that automatically mean that when I have trouble I've sinned? No. Remember Job? He's a classic example of someone who faced adversity though there was no glaring sin in his life. Jesus observed that God sends the rain on the just and the unjust. You're not exempt because you're a Christian. When Paul wanted to encourage the believers of Asia Minor, he said: "We must go through many tribulations to enter the kingdom of God." Adversity comes to all and we should all expect it. If you're a Christian, don't expect God to keep you from tribulation.

2. **Whatever You're Going Through, God Has a Plan to Use It for Good.** God allows adversity in our lives because He wants to strengthen our character. Beethoven did most of his best work after

he was completely deaf. Pascal learned his greatest lessons about life while bedridden with disease. There are things in your life that God allows to come because He knows the end from the beginning, and He knows what's good for you. In fact, He knows what's best for you. So if God allows adversity in your life, He does so because He knows it will lead to good. See Romans 8:28.

3. **Whatever You're Going Through, God Will Not Let You Face It Alone.** Jesus promised, "I will never leave you nor forsake you" (Heb. 13:5). God promises to always be with us in our adversity. See Psalm 94:12–14. He is very interested in you and will never let you go through adversity by yourself. As we learn the lessons of adversity we understand that it's necessary in our lives. We really can't have maturity in our Christian lives without some adversity. Some of us, even those who may be more mature in the Christian faith, sometimes nearly crack under adversity; but we must always remember that God has not abandoned us amid our problems. The great writer, W. T. Purkiser, said, "God does not offer us a way out of testings in life. He offers us a way through them, and that makes all the difference." Adversity teaches us many things about God and about what He wants to accomplish in our lives. For example, it teaches us something about the faithfulness of God. Erwin Lutzer remarked that God often puts us in situations that are too much for us so that we can learn that no situation is too much for Him. What I learn from adversity is that God is always going to be there, and He is always faithful to me. I am not sufficient in myself to overcome the adversities of my life, but through God's strength I am strong. "I can do all things through Christ who strengthens me" (Phil. 4:13).

Conclusion: Hey, listen. Sometimes I don't want adversity to come to my life. But as I mature in my faith, I understand that God allows adversity to come to my life, and it is not always because I have sinned. We're all going to face adversity. God allows it because He has a plan for us that is better than our plans for ourselves, and Jesus Christ has promised to be with us always, even in the valley of the shadow. In this world we will have tribulation, but we can be of good cheer for He has overcome the world.

STATS, STORIES, AND MORE

More from Dr. Kroll

When my mother was a little girl she once had a stone in her shoe. As she took it out, her father who was a very wise man, said, "Now, doesn't that feel good—once you got that stone out? If the stone had never been there, you would never know how good it felt afterward." If there were no adversity in your life, you may not be able to enjoy life.

Sometimes God uses adversity as an opportunity to help you in your own life. A boy was ten years old when he ran away from home. His family had a soap manufacturing business, but he didn't like being in the business; so at age ten he decided to run away from home and go to Chicago. The only thing he knew was soap, so he started to sell soap in order to keep body and soul together. He decided to make some incentive for people to buy his soap. Every bar of soap they bought, he gave them two free sticks of gum. He soon found out people loved the gum more than the soap, and soon he went into the gum business. His name was William Wrigley. It was the adversity of having to run away from home and trying to get away from his family that led him to the thing God obviously called him to—Wrigley's gum. Sometimes God will use adversity simply to bring you to the point where He can bless you.

APPROPRIATE HYMNS AND SONGS

"Have Faith in God," B. B. Mckinney, 1934 Renewed 1962 Broadman Press (ARR Genevox Music Group).

"Love Lifted Me," James Rowe/Howard Smith, Public Domain.

"Embrace This Place," Jason Harrison/Darin Sasser, 1998 Shadow Rock Publishing Group (Shadow Spring Music, Inc.).

"God Leads Us Along," G. A. Young, Public Domain.

FOR THE BULLETIN

Italian mystic Catherine of Siena died on this day, April 29, 1380, exhausted by her efforts to unite rival factions of the church. John of Arc, another woman whose mystical visions captured the fascination of large masses of people, entered the besieged city of Orleans to claim a French victory over the English. ● The first Anglican church in the American colonies was established at Cape Henry, Virginia, on this day in 1607. ● Today, April 29, 1751, is the birthday of the English hymnist, John Rippon, who pastored London's Carter Lane Baptist Church for over sixty years, but is best known for his famous hymnal, *A Selection of Hymns from the Best Authors, Intended to Be an Appendix to Dr. Watts' Psalms and Hymns,* which was reprinted 27 times. Today is also the birthday, in 1795, of missionary Lorrin Andrews who became a highly visible Bible translator in the Hawaiian Islands. He went on to publish Hawaii's first newspaper and become the first associate justice of the Hawaiian Supreme Court. ● Joseph H. Gilmore, American Baptist clergyman and the author of the hymn, "He Leadeth Me, O Blessed Thought," was born on April 29, 1834. ● On April 29, 1848, Thomas Jackson, the famous Civil War general, was baptized at Saint John Episcopal Church in New York City. ● The great Chinese Christian leader and martyr, Watchman Nee, was converted to Christ on April 29, 1920. ● Today heralds the birth of the Navigators. Founder Dawson Trotman began the work in San Pedro, California, on April 29, 1933.

Quote for the Pastor's Wall

The purpose of those who share the "oracles of God" is not primarily to help people with their problems; it is to speak for God who is ultimately the only help.

—DAVID L. LARSON in *The Company of Preachers; A History of Biblical Preaching from the Old Testament to the Modern Era*

WORSHIP HELPS

Call to Worship

I will be glad and rejoice in Your mercy, for You have considered my trouble; You have known my soul in adversities, and have not shut me up into the hand of the enemy; You have set my feet in a wide place . . . Blessed be the LORD (Ps. 31:7–8; 21).

Testimony

One of the missing elements in our worship is the power of testimony. Many hymns are actually testimonies, such as John Newton's "Amazing Grace." Much of Christian autobiography is testimonial in nature. In a smaller church, you might ask if anyone present has a word to say for the Lord. In a larger church, it might be better to plan in advance or videotape a testimony. If it's too late to plan for this week's service, skip ahead a few weeks and plan in advance.

Scripture Reading—James 1:2–5 PHILLIPS

When all kinds of trials and temptations crowd into your lives, my brothers, don't resent them as intruders, but welcome them as friends! Realize that they come to test your faith and to produce in you the quality of endurance. But let the process go on until that endurance is fully developed, and you will find you have become men of mature character with the right sort of independence. And if, in the process, any of you does not know how to meet any particular problem he has only to ask God . . . and he may be quite sure that the necessary wisdom will be given him."

Additional Sermons and Lesson Ideas

It's Well with My Soul
Date preached:

SCRIPTURE: Romans 8:18–39

INTRODUCTION: An old hymn says, "When peace like a river attendeth my way; when sorrows like sea billows roll . . ." Those words acknowledge an obvious truth. Life is a mixed bag, a hodgepodge of good and bad, of joy and sadness, or tragedies and treasures. Romans 8 is just what we need amid the uncertainties of life.

1. We Need Perspective (v. 18). Suppose you were given a free month's vacation at a fabulous resort, but you encountered a short stretch of bumpy road getting there. Would you say, "I'm sorry we ever started out!"? No, you'd say this bit of aggravation isn't worth comparing with the joys of our month-long vacation.
2. We Need Patience (vv. 19–24). We're in the "groaning" period of earth's time span, but better days are coming. Eternity is ahead. We must wait for it patiently.
3. We Need Providence (vv. 25–30). As the Holy Spirit prays for us, the heavenly Father sees to it that all things work together for our good.
4. We Need Praise (vv. 31–39). This chapter ends with a doxology of worship, and that attitude infuses us with triumphant joy. Nothing can separate us from God's love.

CONCLUSION: So when peace like a river attends our way, when sorrows like sea billows roll, take time to read Romans 8 and say, "It is well, it is well with my soul."

Faith: The Spiritual Tool We Can't Live Without
Date preached:
By Dr. Larry Osborne

SCRIPTURE: Various

INTRODUCTION: While it's the most basic of spiritual tools, faith is probably also the one most misunderstood by both non-Christians and Christians alike.

1. What It Is. Faith is trusting God enough to do what He says (Heb. 11:1–40; James 2:14–24; 1 John 2:3–5). Here are some common misconceptions and Scriptures that disprove them:
   A. Faith Has No Room for Doubt (Acts 12:1–19; Dan. 3:16–30).
   B. Faith Has No Room for Fear (1 Cor. 2:1–3; 1 Pet. 3:4).
   C. Faith Has Power in Itself (1 Kin. 18:21–40).
   D. Faith Defies Logic (John 14:11; 20:31).
2. How Important It Is. Without faith it's not possible to please God (Heb. 10:28–30; 11:6; Prov. 3:5–8; Rom. 1:17; 2 Cor. 5:7; Gal. 2:20). We must believe that He exists and that He rewards (Heb. 11:6).
3. How We Can Get the Faith We Need. Remember the mustard seed principle: it's not about having *more* faith (Luke 17:3–6; Mark 9:24; John 3:16), it's about who your faith is in.

CONCLUSION: Who is your faith resting in?

CLASSICS FOR THE PASTOR'S LIBRARY

Foxe's *Book of Martyrs*

John Foxe, born in Lincolnshire, England, in 1516, was a brilliant young man who entered Oxford when only 16. News of Luther's Reformation was infiltrating university life in England, and young Foxe, intrigued, began pouring over the Scripture, trying to determine their true teaching. At length, he turned from Roman Catholicism to Protestantism, accepting the doctrine by justification by grace through faith alone.

His was a sensitive spirit, and often at night he would take long walks, weeping, and pouring out his soul to the Lord in prayer. As a result of his Protestant "fanaticism" he was expelled from Oxford and, through the help of friends, became a private tutor in Stratford-on-Avon. Here he fell in love with Agnes Randall, and the two were married.

Their Protestant views caused them much trouble, for the pope's inquisitors were never far away. Through the help of family and friends, however, he remained secure and at liberty through-out the reigns of King Henry VIII and his son Edward VI, and into the reign of Queen Mary I.

But Mary was fiercely Catholic, and she waged a terrible crusade against the Protestants, forcing the Foxes (along with many others) to flee to the Continent. They traveled through Strasbourg, France, Germany, and on to Switzerland where they took up temporary residence.

It was while in Switzerland that John Foxe heard horrible news filtering in from England. Great Christian leaders such as Hugh Latimer, Nicholas Ridley, and Thomas Cramner, were being cap-tured, tortured, and burned alive. It was a killing time, and scores of believers were perishing amid great pain and persecution.

It came sharply into Foxe's mind that someone should tell their stories. And he decided to do it himself, to compile a record of the persecution of God's people and give personal accounts of those who had suffered and died for Christ, especially during the inquisitions of Queen Mary.

Despite living on the edge of poverty, Foxe spent every spare moment on his project. He labored by day in Oporinus of Basel's printing shop to support his family, but by night he poured over his manuscript. He researched thoroughly, interviewed, and collected reports. His writing style was vivid, giving details, painting word pictures.

Finally the first version was ready, and in 1559, Foxe published his book on the Continent—732 pages in Latin. Returning to England under Protestant Elizabeth, he resumed pastoral work and translated his book into English. John Day published it in London in 1563 under the title *Acts and Monuments of These Latter and Perilous Days Touching Matters of the Church.*

But Foxe wasn't finished. He spent another four years traveling across England, interviewing witnesses, tracking down documents, finding letters. After long days of church ministry, he sat by flickering candlelight, continuing his writing. In 1570, a second edition appeared—two large volumes totaling 2,315 pages—then a third and a fourth.

Foxe's *Book of Martyrs* was one of the most important events in Elizabeth's reign, having an extraordinary impact on Britain. Copies appeared in every cathedral alongside the Bible. Vicars read from it during Sunday services. Francis Drake read it aloud on the western seas. It inspired the Puritans. It took the world by storm. Still today, 400 years later, it is among Christianity's most treasured books.

Foxe's *Book of Martyrs* also took a toll on the author's personal health, and he never recovered. He died from weariness on April 18, 1587. But he had given us his life's crowning achievement.[1]

---

[1]Excerpted from the editor's book, *Real Stories for the Soul* (Nashville: Thomas Nelson Publishers, 2000), pp. 71–74.

MAY 6, 2007

Dealing with Deception

Date preached:

By Dr. Melvin Worthington

Scripture: Various, especially 1 John 2:21
I have not written to you because you do not know the truth, but because you know it, and that no lie is of the truth.

Introduction: When you are tempted to sin, do you feel like you're being led into a trap? Do you feel it's not always coincidence that certain factors work together to tempt you, as if there's an underlying force working against you? The objective of Satan in the world is to deceive and ultimately destroy us. The entire book of Revelation unveils the efforts of Satan to deceive the masses. Let's learn from the Scriptures about deception and how to deal with it.

1. **The Source of Deception.**

    A. **The Devil.** Satan is the author of all deception. In Genesis 3, he used the serpent to deceive Eve. John reminds us that the last days will be characterized by deception (1 John 2:18–19). Paul confirms the source of deceit when he says, "And you He made alive, who were dead in trespasses and sins, in which you once walked according to the course of this world, according to the prince of the power of the air, the spirit who now works in the sons of disobedience" (Eph. 2:2). Satan as the author of deception seeks to seduce, snare, and subdue every human being.

    B. **The Devil's Disciples and Demons.** John describes deceivers who go into the world not acknowledging Jesus Christ as having come in the flesh. He calls these people antichrists, disciples of the devil (2 John 1:7). Paul's letter to Timothy describes the deception of demons clearly, "Now the Spirit expressly says that in latter times some will depart from the faith, giving heed to deceiving spirits and doctrines of demons" (1 Tim. 4:1).

    C. **The Depravity of the Human Heart.** The devil uses the world and the flesh to carry out his seductive activity (1 John 2:15–17).

2. **The Scope of Deception.** Deception affects the entire human race (2 Thess. 2:7–12). It reaches out in specific ways:

A. **Deceitful Use of the Tongue (James 3:1–12).** We can deceive with our talk, our teaching, and our testimony.

B. **Deceitful Use of the Truth (2 Cor. 4:2; 1 Thess. 2).** The truth is used deceitfully when it is distorted, diluted, diminished, and denied.

C. **Deceitful Use of Our Treasures (Acts 5:1–11; Matt. 6:1–8).** We practice deception when we pretend to give more than we really give and when we pretend to care more than we really care. In other words when we are hypocritical regarding the use and giving of our resources.

3. **The Sinfulness of Deception.** Deception and hypocrisy are destructive sins. Jesus addresses these issues in Matthew 23 when He pronounced eight *woes* on the scribes and Pharisees, starting with this one: "But woe to you, scribes and Pharisees, hypocrites! For you shut up the kingdom of heaven against men; for you neither go in yourselves, nor do you allow those who are entering to go in" (Matt. 23:13). Jesus denounced hypocrisy with severe and strong language. Hypocrisy and deceit are unacceptable with God. God will bring swift, sure, and severe judgment on deceivers and hypocrites.

4. **The Specifics of Deception.** Matthew 6:1–21 provides some specific areas where deception and hypocrisy may be found. In each of the following areas, Jesus preaches against hypocritical and deceitful treatment of seemingly spiritual actions.

A. **Almsgiving: Tithing (Matt. 6:1–4).**

B. **Asking: Prayer (Matt. 6:5–15).**

C. **Abstinence: Fasting (Matt. 6:16–18).**

D. **Accumulation: Stewardship (Matt. 6:19–21).**

E. **Allegiance: Faithfulness (Matt. 6:22–24).**

F. **Anxiety: Trust (Matt. 6:24–34).**

Conclusion: The devil uses the depravity of the human heart as a seed bed for deception. When he accomplishes his purpose, he produces hypocrites: people who pretend to be what they are not, those who put on a "spiritual show." Being deceitful and deceptive is wrong wicked sin. We should examine our hearts to root out areas of deception in our own lives.

STATS, STORIES, AND MORE

Raccoons for Pets?

Gary Richmond, a former zoo keeper, explains that raccoons go through a glandular change at about 24 months. After that, they often attack their owners.

Richmond had a friend named Julie who owned a pet raccoon. Since a 30-pound raccoon can equal a 100-pound dog in a fight, he felt compelled to warn her of the coming change.

"It'll be different for me," she replied with a smile. "Bandit wouldn't hurt me. He just wouldn't."

Three months later Julie underwent plastic surgery for facial lacerations sustained when her adult raccoon attacked her for no apparent reason. Bandit was released into the wild.

Sin, too, often comes dressed in an adorable guise, and as we play with it, it's easy to say, "It will be different for me." The results are predictable.[1]

Deception Cream

There's a popular cosmetic product named "Deception Cream," designed to make "wrinkles almost invisible to the naked eye." The advertisements say, "It's cheating, but it works!" Ads go on to say, "There is now a new cosmetic cream which uses something very much like a 'magician's trick' to de-age the appearance of your skin. It's called Deception." The makers claim that rubbing it into your skin will make anyone look up to twenty years younger, and this product is purported to be used by many Hollywood stars and supermodels. Well, it's one thing to have deception on your face; it's another thing to have it in your heart. The devil has his own deception cream and he makes heavy use of it.

APPROPRIATE HYMNS AND SONGS

"We Stand Together," Chris Christensen, 1987 Integrity's Hosanna! Music (Admin. Integrity Music).

"Clean Hands Pure Heart," John Slick, Mark Gersmehl, 1986 Paragon Music Corp. (Admin. Brentwood-Benson Music Publishing).

"I Will Serve Thee," William J. Gaither/Gloria Gaither, 1969 William J. Gaither, Inc. (ARR UBP of Gaither Copyright Management).

"Change My Heart Oh God," Eddie Espinosa, 1982 Mercy/Vineyard Publishing.

---

[1] Adapted from Bob Campbell, "Sin's Delusion," in *Leadership Journal,* Spring, 1988, p. 47.

FOR THE BULLETIN

On May 6, 1536, King Henry VIII ordered that a Bible be placed in every English church. On this same day, May 6, in 1816, the American Bible Society was formed and Elias Boudinot was elected its first president. The Society soon made its first grant of 300 Bibles to the Steuben County Bible Society of Bath, New York, and distributed Bibles to the crew of the USS *John Adams*. ● Today marks the birthday, in 1835, of John T. Grape, an American Methodist layman who composed the tune for the hymn, "Jesus Paid It All." It's also the birthday of the noted missionary and author, Rosalind Goforth. She and her husband, Jonathan, served in China with great evangelistic power. ● Southern Baptist giant, George Truett, was born on May 6, 1867, in Clay County, North Carolina. He pastored the First Baptist Church in Dallas, Texas, for forty-seven years, until his death in 1944. During his ministry, the church's membership swelled from seven hundred to over seventy-eight hundred. ● On May 6, 1892, E. M. Bounds left Nashville for denominational meetings in Memphis, which left him so disillusioned and troubled that he resigned his position, moved to Alabama, and eventually wrote and published his first book about prayer. ● On May 6, 1955, the first student enrolled in L'Abri Fellowship, a ministry which began in Switzerland when Francis and Edith Schaeffer decided to open their home for students seeking answers to their lives.

" *Quote for the Pastor's Wall*

I did it the same way I learned to skate—
by doggedly making a fool of myself
until I got used to it.

—GEORGE BERNARD SHAW (when asked how he learned to speak so compellingly in public)[2]

"

---

[2]Quoted by Dale Carnegie in *The Quick and Easy Way to Effective Speaking* (New York: Association Press, 1962), p. 21.

WORSHIP HELPS

Call to Worship
I will bless the LORD who has given me counsel . . . (Ps. 16:7).

Responsive Reading

Worship Leader: Savage wolves will come in among you, not sparing the flock. Also from among yourselves men will rise up, speaking perverse things, to draw away the disciples after themselves (Acts 20:29–30).

Audience: My sheep hear My voice, and I know them, and they follow Me. And I give them eternal life, and they shall never perish; neither shall anyone snatch them out of My hand. My Father, who has given them to Me, is greater than all; and no one is able to snatch them out of My Father's hand (John 10:27–29).

Worship Leader: Now the Spirit expressly says that in latter times some will depart from the faith, giving heed to deceiving spirits and doctrines of demons (1 Tim. 4:1).

Audience: I am convinced that neither death nor life, neither angels nor demons, neither the present nor the future, nor any powers, neither height nor depth, nor anything else in all creation, will be able to separate us from the love of God that is in Christ Jesus our Lord (Rom. 8:38–39 NIV).

Worship Leader: Many deceivers, who do not acknowledge Jesus Christ as coming in the flesh, have gone out into the world. Any such person is the deceiver and the antichrist. Watch out that you do not lose what you have worked for, but that you may be rewarded fully (2 John 1:7–8 NIV).

Audience: If God is for us, who can be against us (Rom. 8:31)?

Benediction
To those who by persistence in doing good seek glory, honor and immortality, he will give eternal life. But for those who are self-seeking and who reject the truth and follow evil, there will be wrath and anger (Rom. 2:7–8 NIV).

Additional Sermons and Lesson Ideas

Right Wrongs in the Right Way
By Dr. Timothy K. Beougher

Date preached:

SCRIPTURE: 1 Corinthians 6:1–9a

INTRODUCTION: Our generation could be described as the "lawsuit" generation. Someone has calculated that America has almost one million lawyers with around 125 million lawsuits filed per year. What's the right way to deal with wrongs against us?

1. Embrace the Church's Counter-Cultural Nature (vv. 1–5). Believers should deal with each other differently.
2. Avoid Compromising Our Witness (vv. 6–7a). Paul explains that taking cases to unbelievers to judge between two believers is exactly the opposite of Christ's kingdom! The saints will judge the world and not vice-versa!
3. Realize It Can Be Right to Be Wronged (v. 7b; 1 Pet. 2:19–24). Our culture preaches that we *deserve* to have the best of everything. Christ didn't in His time on earth; why should we expect the same?
4. Examine Our Own Heart (vv. 8–9a). Paul gives a serious warning to those who would still cheat and deceive within the church, saying that the wicked will not inherit the kingdom of God!

CONCLUSION: Have you been "wronged"? Are you demanding justice? God may be saying to you today that it can be right to be wrong! Yield your "rights" and give your situation to God.

The Lordship of Christ
Based on a Sermon by Dr. W. Graham Scroggie

Date preached:

SCRIPTURE: Isaiah 26:13

INTRODUCTION: Isaiah's prayer in this passage is a practical example of confession and repentance:

1. A Humble Confession. "O LORD our God, masters besides You have had dominion over us." Here, we see the confession of Israel, that their affections were divided and that sin had mastery over them. Foreign gods and sinful lifestyles ran rampant. How often do we allow other gods or sinful practices to control our lives? Do you recognize those things? Have you confessed them?
2. A Decisive Renouncing. ". . . but by You only we make mention of Your name." Here, Isaiah voices repentance. He conveys that the

King has been enthroned in the hearts of His people who repent. Perhaps you notice sin in your life and confess it regularly, but have you renounced it and changed your lifestyle?

CONCLUSION: What masters have replaced the Lord in your life? TV? Pornography? Selfishness? Alcoholism? God is calling you to renounce those things and enthrone Jesus Christ as your Master and Lord!

Reading the Classics

When I started writing for publication, I had an editor who warned me against quoting well-known, popular, published authors. "If people want to know what Chuck Swindoll and Max Lucado have to say, they'll read these books themselves," he told me. "You should quote dead people. If you include a quotation, make sure it's a classic."

Since then, I've read fewer and fewer Christian books on the current bestseller lists. Instead I study my Bible inside and out, and I'll occasionally read a secular best-seller for insight into the popular culture. Then I keep my eyes open for inspirational authors who are dead and buried, but who nevertheless wander in and out of my study on a regular basis.

My most recent discovery (profiled elsewhere in this *Sourcebook*) is the Puritan Samuel Clarke (1684–1750), who compiled an excellent little book of Scripture promises that was once enjoyed by generations of believers but is virtually forgotten today. Clarke's introduction has blessed me repeatedly, and now I keep one copy of his *Promises* on the shelf above my desk at the office, and another on my bedside table. I go to bed every night with Samuel Clarke and get up with him first thing each morning, though I don't say that too loudly.

I also recently sat down with Aurelius Augustine as he told me his incredible life's story in the *Confessions*. Missionary Hudson Taylor took several hours explaining to me his *Spiritual Secret*. Brother Lawrence was eager to describe the art of practicing the presence of God, and Peter Cartwright regaled me with one adventure after another in his *Autobiography*.

I've attended Charles Spurgeon's *Lectures to My Students* and learned a great deal from the old Prince of Preachers, especially when he talked about the minister's "fainting fits." I've also paid several visits to the parsonage at Wittenberg where I've listened in rapt attention to cranky old Martin Luther's *Table Talk*. John and Charles Wesley have dragged me all over the British Isles

Continued on the next page

with their *Journals,* and Frances Ridley Havergal's poems and devotional books are great companions for little benches in the countryside.

Alfred Edersheim has explained much I didn't understand about *The Life and Times of Jesus the Messiah,* and Eusebius of Caesarea filled in the blanks of my understanding of early Christian history. John Foxe took me on a macabre little tour of the torture chambers of Bloody Queen Mary in his *Book of Martyrs,* but Thomas à Kempis soothed my soul with his *Imitation of Christ* and *Consolations For My Soul.* I'm also grateful for Mrs. Charles Cowman, who continually refreshes my mind with her *Springs in the Valley* and *Streams in the Desert.*

I've traveled with John Bunyan from Destruction Junction to the Celestial City in his *Pilgrim's Progress,* and I've wandered around a deserted island with a castaway named *Robinson Crusoe* as he worked his way to faith in Christ. I spent time in Switzerland with *Heidi,* in the South Pacific with *The Swiss Family Robinson,* and in Russia with *The Brothers Karamazov.*

Christian fiction, it seems, has been around awhile.

I mention fiction because for the record, I'm not a scholar or an academic. At first, I was a little intimidated by the classics, expecting them to be hard to understand. For the most part, they are quite readable, though I do tend to read these books a little slower—not because they are difficult, but because they are deep.

Think about it. Writing a book in those days was a different kind of activity than it is today. Resources and references were fewer, so one's material had to come from his or her own meditation. In the days before media, entertainment, modern travel, and 24/7 living, people had time for solitude and for stillness to think. There were no Internet search engines, so illustrations had to be immediate and personal. There were no cut-and-paste options, so everything was original. Every word was written by hand with pen-in-ink, or perhaps plucked on an old manual typewriter. Corrections and revisions required rewriting the entire manuscript. There was effort in every syllable.

Many of these writers only produced one classic, so the

wisdom of an entire lifetime was distilled between the covers. Yet these are the least expensive books we can buy. Many of them are available for a few bucks at yard sales and used book stores; and since they're old and in the public domain, most of them can be found for free, word-for-word, on various Internet sites.

I'm not suggesting we abandon newly published works. (I'm glad you've bought this book!) But don't underestimate the privilege of populating your study with such personalities as Amy Carmichael, Christopher Love, Charles Spurgeon, Richard Baxter, G. K. Chesterton, Andrew Murray, Watchman Nee, Madame Guyon, Robert Murray M'Cheyne, and the old German hymnist Paul Gerhardt.

These venerated authors are honored guests in my home and they comprise the faculty of my own personal university. They are teachers and mentors who speak a timely word in due season. They never violate a confidence, don't get angry if I quote them without attribution; and when I get tired of one of them, I can shut him up without offending him. Try doing that with a modern writer!

Furthermore, the message of these old divines still resonates with contemporary audiences. After all, pastoring today isn't much different than in generations gone by. We're meeting time-less problems with eternal truth in the name of the One who is the same yesterday, today, and tomorrow. We don't want a lot of "thee" and "thou" in our vocabulary, but who can complain about using this seventeenth-century quote by Thomas Watson: "The word is fading, not filling, and often under silken apparel, there is a threadbare soul." Or this one: "Prayer delights God's ear, it melts His heart, it opens His hand." Or—once I get started I can't stop—"Reading without meditation is unfruitful; meditation with-out reading is dangerous."

Well, I've said about all I have to say on this subject, so I'll let another of my dead friends sign off: "The three practical rules, then, which I have to offer are: 1. Never read any book that is not a year old. 2. Never read any but famed books. 3. Never read any but what you like." —Ralph Waldo Emerson

MAY 13, 2007

SUGGESTED SERMON

The Importance of Mothers and Grandmothers

Date preached:

By Rev. Richard S. Sharpe, Jr.

Scripture: 2 Timothy 1:1–7, especially verse 5

I call to remembrance the genuine faith that is in you, which dwelt first in your grandmother Lois and your mother Eunice, and I am persuaded is in you also.

Introduction: Our families are under attack today. Culture has redefined what constitutes a family. In the process there is a redefinition of what is a mother. The Bible gives some timeless principles that can help us as mothers and fathers to create an atmosphere of family.

1. **Mothers Share the Promise of Life (v. 1).** This first verse teaches us that Paul is an apostle of Jesus Christ. He is doing this according to the will of God the Father in connection to the "promise of life," referring to the spiritual life of those who accept Christ as their Savior. Timothy has this life because of his heritage in Christ—not because his grandmother and mother accepted Christ for him, but because of their faith they taught him what it means to believe.

2. **Mothers Have Beloved Children (v. 2).** Paul considered Timothy his dearly beloved son. He was his spiritual mentor. Leading people to Christ, spiritually mentoring others makes them our children in the Lord. The responsibility is awesome. Paul wishes grace (getting what we don't deserve) and mercy (not getting what we deserve) and peace (contentment in the midst of a storm) to Timothy. We should wish this on all of our children and spiritual children as well.

3. **Mothers Help Foster a Pure Conscience (v. 3).** Paul continues his introduction saying that he serves with a pure conscience as his forefathers did. As a Jew, he was taught the Word of God. He met Christ on the Damascus Road and learned better how to serve the Lord. Part of his pure conscience is also from his life of prayer as he mentions in regards to Timothy here. Paul prayed for Timothy day and night, a great example for us as parents to pray for our children continually.

4. **Mothers Need to Be Filled with Joy (v. 4).** Timothy's mother, grandmother, and father in the Lord want to see how he is doing in the Lord. They would be filled with joy at news that he is continuing to mature in the faith.

5. **Mothers Need to Demonstrate Unfeigned Faith (v. 5).** Paul calls to remembrance Timothy's background in the faith. Paul points out Timothy's mother and grandmother as genuine, faithful believers; they trusted Christ fully. Many wives here in our church have that kind of faith in the Lord, taking things to the Lord in prayer, living each day serving the Lord with a smile. This is the type of parent and grandparent Lois and Eunice were. We need to reflect this lifestyle to our physical and spiritual children and grandchildren.

6. **Mothers Need to Encourage the Gift of God in Their Children (v. 6).** Children have spiritual gifts (at least one) given to them when they accept Christ as their Savior. Paul reminds or re-ignites Timothy's memory regarding his gift. He wants Timothy to be on fire for the Lord. Are we reminding our children and grandchildren of their spiritual gifts from the Lord?

7. **Mothers Should Banish the Spirit of Fear (v. 7).** Paul reminds Timothy that God has not given him a spirit of fear, but of power, love, and a sound mind. God has given the pastors power to preach and teach. This word for power in the Greek gives us our word for dynamite. The Word of God can blow up all false beliefs and teaching. The word used for love here is *agape*. This is God's love to us when He gave us His son to die on the Cross for our sins. This third word here is translated "sound mind," which speaks of a disciplined life. God wants us to have our thinking guided by the Word of God. Timothy was taught the Word of God by his mother and grandmother. We need to continue to teach our physical and spiritual children and grandchildren the Word of God.

Conclusion: Praise the Lord for all the faithful women and wives here amongst us today. Like Paul, we recognize your spiritual heritage, the children you have raised in the Lord. I would like to both encourage and challenge you today to continue fulfilling this high calling. Know that our church members and staff are behind you, and today we are glad to praise the Lord in recognition of you.

STATS, STORIES, AND MORE

Great Mother's Day Quotes

🐾 *Hundreds of dewdrops to greet the dawn, / hundreds of bees in the purple clover, / Hundreds of butterflies on the lawn, / But only one mother the wide world over.* —George Cooper

🐾 *Lessons learned at a mother's knee last through life.*
—Laura Ingalls Wilder

🐾 *The mother is and must be, whether she knows it or not, the greatest, strongest, and most lasting teacher her children have.*
—Laura Ingalls Wilder

🐾 *One mother achieves more than a hundred teachers.*
—Yiddish Proverb

🐾 Notice this line in "Now Thank We All Our God"—*Who from our mother's arms has blessed us on our way . . .*

🐾 *Honor your father and mother, even as you honor God, for all three were partners in your creation.* —Jewish Proverb

An Insight from Pearl Buck

Author Pearl Buck once made a critical observation about being a mother: "I love people. I love my family, my children . . . but inside myself is a place where I live all alone and that's where you renew your springs that never dry up." The apostle Paul told the Ephesian elders to "Take heed to yourselves and to all the flock." We have to have some time alone, time with the Lord, time by ourselves, so that we can renew our springs. The psalmist said, "All my springs are in Him" (Ps. 87:7). Mothers need to find ways of getting away from the stress and strain of their responsibilities for a few minutes each day, a few hours each week, and for a few days each year, just to replenish the inner springs.

The Magi

If the three wise *men* had been three wise *women,* what would have happened? They would have asked for directions, arrived on time, helped deliver the baby, cleaned the stable, made a casserole, and brought practical gifts.

APPROPRIATE HYMNS AND SONGS

"A Christian Home," Barbara Hart/Jean Sibelius, 1965, 1986 Singspiration Music (Brentwood Benson Music).

"My Mother's Gentle Love," Ron Hamilton, 1988 Majesty Music Inc.

"Thank You for Mothers," Ken Young, 1993 Hallal! Music Exc. (LCS Music Group Inc.).

"Bind Us Together," Bob Gillman, 1977 Kingsway's ThankYou Music (EMI Christian Music Publishing).

"For Future Generations," Dave Clark/Don Koch/Mark Harris, 1994 First Verse Music (Admin. Brentwood Benson Music).

FOR THE BULLETIN

Jamestown, Virginia, was officially settled under the leadership of Captain John Smith on May 13, 1607. Most of the members were Anglicans, and under the leadership of Chaplain Robert Hunt, the first Anglican church was established in America. ● Today, May 13, 1779, is the birthday of Jabez Bunting, called the "second founder of Methodism." It's also the birthday, in 1812, of John Sullivan Dwight, best known for his translation of the Christmas Classic, "O Holy Night." Dwight was the son of Timothy Dwight, president of Yale University and author of the hymn, "I Love Thy Kingdom, Lord." ● Just before sunset on May 13, 1828, pioneer evangelist David Marks rode into Ancaster, Ontario, announcing he would preach in the park. A crowd gathered, and Marks asked if anyone had a text he would like. A man mockingly said, "Nothing!" Marks began preaching on "nothing." God created the world from "nothing," he said. God gave us laws in which there is "nothing" unjust. But, Marks continued, we have broken God's law and there is "nothing" in us to justify us—nothing but Christ. ● William Mackay, Scottish physician and pastor, was born on May 13, 1839, in Montrose, Scotland. He is best known as the author of the hymn, "Revive Us Again." Hymn composer Arthur Seymour Sullivan was born on this day three years later. He wrote the music to "Onward Christian Soldiers." ● On May 13, 1852, William Booth and Catherine Mumford were engaged to be married. ● On May 13, 1981, Pope John Paul II was seriously wounded in St. Peter's Square by a gunshot from Turkish assailant Mehmet Ali Agca.

WORSHIP HELPS

Call to Worship

Praise the LORD! Praise, O servants of the LORD, praise the name of the LORD! Blessed be the name of the LORD from this time forth and forevermore! From the rising of the sun to its going down the LORD's name is to be praised. The LORD is high above all nations, His glory above the heavens. Who is like the LORD our God, who dwells on high, who humbles Himself to behold the things that are in the heavens and in the earth (Ps. 113:1–6)?

Word of Welcome

I cannot tell you how joyful I am today. Every one of us should look around at the women here in our congregation with hearts full of thankfulness to the Lord. In a culture and time when it's not necessarily popular to get up and go to church, in an age when Mother's Day is defined by mothers receiving gifts or going out to eat, they found it most important to be here today. There's nothing wrong with gifts or giving mom a break from the kitchen, but I'm simply recognizing these women here as mothers who are more interested in giving. By being here today with their families, they are rightly recognizing God as central to their role as mothers. I want to say thank you, and we praise the Lord for you. Let's give them a round of applause and then I will lead us in a word of prayer for their continued faith and praise for their faithfulness.

Kid's Talk

Have the children come up front and gather around. Sit down with them and tell them about your own mother, grandmother, or wife. Give them an example of one thing specifically for which you're appreciative. Ask them what they love about their moms or grandmothers, allowing them to speak into the microphone if possible. Then tell them how you know that your mother (or whomever you used in the first example) loves the Lord and how it encourages you to love the Lord and live for Him. Again, allow them to answer what ways they know their moms love the Lord. Finish by telling them it's important not only to obey our moms, but to pray for them too; lead them in a prayer for the mothers and caretakers in the church.

Additional Sermons and Lesson Ideas

Comfort for a Tough Mother's Day

Date preached:

By Joshua D. Rowe

SCRIPTURE: Psalm 27

INTRODUCTION: Mother's day is not always a celebration. Many of us may be saddened as we remember our mothers who have passed away. Some of us are estranged from our parents and, though alive, we may not have a relationship that allowed us even a phone call today. Whatever the case may be, Psalm 27 can offer you comfort, as the Lord offers hope:

1. We Are Offered the Lord's Salvation and Strength (v. 1).
2. We Are Safe in the Lord's Dwelling (vv. 4–6).
3. We Are Received into the Lord's Family (vv. 8–11).
4. We Will See the Lord's Goodness in this Lifetime (v. 13).

CONCLUSION: If you find yourself uneasy this Mother's day for whatever reason, take comfort in these verses and remember to, "Wait for the LORD; be strong and take heart and wait for the LORD" (v. 14 NIV).

Lifelines for the Soul

Date preached:

SCRIPTURE: Psalm 119:38, 41, 50, 57, 58, 76, 82, 116, 123, 140, 148, 154, 162, 170 (NIV)

INTRODUCTION: The promises of God are the lifelines of the soul, and the word "promise" is one of the synonyms used by the writer of Psalm 119 for the Word of God. Here we learn that God's precious promises are to be:

1. Discovered (vv. 82, 123, 162)
2. Loved (vv. 50, 76, 140)
3. Pondered (v. 148)
4. Claimed (vv. 38, 41, 58, 116, 154, 170)
5. Reciprocated (v. 57)

CONCLUSION: Many people today leave their spouses, their churches, their jobs, and/or their families, claiming their "needs aren't met." Our deepest needs can only be met by the Lord through actively discovering, loving, pondering, claiming, and reciprocating His promises.

YOUTH SERMON

Sexual Purity

Date preached:

By Dr. Larry Osborne

Scripture: Ephesians 5:3–14, especially verses 3, 8 (NIV)
But among you there must not be even a hint of sexual immorality, or of any kind of impurity, or of greed, because these are improper for God's holy people. For you were once darkness, but now you are light in the Lord. Live as children of light . . .

Introduction: How many of you think that today is probably a more difficult time to live a sexually pure life than any time in history? Most Christian literature you read suggests this culture is particularly difficult, and difficult it is, but in no way does our culture compare to that of the New Testament. Men were expected to be promiscuous. It was not only openly accepted, but it was a part of everyday life for a man to use temple prostitutes. Almost all marriages were arranged, so many had one or more mistresses on the side. The passage we're looking at today is written to people of that culture. Paul expected sexual purity from those who lived in that type of culture, and God expects us to live sexually pure lives too.

I. **Acknowledge that Sexual Purity Is a Big Deal (Eph. 5:3–14; 1 Thess. 4:3–8; Gen. 1:27–28; 1 Cor. 6:9–11; 7:3–5).** The word used here for sexual immorality is defined like this: sex without the commitment of marriage. Adultery, prostitution, homosexual acts, loose promiscuity, pornography, self-gratification, sexually active committed dating relationships, sexually active engaged relationships: all of these are forms of the biblical word for sexual immorality! We often attempt to redefine Scripture to say what we want it to say. Our passage says, "there must not even be a hint of sexual immorality" and goes on to say "Let no one deceive you with empty words, for because of such things God's wrath comes" (v. 6). How does God's wrath come?

A. **Disease.** Sex isn't safe when it's promiscuous. If we followed God's pattern, these wouldn't exist.

B. **Broken Homes.** How many of you come from broken homes? When partners are unfaithful, or if a marriage breaks up which united a couple in sexual intimacy, it tears down the bonds of a home.

C. **Broken Hearts.** Secular resources consistently show us that "living together" before marriage to "try it out" doesn't work. Most relationships like this fail; two broken hearts result.

D. **Confusion.** Sexual intimacy is a glue that holds people together. When people outside the commitments of marriage start with sex, they end up with major emotional scars. They begin by uniting in flesh, and often find out they don't fit together in other ways.

2. **Avoid Sexual Immorality.**

A. **Flee before You're Tempted (Eph. 5:3; Prov. 4:23; 5:8; 7:7–23).** The biblical commands on how to deal with the desires of the flesh. Many Christians know to flee, but wait too long to start running. God tells us to run away from sexual immorality because He understands us. He knows once you start down the path, it's more and more unlikely you will resist. That's why Ephesians says "not even a hint" (Eph. 5:3). We shouldn't ask how far can we go without sin, the question should be how close to righteousness can we get.

B. **Spirituality Is No Match for Sexual Temptation (Matt. 5:27–30; 2 Sam. 11:1–4; 1 Kin. 11:1–14; 1 Cor. 6:18–20; James 4:7).** As Christians, we often flee when attacked spiritually, but attempt to stand up to sexual temptation. That's exactly backwards! Scripture tell us to stand up against spiritual attacks, and to flee sexual temptation.

C. **Only a Fool Sees Danger and Keeps on Going (Prov. 22:3).** Lots of people seem to get by in the sexual area. You may constantly see those who seem happy, disease-free, or popular with the hottest girl or guy in your class, but Scripture teaches us we should never take our cues from lucky fools.

3. **Accountability Is Key to Overcome Sexual Impurity.** Accountability is more than a small group meeting. Most people lie to their accountability partners. Accountability is making our lives and actions as transparent as possible (Eph. 5:8–14). Anonymity breeds sin; transparency breeds righteousness. Live your life with the windows

wide open. When we're in the light, we're not as tempted to do what's shamefully done in the dark.

Conclusion: Acknowledge that sexual purity is a big deal despite what our friends and our culture tell us. When you see an area of temptation, flee before it's close enough to reach out and take. Be accountable by having your life as open as possible: don't take the computer to your bedroom, but leave it in the open; don't go on dates that leave you in the dark, but take a group or go to a public place. As children of the light, God isn't trying to hold out on us, but to allow us to enjoy the fullness of sexuality as He created it in a marriage relationship.

MAY 20, 2007

SUGGESTED SERMON

All Things Work Together for Good

By Dr. Ed Dobson

Date preached:

Scripture: Various, especially Romans 8:28
And we know that all things work together for good to those who love God, to those who are the called according to His purpose.

Introduction: The promise of Romans 8:28 is one to which Christians for centuries have clung. The first three words of this promise are the basis for our study today, "and we know." Scripture gives supporting evidence of this truth. Through personal experience Paul indicated that in all of the circumstances of life, God is at work for good because we love Him. And the God who was at work in Paul's life has an objective for his life, namely, to make him more and more like Jesus Christ. Paul learned this, and we can, too, through:

1. **Unavoidable Sickness (2 Cor. 12:7–10).** Paul wrote that even in sickness and in pain, God works to accomplish His purpose. Scholars have debated for centuries as to precisely what the "thorn" in Paul's flesh refers to. The bottom line is, we don't know. We can be reasonably sure that it was some sort of sickness or disease. Satan works by the permission of God and within the boundaries that God establishes. So, God allowed and God permitted a messenger of Satan to torment Paul with some sort of ongoing physical infirmity, sickness, or disease. Like all of us, when we get sick, Paul prayed for his own healing. The automatic response of all of us in difficulty is deliverance. God can do it, but doesn't always. One main point in Paul's situation, though: he wasn't sickness focused, but Jesus focused. He wasn't circumstance focused, but Christ focused. Paul said, when healing did not come, he discovered the power of Christ in his weakness.

2. **Unfair Circumstances (Phil. 1:12–14).** Paul discovered that even when he was the victim of injustice, and even when his circumstances were the result of unfair treatment, God was still at work, still in control, accomplishing His purpose. Let me pause to remind

you what had happened to Paul. Paul had been active on missionary journeys, preaching the gospel, planting churches, encouraging believers. He became the victim of unfair and unfounded accusations. As a result, he had been illegally arrested. He made his appeal to Caesar because he was a Roman citizen, and was transported to a Roman prison, from which he wrote to the Philippians. Almost everyone had forsaken him. There he was in prison separated from his ministry, forsaken by his friends, the victim of unfair circumstances. But, as these verses reveal, Paul saw every obstacle as an opportunity to advance the gospel. What a perspective! Other believers were encouraged through his imprisonment and he was able to preach to his captors!

3. **Unfair Criticism (Phil. 1:15–18).** Different people have different motives for preaching the same gospel. We don't know exactly what occurred that Paul refers to in these verses except that in Rome there were people preaching the gospel who were sympathetic toward Paul. There were others also preaching Christ who were not sympathetic to Paul, but looking to stir up trouble for him through preaching. If you study the life of Paul, you'll discover that throughout his life, Christians sought to discredit him because he was not one of the original twelve disciples. People continually undermined him, criticized him, and put him down. Paul's answer was basically, "Who cares?" His desire is that the gospel be preached despite what that meant to him.

4. **Inevitable Death (2 Tim. 1:11–12; 4:16–17).** When Paul was nearing the end of his life, he expressed his faith in God and entrusted his soul to Him. Paul was imprisoned twice in Rome. The first time he wrote Philippians and other letters. The second time he wrote 1 and 2 Timothy. Second Timothy was the last letter that he wrote shortly before his death. He writes about those who deserted him during imprisonment, "At my first defense no one stood with me, but all forsook me. May it not be charged against them. But the Lord stood with me and strengthened me . . ." (2 Tim. 4:16–17). Paul wasn't interested in fighting the "unfair" things in life because he *knew* all things work together for good!

Conclusion: Others may forsake you, you may be sick, you may be the victim of criticism or unfair circumstances, but God always stands by us and gives us strength. I must remind you of some harsh theology: the gospel of God and the glory of God are far more important than our personal convenience and circumstance. He will strengthen you through trials so that His gospel will be made known. God works all things together for good for those who love Him, who have been called according to the purpose of God. Do you believe that?

STATS, STORIES, AND MORE

More from Dr. Dobson

My family and I went to Leland, Michigan, for vacation one year. Leland is a beautiful, quaint, picturesque village by the harbor. We stepped off the ferry to receive instructions from the park ranger and then received an official "back country permit." As we walked around Leland, however, I discovered that there were really two groups of people. The vast majority of people are what I would call the L. L. Bean crowd. They looked as if they had stepped out of the pages of the catalogue of the L. L. Bean Company: pressed khaki pants, Birkenstock sandals, lovely shirts, mom and dads dressed up, kids dressed to match each other as they shop in expensive stores, eat at the nicest restaurants, and go back to their yachts or condos. I also noticed scattered throughout Leland were people who looked like me; the backpacking crowd. We all sort of looked alike: shorts or jeans, tee-shirts, backpacks, guys unshaven. As I walked around this little village, I was struck by this contrast.

In our Christian lives, our expectation is that God will create the spiritual equivalent of Leland, Michigan: the L. L. Bean Christian, dressed nice, shopping from quaint little expensive stores, eating at the finest restaurants, barbecuing on the loveliest yachts, staying at the nicest condos. That's a wrong expectation of God. The reality is we are spiritual backpackers. This world is not our home, we're pilgrims, we're aliens, and we're strangers. When we entered the family of God, God issued us a back country permit.

The more I focus on heaven and Christ, the more I realize that in every circumstance of life, God is at work. What is my expectation? To carry my backpack for Jesus knowing that this world is not my home, I'm just passing through. I understand whether on the mainland or on the island, in the midst of plenty or alone in the wilderness, God works all things together for good for those who love Him, who have been called according to the purpose of God.

APPROPRIATE HYMNS AND SONGS

"God Leads Us Along," G. A. Young, Public Domain.

"Trust His Heart," Eddie Carswell/Babbie Mason, 1989 Dayspring Music, Inc./May Sun Music (Admin. Word Music Group, Inc.).

"Firm Foundation," Nancy Gordon Jamie Harvill, 1994 Integrity's Hosanna! Music/Integritys Praise Music.

"I Love You More," Dallas Holm, 1980, 1981 Dimension Music (Brentwood Benson Music Publishing).

FOR THE BULLETIN

This is an important day in Christian history, for on May 20, A.D. 325, the famous Council of Nicea convened in Nicea, Asia Minor (modern Iznik, Turkey). Among the subjects discussed was Arianism, which denied the deity of Christ. The creed of Nicea was one of the first great statements on the divinity of Jesus. ● Pope John XXI, who had served as pope for less than a year, built an apartment onto the papal palace in Viterbo for peace and quiet. On May 14, 1277, while he was alone in the apartment, the roof collapsed on top of him. He died on May 20th from his injuries. ● On May 20, 1310, a new innovation was introduced into human history—shoes for both the right and left feet. ● Christopher Columbus died on May 20, 1506, impoverished, in Spain. ● The Anabaptist leader Michael Sattler, was arrested in the mid-1520s. On May 20, 1527, his tongue was sliced, chunks of flesh were torn from his body with red-hot tongs, and he was burned at the stake. As soon as the ropes on his wrists were burned, Sattler raised the two forefingers of his hand giving the promised signal to his brothers that a martyr's death was bearable. Then the assembled crowd heard coming from his seared lips, "Father, I commend my spirit into Thy hands." Sattler's wife was executed by drowning eight days later. ● May 20, 1690, marks the death of John Eliot, 86, colonial missionary to the American Indians of Maryland.

WORSHIP HELPS

Call to Worship

I call on you, O God, for you will answer me; give ear to me and hear my prayer. Show the wonder of your great love, you who save by your right hand those who take refuge in you from their foes. Keep me as the apple of your eye; hide me in the shadow of your wings (Ps. 17:6–8 NIV).

Offertory Comments

Someone once said, "When it comes to giving, some people stop at nothing." Well, we know that many church-goers in America give virtually nothing to the Lord's work; but this happens to be a generous church, and we're grateful for those who take stewardship seriously. The Lord blesses us for it. Sir John Templeton wrote from his own experience when he said, "I have observed 100,000 families over my years of investment counseling. I always saw greater prosperity and happiness among those families who tithed than among those who didn't." May the Lord bless us today as we bless Him with the giving of our tithes and offerings.

Pastoral Prayer

Our God, we give You thanks for this promise and I pray that this week in every circumstance of life we would begin to understand the larger picture of Your purpose and Your work in our lives. Help us not to get too attached to the things of this world. Remind us that we are resident aliens, we are pilgrims and strangers. We're just passing through. Our home is in eternity. So grant that this week we might live with eternal values in view. In the name of Christ our Lord we pray, Amen.

—Dr. Ed Dobson

Benediction

And the Lord will deliver me from every evil work and preserve me for His heavenly kingdom. To Him be glory forever and ever. Amen (2 Tim. 4:18)!

Additional Sermons and Lesson Ideas

Feed the Flock

Date preached:

By Dr. Melvin Worthington

SCRIPTURES: Various, especially 1 Corinthians 3

INTRODUCTION: Spiritual immaturity cannot be ignored as a threat to progress in God's work.

1. The Danger of Spiritual Immaturity (1 Cor. 3). The Corinthian Church had lost its spirit of unity and become filled with dissension, division, and disgrace as the result of spiritual immaturity. Spiritual immaturity is manifested through *impulsiveness, impatience, intolerance,* and *insinuation.*
2. The Diet for Spiritual Instruction. To grow spiritually, all believers must *desire the milk* of the Word (1 Pet. 2:2; Heb. 5:11–14). We must *diligently meditate* on the Word of God (Ps. 1; Ps. 119). We also must maintain the proper *disposition mandated* by the Word of God (1 Pet. 2; 2 Pet. 1).
3. The Duty of Shepherds Inferred. The pastor has the solemn duty to teach the flock (1 Tim. 3:2), to tend the flock (John 21:16; 1 Pet. 5:2), and to train the flock (1 Tim. 3:2, 1 Pet. 5:2).

CONCLUSION: Is your spiritual diet adequate?

The Practice of Hospitality

Date preached:

By Rev. Billie Friel

SCRIPTURE: Leviticus 19:33–34

INTRODUCTION: Hospitality is a mark of people who know and serve God.

1. The Meaning of Hospitality. The word hospitality comes from two Greek words, when put together basically mean "love of strangers."
2. The Mentions of Hospitality. Christians are commanded to practice hospitality (Rom. 12:13) without grudging (1 Pet. 4:9), in a manner worthy of God (3 John 5–8). Hospitality also marks both a church leader (1 Tim. 3:2) and a genuine widow (1 Tim. 5:9–19).
3. The Misconception of Hospitality. Entertainment does not equal hospitality. Entertainment is often centering on self, showing off, begging for compliments, seeking to move socially upward, and expecting something in return.
4. The Motivations for Hospitality.
   A. The Character of God (Lev. 19:34). We have a God who cares, loves, and shows mercy to all.

B. What God Has Done for Us (Lev. 19:34; Eph. 2:11–13). God calls us to remember. We are no longer strangers because Jesus died to make everyone a member of God's household.

CONCLUSION: As each of us has received the gift of hospitality from God, so let us minister the hospitality of God to one another (1 Pet. 4:10).

PRAYER FOR THE PASTOR'S CLOSET

God's Word

Almighty God, Your Word is cast
Like seed into the ground;
Now let the dew of Heav'n descend,
And righteous fruits abound.
—JOHN CAWOOD (1819)

PATRIOTIC SERMON

Do You Remember?

Date preached:

By Dr. Timothy Beougher

Scripture: 2 Timothy 2:8–9
Remember that Jesus Christ, of the seed of David, was raised from the dead according to my gospel, for which I suffer trouble as an evildoer, even to the point of chains; but the word of God is not chained.

Introduction: Do you ever have trouble remembering things? If you're not sure, the answer is probably "yes." Do you ever forget where you put your keys? Your wallet? Your checkbook? Your Day Timer? Your mind? Tomorrow is Memorial Day, a national Day of Remembrance for those who have lost their lives in service to our country. These men and women have given the ultimate gift, their life, that we might have freedom. Even the freedom to gather together today in worship is a freedom that many Christians around the world do not enjoy. As Americans, it is good to have days like Memorial Day to remind us to be thankful and to express gratitude to those who have served and are serving our country, and to their parents, children, and spouses. As Christians, we are called to remember certain things as well (see Ps. 78:11; 105:5; 106:21; Hos. 13:6). In 2 Timothy 2:8–9, the apostle Paul exhorts Timothy to "remember." As we reflect on this passage from God's Word this morning, we see that we are called to remember five very important things.

1. **The Person of Christ: "Remember that Jesus Christ, of the Seed of David, Was Raised from the Dead" (v. 8).** The word "remember" is imperative; it's a command, not a suggestion. The verb suggests continual action: "keep on continually, moment by moment, re-membering." We must never lose sight of the Person of Christ. Paul refers to Him as Jesus Christ: Jesus represents His humanity, Christ represents His deity. The additional phrases heighten this emphasis: "raised from the dead" Christ's death was a death for sin. His resurrection means the penalty for sin is satisfied. The phrase, "the seed of David" also speaks of Jesus' humanity. He was born into this world as a baby, in the lineage of David. We are called

to remember Jesus Christ as the Son of God and the Son of Man, as One who was fully God, yet fully human.

2. **The Power of the Resurrection: "Raised from the Dead" (v. 8).** We are called to remember the power of the Resurrection. Would you agree that some of life is unmanageable? Life is not always easy! We can't possibly manage everything that life is going to throw at us. But God can! And that is good news! You can't control everything in your life, but God can! And that is good news! Some people today are admitting, "My life is in trouble." I feel powerless to overcome a bad habit; I feel powerless in my relationships; I feel powerless to deal with my circumstances. What you need is a power greater than yourself! You were never meant to live your life just on your power; God wants to have a relationship with you!

3. **The Promises of God: "The seed of David" (v. 8).** I mentioned a moment ago that this focuses on His humanity. We remember Jesus Christ as One who has walked on this earth, who knows and understands the struggles we face (Heb. 4:14–16). Not only does this phrase highlight Jesus' humanity, it's also Paul's way of emphasizing that Jesus is the Messiah, the Promised One, the Son of God. He is the fulfillment of the hopes and dreams, not only of Israel but of the whole world. As you read through the Gospels you are struck with a phrase over and over again: [These things happened] so that the Scripture would be fulfilled?" Did you know that over 300 prophecies were fulfilled by Jesus Christ, most of which were made hundreds of years before His birth?

4. **The Priority of the Gospel: ". . . According to My Gospel, for Which I Suffer Trouble as an Evildoer, Even to the Point of Chains . . ." (vv. 8–9).** The gospel is the most important message in the world. Paul was willing to endure any hardship, any suffering to share the gospel, because He remembered (Eph. 2:12–13). We are to remember the priority of the gospel.

5. **The Paradox of Suffering: ". . . For Which I Suffer Even to the Point of Chained; but the Word of God Is Not Chained" (v. 9).** Paul affirmed that even though he was imprisoned, the Word of God was not imprisoned. The Roman government could not construct a prison that could contain the Word of God! The Word lives as a lamp to our feet, as a light to our path, as food for the hungry, as

water for the thirsty, as rest for the weary, as salvation for the sinner, and grace for the Christian. God's Word was not chained; the gospel was continuing to spread! Paul's perspective allowed him to see the good coming out of his circumstances. A believer must look at the result of the adversity, not at the adversity itself. For Paul the prison wasn't a punishment for preaching the gospel but a platform for preaching it to new people! Oftentimes it is in the most difficult circumstances that God can do the most in us and through us.

Conclusion: How's your memory this morning? "Do you remember?" God has given us something much greater than a Kodak camera to help remember. He has given us His Word and His Spirit so we will remember Him and all His blessings and not forget. As Americans, we remember the sacrifice of those who have fought for our freedom. At funerals we present an American flag to the family with the words, "on behalf of a grateful nation." As believers, should we not present our bodies to God as a living sacrifice and say, "on behalf of a grateful sinner who has been redeemed by the blood of Jesus"? Remember Jesus. Remember that God has provided for you a divine Companion, One who has promised never to leave you or forsake you. Remember that Jesus is a divine Friend, who understands what you feel and knows what you are going through. Remember that Jesus is an all-powerful Companion who can take you through a time of trial and suffering and work it out for His glory and for your good. Remember Jesus Christ!

MAY 27, 2007

Spirit Filled

Date preached:

By Dr. Larry Osborne

Scripture: Ephesians 5:15–20, especially verse 18
And do not be drunk with wine, in which is dissipation; but be filled with the Spirit.

Introduction: Those of you here today who have been Christians for a long time will realize that I am not covering every detail of the Holy Spirit. Those of you who are newer Christians may feel somewhat overwhelmed. The Holy Spirit is too vast of a topic for us to cover in one sermon, so let's look at some basics of the Holy Spirit and then some practical applications.

I. **Who Is the Holy Spirit and What Does He Do?**

   A. **He's God (Acts 5:3–4).** This passage equates lying to the Holy Spirit with lying to God Himself. A word of advice: take this as a simple truth and don't get too hung up on trying to completely grasp the idea of the Trinity. We live in a three-dimensional world and this is a fourth-dimensional spiritual truth (Deut. 29:29).

   B. **The Spirit Is the Source of All Spiritual Knowledge and Power.** Jesus, just before going to the Cross, spoke to His disciples about the Spirit whom He would send. He told them the Spirit would bring truth. The disciples were grieved that Jesus would leave them, but Jesus told them it was better that He go and the Holy Spirit come (John 14:12, 15–18; 16:5–15). When Jesus was with them, they had the Spirit *with* them. When the Spirit came at Pentecost, the Spirit was then *in* them, never to leave (Acts 1:8).

   C. **He Has Always Been the Same.** The Holy Spirit has always been the source of any act of spiritual knowledge and power in any human being. The miracles of Christ were many of the same miracles done by the Old Testament prophets (1 Kin. 17—2 Kin. 13:20). Only after His being baptized with the Holy Spirit (Matt. 3:16) did Jesus really begin His earthly public ministry.

2. How Do We Get the Holy Spirit and What Is It to Be Filled?

A. **We Receive the Spirit When We Choose to Follow Jesus.** Paul taught that we were sealed with the Holy Spirit when we came to Christ (Eph. 1:13–14). In Romans, he tells Christians that they are not controlled by the sinful nature, but by the Spirit; if we don't have the Spirit, we are not true believers (Rom. 8:9).

B. **Filled Simply Means "Controlled By."** For many people, being filled with the Holy Spirit means being weird: fainting "in the spirit," being manic for God, or acting outlandish. This definition is simply not scriptural. The Greek word for "being filled" means to be controlled by (Eph. 5:18; Gal. 2:20; 5:16, 22–25). Paul contrasts being filled with alcohol, which controls a person's actions when he's drunk, with being filled with the Spirit, who controls us when we're filled! This can come through inner spiritual prompting, or simply reading and obeying a Scripture verse.

3. How Does the Spirit Guide and Change Us from the Inside Out?

A. **Sometimes It's Spectacular, Most Often It's Subtle.** Elijah, after experiencing the spectacular work of the Spirit, is threatened by the queen. He runs away and hides in a cave, discouraged and complaining to God. God tells him to go outside the cave and that God would, in some physical way, interact with Elijah. Elijah went out and saw fire, an earthquake, and powerful wind, none of which were the interaction God spoke of. Finally, Elijah heard a still small voice, the whisper of God (1 Kin. 19:11–13). God taught Elijah that the Spirit isn't only in the big things.

B. **We're All Unique and So Is Our Relationship with the Holy Spirit.** We do not have a special formula to follow, nor do we need to simply mimic every detail of others' relationship to the Spirit. We need to allow Him to be God and expect a unique relationship to fit our own unique personality and circumstances (see Luke 7:31–35; 1 Cor. 12:1–27; Rom. 12:3–8).

C. **To Be Filled with the Spirit, We Need to Follow the Spirit (Eph. 5:18; Gal. 5:16–23; Prov. 4:18).** This principle is so simple, and yet the most practical. The things you know are of the Spirit, do!

D. To Hear the Spirit, We Need to Stop and Listen. Why don't many Christians understand what it's like to have God guide them? We run our lives so fast, we never stop to listen (see 2 Tim. 3:16–17; Ps. 119:105; Prov. 8:34; 12:15).

Conclusion: If you're a follower, the Spirit is in you, but you've got to listen to what He says and do it!

STATS, STORIES, AND MORE

Calvary Must Precede Pentecost

"There can never be a Pentecost in your life until there's been a Calvary in your life. Pentecost can only be a reality when Calvary is a finality; when I know what it is daily, and I mean daily, by the power of the indwelling Spirit to reckon myself indeed dead unto sin but alive unto God through our Lord Jesus Christ." —Dr. Stephen Olford

More from Dr. Osborne: If Jesus Showed Up at Church

Christians today have the wrong idea about Jesus and the Holy Spirit. If you knew that Jesus was going to show up at church on Sunday, how many of you would go? But, you have to understand, crowds would be around Him, He would be most likely far away from you. You might glean a little insight from hearing His words, but who knows how much you would see? Jesus explains in John 14–16 that His Holy Spirit will (now does) live within His people to guide them into truth, and that this is better for the disciples and all believers! Right now, it's to our advantage that Jesus went to sit exalted at the right hand of the Father, for His Spirit now lives within us, not within one divine human in the Person of Christ on earth.

Manipulating the Spirit or Allowing Him to Manipulate You

When we learn that the Holy Spirit is responsible for every miracle in Scripture, we may begin to think that we can just go home and call down fire from heaven on evil people, or that we can know what our neighbors are thinking. After all, the same Spirit that did these things in Scripture can do them through us. We *must* understand that the Holy Spirit has His own agenda: to do the will of the Father only. The Holy Spirit is not a power that, as you grow spiritually, you learn to plug into and manipulate. Many Christians get this wrong. In fact, religious movements with this philosophy happen all the time, some are going on even now. They teach that you can simply learn the secrets of the Holy Spirit, He is at your beckoning call. They teach that you can plug into and manipulate this power to do what you want. The truth is that the Holy Spirit isn't a power, but a person: God living through you. When God is living through you, guess who sets the agenda?

APPROPRIATE HYMNS AND SONGS

"Holy Spirit Come," 1988 Paragon Music Corp. (Brentwood Benson Music Publishing, Inc.).

"Be Filled with the Spirit," Louise Nankivell, 1957 Gospel Publishing House (Admin. Lorenz Corp.).

"Channels Only," Mary E. Maxwell/Ada Rose Gibbs, Public Domain.

"Holy Spirit Rain Down," Russell Fragar, 1997 Russell Fragar (Hillsong) (Admin. Integrity Music, Inc.).

FOR THE BULLETIN

On May 27, 1524, the great translator of the English Bible, William Tyndale, registered as a student at the University of Wittenberg under the name William Daltici of England in an attempt to foil British agents who were seeking to arrest him. ● On May 27, 1525, the German reformer, Thomas Muenzer, died. He took Luther's teachers further than Luther, stirring up revolutionary turmoil and helping to spark the bloody Peasant's War, during which he was captured and executed. Interestingly, John Calvin also died on the same day, May 27, of the year 1564, just as the sun was setting. ● On May 27, 1647, Achsah Young was hanged as a witch in the first recorded execution of this kind in Massachusetts, and on May 27, 1661, Scottish evangelical Archibald Campbell, was beheaded for his faith in Christ. He was accused of treason because of his association with the *Scottish Covenanters.* ● May 27, 1676 also marks the death of the great German hymnist Paul Gerhardt, the "Charles Wesley of Germany," a prolific hymnist who gave Lutheranism some of its warmest hymns. His hymnody reflects the shift from the rugged theological hymns of Luther to the more subjective, devotional songs of the German Pietistic revival. ● Peter Marshall, the Scottish preacher who became Chaplain of the United States Senate, was born on May 27, 1902. Following his death of a heart attack, his wife, Catherine, immortalized his life's story in her book, *A Man Called Peter.*

WORSHIP HELPS

Call to Worship

> Spirit, aiding all who yearn
> More of truth divine to learn
> And with deeper love to burn;
> Hear us, Holy Spirit . . .
>
> Holy, loving, as Thou art,
> Come and live within our heart,
> Never from us to depart;
> Hear us, Holy Spirit.
>   —"Spirit Strength of All the Weak,"
>   THOMAS B. POLLOCK (1836–1896),
>   date written unknown

Pastoral Prayer

Father, I thank You for this incredible gift of You actually coming inside our lives to change us from the inside out so that we don't have to do it on our own. I pray that You will help us understand more and more what it means to yield to You in that way. Moment by moment, help us to ask "what do You want me to do." Help us have margins built into our lives where we can take time to hear from Your Word, from others, from You what You want us to do.   —Dr. Larry Osborne

Invitation

I want to speak to those of you who have been "window shopping" Jesus. Today we've been speaking of the most incredible aspect of what it means to turn your life over to Him: you receive His Spirit! You may have attended our services or some Bible studies; they've been making sense to you, but you have yet to really make the final step in handing over control of your life to God. If you've never done that and you would like to take Him up on His offer to forgive your sins through His shed blood on the Cross, if you want to ask Him to come inside you and begin to change your life from the inside out, I invite you to make that decision today. Pray with me: "Dear Jesus, I ask You to forgive my sins. I ask You to adopt me into Your family. Would You come and start changing me from the inside out? Here is the steering wheel of my life: You take control. Take me where You want me to go, and change me as You want me to change."   —Dr. Larry Osborne

Additional Sermons and Lesson Ideas

Holiness in Relation to the Holy Spirit
Based on a Sermon by Rev. E. H. Hopkins

Date preached:

SCRIPTURE: John 16:13

INTRODUCTION: There can be no holiness without the truth of God, and there can be no holiness without the Spirit's guidance in that truth.

1. The Guide. The Holy Spirit is a *personal guide,* for He is referred to by a personal pronoun and identity. He is a *divine guide,* for this verse tells us He speaks what He hears and will tell of what is to come. He is an *indwelling guide* (Eph. 1:13; 3:17).
2. The Guidance. The Holy Spirit guides us through the Word of God (John 16:13) and through conscience (16:8).

CONCLUSION: This brings us to our responsibility as *The Guided.* The Holy Spirit will guide us practically and daily as our lives are given in submission to Him. Our greatest responsibility is to obey!

Names of the Holy Spirit
Based on an Outline by R. A. Torrey

Date preached:

SCRIPTURE: Various

INTRODUCTION: Scripture refers to the Holy Spirit using many names, each of which can teach us more about who He is. Let's look at a few:

1. The Spirit of Holiness (Rom. 1:4). The Holy Spirit is holy in character; He imparts holiness to believers.
2. The Spirit of Grace (Heb. 10:29). The Holy Spirit is the administrator of the grace of God.
3. The Spirit of Glory (1 Pet. 4:14). He imparts the glory of God to us more and more, until we are filled with the fullness of God.
4. The Spirit of Truth (John 16:13). The Holy Spirit makes real to us the truth of God.
5. The Spirit of Life (Rom. 8:2). He imparts to us daily the life of God.

CONCLUSION: The Holy Spirit of Jesus Christ is God's gift to those who believe in Him; won't you allow Him to take over your life?

SUGGESTED SERMON
What Authentic Conversion Looks Like

By Dr. Al Detter

Date preached:

Scripture: Luke 19:1–10, especially verse 10
. . . for the Son of Man has come to seek and to save that which was lost.

Introduction: The story of Zacchaeus demonstrates for us three clear aspects of authentic conversion. We need to know them, as God's will is for us to enter into them. Authentic conversion means:

1. **You Must Successfully Overcome the Barriers Keeping You from Christ (Luke 19:1–4).** For every person, there are barriers that stand between them and a dynamic relationship with Jesus. There are no exceptions to this. Until those barriers are overcome, authentic conversion is impossible. Zacchaeus had some barriers to hurdle.

   A. **Means of Wealth.** Zacchaeus was a rich chief tax collector. Being a chief tax official is a neutral line of work, and there's nothing wrong with being a man of means. The problem was his approach to the job. He was known as a thieving tax collector. He lived life for what he could get, with no compassion for others. He was a crass opportunist. An authentic conversion would mean that all of this would need to change.

   B. **Stature.** Zacchaeus was a short man. In those days, people in general were not as tall as Americans. So Zacchaeus might have been somewhat less than five feet tall. This story occurred about a week before the crucifixion of Jesus. Jesus was on His way to Jerusalem. He was popular among the people and wherever He went He drew a crowd. Zacchaeus was too short to see Jesus in the crowd, so he ran ahead to climb a sycamore tree along the path Jesus surely would take.

Application: Until conversion, every one of us has barriers that stand in the way of seeing Jesus like we need to see Him. You may think yourself unworthy to be loved by Jesus. Maybe you think you're not good enough or that you don't really need the Savior. We have to get over hurdles like these if we are going to have an authentic conversion to Christ.

2. **Jesus Must Intersect Your Life in Some Fashion (Luke 19:5–6).** It's important to be able to see Jesus, but you can't be converted unless Jesus has made an evident entrance into your life. When Jesus came to the tree, He looked up and said, "Zacchaeus, make haste and come down, for today I must stay at your house." This verse is loaded with meaning.

    A. **Jesus Knew His Name.** Jesus knew his name just like He knows every star by name and just like He knows you and me by name. He knew all about Zacchaeus and loved him in spite of his sin. He knows everything about us and loves us as well.

    B. **This Meeting Wasn't by Chance.** Jesus said, "I must stay at your house" (v. 5). The key word here is "must." The Greek word for "must" means "necessity." It's not only the proper thing to do but the unavoidable thing to do. Jesus had to meet Zacchaeus if he was going to be converted. Nobody is ever converted without this "divine must." Jesus must intersect our lives in some fashion in order for us to respond to Him. If we have no encounter with Jesus, we cannot be converted.

Application: Jesus, though headed to the Cross, had time to stop for Zacchaeus. Often our days are busy. We have plans. We are working on a specific thing or needing to go to a specific place. We meet someone along the way. The phone rings. It's not part of our plans. It may even seem like an intrusion. But guess what? It may be a divine "must."

3. **Your Life Must Be Radically Changed (Luke 19:8–10).** Zacchaeus opened his life to Jesus and Jesus changed him from the inside out. Zacchaeus promised half of what he owned to the poor; he saw their plight for the first time. He went on to promise restitution according to the Old Testament standard (Lev. 6:5; Num. 5:7; Ex. 22:1; 2 Sam. 12:6) to those he defrauded. It was going to cost him a bundle! When Zacchaeus was finished, Jesus said, "Today salvation has come to this house, because he also is a son of Abraham" (v. 9).

Application: The problem we face today is religion without changed lives. When Jesus truly saves immoral people, they stop sleeping around. When He saves drunks, they leave their booze. When He saves people who mistreat others, they become kind. When He saves people with money, they become generous. True conversion does not mean that we become perfect. We will fail in our walk with Jesus until we die. But we won't live the way we used to.

STATS, STORIES, AND MORE

Before He Met Jesus, What Was So Wrong with Zacchaeus?
Jericho, a famous Old and New Testament city, was about fifteen miles
northeast of Jerusalem. It was a major stop on a trade route. Taxes were
imposed on commerce as well as on real estate. Zacchaeus was a turncoat
Jew. He held his job as an agent of the Roman government, which was
oppressive to the Jews. He was collecting excessive taxes even from his
own people, giving the required amount to Rome, and pocketing the rest.
He loved his money but he was a hated man.

A Zacchaeus Experience
I did something like Zacchaeus once. John F. Kennedy was shot on a
Friday. They brought his body down Pennsylvania Avenue to the capitol
building to lie in state on a Sunday. Early that morning, my father gathered
our family together and we drove several hours to Washington, D.C., to see
the casket processional. Thousands lined the streets. We waited for hours.
Suddenly a charge went through the crowd as we heard the drum rolls.
The cortege was approaching. But I was too short to see. So I climbed a
tree. It was that or miss the whole thing.   —Dr. Al Detter

A Divine Must
One week, I had a full schedule, all planned out with no margins. The
phone rang; it was a funeral director. A man in his thirties had a tragic
death and the director wondered if I would take the funeral. My first
thought was, "No wiggle room. Can't do it." But in my heart of hearts the
Spirit spoke to me and said, "You must take this funeral." When I
approached the funeral home, I couldn't believe what I saw. Perhaps 200
people filled the funeral home out into the lobby and hallways. Over 80
cars went to the cemetery. Hardly anybody knew Jesus there and I had
the opportunity to share Him with a whole crowd of people.
                                                                —Dr. Al Detter

APPROPRIATE HYMNS AND SONGS

"Amazing Grace," John Newton/Edwin Excell/John P. Rees, Public Domain.

"Deliverance," David Ingles, 1976 David Ingles Music.

"Grace So Amazing," Eugene M. Bartlett, 1964 Albert E. Brumley And Sons
    (Admin. Integrated Copyright Group, Inc.).

FOR THE BULLETIN

On June 3, 1098, the armies of the First Crusade captured the city of Antioch from the Muslims. ● Thomas à Becket was consecrated as Archbishop of Canterbury on this day in 1162 at the instigation of King Henry II, who later regretted the decision. ● On June 3, 1647, the Puritan Parliament in Great Britain banned the observance of Christmas. ● Today is the birthday, in 1726, of German reformed pastor, Philip William Otterbein, who helped begin the Church of the United Brethren in Christ in America, an early branch of the modern United Methodist Church. It's also the birthday, in 1796, of Dyer Ball, missionary doctor to Asia. ● Baseball uniforms were worn for the first time on June 3, 1851, when the New York Knickerbockers suited up in white shirts, blue trousers, and straw hats. ● Hymnist Frances Ridley Havergal, 42, died on June 3, 1879. Among her last words: "Splendid to be so near the gates of heaven . . . I thought He would have left me here a long while; but He is *so* good to take me now . . . Come, Lord Jesus, come and fetch me." ● Missionary hero J. Hudson Taylor, founder of China Inland Mission, died on this day in 1905. Pastor A. T. Pierson passed away on this day in 1911 after returning from a trip to Asia. Pope John Paul XXIII died on this day in 1963.

WORSHIP HELPS

Call to Worship
The LORD is my strength and song, and He has become my salvation; He is my God, and I will praise Him; my father's God, and I will exalt Him (Ex. 15:2).

Word of Welcome
As we gather today, we are extremely fortunate. You see, in this country most every church has the means to provide pews or chairs, microphones and speaker systems, and seating arrangements so that everyone can be comfortable and see everything going on as we worship together. As we begin to worship, I want you all to consider an important question, keeping in mind that the Church is the body of Christ: what would you give to be a part of what Jesus does each week? You see, our culture is one of convenience where it's not so hard to get to church and be comfortable here. What if it just wasn't so? What if, like Zacchaeus, we had to climb a tree just to see a glimpse of Jesus? Consider other countries, where services are

standing-room only. Some members literally climb trees to see in the windows or to see the service in an outdoor setting! Poorer congregations meet in non-air-conditioned, smelly rooms to study the Scriptures and hear the Word of God. Many must travel for hours by foot to reach the nearest church, and they stay for hours and hours. Persecution, war, or depression could hit even this country at any time and we could be put in similar situations as those other countries. We want you to be comfortable here, but I challenge you as we begin worship together, to reflect on the importance of being a part of the body of Christ. Commit to endure any circumstance and overcome any obstacle to be a part of what Jesus is doing.

Suggested Scriptures

- Exodus 22:1
- Leviticus 6:5
- Numbers 24:14
- 2 Samuel 12:6
- Matthew 2:49
- Mark 8:31; 13:10
- Luke 2:49; 18:18–30; 19:1–10
- John 3:7; 4:29; 20:9
- Acts 1:8
- 1 Corinthians 5:10

Additional Sermons and Lesson Ideas

Jabez Times Four

Date preached:

SCRIPTURE: 1 Chronicles 4:8–9

INTRODUCTION: A few years ago, the prayer of Jabez was popularized in a book indicating that God wanted us to ask for His blessings and for the enlargement of our influence and ministry for the sake of the kingdom. There are actually four versions of this prayer in the Bible, which, taken together, teach us to be bold and ambitious about our praying for His sake.

1. "Enlarge My Territory" (1 Chr. 4:8–9).
2. "Enlarge My Tent" (Is. 54:2).
3. "Enlarge My Area of Activity" (2 Chr. 10:15–16).
4. "Open Doors for Our Message" (Col. 4:3).

CONCLUSION: None of these prayers are for our own health, wealth, glory, or consumption. We're to pray them for the sake of God's work on this earth through us and our church.

Commitment in Marriage

Date preached:

By Dr. Timothy Beougher

SCRIPTURE: 1 Corinthians 7:10–16

INTRODUCTION: Scripture gives us insight on how to carry out our marriage commitments whatever circumstance we are in as believers:

1. Two Foundational Truths. Before we discuss God's standards for marriage, we need to understand two basic things:
   A. God loves us (Rom. 5:8)!
   B. God's Standards Are for Our Good (1 John 5:3)!
2. A Christian Married to a Christian Is to Stay Married (vv. 10–11).
3. A Christian Married to a Willing Unbeliever Is to Stay Married (vv. 12–14).
   A. A Christian Shouldn't Take the Initiative to Break Up a Marriage (vv. 12–13).
   B. The Christian Partner Has a Sanctifying Effect on the Lost Partner and the Children (v. 14).
   C. Suggestions for Witnessing to an Unbelieving Spouse: Pray (Rom. 10:1) and Remember the Walk-to-Talk Balance (1 Pet. 3:1).
4. A Christian Married to an Unwilling Unbeliever Is to Seek Peace (vv. 15–16).

CONCLUSION: Live up to your commitment!

Preaching that Connects
An Interview with Dr. Larry Osborne

For many preachers, the hardest part of sermon preparation is application, but that seems to come naturally to you. What are your secrets for preparing relevant and applicable sermons?

One of the things that works well with me is to follow this procedure. The first time I read through a text I try to avoid any grammatical work; I just look at it devotionally and ask myself, "What does it mean?" I use a form of mind-mapping. I draw a circle around a verse, reference or the main idea of the text and then I'll jot down every idea, verse, concept, or illustration that it triggers—connecting them by little spokes and circles. That often brings to mind places and people where I've seen this verse or the principles at work in someone else's life besides my own; greatly broadening my illustration base. Once I get to principles, illustrations come quite easily. When I go directly from text to illustration, I struggle because it's so narrow. But when I go from text to principle to illustration, I have many more applications I can tap into. I pretty much always try to pull an illustration out of my life or someone's life I've seen first hand, just making sure that I'm appropriate in what I say and how I apply it.

Do you ever disguise illustrations?

I seldom use a story within a three-to-five-year period of time, so I don't feel a need to disguise it too much as a rule. Sometimes I hide or alter just enough details to be appropriate, because it would be hurtful to the person if they hear about it or are in the congregation. So I might occasionally disguise it by simply saying, "I was once in a situation very similar to this. Let me tell you the story." And then I might say, "A man I know . . ." (it was really a woman) and go on with the story.

Continued on the next page

CONVERSATIONS IN THE PASTOR'S STUDY—*Continued*

Do you ever ask permission from the people? Or do you feel instead that after a period of time the story has merged into the general flow of humanity, so to speak, and is indistinguishable?

I seldom ask permission, because if it's a negative story, it's long ago, far away, in another galaxy. And if it's a positive story, I've never known anybody to be bothered by it. When it's my own family . . . well, I just have an intuitive sense about that. I think I know them well enough and understand where the lines are. Each member of my family is very different, and I occasionally weave them into my sermons accordingly. I have one kid who can handle being ribbed, but I have two others who . . . no, I wouldn't do that to them.

Do you ever import illustrations from other sources? From your reading?

I seldom import illustrations per se. Because our ministry is taped for longer term use with our video venues, I try to be more timeless. Rather than saying, "This week," I might say, "Recently . . ." I am, however, involved in some business interests which I find is a powerful way to reach men—much more than sports illustrations—and I will occasionally pull in a business illustration.

How, then, do you go from text to principle and application?

I imagine I'm in Starbucks, sitting down with a cup of coffee, talking to someone about the truth I've been studying. Here's what the passage says, and here's what it doesn't mean and here's what it does mean. Here's how it impacts my life. Here's how it intersects with your life.

Are your outlines always principle- or application-centered rather than expositional in tone?

Yes. Sometimes I give a running commentary of a longer text or even a short verse, almost in the old J. Vernon McGee style; but I'm done with that in five or ten minutes. The next part of the message always flows out of the question: "So what? What does it mean to us? How does it work?" I will seldom say: "Three Things Moses Did." I'll say, "Three Things Great Leaders Do." Then boom—point one—and I look at Moses to illustrate it; boom, point two—then another look at Moses; and so on. This approach seems to makes a huge impact on people, especially on the unchurched.

Has that been a life-long pattern in your sermon preparation, or was there a point where you said, "My sermons aren't relevant enough. What can I do to preach more practically?"

I made a change about twenty years ago. I had always received a lot of positive feedback from my teaching. I was highly influenced by the Chuck Smith model, because I was a Jesus freak in Southern California and came to Christ in the early days of that movement. Then I went to a seminary that was very expository-oriented. One day it dawned on me that when I was in the pulpit I communicated differently than I did with a person in real life. Here was the difference: In the pulpit I taught the Bible and applied it. In real life I would teach you how to live the Christian life from the Bible with the Bible as my only authority. But what a huge difference that was! So now whenever I struggle with a passage, I will still to this day write, "Instruction in Christian Living," in the upper right hand corner to remind myself that (it sounds like heresy till you hear me out) I'm not teaching the Bible; I'm instructing people how to live the Christian life with the Bible as my only authority. This might involve long, expository sections, of course—right now I'm preaching through the book of Ephesians. Or it might be systematic theology or a topical study. But whatever the sermon may be on any particular day, I think in *So What?* terms.

So you spend some time on the front end getting the setting and exposition, then devote the major part of the message to drawing out and applying the principles?

It will vary. In my current series from Ephesians chapter four (we're calling it "Pit Stop Christianity" because the verses are

Continued on the next page

short and packed with instructions for putting off an old pattern and putting on a new one), I'll spend the first seven to ten minutes on the verse or text, then devote the rest of the message to the principles and application. For instance, this week we were looking at the verse that says, "Let no unwholesome speech come out of your mouth except that which benefits." I opened by saying, "Normally I don't critique Greek, but right now notice there are three key phrases—the words 'unwholesome,' 'build up' and 'benefit.'" Unwholesome is used eight times in the Greek New Testament, and in the other seven occasions it's translated 'rotten.' That's a powerful, visual word. 'Build up' is self-explanatory. 'Benefit' is the Greek word for grace, a key Christian concept having to do with getting way better than we deserve. So this passage is about whether we say rotten things or constructive things to others. It says everything we say should build people up, and it should actually 'grace' them." And the hurtful things we say aren't just unwholesome—they're "rotten." Then I went into five questions to ask before we speak, like: Is it true? Is it helpful? Is it right for the situation? As I said, my goal is not to teach the Bible, but to teach people how to live the Christian life with the Bible as my only authority. That, I think, is preaching that connects.

JUNE 10, 2007

SUGGESTED SERMON

Bring the Joy Back!

Date preached:

By Dr. David Jeremiah

Scripture: John 15:11 and Galatians 5:22–23, especially verse 22
The fruit of the Spirit is . . . joy.

Introduction: I don't know if you've noticed, but folks aren't smiling much these days. Jesus wants us to smile, to exhibit joy. He said, "These things I have spoken unto you that My joy may remain in you and that your joy may be full" (John 15:11). I've been reading the Bible this week with joy in mind, and everywhere I turn I find it. Joy is the atmosphere in which Christians live. We rejoice in the Lord always (Phil. 4:4); we "rejoice evermore" (1 Thess. 5:16). As someone put it, "Joy is the gigantic secret of the Christian."

1. **The Source of Joy in Your Life (John 15:11).**

    A. **The Center of Joy for the Christian Is Christ.** "My joy," He says, ". . . in you." Christian joy is Christ's joy in us.

    B. **The Characteristic of Joy.** Jesus wants our joy to be full. Peter called it "joy unspeakable and full of glory" (1 Pet. 1:8). It's not an incomplete, imperfect, almost-type of joy. It is fully orbed and rich.

    C. **The Continuity of Joy.** "These things I have spoken to you, that My joy may remain in you." Have you noticed how easily earthly joy can leave? Nothing seems stable in the world, does it? But the joy of Christ is a continual, never-ending, absolutely constant joy when we follow the principles of Scripture. This joy even survives the difficult times in life. It isn't intermittent or hinged on happenings but on a person (John 16:22; James 1:2; and Acts 16:25). That's why Nehemiah 8:10 says, "The joy of the Lord is your strength." I was a hospital chaplain while in seminary, and I found it quite easy to determine whether people were saved when I walked into the family room. Oh, there were tears and sorrow, but there was a kind of deep abiding stability in the lives of people who knew Jesus Christ. At that moment you wouldn't call it the joy of the Lord, but that's what the Bible calls it.

2. **The Secret of Joy in Your Life.** You say, "Pastor, I am a Christian, but why don't I have the joy of the Lord?" Well, I can't answer that question for all of you, but let me go through some basic things we need if we're going to have the joy of the Lord.

   A. **Surrender Your Life to Christ.** The secret of joy begins when you surrender yourself to Him. David prayed, "Restore to me the joy of my salvation" (Ps. 51:12; also see Ps. 35:9; Acts 8:8, 39).

   B. **Submit Yourself Totally to the Spirit of God (Rom. 14:7; 1 Thess. 1:6).** Joy and the Holy Spirit go together. Galatians 5:22 calls joy a fruit of the Spirit. An interesting testimony to this comes from the life of a great teacher of the past named Walter Wilson. In his early days of ministry, Wilson felt fruitless. He was a hard worker, but there was little evidence of God's working through him. One day a friend asked: "Dr. Wilson, what is the Holy Spirit to you?" Wilson replied, "He's one of the persons of the Godhead, a teacher, a guide, a third person of the Trinity." His friend said, "You haven't answered my question—what is the Holy Spirit *to you?*" Wilson answered truthfully, "He is nothing to me. I have no contact with Him . . . I could get along quite well without Him." Later Wilson heard Dr. James Gray preaching about the filling of the Holy Spirit. At the end of the service, Wilson returned to his motel, fell on the carpet, and began to pray, offering himself to the control of the Holy Spirit. Dr. Wilson was a changed man from that moment and went on to become one of the most joyful and powerful preachers of his generation.

   C. **Study the Word of God.** In 1 John 1:4, we read, "These things we write to you that your joy may be full." Jesus said, "These things I have spoken to you that you . . . that your joy may be full" (John 15:11).

   D. **Spend Time with God in Prayer.** John 16:24 says, "Ask, and you will receive, that your joy may be full" (also see Ps. 16:11).

Conclusion: I'm sure you're wondering, "Pastor, can't you come up with anything more original then receiving Christ, submitting to the Spirit, reading the Bible, and praying?" Well, you know I like to be original but that's just the bedrock simplicity of what it means to have joy in Christ. It's not joy without tears or without sorrow. But it is a kind of joy you will never experience any place else until you find Christ in your own life.

STATS, STORIES, AND MORE

More from Dr. Jeremiah
I have a preacher friend named Tom Wallace who used to pastor a church in Maryland, and he told of a fellow who came into his congregation one Sunday morning. He just walked in off the street. He was an unkempt fellow who obviously hadn't been in church for a long time. He came about half way into the congregation and sat down. That morning, Dr. Wallace preached in great power, and this man heard the clear presentation of the Gospel of Jesus Christ. When the invitation was given, he slipped out from where he was standing and came forward to give his life to Christ. Now, Dr. Wallace was involved in a church where they didn't mess around with long periods of time between conversion and baptism. If you come forward in the morning to get saved, they baptized you after the service. And so they told this fellow that he was going to be baptized and he was excited because he was really happy in the Lord. Dr. Wallace said something happened that day that never happened before in all his ministry. This uncultured, uneducated man, who had found Christ, went down into the water in his baptism, and when he came out of the water, he jumped up and down clapping his hands shouting, "Hot dog! Hot dog!" He hadn't had time to learn proper etiquette, that you are supposed to say, "Amen! Praise the Lord! Hallelujah!" All he knew was "Hot dog!" but it conveyed his joy in Jesus.

APPROPRIATE HYMNS AND SONGS

"All I Once Held Dear," Graham Kendrick, 1993 Make Way Music (Admin. Music Services).

"Sing for Joy," Lament Hiebert, 1996 Integrity's Hosanna! Music.

"Let It Rise," Holland Davis, 1997, 1999 Maranatha Praise, Inc. (Admin. The Copyright Co.).

"Joy Unspeakable," Barney E. Warren, Warner Press.

FOR THE BULLETIN

John Hus, the Reformer of Prague, was summoned to Constance in 1414 on charges of heresy. Though promised safe conduct, he was quickly arrested. On June 10, 1415, he wrote to his followers in Bohemia: *I write this letter to you in prison, bound with chains and expecting on the morrow the sentence of death, yet fully trusting in God that I shall not swerve from his truth nor swear denial of the errors, whereof I have been charged by false witnesses. What grace God hath shown me, and how he helps me in the midst of strange temptations, you will know when by his mercy we meet in joy in his presence.* Twenty-six days later, Hus died at the stake. ● Thomas Hawkes was martyred in England on June 10, 1555, for refusing to baptize a baby. ● On June 10, 1752, Benjamin Franklin's kite was struck by lightning. ● The American Bible Union was founded on June 10, 1850, by Baptists who had withdrawn from the American and Foreign Bible Society. ● Richard Allen was ordained a minister in the Methodist Episcopal Church on June 10, 1854. ● Edwin O. Excell died on this day in 1921. Excell, who was saved during a Methodist revival, became a popular gospel songwriter and publisher during the Ira Sankey era. His hymns number more than 2,000, including "Since I Have Been Redeemed" and "Count Your Blessings." He died while on an evangelistic tour with Gypsy Smith. ● Alcoholics Anonymous was founded on this day in 1935 in Akron, Ohio, by William G. Wilson and Robert Smith.

WORSHIP HELPS

Call to Worship
Therefore my heart is glad, and my glory rejoices . . . You will show me the path of life; in Your presence is fullness of joy; at Your right hand are pleasures forevermore (Ps. 16:9, 11).

Pastoral Prayer
Lord God, I pray that You will place within each of us today in this service the determination that we will be thankful at all times, for all things. Whatever You bring into our lives, whatever You allow us to experience, give us the spirit of gratitude. For Lord, we are of all people, most blessed. We give You praise for eternal life and salvation in Jesus Christ. We lift up our voices in gratitude and thanksgiving to You for You alone are worthy. We praise Your name. We honor You and magnify You, and with thanksgiving in our hearts, we bring this prayer to You today. In Jesus' name I pray, Amen.   —Dr. David Jeremiah

Kid's Talk

Ask the children if they know the difference between jokes and joy? You might tell them a couple of "why did the chicken cross the road" jokes. Why did the rooster cross the road? To cockadoodle dooo something. Why did the chicken cross the basketball court? He heard the referee calling fowls. Why did the chicken cross the road, roll in the mud, and cross the road again? Because he was a dirty double-crosser. Why did the chicken cross the playground? To get to the other slide. Explain that jokes make us laugh, but joy makes us smile. It's harder to smile than to laugh, because our faces should almost always have a smile on them, while laughter occurs when something strikes us as funny. Joy comes from within, and it depends on Jesus. That's why joy is even better than jokes.

PRAYER FOR THE PASTOR'S CLOSET

Patience for the Wayward

Lord, help me not to be impatient with Thy sheep! They may be diseased and willful and wayward, but help me to remember they are not wolves. Help me to feed, not club, Thy Sheep!

—SAMUEL LOGAN BRENGLE[1]

---

[1] Clarence W. Hall, *Samuel Logan Brengle: Portrait of a Prophet* (Atlanta: The Salvation Army Supplies and Purchasing Department, 1933), p. 148.

Additional Sermons and Lesson Ideas

Dreams and Goals

Date preached:

By Dr. Larry Osborne

SCRIPTURE: Various, especially Proverbs 16:9

INTRODUCTION: Scripture gives us some great principles to put our dreams and goals into perspective.

    1. How Dreams Become Nightmares:
       A. We Choose the Wrong Goals (Eccl. 2:1–11).
       B. We Take the Wrong Path (Prov. 14:12; 16:25).
    2. Pursuing Your Dreams:
       A. Dream Big, but Be Realistic (1 Chr. 4:9–10; Rom. 12:3; Prov. 12:11; 13:16; 14:8; 28:19).
       B. Just Because I Could, Doesn't Mean I Should (Matt. 16:26; 1 Chr. 22:5–10; John 8:28; Prov. 16:2).
       C. Never Trade Your Family for Your Dream (1 Tim. 5:8; Eph. 5:22—6:4).
       D. Be Patient: Glaciers Produce More than Avalanches (1 Pet. 5:6; Acts 7:23–36; Prov. 12:24; 13:4; Prov. 19:2).
       E. If I Can't Be Happy Here: I Won't Be Happy There (Phil. 4:11–13).

CONCLUSION: A man's heart plans his way, but the Lord directs his steps (Prov. 16:9).

The God of Jacob

Date preached:

Based on a Sermon by Rev. C. G. Moore

SCRIPTURE: Selections from Genesis 25—48

INTRODUCTION: From Jacob's life as recorded in Genesis, we can be encouraged by some key characteristics of The God of Jacob:

    1. He Planned and Sought the Very Best for His Servant (Gen. 25:23).
    2. He Appointed His Servant's Discipline and Sustained Him Under It (Gen. 30:27; 31:5, 42).
    3. He Helped His Servant Through Life's Sore Dreads (32:3—33:11).
    4. He Redeemed His Servant from All Harm and Crowned His Life with Grace (48:15–16).

CONCLUSION: Will the God who sought the best for Jacob, who disciplined and sustained him, who helped him through life's dreads to his dying day, will He not also do the same for us? "Happy is he who has the God of Jacob for his help, whose hope is in the Lord his God" (Ps. 146:5).

HEROES FOR THE PASTOR'S HEART

John Newton

You probably know something of the remarkable life of John Newton. He was a prodigal, an infidel, a slave trader, a backslider, and a miserable failure who deserted his post, was flogged aboard ship, and eventually became the slave of a slave. But he was later claimed as a trophy for Christ, becoming one of England's greatest preachers and the author of "Amazing Grace."

What you may not know is that he wrote many other great hymns that have been largely lost to general usage. Newton worked as hard each week on his Sunday hymn as on his weekly sermon. His poetry came right out of his Bible study, and many of his hymns are poetic renditions of the Bible stories from which he was preaching, particularly from the Old Testament. Examples include "Alas! Elisha's Servant Cried," "The Lion that on Samson Roared," and "Poor Esau Repented Too Late."

Other hymns merge great theology with autobiographical insight. Newton wrote through the sieve of his own experience, so that—just as in "Amazing Grace"—his personal testimony shines through in ways that allow us to identify with him. And Newton was very honest.

I'll give you one example, and then let you search out the others for yourself.

Here is Newton's hymn, "Conflicting Feelings," also known by its first line, "Strange and Mysterious Is My Life." As you read it, you'll probably be reminded of the apostle Paul's confession in Romans 7 of the conflicting passions ricocheting within him.

If you want to sing this hymn, it's often set to the tune SOLID ROCK ("My Hope Is Built on Nothing Less"), with the last line of each stanza repeated. Let it whet your appetite for more spiritual contemplations on the forgotten hymns of John Newton.

Strange and mysterious is my life.
What opposites I feel within!

Continued on the next page

HEROES FOR THE PASTOR'S HEART—*Continued*

A stable peace, a constant strife;
The rule of grace, the power of sin:
Too often I am captive led,
Yet daily triumph in my Head,

I prize the privilege of prayer,
But oh! what backwardness to pray!
Though on the Lord I cast my care,
I feel its burden every day;
I seek His will in all I do,
Yet find my own is working too.

I call the promises my own,
And prize them more than mines of gold;
Yet though their sweetness I have known,
They leave me unimpressed and cold
One hour upon the truth I feed,
The next I know not what I read.

I love the holy day of rest,
When Jesus meets His gathered saints;
Sweet day, of all the week the best!
For its return my spirit pants:
Yet often, through my unbelief,
It proves a day of guilt and grief.

While on my Savior I rely,
I know my foes shall lose their aim,
And therefore dare their power defy,
Assured of conquest through His Name,
But soon my confidence is slain,
And all my fears return again.

Thus different powers within me strive,
And grace and sin by turns prevail;
I grieve, rejoice, decline, revive,
And victory hangs in doubtful scale:
But Jesus has His promise passed,
That grace shall overcome at last.

JUNE 17, 2007

FATHER'S DAY   SUGGESTED SERMON

Walking with Christ: A Fresh Vision for Discipleship

Date preached:

By Dr. Timothy Beougher

Scripture: Colossians 2:6–7; Ephesians 4:11–13, especially Colossians 2:6–7
As you therefore have received Christ Jesus the Lord, so walk in Him, rooted and built up in Him and established in the faith, as you have been taught, abounding in it with thanksgiving.

Introduction: Often we ask children, "What do you want to be when you grow up?" We typically get a variety of responses: a fireman, a professional athlete, a teacher, a doctor, a race car driver, etc. Most of us changed our answers over the years and probably ended up doing something different than we thought. I want us to reflect this morning not on the first part of the question, but on the last part, ". . . when you grow up." In the New Testament, the word "disciple" means a learner or a follower. A disciple is one who walks with Christ, who grows in his or her relationship with Christ. Just as is true in the physical world, growth in one's spiritual life requires food and exercise. Spiritual maturity is not automatic, but it is God's goal for us.

1. **Walking with Christ Has a Beginning (Col. 2:6a).** Walking with Christ has a beginning, and that beginning is to receive Christ Jesus as Lord, "As you therefore have received Christ Jesus the Lord . . ." (v. 6a). So how do we do that? How do we receive Christ Jesus as Lord? We hear the message of the gospel and respond with repentance and faith. You can't walk with Christ until you first receive Him as Lord and Savior. Have you received Christ as your Lord and Savior?

2. **Walking with Christ Involves Action (Col. 2:6b–7; Eph. 4:11–12a).** Coming to know Christ as Lord is wonderful, but it is only a beginning. Walking with Christ involves action. The believer's life must be lived in constant fellowship with Christ. Colossians 2:7 amplifies how this is possible: "rooted and built up in Him and established

in the faith . . ." One image here is that of a tree. We only see what is above ground; we can't see the roots. But it is the root system that provides support and nourishment to the tree. Strong roots stabilize growth. Another image in this verse is that of a building. We must build on the foundation, which is Jesus Christ (see 1 Cor. 3:11–15). So what materials are we using to build? The verse continues, ". . . as you have been taught" (Col. 2:7b; see also Eph. 4:11–12a). If God has provided individuals to help us learn and grow, are we taking advantage of those opportunities? You will never grow physically if you don't eat and exercise. You don't grow spiritually if you don't eat and exercise spiritually.

3. **Walking with Christ Produces Results (Col. 2:7; Eph. 4:12–13).** What are the results of walking with Christ? One result is that we become strengthened or established in the faith. When the storms of life howl around us, we are able to hold our ground securely. Another result is that we will be abounding with thanksgiving (Col. 2:7b). Gratitude implies dependence. When we walk with Christ, one result will be that our lives will overflow with thanksgiving. Ephesians 4:12–13 give us additional results of walking with Christ, "so that the body of Christ may be built up until we all reach unity in the faith and in the knowledge of the Son of God and become mature, attaining to the whole measure of the fullness of Christ" (NIV). When we walk with Christ, the body of Christ, the church, is built up.

Evaluation: Are you further along in your walk with Christ today than you were when you first came to know Christ as Lord and Savior? Are you more mature spiritually than you were last year at this time? We will all face setbacks, but what is the trend of your life? It is growth or stagnation? Are you growing? Remember the starting point: receiving Christ. If you know Christ, are you growing?

Conclusion: Fathers, I want to take just a moment to speak to you on this Father's Day. You must first be concerned about your own spiritual maturity, for your child watches what you do more than he or she listens to what you say. Secondly, I want to challenge you to make the spiritual development and mentoring of your entire family of highest priority in your life. You are the leaders of your household, and the Lord will hold you accountable for your spiritual leadership.

STATS, STORIES, AND MORE

Both Glad and Sorry
A fable was once told about three men traveling across the desert. They encountered an old prospector who told them a few miles ahead was a dry creek bed. He told them they should gather as many rocks out of the bottom as they could, and in the morning they would be both glad and sorry. The next morning they discovered the stones had turned into diamonds and the words of the prospector came back to them, "you'll be both glad and sorry." They were glad for what they had picked up, but sorry they had not taken the time to gather even more. That fable is a picture of our life. It costs us energy, time, and discipline to mature spiritually, but in hindsight we are sorry we didn't invest more!

Tap into the Power
Jim Davis tells the story of a lady who owned a small house on the seashore of Ireland at the turn of the century. She was wealthy, but frugal. When electricity was offered along the coast, some of her friends were surprised that she had it installed in her home. Several weeks after the installation, a meter reader came to her door, and asked if her electricity was working okay. She assured him that it was. He then said, "Could you explain something to me? Your meter shows hardly any usage. Are you sure everything is okay?" "Certainly," the woman said. "Each evening when the sun sets, I turn on my lights just long enough to light my candles, then I turn them off." The woman had tapped into the power of electricity, but wasn't using it. Her house was connected, but her habits had not changed to draw upon that power. If you know Christ, the power of Christ has saved you. Will you let the power of Christ now transform you?

More from Dr. Beougher
When my wife and I got married, we knew we were supposed to be one, but the problem was figuring out which "one" it was! I say that with a twist of humor, but in all seriousness, we had to learn quickly that Christ is the One. He is the decision maker, the head of our marriage, and the head of our family.

APPROPRIATE HYMNS AND SONGS

"Faith of Our Fathers," Frederick W. Faber/Henri F. Hemy, Public Domain.

"Walking in the Spirit," David Morris, 1986 Integrity's Hosanna! Music.

"I Am a Man," Jack Hayford/Jean Sibelius, 1994 Annamarie Music (Admin. Maranatha Music).

"Make Me a Servant," Kelly Willard, 1982 Maranatha Music (Admin. Copyright Co.) (Willing Heart Music).

"God of Our Fathers," Daniel C. Roberts/George Warren, Public Domain.

FOR THE BULLETIN

Another wave of persecution in the Roman Empire began on June 17, 362, when Emperor Julian the Apostate ordered that all educators be licensed before teaching, in an effort to prevent the Christian education of young people. On this same day in 1963, the U.S. Supreme Court outlawed classroom prayer and Bible reading in American schools. ● Today is the birthday, in 1703, of John Wesley, the founder of Methodism. This is also the "birthday" of the village of Herrnhut on the eastern flanks of Germany, which began after Moravian refugees asked Count Ludwig von Zinzendorf for shelter. Christian David felled the first tree to establish this Moravian center on June 17, 1722. ● On June 17, 1822, the first elders were elected in the African Methodist Episcopal (A.M.E.) Church in New York City. ● Presbyterian evangelist J. Wilbur Chapman was born on June 17, 1859, in Richmond, Indiana. He held pastorates in four different states before devoting most of his ministry to evangelism. He worked closely with D. L. Moody, and, along with his songleader, Charles M. Alexander, become the first to circle the globe with the Gospel. ● On June 17, 1873, evangelist D. L. Moody and his songleader, Ira Sankey, arrived in Liverpool, England, for their first evangelistic endeavor there. Unfortunately, the three men who invited them were unavailable to help them. Two had died, and the third had forgotten about the invitation. It nonetheless was the beginning of a powerful evangelistic period in Moody's life in which millions in England heard him preach. ● On June 17, 1885, the Statue of Liberty arrived in New York City aboard the French ship *Isere*.

Quote for the Pastor's Wall

The preacher is not sent to merely induce men to join the church . . . The work of the ministry is to change unbelieving sinners into praying and believing saints.

—REV. E. M. BOUNDS

Call to Worship

Stand up and bless the LORD your God forever and ever! Blessed be Your glorious name, which is exalted above all blessing and praise! You alone are the LORD; You have made heaven, the heaven of heavens, with all their host, the earth and everything on it, the seas and all that is in them, and You preserve them all. The host of heaven worships You (Neh. 9:5–6).

An Invitation to Salvation

During His time on earth, Jesus was always inviting people to become His followers. He said to those by the Sea of Galilee, "Follow Me." He invited His listeners to come to Him, to come by faith, to come for healing, to come for hope, to come for happiness. He said, "Come to Me, all you who labor and are heavy laden, and I will give you rest" (Matt. 11:28). He said, "If anyone desires to come after Me, let him deny himself, and take up his cross, and follow Me" (Matt. 16:24).

Perhaps today you feel that Christ Himself is speaking just to you. Imagine if He were in this room, giving this invitation. What would you do? He really is in this room. He really is inviting you to become His child, His follower, His disciple. I'm going to ask you to leave your seat and come down one of the aisles. Someone will meet you here and pray with you. Come now. Come willingly. Come courageously. Don't worry about what anyone else thinks; this is your time with Christ. He is calling you as an individual, calling you as a couple, calling you as a family. He died for you and rose again. His blood washes away your sins, and He can give you new life if you'll come. Come to Christ now, while there's still time, while you still can.

> *Only a step to Jesus!*
> *O why not come and say,*
> *"Gladly to Thee my Savior,*
> *I give myself away."*
> —FANNY CROSBY

Additional Sermons and Lesson Ideas

A Choice Each Day

Date preached:

SCRIPTURE: Psalm 106 (NIV)

INTRODUCTION: Every day brings its own set of challenges. The writer of Psalm 106 presents a decision we have to make each morning that will determine our attitude for the next twenty-four hours.

1. We believe His promises and sing His praise. Verse 12 says: "Then they believed His promises and sang His praise." This passage recounts the story of the Israelites at the Red Sea. When we search out and claim God's promises for each new day, our hearts are dominated by an attitude of praise.
2. We don't believe His promises and grumble. Verse 24 says: "They did not believe His promise. They grumbled in their tents." This tells about the Israelites in the wilderness and show us that an attitude of grumbling, depression, and irritability is the result of acting as though the promises of God were not true.

CONCLUSION: What promise do you need for this week? Remember how Psalm 106 ends: "Blessed be the LORD God of Israel, from everlasting to everlasting! And let all the people say, 'Amen!' Praise the LORD."

Moses My Man

Date preached:

By Dr. Melvin Worthington

SCRIPTURE: Hebrews 11:23–29

INTRODUCTION: This Father's Day, let's look at the characteristics of a man of God:

1. The Parental Faith (v. 23). Moses' parent's faith kept them from killing him as instructed by the Egyptians when he was born.
2. The Personal Faith (vv. 24–25). Moses' personal faith includes *his circumstances: a refusal* (v. 24) and *his choice: a rejection* (v. 25).
3. The Perceptive Faith (v. 26). Moses' perceptive faith includes *his recognition* and *his respect.*
4. The Pioneering Faith (v. 27). Moses' pioneering faith includes *his forsaking* and *focusing.*
5. The Persevering Faith (vv. 28–29). Moses' persevering faith includes *the observance of the Passover* and *the Omnipotent's power.*

CONCLUSION: Moses illustrates in a powerful way the truth, "the just shall live by faith" (Rom. 1:17).

Hit the Road, Jack: The Pastor's Family Vacation

We pastors should take our vacations religiously. No one needs getaways more than preachers, and you should probably start planning one right now. We try our hardest to be super-human (in a sanctified way, of course); but our work, when seriously undertaken, is exhausting even for superheroes. Jesus said that "virtue" went of Him, and most of us have little enough of *that* to begin with. Remember that God Himself rested on the seventh day; and our Lord Jesus took breathers during His earthly ministry. He came apart to rest awhile, and He told His followers to do the same.

If vacations provide relief from the stress and strain of pastoring and offer irreplaceable family time, why do pastors skimp on R & R?

One reason is guilt. Many pastors feel badly for taking time away from their responsibilities. There's nothing like the pangs of guilt that hit me on a Sunday morning when I'm splashing in the surf instead of standing in the pulpit. But I've learned that if I take a deep breath, say a prayer, and apply another coat of suntan lotion, I can get over it.

Yes, but someone has to be with Deacon Jones as he faces a life-threatening outpatient surgery at 5 A.M. Monday morning. And who will conduct prayer meeting while you're away, lock up the building, drain the baptistery, visit the hospital, console the afflicted, counsel the troubled, bury the dead, turn off the lights, and change the witticism on the church sign? And who, oh who, will preach on Sunday morning?

How can we possible leave these things in the hands of *amateurs?*

Well, not to be too blunt—we're not as indispensable as we think. If we had a heart attack, plane crash, or nervous breakdown, the work would go right on. If you keeled over today, the world would keep spinning at the same speed. The Lord's church did

Continued on the next page

HELPS FOR THE PASTOR'S FAMILY—_Continued_

all right before we came, and it'll manage after we're gone. The kingdom will survive for ten or so days without you and me.

Still worried? Try this. Gather your board informally and, using a suitably grave ministerial voice, explain that the Lord is calling you away for a few days. You'll be in a remote location without phone service, fax machines, Internet access, cellular communications, or smoke signals. "If an emergency should arrive," you can say after a somber pause, "here's a number to notify authorities who will send a search team for us." Pause again, then say: "It's my wife's fault. She planned this trip. She felt I needed to get away . . . (cough slightly) . . . for my health."

Find a few faithful souls and deputize them; and then take off and don't look back. There's nothing as refreshing as the sight of our churches disappearing in the rearview mirror for a few days. Someone once said, "A vacation is what you take when you can't take what you're taking any more."Here's something else to keep in mind. Believe it or not, the Lord can actually bless your people in your absence. No one can preach like you, of course— but perhaps your people need a break from excellence. When the great Scottish preacher, Robert Murray McCheyne took an extended trip to recover his health, he left his congregation in the hands of an inexperienced young man named William Burns— and revival broke out.

Sometimes we pastors fear being criticized for our time away. Not to worry; you could be criticized for worse things. In his biography of Charles Haddon Spurgeon, Lewis Drummond told of a time when the great preacher was standing on the platform of a train station, chatting with a fellow minister. As the train boarded, the other minister cast a critical eye at Spurgeon's first class ticket. He said to Charles, "I am going to the third class section of the train to save the Lord's money." To which Spurgeon replied, "Well, I am going to the first class section of the train to save the Lord's servant."

Reminds me of another well-known preacher who advised a group of elders to take _heed to themselves_ and to all the flock over which the Holy Spirit had made them overseers. There comes a time when the best way of taking care of others is to first take care of ourselves.

Call it decompression—time to unbuckle your belt, rest your oars, take off your shoes, relax your load, close your eyes, catch your breath, enjoy your kids, love your wife, sharpen your ax, practice your backstroke, and read your Bible looking for personal nourishment rather than sermon outlines.

Perhaps you're thinking you can't afford the money, but it can be done cheaply. If you shop around, you can even find Alaskan cruises or European packages for a few hundred dollars. My wife and I found a great deal by booking a cruise during hurricane season. We paid and prayed! Some of America's finest hotels have off-season rates, and by comparison shopping you can book a five-star room for what Trucker Joe is paying for an eight-by-twelve two-bit room, no phone, no pool, no pets.

Try state and national parks; and if you can't afford a mansion over the hilltop, try a tent or a cottage—why should you care? Just find some peace in the valley down by the riverside.

Remember that the Lord is a great believer in vacations. Notice how many feasts and festivals He built into the calendar for the ancient Israelites. One day every week, a bunch of weeks each year, and one whole year off every fifty.

Jesus had His remote spots. David preferred green pastures, John the Baptist liked the desert, and Isaiah went native. Elijah knew a nice little spot under a juniper tree, and Jonah . . . well, don't follow his example. His voyage was interrupted mid-cruise, and he didn't get a refund on the cancelled portion of the trip.

It'll turn out better for you. Why not gather your family around a calendar later today. Find a week or two that will work for everyone, draw a line through it, make sure it's on everyone's schedule, decide where you want to go, and pack your bags. Get on the bus. See the USA in a Chevrolet. Let Hertz put you in the driver's seat. Fly the friendly skies. Put a tiger in your tank. Hit the road. Head for the border.

Just pick your slogan and go. Chances are your church will still be standing when you return.

JUNE 24, 2007

SUGGESTED SERMON

The Mysteries of His Love and the Testing of Our Faith

Date preached:

By Rev. Larry Kirk

Scripture: John 11:1–27, especially verse 4
. . . "This sickness is not unto death, but for the glory of God, that the Son of God may be glorified through it."

Introduction: During our trials, we all have asked, "If God loves me so much, why would this be happening?" The story that follows taught Mary, Martha, and Lazarus, the disciples of Jesus, and can teach us all today this invaluable lesson: many things that seem mysterious to us are ordained by love for God's glory and our good.

1. **Sometimes It Seems the Love of Christ Makes Little Difference (11:3–6).** Verse 3 introduces a difficult concept to understand: the relationship between the love of Christ and the suffering of His loved ones.

   A. **If Jesus Loved Lazarus, Why Was He Sick (vv. 3–4)?** John, in his Gospel, went way out of his way to stress the special relationship that Jesus had with this family. Staying with this family in Bethany was not just a matter of convenience but of companionship. As John wrote, Jesus loved them. It is the fact of this special love for them that explains the unique way the sisters worded their message to Jesus: "Lord, behold, he whom You love is sick" (John 11:3). Jesus answers in verse four, that it will ultimately be for His glory.

   B. **Why Did Jesus Tarry (vv. 5–6)?** Why does He make them wait? Later on verse 17 tells us that when Jesus finally walked into the village Lazarus had already been in the tomb for four days. It probably took the messenger one day to reach Jesus, after which Jesus waited two more days before leaving; it would have then taken Him one full day to get to the village of Bethany. That also means Lazarus must have died soon after the messenger left. It must have seemed like four long days! We will see that Jesus didn't want to heal a sick man, but raise a dead man!

2. **Sometimes It Seems the Word of Christ Isn't True (v. 4).** Jesus says something very perplexing when the messenger told Jesus of Lazarus, "This sickness is not unto death, but for the glory of God, that the Son of God may be glorified through it" (v. 4). I imagine that to the sisters and anyone else who heard what Jesus said it may have seemed as if His words had not been true. Lazarus had died after all. We learn that the relationship between God's promise and providence can be puzzling. Sometimes we need to trust to take us where understanding cannot go. We often have to say: "Lord I do not understand but I trust in You."

3. **Sometimes It Seems the Way of Christ Doesn't Make Sense (vv. 5–16).** Jesus, after waiting for two days, told the disciples they would return to Judea. To the disciples it seemed incredibly foolish to return there where the Jews sought to stone Him.

4. **In the Midst of Mysteries, We Must Trust in Jesus Christ (vv. 17–44).** We also know that in every way Christ proves worthy of all our trust.

   A. **The Love of Christ Makes All the Difference.** Christ delayed coming to Bethany for two days, not in spite of His love but because of His love. Because of His great love for His friends He submitted to His Father's timetable. Waiting is allowed for the same reason that the test was sent. The delays of Christ are the delays of love; the help of Christ always comes at the right time. In the end, Christ's love makes all the difference in the world.

   B. **The Word of Christ Proves Itself Completely True.** In the end the death of Lazarus, the delay of Jesus in returning, the danger that Jesus and the disciples faced in returning to Judea, all served a higher purpose in the plan of God. The waiting made the miracle more wonderful! This whole incident was preparing the disciples for what they were about to experience with the resurrected Jesus!

   C. **The Way of Christ Proves to Be Absolutely Right.** One thing that is clear in the Bible is that the love of God and of Christ is not synonymous with safety as we often think of it. God's love is real and reliable but is not tame and predictable. God knows what you are made for and in love He calls you into a drama that is not only good but glorious for you and for Him.

Conclusion: Trust Jesus Christ, for His love will rescue you at just the right time, even if not in this lifetime. Remember that through His love, through His own resurrection, if you have committed your life to Him, He has rescued you eternally.

STATS, STORIES, AND MORE

Feeling Puzzled by God's Ways
St. Theresa, a 16th century reformer stood mired in the mud on one of her journeys and she cried out to God, "If this is the way You treat Your friends, no wonder You don't have many!" Lots of people have felt that way at times.

The Mysteries of God's Ways
There is an old Jewish story about trusting in the truth of God's Word even when faced with the mysteries of God's ways. It's the imaginary story of the prophet Elijah on a journey with a Rabbi Jachanan. Both the Rabbi and the prophet were well aware of the teachings of God's Word but the prophet had revelation into the mysteries of God's ways.

The story says that they walked all day and at nightfall they came to the humble cottage of a poor man whose only treasure was a cow. The poor man ran out of the cottage, and his wife ran, too, to welcome the strangers for the night and to offer them all of the simple hospitality that they were able to give in their poor circumstances in life. Elijah and the Rabbi were given plenty of the cow's good milk and sustained by homemade bread and butter and they were put to sleep in the best bed while their kind hosts lay down on the floor. In the morning, the poor man's cow was dead.

They walked all day the next day, and came that evening to the house of a very wealthy merchant, whose hospitality they craved. The merchant was cold and proud and rich and all that he would do for the prophet and the rabbi was to lodge them in a cow shed and feed them on bread and water. In the morning however Elijah thanked him very much for what he had done and sent for a mason to repair one of his walls which happened to be falling down as a return for his kindness.

The Rabbi Jachanan was unable to keep silence any longer and he begged the prophet to explain these dealings with people. The prophet said, "In regard to the poor man who received us so hospitably it was decreed that his wife was to die that night but in reward for his goodness, God took the cow instead of the wife. I repaired the wall of the rich man because a chest of gold was concealed near the place and if the miser had repaired the wall himself, he would have discovered the treasure. Say not therefore to the Lord, what doest thou. But say in thy heart: 'Must not the Lord, of all the earth do right?'"

APPROPRIATE HYMNS AND SONGS

"'Tis So Sweet," Louisa M. R. Stead/Steve Adams, 1981 Bridge Building Music (Brentwood Benson Music Publishing Inc.).

"Dare to Be a Daniel," Philip P. Bliss, Public Domain.

"Have Faith in God," B. B. McKinney, 1934. Renewed 1962 Broadman Press ARR (Distributed by Genevox Music Group).

"His Eyes," Steven Curtis Chapman/James Isaac Elliot, 1988 Careers BMG Music Publishing, Inc./Sparrow Song (div. of EMI Christian Music Publishing).

"My Faith Has Found a Resting Place," Lidie H. Edmunds/Andre Gretry, Public Domain.

FOR THE BULLETIN

On June 24, A.D. 64, the Roman Emperor Nero unleashed a horrific period of persecution against Christians. ● Today is the birthday, June 24, 1485, of the German reformer Johannes Bugenhagen. He assisted Martin Luther with his German Bible translation and become one of Luther's staunchest allies. On this day in 1499, another Luther ally was born—Johann Brenz who advanced the reformation in southern Germany. John Calvin's associate, disciple, and successor, Theodore Beza, was born on this day in 1519. ● Henry Venn died on June 24, 1797. He was a pastor and revivalist in England during the days of George Whitefield, with whom he was close friends. During his final debilitating illness, his role as a prayer warrior was described by a grandson: "He often declared that he never felt more fervency of devotion than whilst imploring spiritual blessings on his children and friends, and especially for the success of those who were still engaged in the ministry of the blessed gospel, from which he was himself laid aside. For himself, his prayer was that he might die to the glory of Christ." The doctor treating him observed that the joy he felt at his near departure was actually counterproductive and giving stimulus to his life. ● Other birthdays today include George J. Webb (1803), American church organist best known for composing the melody to the hymn, "Stand Up, Stand Up for Jesus." And American pulpiteer, Henry Ward Beecher, who was born in 1813.

WORSHIP HELPS

Call to Worship

Be exalted, O LORD, in Your own strength! We will sing and praise Your power (Ps. 21:13).

Reader's Theater (Or Responsive Reading)

Reader 1: The LORD is my rock and my fortress and my deliverer; the God of my strength, in whom I will trust; my shield and the horn of my salvation, my stronghold and my refuge; my Savior, You save me from violence. I will call upon the LORD, who is worthy to be praised; so shall I be saved from my enemies (2 Sam. 22:2–4).

Reader 2: In my distress I called upon the LORD, and cried out to my God; He heard my voice from His temple, and my cry entered His ears (2 Sam. 22:7).

Reader 3: He delivered me from my strong enemy, from those who hated me; for they were too strong for me. They confronted me in the day of my calamity, but the LORD was my support. He also brought me out into a broad place; He delivered me because He delighted in me (2 Sam. 22:18–20).

Reader 1: For You are my lamp, O LORD; the LORD shall enlighten my darkness (2 Sam. 22:29).

Reader 2: As for God, His way is perfect; the word of the LORD is proven; He is a shield to all who trust in Him. For who is God, except the LORD? And who is a rock, except our God? God is my strength and power, and He makes my way perfect (2 Sam. 22:31–33).

Reader 3: The LORD lives! Blessed be my Rock! Let God be exalted, the Rock of my salvation (2 Sam. 22:47)!

Additional Sermons and Lesson Ideas

A Hope, a Promise, and a Message

Date preached:

SCRIPTURE: Titus 1:1–3

INTRODUCTION: Writing to his friend and associate, Titus, the apostle Paul began his letter with a dose of deep truth about eternal life. Speaking of those who share "the faith of God's elect and the acknowledgment of the truth" (v. 1), Paul said that in Christ we have everlasting life, which he described as:

1. A Hope (v. 2: "in hope of eternal life"). It is a sure and certain prospect which should make our lives hopeful and optimistic.
2. A Promise (v. 2: ". . . which God, who cannot lie, promised before time began").
3. A Message (v. 3: ". . . but has in due time manifested His word through preaching"). It's our message to the world, the Good News that death is destroyed through the Cross and empty tomb of Christ, giving us the right through Him of living forever.

CONCLUSION: Almost everyone wonders, often late at night when darkness fills our bedrooms, how much longer we have to live. For the Christian, the answer is—forever! Eternal life is *your* hope, *your* promise, and *your* message.

The Flesh or the Spirit?

Date preached:

Based on a Sermon by Dr. W. Graham Scroggie

SCRIPTURE: Galatians 5:17–18

INTRODUCTION: These two verses offer great insight to the biggest spiritual conflict in every human's life:

1. Man's Fallen Nature (v. 17). The idea of the "lust" in this passage refers not to a sexual lust, but to a universal state of being. All men and women have sinned and thus are separated from God (Rom. 3:23).
2. The Human Personality (v. 17). A great conflict is introduced into the human personality in these verses. The Spirit and the flesh are in opposition to one another.
3. The Way of Blessing (v. 18). The key to overcoming our fallen nature and the opposition between the flesh and the Spirit is simple: follow the Spirit's leading.

CONCLUSION: Are you being constantly dragged along by your flesh and its selfish desires? Enthrone Christ as Lord in your life and allow His Spirit to win the battle against your flesh!

Finding New Words for Old Truths: From Humdrum to Hallelujah

The American writer Barnaby Conrad was badly gored in a bullfight in Spain in 1958. Later, two actors, Eva Gabor and Noel Coward, were overheard talking about the incident in a New York restaurant. "Noel, dahling," said Eva, "have you heard the news about poor Bahnaby? He vas terribly gored in Spain."

"He was *what?*" asked Coward in alarm.

"He vas gored!"

"Thank heavens. I thought you said he was bored."[1]

Today's society can't think of anything worse than boredom, and that's why our world is so hobby-driven, entertainment-driven, media-driven, gadget-driven, and leisure-driven.

That leaves the preacher on the horns of a dilemma, so to speak. There's nothing new about our message. It's two thousand years old, and many people in most churches have heard and re-heard the gospel, some since childhood. Though an old song says, "Those who know it best seem hungering and thirsting to hear it like the rest," that's not completely true. Our hearts are constantly hungry for the old truth, but sometimes we'd like to hear it in new ways.

I tell young ministers that every sermon should either tell people something they've never heard before or tell them something they have heard in a way that makes them think they're hearing it for the first time. Every sermon should be served hot and fresh from an overflowing heart. We've got to dig into the Scriptures; and instead of going back to John 3:16 every week, we should ferret out some neglected passages and preach the "whole counsel of God." The Bible is a big book, and I've found that parishioners like to make new discoveries of old truths. They occasionally like to learn something from the minor prophets, the obscure characters, the Levitical sacrifices, and the Old Testament types.

---

[1] Donald W. McCullough, "Anything But Boredom!" in *Christianity Today,* August 19, 1991, p. 30.

A primary means by which our message remains fresh is in our application, of course. "Thou shalt not covet" is an old commandment with a long history, but it's never been more relevant than now, with our constant commercials, endless billboards, pop-up ads, wall-to-wall advertising, affluent living, and rows of shopping malls and Internet stores.

We can also be creative in the way we present the message, using video, movie clips, drama, first-person narrative sermons, testimonies, interviews, original poems, creative staging, and object lessons.

We can also vary our sermonic styles. My bread-and-butter style of preaching is expositional, but occasionally I'll throw in a textual, topical, narrative, or even a story-stacking sermon. I also try to occasionally vary the length. Ninety percent of my sermons fall between twenty-five and thirty-five minutes, but sometimes ten minutes will do the trick, especially on Sunday night. Recently I settled down for a good half-hour Internet sermon by John Stott at London's All Souls Church, and was surprised to find it lasted only ten minutes. But he said more in those ten minutes than I say in a half-hour.

But there's another way to avoid the humdrum too. Ask yourself, "Are there some phrases I wear each week, like the same, predictable tie?" Try breaking up your speaking patterns and using some new words. Switch up your phraseology. I learned this from the apostle Paul who presented the Gospel hundreds of times but almost always using new phrases. He seldom presented a rote recitation of the gospel. Every time he spoke or wrote, it was fresh.

Notice how these examples demonstrate slight variations in phraseology.

> ❧ Therefore let it be known to you, brethren, that through this Man is preached to you the forgiveness of sins; and by Him everyone who believes is justified from all things from which you could not be justified by the law of Moses (Acts 13:38–39). *Continued on the next page*

TECHNIQUES FOR THE PASTOR'S DELIVERY—*Continued*

❧ . . . our Lord Jesus Christ, who gave Himself for our sins, that He might deliver us from this present evil age, according to the will of our God and Father (Gal. 1:3–4).

❧ But when the kindness and the love of God our Savior toward man appeared, not by works of righteousness which we have done, but according to His mercy He saved us, through the washing of regeneration and renewing of the Holy Spirit (Titus 3:4–5).

❧ Believe on the Lord Jesus Christ, and you will be saved (Acts 16:31).

❧ If you confess with your mouth the Lord Jesus and believe in your heart that God has raised Him from the dead, you will be saved. For with the heart one believes unto righteousness, and with the mouth confession is made unto salvation (Rom. 10:9–10).

The same truth is expressed, but Paul seldom used exactly the same words. He was always turning phrases, switching vocabulary, bringing in new idioms and axioms, as though he were constantly asking himself, "Now, how can I say this just a little differently?"

Beware getting locked into a series of stock phrases that you repeat with conventional, weekly regularity. We have a message as big as the Montana sky, as big as the Milky Way! We serve a God whose specialty is creation and creativity. We have people suffering from a million different needs. Let's do all in our power to avoid the sin of staleness, remembering the eleventh commandment for public speakers: Thou Shalt Not Bore.

JULY 1, 2007

SUGGESTED SERMON

Divine Direction

Date preached:

By Rev. Todd M. Kinde

Scripture: Genesis 24:26–67, especially verse 27
And he said, "Blessed be the LORD God of my master Abraham, who has not forsaken His mercy and His truth toward my master. As for me, being on the way, the LORD led me . . . ."

Introduction: As we study this passage today, we should note that we stand on this side of the Cross the same distance as Abraham did on the other side of the Cross. Abraham lived 2,000 years before Christ. We live 2,000 years after Christ. Yet, despite such a time gap, we live by faith just as Abraham did. God took great care in providing a wife for Isaac to fulfill His plan for the coming of Jesus some 2,000 years later. In this passage, we will discover further the greatness of the Lord's leading in our lives, our response to His leading, and how we interact with His providence.

1. **Focus on God's Plan (vv. 28–33).** Rebekah ran back to her home with great enthusiasm at the news of this servant's arrival from Abraham. Laban saw the ring and bracelets and quickly left the house for the spring. His greetings to the servant were overly warm and gracious. We get the sense that Laban is greedy and opportunistic, pursuing riches over and above the Lord. In contrast to Laban, the servant would not be distracted from his oath and assignment. Even the lavish feast before him didn't divert his attention from God's plan (see Prov. 23:1–7; John 4:31–34). We often face the temptation to lose focus when the cares of this life cloud our vision of God's glory. Let us fix our eyes on Jesus, the author and perfector of our faith (Heb. 12:2).

2. **Acknowledge God's Provisions (vv. 34–54a).** The servant, staying focused on God's plan, rehearsed the story of God's provisions for Abraham and for this quest. We are quick to recognize that Abraham is in fact a man of great wealth. Riches are not a sin. Rather, it is the attitude toward riches that is of concern. The servant emphasizes God's provision not the provisions themselves (vv. 35–36).

Specifically, the servant gives attention to the success that the Lord has given to him on the journey. The purpose for recording the story a second time is to ensure that we get the point of God's absolute control over His creation. Living becomes simplistic when we acknowledge the providence of God in all things and submit to His Word.

3. **Resolve to Fulfill God's Purpose (vv. 54b–61).** The servant was no sluggard "sleeping in late after the party last night." He showed the same resolve as his master Abraham—up early the next morning to complete the task (see Gen. 21:14; 22:3). The servant, however, was asked to delay his return for at least ten more days. As we learn more of Laban's manipulative techniques and shrewd business dealings in the chapters to come, we understand that Laban was seeking to get more treasure; he wondered what else there might be stowed away on those ten camels. Probably confident that Rebekah inherited some greediness, Laban and his wife suggest that Rebekah should decide. Rebekah's response is one of resolve like that of the servant. She says, "I will go." We, too, are to follow the Lord's leading with resolve and determination to fulfill God's purpose for us. This is the mark of one who follows Christ, for our Lord Jesus also was resolved to do the will of the Father (Luke 9:51).

4. **Meditate on God's Promises (24:62–67).** The scene now changes to Beer-lahai-roi. You may remember this place form chapter 16 when Hagar had run away from Sarai. There God had seen her distress and helped her. Now in his loneliness, Isaac is at the same well. Here he meditates. The psalmist writes of meditation on the Word of the Lord (Ps. 119:9, 15–16, 147–148). To meditate on the promises of God's Word is to think on them, to let them shape and form our thinking and acting. This is the means by which the Lord leads us (see Rom. 12:2).

Conclusion: We should interact with the sovereign control of God. We should respond to His leading as we focus on God's plan, acknowledge His provisions, resolve to fulfill His purpose, and meditate on His promises. This we endeavor to do by His grace and in His Son, Jesus Christ, who has accomplished this for us.

STATS, STORIES, AND MORE

Guides Galore

The world is looking for good guides—and I don't just mean the ones who can lead you on a hiking trip through the wilderness. One of America's popular magazines is TV Guide, designed to guide our television viewing habits. Travel guides help us plan our trips, and a host of books have the word "Guide" in their title, such as Beginners Guides, Study Guides, Official Guides, Unofficial Guides, Ultimate Guides, Dating Guides, Marriage Guides, Pregnancy Guides, and Parenting Guides. But there's one guide that out-guides them all, and one book that is our ultimate guidebook in life.

> I will instruct you and teach you in the way you should go; I will guide you with My eye (Ps. 32:8).

> You in Your mercy have led forth the people whom You have redeemed; You have guided them in Your strength (Ex. 15:13).

> For this is God, our God forever and ever; He will be our guide even to death (Ps. 48:14).

> You will guide me with Your counsel, and afterward receive me to glory (Ps. 73:24).

Zigzagging?

Charles Swindoll tells of being in the Marine Corps on a ship stationed near Taiwan. The ship stopped at the harbor of Taipei and waited for the arrival of the harbor pilot who came and took the wheel of the ship and began to weave through the pathless waters toward the dock. It seemed like useless zigzagging until the Marines looked over the side of the ship into the crystal clear waters. There were mines located randomly beneath the surface of the water. If the hull of the ship had nudged a mine just enough, disaster would have occurred. But the pilot of the harbor knew where every mine was located.[1]

---

[1] Charles R. Swindoll, *The Tale of the Tardy Oxcart* (Nashville: Word Publishing, 1998), p. 254.

APPROPRIATE HYMNS AND SONGS

"Gentle Shepherd," William J. Gaither/Gloria Gaither, 1974 William J. Gaither, Inc. (ARR UBP of Gaither Copyright Management).

"God Will Make a Way," Don Moen, 1990 Integrity's Hosanna! Music.

"Guide Me O Thou Great Jehovah," William Williams/Harry E. Fosdick/John Hughes, Public Domain.

"He Leadeth Me," Joseph H. Gilmore/William B. Bradbury, Public Domain.

"Place in This World," Michael W. Smith/Amy Grant/Way Kirkpatrick, 1990 Careers BMG Music Pub., Inc./Milene Music, Inc. (Admin. Opryland Music).

FOR THE BULLETIN

Two young monks, Johann Esch and Heinrich Voes, little more than teenagers and followers of Martin Luther, became the first martyrs of the Reformation when they burned at the stake in Brussels for their faith on July 1, 1523. News of their murders inspired Martin Luther to write a ballad entitled, "A New Song Now Shall Be Begun." ● On July 1, 1535, Sir Thomas More was indicted for treason for refusing to acknowledge Henry VIII as head of the church. ● One of America's premier evangelists, Charles Finney, was ordained on this day in 1824 at the age of 32. He has been called the "Father of Modern Revivalism." Another pulpit great was licensed to preach on this day in 1835—Robert Murray McCheyne. He pastored in the Scottish city of Dundee where his congregation grew quickly to number over a thousand souls. His death at age 29 left a lasting mark on Scottish church history, and his biography by Andrew A. Bonar is a Christian classic. ● On July 1, 1838, the first converts were baptized under the ministry of missionary Titus Coan in the Sandwich Islands (Hawaii). On that day, 1,705 were baptized, and by 1853, there were 56,000 native Hawaiians professing Christ as Lord. ● The first United States Postage Stamps went on sale on July 1, 1847. ● Today marks the death in 1892 of the Prince of Preachers, Charles Haddon Spurgeon, who passed away in a hotel on the coast of France where he was vacationing and trying to recover his health. ● The Gideons were organized on July 1, 1899.

WORSHIP HELPS

Call to Worship

The LORD be exalted, who delights in the well-being of his servant. My tongue will speak of your righteousness and of your praises all day long (Ps. 35:27–28 NIV).

Offertory Comments

The other day a message appeared on a church sign that said: "Tithe if you love Jesus. Anybody can honk!" Well, of course, anybody can tithe, too, and it is an expression of our love for the Lord Jesus. Today we invite you to give to the Lord as He has prospered you.

Invitation

A Christian without a church is like a child without a family or a man without a country. In this cold world of cynicism and criticism, we need a place of love, fellowship, prayer, and happiness. We need the church. Perhaps today you'd like to officially join our church. We'd love to make you a part of our family. Come join us today. If you know Christ as your Savior and you want to make this your "church home," just step out from where you are sitting, come to the front, and someone will be glad to talk and pray with you about it.

If your membership is at another church, it can be transferred here to us. If you've never been baptized, we would be glad to talk with you about the meaning of baptism. If you've been saved and baptized, but have never joined a church, you can become a member here upon the simple statement of your faith in Christ. "Come with us, and we will treat you well; for the LORD has promised good things . . ." (Num. 10:29).

Additional Sermons and Lesson Ideas

What Is the Gospel?
Date preached:

By Dr. Timothy K. Beougher

SCRIPTURE: Various

INTRODUCTION: The Gospel is a message to you:

1. A Message About God (Gen. 1:1; Lev. 11:44; Ps. 89:5–15). The Bible tells us that God is the Holy and Loving Creator. As such, God has an absolute claim on our lives. We are accountable to live as God tells us to live.
2. A Message About Man (Rom. 3:23; 6:23). We haven't chosen to live as God wants us to live, but have stubbornly chosen our own way. We have rebelled against God's authority in our lives: this is what the Bible calls sin. Our sin earns us spiritual death and separation from God.
3. A Message About Christ (1 Pet. 2:24; John 3:16). Christ is the merciful Redeemer. He is Himself God, but came to earth to live a perfect life and die on a cross for sinners as the perfect substitute.
4. A Message About Response (John 1:12). The gospel message, the Good News calls for a response. Our necessary response is repentance and faith, that is, turning from our sin and placing our trust completely in Him.

CONCLUSION: Receiving Christ is not something we earn (Eph. 2:8–9). It's a gift. I beg you to accept Christ today.

Great and Precious Promises
Date preached:

Based on a message by Samuel Clarke (1675–1729)

SCRIPTURE: 2 Peter 1:3–4

INTRODUCTION: Whatever your situation today, there's a promise from God to meet every need.

1. The Nature and Variety of the Blessings Contained in the Promises. The promises of God are of an excellent nature and suited to every circumstance. They address our needs, both of body and spirit. They address the various troubles and calamities that befall us.
2. The Manner in Which They Are Expressed. They are not expressed in general or ambiguous terms, but are specifically stated to meet our practical needs.

3. The Certainty with Which We May Depend on Them. God has confirmed His promises with an oath and ratified them with His own blood.

4. Their Happy Influence on the Mind. As Puritan Samuel Clarke quaintly put it: "A fixed, constant attention to the promises, and a firm belief in them, would prevent solicitude and anxiety about the concerns of life. It would keep the mind quiet and composed in every change and support and keep up our sinking spirits under the several troubles of life."

CONCLUSION: Christians deprive themselves of their most solid comforts by their unbelief and forgetfulness of God's promises. For there is no extremity so great but there are promises suitable to it, and abundantly sufficient for our relief in it.

JULY 8, 2007

SUGGESTED SERMON

The Seriousness of Sin

Date preached:

By Dr. Melvin Worthington

Scripture: Various, especially Romans 6:23
For the wages of sin is death, but the gift of God is eternal life in Christ Jesus our Lord.

Introduction: One word that makes people shudder is a little three-letter word. Can you guess it? Sin. Our culture clearly teaches that, "What I like makes it right." Scripture, however, is very serious on this subject. When the Bible is serious about a subject, we should be too. Let's look together at what Scripture tells us about this uncomfortable doctrine of sin:

1. **The Definition of Sin.** The apostle John says, "Whoever commits sin also commits lawlessness, and sin is lawlessness" (1 John 3:4). Again John declares, "All unrighteousness is sin . . ." (1 John 5:17). James declares, "Therefore, to him who knows to do good and does not do it, to him it is sin" (James 4:17). Paul states, "But he who doubts is condemned if he eats, because he does not eat from faith; for whatever is not from faith is sin" (Rom. 14:23). The two most familiar types of personal sin are omission and commission. The sin of omission is when one fails to do what God prescribes. The sin of commission is when one does what God prohibits.

2. **The Devastation of Sin.** When Adam disobeyed God in the garden (Gen. 3) he was separated or alienated from God. As an individual he became sinful, dying spiritually as God had warned. As a result of sin he began to die physically. God pronounced a curse on the serpent, the woman and Adam (Gen. 3). God also provided salvation for Adam and Eve and then drove them out of the Garden of Eden lest they eat of the tree of life (Gen. 3). Sin infected the individual, the family and the entire human race (Rom. 3; 5).

3. **The Destruction of Sin.** Genesis 6—8 records the destruction that resulted from Adam's disobedience. The human race was corrupt and every imagination of the hearts of the inhabitants of the earth

was evil continually. Noah found grace in the eyes of the Lord and he and his family along with two of every animal were spared the waters of the flood (Gen. 6:17). Peter reminds his readers of the destructive nature of sin when he cites the illustrations of the angels that sinned, the flood that destroyed and the judgment of Sodom and Gomorrah (2 Pet. 2:4–6).

4. **The Disillusionment of Sin.** Sin always promises far more than it ever delivers (2 Sam. 13; Luke 15 and Eccl. 1—2). Sin never brings lasting joy. There is no peace to the wicked, they are like the troubled sea.

5. **The Distress of Sin.** Sin produces physical, emotional, psychological, and spiritual stress. Genesis 37, Acts 9, and Joshua 7 serve as classic passages that deal with the distress caused by sin.

6. **The Deceitfulness of Sin.** Sin is always deceptive and destructive. Scripture constantly reminds us of this truth (Heb. 11; Judg. 12—16; Gen. 19).

7. **The Degeneration/Depravity of Sin.** Romans 1—3 provides a divine record of the progressive nature of sin. It follows a downward spiral until the only remedy is judgment.

8. **The Deliverance from Sin (Rom. 6:23).** God has provided redemption through the person and work of the Lord Jesus Christ. God's method for saving man is by grace through faith. The prerequisites for salvation include: recognition of our sin, repentance of our sin, reception of Christ's payment for our sin, and reliance on Christ for salvation from our sin.

Conclusion: The seriousness of sin cannot be overlooked. Sin will be judged by God Himself. The saints will be judged (1 Cor. 3; Rom. 14; 2 Cor. 5). Societies will be judged (Matt. 25) and sinners will be judged (Rev. 20). God has provided redemption for the sinner through the redemptive work of the Lord Jesus Christ. Have you recognized your sin, repented of your sin, and received Christ as your savior? Are you relying on Him for salvation?

STATS, STORIES, AND MORE

Quotes About Sin

> *Life is short / Death is sure / Sin the cause / Christ the cure.*
> —Anonymous

> *It is impossible for a man to be freed from the habit of sin before he hates it, just as it is impossible to receive forgiveness before confessing his trespasses.*
> —Ignatius

> *We have a strange illusion that mere time cancels sin. But mere time does nothing either to the fact or to the guilt of a sin.*
> —C. S. Lewis

> *Sin and the child of God are incompatible. They may occasionally meet; they cannot live together in harmony.*
> —John R. W. Stott

A Glistening Rainbow

Dr. J. Sidlow Baxter, the well-known Bible teacher who is now with the Lord, told of a time when he was hospitalized in Santa Barbara, California, low in both body and spirit. In the morning hours, as Sid emerged from sleep into a hazy semi-consciousness, he seemed to suddenly see a bright amber background, and in the foreground an opened Bible. A hand and index finger was pointing to Psalm 103:3: ". . . who forgiveth all thine iniquities." Baxter later recounted, "What those words conveyed to me at that moment I could hardly get over to you vividly enough. They seemed to say, 'Sid, what does it matter basically whether you live or die, whether you are well or ill, compared with knowing that you are saved, that you have a full, free, final, and forever forgiveness, a forgiveness which is not merely a pardon but a welcome to the heavenly Father's heart . . .'" Those words were like "a glistening rainbow" overarching him all day long.[1]

APPROPRIATE HYMNS AND SONGS

"In the Arms of Sweet Deliverance," Mosie Lister, 1970 Lillenas Publishing Co. (Admin. The Copyright Co.).

"You Are My Hiding Place," Michael Ledner, 1981 Maranatha Music (Admin. The Copyright Co.).

"Song of Deliverance," Bob Fitts, 1993 Integrity's Hosanna! Music (Admin. Integrity Music, Inc.).

"I Waited Patiently," Danny Chambers, 1993 Praise on the Rock Music.

---

[1] J. Sidlow Baxter's account of this story is related by E. A. Johnston: *J. Sidlow Baxter: A Heart Awake* (Grand Rapids: Baker Book House, 2005), p. 101.

FOR THE BULLETIN

Peter the Hermit died on this day in 1115. He was a French monk who, following a pilgrimage to the Holy Land, complained to Pope Urban II about the brutalities committed by the Mohammedan Turks against Christians. Peter's rhetoric led to the forming of the first Crusade. ● On Sunday, July 8, 1741, Jonathan Edwards stood in the pulpit of his church in Enfield, Connecticut, and preached *Sinners in the Hands of an Angry God*, saying "O sinner! Consider the fearful danger. The unconverted are now walking over the pit of hell on a rotten covering, and there are innumerable places in this covering so weak that it will not bear their weight, and these places are not seen." Five hundred were converted that day, sparking the Great American Awakening. ● Today is the birthday, in 1782, of hymnist Lowell Mason, who composed over a thousand hymn tunes, including the melodies to hymns like "Nearer, My God, to Thee," "Bless Be the Tie that Binds," and "When I Survey the Wondrous Cross." Mason was passionate about training children in sacred music. Recognizing that young William Bradbury had an inborn talent, Mason sought to encourage him at every turn and mentored him into a giant figure in the era of Gospel music. ● On July 8, 1939, Dietrich Bonhoeffer, who had come to America to teach and to find safety, left the United States for Germany where he knew he was facing a catastrophic conflict with Adolf Hitler. As he wrote in *The Cost of Discipleship*, he felt drawn to serve his God through the suffering of his homeland. He was a willing martyr. Bonhoeffer arrived on September 1, 1939, the very day that Hitler invaded Poland. He was martyred for his faith.

Quote for the Pastor's Wall

When I pastored a country church, a farmer didn't like the sermons I preached on hell. He said, "Preach about the meek and lowly Jesus."

I said, "That's where I got my information about hell."

—Vance Havner

WORSHIP HELPS

Call to Worship
Yours, O LORD, is the greatness, the power and the glory, the victory and the majesty; for all that is in heaven and in earth is Yours; Yours is the kingdom, O LORD, and You are exalted as head over all. Both riches and honor come from You, and You reign over all. In Your hand is power and might; in Your hand it is to make great and to give strength to all. "Now therefore, our God, we thank You and praise Your glorious name" (1 Chr. 29:11–13).

Pastoral Prayer
Lord, we pray with David, "Who can understand his errors? Cleanse me from secret faults. Keep back Your servant also from presumptuous sins; let them not have dominion over me. Then I shall be blameless, and I shall be innocent of great transgression. Lord, this is our corporate prayer, not just for me, but for us. Let the words of our mouths and the meditations of our hearts be acceptable in Your sight, O Lord, our strength and our Redeemer.

Benediction
God has exalted Jesus Christ to His right hand to be Prince and Savior, to give repentance to Israel and forgiveness of sins. And we are His witnesses to these things, and so also is the Holy Spirit whom God has given to those who obey Him (Acts 5:31–32).

Kid's Talk

Ask to see the children's hands. You might pass out some hand sanitizer or wipes, and talk about how important it is to wash our hands, how that helps to prevent our getting sick. But we cannot wash the heart. We can't sanitize our souls. Only Jesus can do that, and that's what we call forgiveness.

Additional Sermons and Lesson Ideas

Shameless or Blameless

Date preached:

SCRIPTURE: Psalm 101

INTRODUCTION: Our society is forging a new mentality, that there's nothing to be ashamed of. Behavior that was once "evil" is now "alternative" and "mainstream." King David, in Psalm 101, determined to live a blameless life according to God's standards, saying:

1. I Will Sing of Holiness (v. 1). We not only sing of God's love, but of His justice.
2. I Will Be Careful to Lead a Blameless Life (v. 2a). "I will behave wisely in a perfect way" (NKJV); "I will be careful to live a blameless life" (NIV).
3. I Will Be Blameless at Home (v. 2b). We must be pure and blameless in our fidelity to our families.
4. I Will Be Blameless with My Eyes (v. 3a). This includes entertainment and Internet viewing. Compare Psalm 119:37.
5. I Will Be Blameless in My Choice of Friends (vv. 3b–8).

CONCLUSION: In a shameless world, Christians must live blameless lives.

Trust and Obey
By Dr. David Jeremiah

Date preached:

SCRIPTURE: 1 John 2:3–11

INTRODUCTION: If you were in a small aircraft and the pilot slumped over with a heart attack, you would try your best to do exactly what the control tower told you to do. Obedience is a crucial quality in critical times, and it's a crucial quality all the time as it relates to the Lord.

1. Obedience Is the Sign of Relationships (1 John 2:3–5).
   A. Obedience Proves the Reality of Our Faith (1 John 2:3–4).
      (1) The Positive Statement (1 John 2:3).
      (2) The Negative Statement (1 John 2:4).
   B. Obedience Proves the Reality of Our Love (1 John 2:5).
2. Obedience Is the Secret of Fellowship (1 John 2:6–8).
   A. The Expectation of Obedience (1 John 2:7).
   B. The Explanation of Obedience (1 John 2:8).
   C. The Example of Obedience (1 John 2:6).
   D. The Expression of Obedience (1 John 2:9–11).

CONCLUSION: Life is like sitting in the pilot's chair for the first time. But Someone out there is telling you how to fly. Take what He says seriously. He's the Captain of your salvation. He can guide you safely to your destination but you have to trust Him, and you have to obey.

JULY 15, 2007

SUGGESTED SERMON

Down a Mine Shaft

Date preached:

Scripture: Exodus 40:43—Leviticus 1:1, especially 1:1
Now the LORD called to Moses, and spoke to him from the tabernacle of meeting . . .

Introduction: Leviticus doesn't have the loftiness of Ephesians, the practicality of Proverbs, or the scenery of the Gospels, but it has a vital message. Preaching from Leviticus is like descending a mineshaft. We have to plunge in and chip away at the rock, but there we'll find jewels. The first thing to notice is that Leviticus is simply a continuation of Exodus, telling us what happened as the Israelites camped at Sinai. God told them two things: He is a holy God; and He had delivered them from Egypt to be His holy people.

1. **A Monotonous Book.** Leviticus has a reputation of being the dullest book in the Bible. One man called it "101 Ways to Kill a Bull." Many people decide to read through the Bible until they come to Leviticus; then they get bogged down.

2. **A Meaningful Book.** One commentator suggested Leviticus wasn't meant to be read, but to be studied. It's full of diamonds for those who will dig them out. Leviticus was the first book studied by Jewish children. It was quoted about forty times in the New Testament, and much of the New Testament cannot be understood without knowing Leviticus.

3. **A Methodical Book.** It is a well-arranged book. The theme of Leviticus is *holiness*. The word *holy* occurs 95 times in this book!

   A. **Leviticus 10:3ff:** *This is what the Lord spoke, saying: "By those who come near Me I must be regarded as holy."* That's the theme of Leviticus in a nutshell.

   B. **Leviticus 11:45:** *I am the LORD who brings you up out of the land of Egypt to be your God. You shall therefore be holy, for I am holy.*

   C. **Leviticus 15:31:** *You shall separate the children of Israel from their uncleanness, lest they die in their uncleanness when they defile My tabernacle.*

D. Leviticus 19:1ff: *'You shall be holy, for I the LORD your God am holy.'"*

E. Leviticus 20:7–8: *Consecrate yourselves therefore, and be holy, for I am the LORD your God . . . who sanctifies you.*

F. Leviticus 20:16: *And you shall be holy to Me, for I the LORD am holy, and have separated you from the peoples (to) be Mine.* Holiness is God's infinite, unchangeable moral excellence. There is a holiness perimeter around God, and everything unholy that enters that zone is consumed by His blazing purity. It's like flying into the sun. How long would we last if we were flying into the sun? See Isaiah 6:1–5. Leviticus establishes the foundation for this central column of biblical truth—the holiness of God. The theme of Leviticus is that God is holy, and His holiness is to be the standard of our conduct and behavior. *Be ye holy, for I am holy.* Holiness is not a standard to which God conforms. Holiness is that which God is, and everything else must conform to that standard or be ruined. Everything in the universe is good as it conforms to God's holiness and evil as it does not. The holiness of God provides the basis for moral absolutes—the very truth that is under attack today. If there was ever a generation that needed to rediscover this great biblical theme, it's ours. One way of doing so is to descend into the mineshaft of Leviticus where we find the diamond-like truth of God's holy character.

4. **A Messianic Book.** It is all about Atonement, about Divinely engineered Offerings, about the Reconciling Savior. Leviticus gives us a series of sacrifices; it tells us of shedding of the blood, about the burnt offerings, about the priesthood which points toward the Lord Jesus. At its very center is the description of the Day of Atonement in chapter 16. The purpose of Leviticus is to show us how a Holy God provides atonement through blood-sacrifice that we might be reconciled to God and made holy in His sight. See Romans 3:21–26.

Conclusion: Leviticus provides the deep moral and biblical foundations for the Book of Romans and gives us the theological underpinnings for our salvation. Oh, that we might see God in His holiness. Oh, that we might see ourselves in our sinfulness. Oh, that we might see how

Christ—by His atoning sacrifice—pardons our sinfulness and clothes us in His holiness that we might be reconciled to God for eternal life! As John Newton put it:

> O, can it be upon a tree,
> The Savior died for me?
> My soul is thrilled, my heart is filled,
> To think He died for me.

STATS, STORIES, AND MORE

There was once a sort of consensus in America about universal, absolute moral law, and that's what propelled America in a war of liberation in Europe. By the same token, the Nazis rejected such standards. Hitler rejected the idea of a personal God who decreed absolute truth. One of the reasons he hated Jews was because they represented transcendent monotheism. By killing Jews, Hitler thought he could eradicate those who had 'invented' God." Morality thus became fluid. It could be whatever a man or a society wanted it to be. Now, sixty years later, this is the philosophy being espoused by modern America, and those who dare stand in opposition are called "right-wing religious extremists."

The other day I bought a clock. The directions told me not to set the clock, only to push a little button. Something within the clock beamed signals to the U.S. Naval Observatory in Colorado. The hands started moving as if by magic and automatically synchronized to the absolute standard of the master clock operated by government. What if I gathered a people in the room and said, "What time do you want it to be? There's no absolute standard. We can set this clock however we want." Our society has disconnected itself from the absolute standard of the holiness of God, and we think we can set the clock however we'd like. But it's really getting closer and closer to midnight. We have lost the message of the Book of Leviticus. God is holy, and His holiness is the basis of our conduct and morality.

APPROPRIATE HYMNS AND SONGS

"Great Is Thy Faithfulness," Thomas O. Chisholm/William M. Runyan, 1923. Renewed 1951 Hope Publishing Co.

"Holy, Holy, Holy," John B. Dykes/Reginald Heber, Public Domain.

"Holy Is the Lord," Dennis Jernigan, 1994 Shepherds Heart Music (Admin. Word Music Group).

"Take Time to Be Holy," William D. Longstaff/George C. Stebbins, Public Domain.

"We Fall Down," Chris Tomlin, 1998 WorshipTogether.com Songs (Admin. EMI Christian Music Publishing).

FOR THE BULLETIN

Jerusalem fell to the crusaders from Europe on July 15, 1099. They had been inspired by Pope Urban II's electrifying sermon describing the plight of the Eastern Church inundated by Islamic infidels who controlled the Holy Land. All Europe was stirred by the thought of Christian holy sites being controlled by Muslims, and hundreds of thousands of people set out to liberate Jerusalem. The city finally fell on Friday, July 15, 1099, at three o'clock, the day and hour of the Savior's death, it was noted. Jubilant Crusaders sang hymns as they waded through a sea of bodies to the holiest spot in Christendom, the Church of the Holy Sepulcher. ● Bonaventura, medieval Christian scholar and close friend of Thomas Aquinas, died on this day in 1272. The suddenness of his death at age 53 caused widespread speculation he was poisoned, though most scholars believe he died of the plague. The devotional and mystical style of his writings has led him to be called the "The Seraphic Doctor." ● Julins Palmer, a zealous English Catholic, was converted to the Protestant cause by observing how bravely the English reformers, including Latimer and Ridley, died at the stake. His conversion brought him the same condemnation, and on July 15, 1556, Palmer was condemned to death. The next day, he was executed in the flames. His last words were: "Be strong and take courage, all you who put your hope in the Lord." ● Today is the birthday of the Dutch painter, Rembrandt van Rijn, in 1606; and of Clement C. Moore, in 1779. Moore was an Episcopal theologian and a professor in New York City, who is best known for his poem, "T'was the Night before Christmas." It's also Edward Caswall's birthday, in 1814. He's the hymnist who translated "Jesus, the Very Thought of Thee" and "When Morning Gilds the Skies."

WORSHIP HELPS

Call to Worship
The LORD lives! Blessed be my Rock! Let the God of my salvation be exalted (Ps. 18:46).

Pastoral Prayer
Our Heavenly Father, we so often pray over our own prayer requests while forgetting that You have given us some prayer requests too. On this Sunday, as we remember our national day celebrating our independence, we recall Your instructions in 1 Timothy 2, that we pray for those in authority over us. We ask You to bless our President and Vice President, giving them wisdom for their tasks. Give good hearts and minds to our Congress and Judiciary. Guide our state's governor and our city's mayor. And grant peace to our nation, Lord, and to our world that Your gospel might be proclaimed freely to the ends of the earth.

Offertory Comment
We call this next portion of our worship service the "offering," but that really isn't a very good term for it. It's true that we are offering some of our money to the Lord for His purposes, but that's not the best term. Ever worse is that old term "collection." I like the term "worship," don't you? Or the phrase "honoring God." Proverbs 3:9 says, in the Living Bible: "Honor the Lord by giving Him the first part of all your income." So this isn't just the offering or collection; it's the God-honoring portion of our service. May the Lord bless us as we honor Him with our "offerings."

Additional Sermons and Lesson Ideas

Ranking Responsibilities

Date preached:

By Dr. Melvin Worthington

SCRIPTURE: Various

INTRODUCTION: Christians often feel there's not enough time to get everything done. The pace, problems, and pressures of today's complex and corrupt society cause us to misplace our priorities. What is the order of priorities for the Christian?

1. The Relationship to Our Heavenly Father (Matt. 22:37–38). The first priority is our relationship to our heavenly Father.
2. The Role within Our Human Family (Matt. 22:39). This role includes the husband, help, and the heritage. Christianity must work in the home before it is put on display in the community.
3. The Responsibility to Our Honored Functions. Our responsibility includes our function within the *church* (1 Cor. 12:3–8), within our *communities* (Rom. 13:1–7), and as citizens of our *countries* (1 Pet. 2:17).

CONCLUSION: God is honored when our priorities are structured according to Scripture.

A Glimpse of History

Date preached:

By Rev. Larry Kirk

SCRIPTURE: Various

INTRODUCTION: The gospel can be summarized by an overview of our H-I-S-T-O-R-Y:

H—How it all began: A good creation (Gen. 1:31).
I —Iniquity. Sin entered creation (Gen. 3) and grew.
S —Selection. God selected a people to be a channel of His grace, yet they rebelled (Rom. 9:1–5).
T—Truth. God sent messengers of truth but they were mocked and murdered (Matt. 23:37).
O—God's only Son. Christ lived and died for our salvation (John 3:16).
R—Redemption. Christ dying on the Cross for our salvation (Gal. 3:13).
Y—Your choice. God's salvation is freely given to anyone and everyone who will receive (John 1:12).

CONCLUSION: No matter what your history may be, the God of all history desires that you come to faith in Jesus.

CLASSICS FOR THE PASTOR'S LIBRARY

Samuel Logan Brengle:
Portrait of a Prophet

Biographies are my favorite genre of literature, and the biographical shelves at the bookstores are brimming with new titles every week—all except in Christian bookstores. For some reason, Christian biography isn't selling very well unless the subject is a celebrity or sports star. That means we have to look for older biographies, and here's a treasure: *Samuel Logan Brengle: Portrait of a Prophet* by Clarence W. Hall, published in 1933 by the Salvation Army. It may take a little searching, but you can find a copy, or at least a reprint; and it'll be worth the effort.

Brengle was an American evangelist and holiness preacher who traveled widely for the Salvation Army. He was born in Indiana at the onset of the Civil War. His father left for the war when Samuel was two and returned home an invalid, dying shortly afterward. Samuel's mother, a devout Christian, raised him; and Samuel himself became a Christian at the onset of his teen years.

As a young man, Brengle was greatly taken with General William Booth of the Salvation Army, and on June 1, 1887, he showed up at the Army's Headquarters in London, walked into Booth's office, and said, "General, I have come." Booth stared at the young man for a few moments before saying, "Brengle . . . I don't think you will want to submit to Salvation Army discipline. We are an army, and we demand obedience."

"Well, General," Brengle stammered, "I have received the Holy Spirit as my Sanctifier and Guide. I feel He has led me to offer myself to you. Give me a chance."

That was the beginning of a lifetime of ministry in which Brengle became one of the Salvation Army's best known and most loved ambassadors. His itinerate preaching led thousands of people to Christ, and his writing endures to this day. His six little books are classics. (For a sample of Brengle's writings, see the segment on page 61 entitled "Thoughts for the Pastor's Soul:

Worry and Holiness," which is excerpted from his book, *The Way of Holiness*.)

Clarence Hall's biography of Brengle is so sprinkled with probing quotes that I read it with a highlighter in my hand. Brengle was a great letter-writer who maintained a mountain of correspondence with people around the world, some of which Hall wove into his story. To one person, Brengle wrote about his expanding career with the Army, "I want to be useful. God save me from wanting to be famous."

Later, comparing himself to the better known evangelists of his day, he wrote, "When the General (Booth), or Moody, or Chapman, goes into a city, the whole city takes notice. But when I come, only a handful out of the quarter of a million inhabitants know I am here. Oh, that I might reach the multitudes with the Gospel! I seem so like a man picking up a few handfuls of pebbles here and there along the shore . . . . But I remember that when Paul went into Athens, no one knew it till he began to talk to a few people in the markets."

One evening only nine people showed up for his meeting. One of the organizers suggested they conduct a brief prayer meeting and send the people home. "Certainly not," said Brengle, "these nine have taken the trouble to come long distances at probably great inconvenience on this wet afternoon. I shall go and give them my very best." As a result, six of the nine made decisions for Christ at the altar.

On another occasion, a deaf woman came to the meeting and sat on the front row. Afterward, sobbing, she made a decision at the altar. Her daughter, thinking perhaps the woman had recovered some of her hearing, motioned the question, "Did you hear the sermon?" The woman replied, "No, I heard nothing, but I saw Jesus in that man's face."

The life of a traveling evangelist was lonely and difficult in those days, but Brengle pressed on for years, separated from his wife and family for long stretches of time. He once described himself this way: "I am a lonely man, and yet I am not lonely.

Continued on the next page

CLASSICS FOR THE PASTOR'S LIBRARY—*Continued*

With my open Bible I live with prophets, priests, and kings; I walk and hold communion with apostles, saints, and martyrs, and with Jesus, and mine eyes see the King in His beauty. . . . My daily reading has brought me into company with the great prophets—Isaiah, Jeremiah, Ezekiel, Hosea, Micah, Malachi and others—and I live again with them in the midst of the throbbing, tumultuous, teeming life of old Jerusalem. . . . These prophets are old friends of mine . . . They have blessed me a thousand times."

I took my time reading this biography—just a page or two every day, and I now feel that Samuel Logan Brengle is a friend of mine. I'd like to introduce him to you, for his life and his writings can still bless us a thousand times.

JULY 22, 2007

PARENT'S DAY   SUGGESTED SERMON

Husbands and Wives

Date preached:

By Dr. Robert Norris

Scripture: 1 Peter 3:1–7, especially verses 1 and 7
Wives, likewise be submissive to your own husbands . . . Husbands, likewise, dwell
with them with understanding, giving honor to the wife . . .

Introduction: This Sunday happens to be Parent's Day. If you look around this room at all the parents here, you won't see famous athletes or movie stars who are supposed to make such a difference in children's lives. No, you will see an influence far greater. The family is such a sacred institution, such an undeniably essential part of raising children according to God's Word, and yet our society has tragically warped God's standards and design for the family unit. I want to spend some time this morning in the Scriptures dealing with God's design for a family—particularly focusing on the foundation of every family—the relationship between a husband and wife.

1. **Marriage Is Ordained by God.** Peter understood that family was a divine institution, and he makes this very clear in the text in several different ways. He makes clear that, though there may be difficulties that arise from marriage between Christians and non-Christians, nowhere does he suggest the possibility of divorce (cf. 1 Cor. 7:12–16). In fact Peter uses the picture of the creation principle of "subordination" in such a way as to make clear that this is not simply a matter of human convention but a part of the way in which the whole creation has been ordered by God. There is nothing dishonorable implied in this designation, for the woman is only subordinate to man in the same way in which Christ is subordinate to God!

2. **Marriage Is a Partnership.** As he deals with the nature of marriage as a partnership, Peter makes clear that there are differences of role within the partnership. He begins by outlining the role of the Christian wife. Peter says in a very straightforward way that (if the husband is not saved) the goal is the salvation of the partner: "they . . . may be one . . ." This does not give license to marry an unbeliever, for Paul already addressed that issue (2 Cor. 6:14), but

the backdrop of the early church was often a situation of one spouse, converted after marriage. The Christian wife is not to abandon hope! He gives three practical ways this works out in a marriage:

A. **A Wife's Conduct (v. 1):** "they . . . may be won by the conduct of their wives." Peter puts emphasis on fidelity. He tells them to never let any occasion arise that would give your husband any reason to suspect your fidelity or commitment to the marriage. He is saying, in fact, that to give your husband this loyalty is a demonstration of your regard for God Himself.

B. **A Wife's Character (vv. 3–4):** "Do not let your adornment be merely outward . . . let it be the hidden person of the heart . . ." Peter is not suggesting a "ban" on the braiding of hair, or using gold jewelry or the like. Rather, he insists that Christian women should be more concerned about the beauty of character than outward appearances. He does this by contrasting the perishable ornaments of the "outward" with the imperishable ornaments of the soul: gentleness and tranquility of spirit. These are characteristics of Jesus, who described Himself in these terms: "Come to me . . . and I will give you rest . . . for I am gentle and lowly in heart" (Matt. 11:28–29).

C. **A Husband's Consideration (v. 7):** ". . . dwell with them with understanding . . ." Peter uses a construction that is used to describe the nature of sexual relationships, though includes all interactions. He reminds husbands of their need to deal with their wives with understanding, care, and sensitivity.

D. **A Husband's Courtesy (v. 7):** ". . . giving honor to the wife . . ." Neither the noun "vessel" nor the adjective "weaker" is intended to be derogatory. In fact there is no sense of inferiority suggested ever. The difference between husband and wife is a difference of function and not of status. Indeed Peter warns the husband of the fact that to fail in his husbandly duties carries the danger of breaking communion with God: "that your prayers may not be hindered." With these words he reminds us of another great truth.

Conclusion: We are thankful for every parent represented here today. I pray that you would, on this Parent's Day, devote yourselves to living out your family life according to God's Word.

STATS, STORIES, AND MORE

A Wife's Submission
Augustine gives an illustration of how the principles of this passage worked out in the life of his own mother Monica. In his "Confessions" [IX.,19,22] he says: "When she became of marriageable age, she was bestowed upon a husband and served him as the Lord, and she did all that she could to win him to Thee, speaking to him of Thee by her deportment, whereby Thou madest her beautiful and reverently lovely and admirable to her husband. . . . Finally, when her husband was now at the very end of his earthly life, she won him to Thee."

More from Dr. Norris About the Background of 1 Peter 3:1–7
As we look at these verses, we see that Peter addresses the bulk of what he says to women. The status of women in the ancient world was exceedingly low in Roman and Jewish culture. In Roman law, a woman never lost her child status. While in her father's care, he had the power of life and death over her, and that same authority passed to her husband when she married. The husband also had the right of divorce for any trifling excuse. Even in Israel a husband was free to repudiate his wife, but she could not claim divorce. A wife could not inherit from her husband, nor daughters from their fathers except when there was no male heir. Thus Peter is concerned with the changed place of a woman and spends more time dealing with women's issues. He is especially thinking here of the situation of post marriage conversions, where only one partner became a Christian. Whereas the wife would normally be expected to follow her husband in his religion, it was something very different for a woman to change her faith without her husband's lead. Indeed consequences could be very grave, and it is against that background that Peter needs to be heard.

APPROPRIATE HYMNS AND SONGS

"We Will Serve the Lord," Tom Brooks/Rick Riso, 1994 Integrity's Hosanna! Music.

"A Christian Home," Barbara Hart/Jean Sibelius, 1965, 1986 Singspiration Music (Admin. Brentwood-Benson Music Publishing).

"Love Will Be Our Home," Steven Curtis Chapman, 1988 Careers BMG Music Publishing, Inc./Sparrow Song (div. of EMI).

"O Perfect Love," Dorothy Gurney/Joseph Barnby, Public Domain.

FOR THE BULLETIN

Dionysius became pope on July 22, 259, at the end of the period of persecution by Emperor Valerian I. Dionysius reorganized the Roman church and did much to advance the cause of the gospel. He is the first pope who is not listed as a martyr. ● On July 22, 1604, England's King James I announced the appointment of 54 men to translate the Old and New Testaments into English. This Authorized Version that commonly bears his name, was published in 1611. ● Although King James authorized a new translation of the Bible, he rejected most other demands by the Puritans and generated such persecution that many of them left for Holland for refuge. One group of Separatists, led by William Brewster and John Robinson, remained in Holland until July 22, 1620, when with packed bags and children in tow, its members sailed back to England and there boarded the *Mayflower* for the New World. The Pilgrims arrived off the coast of Cape Cod in November of that year and paused long enough to draw up an organizing charter, the Mayflower Compact, which says: *In ye name of God Amen . . . Having undertaken, for ye glories of God, and advancement of ye Christian faith and honor of our king & country, a voyage to plant ye first colony in ye Northern parts of Virginia, doe by these presents solemnly & covenant, & combine ourselves together into a Civil body politick; for our better ordering, & preservation & furtherance of ye ends aforesaid . . .* ● Today is the birthday, in 1886, of hymnist B. B. McKinney, who wrote such classics as: "Breathe on Me," "Have Faith in God," "Send a Great Revival," "Wherever He Leads I'll Go," and "The Nail Scarred Hand." On Sunday, September 7, 1952, McKinney left a conference in Ridgecrest, North Carolina, heading for Gatlinburg, Tennessee. Near Bryson City, North Carolina, he was killed in a car wreck.

WORSHIP HELPS

Call to Worship
Be exalted, O LORD, in Your own strength! We will sing and praise Your power (Ps. 21:13).

Hymn Story: At Calvary ("Years I Spent in Vanity and Pride")
R. A. Torrey, president of Moody Bible Institute, once received a letter from the father of a prodigal asking him to let the boy enroll at Moody. Torrey declined at first but eventually agreed, but the arrangement didn't go well at first. Eventually, however, that boy—William R. Newell—himself became a beloved professor at Moody. In 1895, William began thinking of putting his testimony into verse form. One day on his way to lecture, the lines came to him. Ducking into an empty classroom, he jotted down the words on the back of an envelope. As he hurried on to class, he happened to meet Dr. Daniel Towner, director of music at the Institute. Handing him the verses, William gently suggested they could use a good melody. By the time Dr. Newell finished his lecture, the completed tune was ready. The two men sang it together, and it was published shortly after. We've been singing it ever since: "Years I spent in vanity and pride, caring not my Lord was crucified . . ." How good God is to reclaim and rebuild our lives. Bill Newell once said that had he not gone through his troubled years, he might never have fully understood the importance of Calvary's grace.[1]

---

[1]Adapted from the editor's volume of hymn stories entitled *Then Sings My Soul*, published by Thomas Nelson Publishers.

Additional Sermons and Lesson Ideas

The Bible: God's Instruction Manual

Date preached:

By Dr. Larry Osborne

SCRIPTURE: Various

INTRODUCTION: Many people hold the Bible in highest regard. Year after year, it remains at the top of the best-seller list. But, ironically, while lots of people have a Bible, few actually read it. Fewer still regularly consult it for life direction.

1. What Is It? The Bible is a collection of 66 books and letters written by over 40 different authors over a 1,600 year time span. It claims to be composed by God (2 Tim. 3:16; 2 Pet. 1:20–21).
2. Its Two Primary Purposes. Scripture is concerned with *proving that Jesus is God's Son* (Luke 24:24–27, 44–48; 1 Pet. 1:9–12). The Bible also *teaches us how to live God's way* (2 Tim. 3:16–17; Rom. 12:2; Acts 17:11; Ps. 119:11, 105; John 17:14–17).
3. How to Put It to Use. Read it whenever you possibly can. Treat it as a text book or life manual (James 1:22–25; Ps. 1:1–3; Josh. 1:7–8; Prov. 2:1–6). Look for the big four: *context, commands, promises, implications.*

CONCLUSION: The Bible was never meant to be a religious decoration on someone's coffee table. It was meant to be our instruction manual for life.

Serious Business

Date preached:

SCRIPTURE: Psalm 62:8

INTRODUCTION: John Bunyan (1628–1688) is best known for his book, *Pilgrim's Progress,* but he wrote over sixty other books, most of them while imprisoned in Bedford Jail for preaching the gospel. His book on prayer begins with this definition: "Prayer is a sincere, sensible, affectionate pouring out of the heart or soul to God, through Christ, in the strength and assistance of the Holy Spirit, for such things as God has promised, or according to His Word, for the good of the church, with submission in faith to the will of God."

1. Prayer Is a Sincere, Sensible Pouring Out of the Soul to God.
2. Through Christ
3. In the Strength of the Holy Spirit
4. For Things God Has Promised in His Word
5. For the Good of His Church
6. With Submission to His Will

CONCLUSION: Have you been taking prayer seriously? It is a serious business that achieves serious results.

JULY 29, 2007

SUGGESTED SERMON

Ripe for Judgment

Date preached:

By Rev. Peter Grainger

Scripture: Amos 8:1–14, especially verse 2
"The end has come upon My people Israel; I will not pass by them anymore."

Introduction: Imagine turning up at church for a Harvest Thanksgiving Service only to discover it is a Funeral Service; and, even worse, says the preacher, it's your funeral service for you are about to die and there is nothing you can do about it. That is the kind of shock that Amos receives and then communicates to the people of Israel in the fourth of the five visions he receives from the Lord. *"Amos, what do you see?"* the Lord asks. *"A basket of summer fruit,"* Amos answers (v. 2). But they are in for a terrible surprise for the Lord says, using a play on very similar sounding words in the original Hebrew, that they are the fruit, about to be plucked and consumed. After decades of opportunity to change their ways and countless warnings from the prophets, it is now too late. The people of Israel, God's chosen people, are ripe for judgment. Harvest-time is here. So look with me at the two sides of the process—sowing and then reaping.

1. **Sowing the Seeds (vv. 4–6).** Here, the Lord describes what the people of Israel, and especially the leaders of Israel, have sown: the seeds of selfishness and self-interest. They have one goal in life and that is to make money, to make a profit. Now, nothing is wrong with making money providing that it's not your goal in life, or more accurately your god.

   A. **Profit before People.** When you put profit before people it is always the poor who suffer and who you profit by, for they have no money or power with which to fight back. Like the game of Monopoly, the weaker players and their possessions are swallowed up by the stronger. Compassion goes out of the window and with it honesty and integrity. So in the days of Amos, the rich landowners swallowed up the landholdings of the poor, land that was supposed to be safeguarded in perpetuity for each family by the Law of Moses. And, in telling words, the poor are even sold into slavery and forced to eat wheat mixed with the sweepings from the floor (v. 6).

B. Profit before God. The great tragedy in Israel was not social injustice, for such things went on in every country in the ancient world. No, the tragedy in Israel was that they should have known better and so should have done better. They knew the one true God who had revealed His laws to them. However, instead of setting an example to the rest of the nations, they had followed the example of the rest of the nations.

2. **Reaping the Results (vv. 7–14).** There is nothing new in the Lord's charges against the people of Israel. They heard them before, not only through Amos, but through many other prophets. Now finally what they had sown had come to fruition, harvest-day, judgment-day had arrived. No more forgiveness or mercy is available. The Lord's judgment is expressed in terms of three natural phenomena which people in those days feared above all else—earthquake (v. 8), eclipse (vv. 9–10) and famine (vv. 11–14). The third of these (famine) is not literal but a picture of a spiritual hunger and thirst. Whether the other two are literal or not is unclear but we should note two things:

A. The Effects of the Fall on Creation and Humans. In Romans 8, the apostle Paul writes of all creation groaning as a result of sin and likewise human beings, in particular, Christians, groaning also—both in anticipation of a final restoration by God of how things should be and once were.

B. God Uses Natural Disasters to Warn of Greater Disaster. In Amos 4, we read that the Lord reminds the people of Israel that in the past he withheld rain and sent famine, struck down their crops with diseases and sent locusts, sent plagues and invading armies—all with one purpose: to get the people to return to Him. Yet they did not listen, and no one heeded the final judgment was about to come.

Conclusion: Thankfully, the Book of Amos doesn't stop here, but looks forward in its final chapter to an unending harvest and a restoration of God's people. However, with these Scriptures before us today, how do you need to respond? Have you placed profit before people and before God? Do you live for the stuff you can attain? Do you feel a spiritual famine in your life because you have neglected God's Word? The fulfillment of the restoration of God's people was completed in Jesus Christ; won't you turn to Him in repentance and faith?

STATS, STORIES, AND MORE

More from Rev. Grainger: Earthquakes and Eclipses
Earthquakes were a frightening phenomenon in the ancient world as they still are today. The Book of Amos begins with a mention of a notable such occurrence referred to as "the earthquake" (Amos 1:1). The land trembles and shakes and everything is thrown into confusion and disarray. In the ensuing devastation, familiar landmarks disappear, leaving the people in mourning at the loss of security. We only need to think of the effects of the events of September 11th to imagine that kind of scenario, yet on a nationwide scale. An eclipse was often seen as a portent of doom in ancient times, unable as they were either to explain its cause or predict its occurrence. It has been calculated that two such eclipses occurred during the time of Amos: in 784 and 763 B.C. The ensuing gloom with no certainty of a return to normality produced deep despair, expressed in public acts of penitence and mourning, as devastating as that felt in the loss of an only son.

Fire Safety
Many years ago, a father and his daughter were walking through the grass on the Canadian prairie. In the distance, they saw a prairie fire; eventually, they realized, it would engulf them. The father knew there was only one way of escape: they would quickly begin a fire right where they were and burn a large patch of grass. When the huge fire drew near, they then would stand on the section that had already burned. When the fire actually did approach them, the girl was terrified by the raging flames. But her father assured her, "The flames can't get to us. We are standing where the fire has already been."

Are you afraid of God's judgment? If you have trusted Christ as your Savior, you can never come under His wrath. When we depend on Him, we are secure; we are where the wrath of God has already been.[1]

APPROPRIATE HYMNS AND SONGS

"Living for Jesus," Thomas O. Chisholm/Harold C. Lowden, Public Domain.

"One Drop of Blood," Ray Boltz/Steve Milikan, 1996 Shepherd Boy Music (Admin. Word Music)/Weedom & Reap.

"Revive Us Again," William P. Mackay/John J. Husband, Public Domain.

"Set My Soul Afire," Eugene M. Bartlett, 1965 Albert E. Brumley And Sons (Admin. Integrated Copyright Group).

---

[1]Adapted from Erwin W. Lutzer, *Failure: The Back Door to Success* (Chicago: Moody Press, 1975), p. 53.

FOR THE BULLETIN

The Patron Saint of Norway, King Olaf II, was killed in battle on this day in 1030, bringing to an end his campaign to establish Christianity in Norway. ● Richard Allen, who grew up in slavery in Delaware, was converted after hearing a Methodist preacher proclaim the Gospel. In 1786, he joined the staff of Philadelphia's St. George's Methodist Episcopal Church, the mother church of American Methodism, where he conducted the 5 A.M. Sunday services. His powerful preaching brought many blacks to St. George's, causing tension in the congregation. With the church's blessing, Allen assembled a group of black Christians on July 29, 1794, in a converted blacksmith's shop. The Bethel African Methodist Episcopal Church was formed, the mother church of the African Methodist Episcopal Church, now known throughout the world. Allen became the first consecrated bishop in the growing movement which today is among the largest Methodist groups on earth. ● William Wilberforce, English Christian, political leader, and anti-slavery advocate, died in London on July 29, 1833. ● Today is the birthday, in 1866, of Thomas O. Chisholm, American Methodist school teacher, newspaper editor, and insurance salesman. He is best known for his hymn, "Great Is Thy Faithfulness." ● On Sunday, July 27 1890, artist Vincent van Gogh returned to the Ravoux Inn and went straight to his attic room. It was later learned that he had been out trying to kill himself, but the self-inflicted bullet had entered his side instead of his heart. He was able to walk home where he died in his own bed on July 29th.

Kid's Talk

Talk with the children about obedience. Perhaps share a time from your childhood when you got into trouble for disobeying. Ask: Are you a good obey-er? There are two reasons we obey our moms or dads. The first is because we don't want to get into trouble. The second reason is even better—because we love them. We obey the Lord for those same two reasons, but especially because we love Him.

WORSHIP HELPS

Call to Worship

Let all those who seek You rejoice and be glad in You; let such as love Your salvation say continually, "The LORD be magnified" (Ps. 40:16)!

Responsive Reading from Psalm 121

Worship Leader: I will lift up my eyes to the hills—from whence comes my help?

Congregation: My help comes from the LORD who made heaven and earth.

Worship Leader: He will not allow your foot to be moved; He who keeps you will not slumber.

Congregation: Behold, He who keeps Israel shall neither slumber nor sleep.

Worship Leader: The LORD is your keeper; The LORD is your shade at your right hand.

Congregation: The sun shall not strike you by day, nor the moon by night.

Worship Leader: The LORD shall preserve you from all evil;

Congregation: He shall preserve your soul.

Everyone: The LORD shall preserve your going out and your coming in from this time forth, and even forevermore.

Offertory Prayer

Lord, not many of us are rich in money, but make us rich in the willingness of our hearts. Make us rich in the grace of our Lord Jesus Christ. Make us rich in good works. Make us recipients of Your abundant life, and may we give, not out of necessity nor grudgingly, but from willing and cheerful hearts. We pray in Jesus' name, Amen.

Additional Sermons and Lesson Ideas

Earthquake, Eclipse, Famine
Date preached:

By Rev. Peter Grainger

SCRIPTURE: Amos 8:8–14 with Matthew 27:4—28:2 and John 19:28

INTRODUCTION: Three curses were pronounced on Israel for their rebellion in Amos 8:8–14: earthquake, eclipse, and famine. Jesus Christ both endured each of these curses and became the answer to them, as the One who has broken sin's curse!

1. Earthquake (Amos 8:8; Matt. 27:50–54; 28:2–4). As Jesus gave up His spirit in agony, a great earthquake occurred, splitting the temple curtain, which had once symbolized the separation between God and man (Matt. 27:50–54). Not only this, but another earthquake three days later marked His Resurrection (Matt. 28:3–4)!
2. Eclipse (Amos 8:9–10; Matt. 27:45). As Jesus endured the Cross, darkness came upon all the land (Matt. 27:45). However, speaking of Christ, John says, "In Him was life, and the life was the light of men" (John 1:4 NIV).
3. Famine (Amos 8:11–14; John 19:28). Again, Jesus on the Cross speaks of His physical and spiritual famine, "I am thirsty" (John 19:28) as He endured this, our punishment for us. He also became the answer to our spiritual famine: "I am the bread of life" (John 6:35).

CONCLUSION: The curses of Amos 8:8–14 are what we deserve. Christ endured them all, however, and offers us stability in a shaky world, light in a dark society, and spiritual food in a land of famine. Doesn't such a Savior and God deserve our complete trust and devotion?

Christian Certainties
Date preached:

By Dr. Melvin Worthington

SCRIPTURE: Various

INTRODUCTION: Biblical conversion makes a significant change in those who experience it. What are the dividends of becoming a Christian?

1. Honest Living (Acts 6:3; Rom. 12:17; 2 Cor. 8:21; 13:7; Phil. 4:8; 1 Pet. 2:12; Rom. 13:13; 1 Thess. 4:12; Heb. 13:18; 1 Tim. 2:2).
2. Hopeful Living (1 Thess. 1:3; 5:8; 1 Tim. 1:1; Titus 2:13; 3:7; Heb. 6:19; 1 John 3:3; 1 Pet. 1:3; 3:15).
3. Happy Living (John 13:17; Acts 26:2; Rom. 14:2; James 5:11; 1 Pet. 3:14; 4:14; Phil. 4).

4. Helpful Living (Rom. 16:3; 1 Cor. 16:16; 2 Cor. 1:11, 24).
5. Holy Living (1 Pet. 1:15–16; 2:5; 2 Pet. 1:21; 3:11; Col. 1:27; 3:12; Eph. 1:4; 5:27).
6. Hallowed Living (Phil. 3; 1 Thess. 1; 2 Pet. 1).
7. Humble Living (Phil. 4; 1 Pet. 5:5–6; James 4:6, 10; Prov. 16:19; 29:23; Is. 57:15).

CONCLUSION: Have you put your complete trust in Christ, turning from sin and submitting to Him as Lord?

AUGUST 5, 2007

SUGGESTED SERMON

Speech

Date preached:

By Dr. Larry Osborne

Scripture: Ephesians 4:29 (NIV)
Do not let any unwholesome talk come out of your mouths, but only what is helpful for building others up according to their needs, that it may benefit those who listen.

Introduction: Speech: how many of you have been hurt by the words of somebody in your life? The tongue is an amazing thing isn't it? With it we can be the wind beneath someone's wings, or we can take the wind right out of their sails. Whether you are a parent, a teacher, a supervisor, or a friend, you have an incredible power to encourage or deflate others with your words.

1. **Rotten Words.** The word translated here "unwholesome" in the original Greek could literally be translated "rotten." You can ask yourself two questions to know whether you're speaking rotten words:

    A. Are Your Words Shameful? If you say something in someone's presence that you wouldn't say in front of someone else, those words are rotten. This might be crudeness, or it might be speaking of someone else in a negative way.

    B. Are These Words Hurtful? The angry parents who yell at their children excessively, or the married couple who scream at each other constantly: this is an example of rotten speech.

2. **Helpful Words.** The Greek word for "benefit" is literally "grace-giving." Again, two questions you can ask yourself to know whether your words are offering grace to someone else:

    A. Are These Words Helpful? Helpful words aren't always easy to hear, but they are always meant to build up.

    B. Do These Words Offer Grace? If I've been insulted and I insult in return, it's a "fair deal," but if I give kindness for rudeness, I've offered grace, unmerited favor.

3. **Before You Speak: Five Profound Questions.** I know none of us will carry around our list of five questions, but there may be one or two of these that really apply to you that you need to go home and pray about:

A. **Is It True (1 Thess. 2:5; Prov. 29:5)?** Helpful words are always true words. Do you give out false encouragement? The Bible calls this flattery. Words should be true, not just happy words. Do you spread unchecked rumors? Have you ever gotten an email from a Christian brother or sister warning you about something, only to find out later that it's not true? Do you spread negative information about others that you don't know to be true?

B. **Is This Appropriate for This Situation (Prov. 10:32)?** Timing is equally important as truth. Here are some examples to consider in the timing of our words:

(1) **Anxious Hearts Need Kindness (Prov. 12:25).**

(2) **Broken Hearts Need Tears (Prov. 25:20; Rom. 12:15).**

(3) **Teaching Needs Pleasantness (Prov. 16:21).**

(4) **Annoyance Calls for Silence (Prov. 11:12; 29:11).**

(5) **Age Calls for Respect (1 Tim. 5:1).**

C. **Will These Words Be Heard (Prov. 25:11–12; Matt. 7:6)?** If someone isn't open to listen to you, there's no reason to continue speaking (Prov. 9:8).

D. **Is My Motivation to Help or Hurt (Prov. 12:18; 27:5–6; 1 Pet. 3:9; James 3:9–12)?**

E. **Is This My Responsibility (Prov. 24:11–12; 26:17; Lev. 19:17; Luke 17:3)?**

Conclusion: I don't know which of these questions may have your name on it, but I pray that this week you will think about these and consider which of these questions you need to personally consider. May we all continue to throw out the words that are rotten, and become wise in our speech.

STATS, STORIES, AND MORE

More from Dr. Osborne

When I was an early college student, having just come to the Lord a couple of years before, I had the opportunity to lead a college Bible study. By the grace of God, it kept growing and growing, and finally the Lord led me to understand He had not only put a passion inside me for ministry, but He had also gifted me. Along the way were many important people, but two in particular stand out to me. One was my youth pastor, Charlie Bradshaw, who said to me something along these lines, "Someday, I'm going to say, 'I knew Larry Osborne when . . .'" More importantly than that, someone once came and told me they heard him say that. Another couple, we will call "the Jones," were involved in the same study, a couple older than I, whom I looked up to. One day I told them that I wanted to be a pastor, and that I would like to be a pastor of a large church with lots of influence if the Lord would lead me to it. I remember their words as fresh as if they said them now: "What makes you think you could ever do that?" It's funny that through the years in the dark moments of my life, I've remembered both, thinking, "Yes, someone once saw something in me, so this is what I should be doing," and "Who do I think I am to be able to do these things?"

Studies have shown that in passing along stories about others, we attach a contagious emotional aspect to the story. What does this mean? When others hear us spreading rumors, they immediately feel a certain emotion toward whomever the rumor is about. Later, when you go back and tell them it wasn't true, or if they find out the rumor was a half-truth, the negative emotion toward that person still lingers. Damage is done that cannot be undone.

APPROPRIATE HYMNS AND SONGS

"Keep Your Tongue from Evil," Frank Hernandez, 1990 Birdwing Music (div. EMI Christian Music Publishing).

"Let the Words of My Mouth," Dieter Zander, 1985 Vi Ray Publishing (Admin. Vi Ray Publishing).

"Let Them Praise," Twila Paris, 1985 Ariose Music/Mountain Spring Music (Admin. EMI Christian Music Publishing).

"Psalm 19," Sonny Salsbury, 1968 Word Music, Inc. (div. of Word Music Group).

FOR THE BULLETIN

August 5, 1503, was a blistering day in Rome, and the Borgia pope, Alexander VI, one of the most corrupt and vile on record, dined in the open air to avoid the indoor heat. Shortly after, he was attacked by a severe fever and died. Historians agree that the cause of death was malarial infection brought on by exposure to the night air of midsummer Rome. ● Spanish Jesuits arrived in Chesapeake Bay on August 5, 1570, for the purpose of evangelizing Native Americans, a project that didn't go well as the group was massacred by the very Indians they had hoped to reach. A more successful missionary to Native Americans, John Eliot, was baptized on this same day in 1604. He is known as "the Apostle to American Indians," and he first preached to the Native Americans in their own tongue in 1646 and published a Bible in their language in 1661. It was the first Bible published in America. ● Mary Slessor worked in mission halls near her home in the slums of Dundee, Scotland, facing down gangs and reaching the hardest of the heard. She felt led to apply for missionary service in Calabar, and on August 5, 1876, she sailed for West Africa aboard the SS *Ethiopia*. She was dismayed to find the ship loaded with hundreds of barrels of whiskey. Remembering how alcohol had ruined her own family, she frowned. "Scores of barrels of whisky," she muttered, "and only one missionary." ● This is a day of "firsts" in American history. The first traffic light in the United States was installed on this day in 1914 in Cleveland, Ohio. The first radio broadcast of a baseball game occurred on this day in 1921, and the first American to swim the English Channel, Henry Sullivan, did so on August 5, 1923.

WORSHIP HELPS

Call to Worship

Be still, and know that I am God; I will be exalted among the nations, I will be exalted in the earth (Ps. 46:10).

Other Appropriate Scriptures

- Psalm 12:1–4
- Proverbs 15:4
- James 3:1–12

Offertory Comments

Just before receiving today's tithes and offerings, I'd like to tell you the story of a young man named Robert Nicholas who moved from Canada to Chicago and came into real money. It was the year 1900, and he wrote home that he was making the incredible sum of six dollars for a sixty-hour week. His father wrote back a lengthy letter, warning his son of the dangers of money. Some people are financially blessed, said the old man, so they can be generous in the Lord's work. Mr. Nicholas quoted Proverbs 11:24: "There is one who scatters, yet increases more; And there is one who withholds more than is right, but it leads to poverty." Robert did begin giving his tithes and offerings to the Lord, and God prospered him. He later became a financial giant in the Chicago area, and many missionaries, churches, and students received aid from him, the gifts often coming anonymously. His life overflowed because he never forgot his father's counsel: Scattering leads to increasing more, but withholding brings poverty.

Pastoral Prayer

Father, would You take these words and help us to see where they fit and where they apply in our right now, day-to-day living, that we might be the men and women You want us to be. In Jesus' name, Amen.

Benediction

He stores up sound wisdom for the upright; He is a shield to those who walk uprightly; He guards the paths of justice, and preserves the way of His saints (Prov. 2:7–8).

Additional Sermons and Lesson Ideas

What Is Jesus Doing Right Now?   *Date preached:*

SCRIPTURE: Hebrews 4:14

INTRODUCTION: If we had a telescope capable of peering into the highest heaven, what would we see Jesus doing right now? What is His present ministry?

1. He Is Ruling from His Heavenly Throne (Eph. 1:20; Mark 16:19; Phil. 2:9, 1 Pet. 3:22).
2. He Is Directing and Empowering His Church (Matt. 16:18; Acts 1:1–2; Rom. 15:18).
3. He Is Interceding for Believers (Rom. 8:42, 1 John 2:1; Heb. 2:17–18, 7:25).
4. He Is Preparing a Place for Us (John 14:1–3).
5. He Is Receiving the Souls of Those Who Die in Christ (Acts 7:54–59).
6. He Is Being Praised by Angels (Rev. 5).

CONCLUSION: If Christ is doing all this for us in heaven, what are we doing for Him on earth?

Paul's Prison Prayers   *Date preached:*
Based on a Series of Published Sermons by Dr. W. Graham Scroggie

SCRIPTURE: Various Prayers from the Pauline Epistles

INTRODUCTION: The prison letters of Paul give the church amazing direction and insight. The prayers as recorded in these letters can give us a glimpse of what we should pray for the church of Christ all over the world.

1. Pray for Discerning Love (Phil. 1:9–11).
2. Pray for Enlightened Behavior (Col. 1:9–12).
3. Pray for Spiritual Illumination (Eph. 1:15–23).
4. Pray for Divine Plentitude (Eph. 3:14–21).

CONCLUSION: How often do you pray for the church? Paul serves as a wonderful example. If you haven't devoted yourself to this discipline in the past, I encourage you to take these Scriptures, and use them as a guide to jump-start your prayer life for God's people.

Keeping the Sound of Music in the Pastor's Soul

An Interview with Rosemarie Trapp

This interview, conducted some time ago, is just for fun, to keep music in the minister's soul (and to provide a couple of good sermon stories). Rosemarie Trapp is one of the famous *Sound of Music* siblings who now lives in Stowe, Vermont. She is a former teacher and now travels extensively as a missionary. Miss Trapp (she officially dropped the "Von" several years ago because it was too long to sign autographs), spoke in a lilting voice with a hint of an accent. She discussed candidly her family's faith and her own remarkable journey to God.

How much of* The Sound of Music *is true?

The whole first part of the movie. My mother wanted to become a nun, and for a year she stayed in a convent in Salzburg. But the Reverend Mother said she wasn't right for a convent, and she was sent to my father's home as a teacher. They fell in love and married. But there was a ten-year lapse between their marriage and their leaving Europe when Hitler came in, so the movie ending was more dramatic than what really happened. We left Austria by train to Italy, then we went on to France where we took a boat to the United States. I was born after they married. Maria is my real mother.

Was your mother like the "How do you solve a problem like Maria?" song describes her?

She certainly was unpredictable. In fact, it was quite a trip to take a ride with her in the car. She was very accident-prone, and broke her legs and arms several times. She rode horses until she was 70 and skied until she was 75.

Did she really make clothing out of curtains?

Servants in the house helped with the sewing when she came there. But when we came to America, we wore Austrian peasant clothes, and in Vermont we kept making our own clothes to save money.

Did you ever meet the cast of The Sound of Music?

Yes, by accident. My mother managed the gift store in our lodge in Vermont, and she took trips to Europe for gift buying. One year in the 1960s she took me along with her. We happened to go through Salzburg, through the main plaza, and there was the whole *Sound of Music* cast making a shot of Julie Andrews walking through a doorway. My mother asked the producer, Robert Wise, if we could be in one of the shots, and he let us walk across the street in the background while Julie Andrews was walking through the doorway singing her song about confidence. We had to do that about eighteen times!

Did Maria have a commitment to Christ?

Very much so. She was orphaned in childhood and eventually ran away from an abusive situation and ended up in Vienna, going to school to be a teacher. She fell in with a modern, new-age-type crowd that didn't believe in God. They just did their "own thing." She thought the only reason to go to church was to hear music. So every Sunday she would go to a different church for a concert. When she was eighteen, she went to church during a holy week revival, though she didn't realize it until she found herself seated near the front, unable to get out. She had to listen to the preacher, but during the sermon she called out loudly, "I don't believe a word you're saying!" The preacher looked down and said, "Young lady, I want to see you after the service." Well, she went and he led her to Christ. After that, she wanted to become a nun and ended up in the Salzburg convent. Later, when she came to my father's house she wanted to take the convent with her. She had a chapel set apart in the house, and we grew up with Christ's consciousness embedded in our minds.

Continued on the next page

CONVERSATIONS IN THE PASTOR'S STUDY—*Continued*

Was your father, Captain George Von Trapp, actually an officer in the German Navy who blew his captain's whistle at home?

Yes he did! I think he was frustrated because his children didn't act like disciplined sailors. But he was a very gentle, loving man. He loved to play violin. He loved to sing with his children, and he started them out in their singing career. When my mother came she perfected it, and he became the manager. He never sang in public, but he took care of the business end.

Was your father a Christian?

Yes. He had deep religious convictions, and he read the Bible. It was a verse of Scripture, in fact, that encouraged him to lead us out of Austria. He found the Scripture where God told Abraham he should get out of his country and go to a land that God would show him.

Did your parents' faith have an influence on you?

They lived their faith. I think that gave us a foundation. When your life centers around religion and worship, it becomes natural. Our schooling, worship, and everyday life just sort of gelled together.

What happened to your family after you arrived in America?

We stayed in Pennsylvania for the first few years. Then my mother missed the mountains of Austria, so we moved to Stowe, Vermont, and that became our headquarters. Our income still comes, for the most part, from our lodge there which my brother manages.

Your father's death was traumatic for you, wasn't it?

Yes. In 1947, he died from cancer, and watching him die shook me up. I was also very disturbed by the stress afterward within the family. I even ran away and when I was found I was taken to a psychiatrist because I wasn't talking. I stayed home that next year, and while everyone else went on a singing tour, I worked at the lodge.

What happened in the years that followed?

I went to New Guinea for three years to live with my sister, a missionary there. When I returned to take a course in nursing in Connecticut, I became stressed out again and entered a hospital for a year. After that, I lived in a bad situation and was very miserable in my sin. Finally, at forty years of age, I heard a gospel evangelist on the radio. He explained that we are all sinners, but that Jesus had given His life for us. I said the sinner's prayer and the Lord found me.

Was it like rediscovering the sound of music?

When the Lord found me, I became happy. I came to realize that Jesus makes us special in God's eyes. Until then I thought I was just special because of the movie about us.

What impact do you think your mother's faith and prayers had on you?

A lot. I believe God answers mothers' prayers and that every answer from God is in His own good time, because He sure waited for me. I know my mother loved God. And I think every child is blessed who has a mother who prays for him or her and who wants to bring him or her to Christ.

Were you very close to your mother?

My mother put her whole soul into my brothers and sisters, and that was a good thing. They needed her. But then she let them raise me. As a result, I never communicated with my mother very much. She read us stories and she read us the Bible. I had some questions growing up that I never got to talk to her about . . .

But . . . ?

But you know, when I started reading the Bible, I remembered that my mother gave me a big picture Bible once when I was young. All of a sudden those pictures flashed back to me, and I said, "Those are my old friends!" The Bible became more real to

Continued on the next page

CONVERSATIONS IN THE PASTOR'S STUDY—*Continued*

me. So though our parents aren't perfect, I believe that God blesses mothers and fathers to be channels of grace for their children.

You seem to have a lot of enthusiasm for life.

Thank you. That's the Lord, because when I was young I used to be very bored. But now that I have Jesus, He makes life interesting. Only yesterday I talked to high school students about the Holocaust and Hitler. I told them that Hitler gave us a symbol of a cross with hooks on it. But our Christian faith gives us a symbol of a cross that brings freedom and resurrection. The world, you know, offers us a glossy cross with hooks in it. My father and mother had to make a choice. They chose the Cross of Christ. And I think that's a great thing for children to learn.

AUGUST 12, 2007

SUGGESTED SERMON

Partnership

Date preached:

By Rev. Richard S. Sharpe, Jr.

Scripture: 1 John 1:1–8, especially verse 3:
Our fellowship is with the Father and with His Son, Jesus Christ.

Introduction: When you hear the word "partner," what comes to mind? Many of us think of a work setting, whether partners in ownership of a business, or partners of a law firm. We also might immediately think of our spouse. These are great examples, but incredibly, our commitment to Christ makes us partners with God Himself, and with fellow Christians to reach the world with the gospel. The Greek word used in 1 John for fellowship conveys this idea of partnership. Scripture teaches us three important aspects of this fellowship:

1. **Partnership within the Trinity (Gen. 1:26; 2 Cor. 13:14).** The first fellowship or partnership we find in Scripture is that between the Godhead. The Father, Son, and Holy Spirit were present at creation.

2. **Partnership with Fellow Christians (1 John 1:7).** Once a relationship is established between man and God, there begins a relationship between fellow Christians. We are made clean by the blood of the Christ. That is the only way we establish fellowship with the Godhead and with fellow believers. Our partnership with each other is carried out mainly in the local church. We are one body that needs to serve the Lord in our world. As a body we have certain functions that we are to partner in with one another:

A. **Partnership as Students of the Word (Acts 2:42).**

B. **Communion of the Lord's Table (1 Cor. 10:16).**

C. **Prayer (Acts 2:42).**

D. **Care for the Poor (Rom. 15:26–27; Gal. 2:9–10).**

E. **Trust in God (1 Cor. 1:9; Philem. 6).**

F. **Encouragement (2 Cor. 8:4).**

G. Fellowship in the Gospel (2 Cor. 4:19; Phil. 1:5; 4:15).

H. Fellowship in Taking the Gospel to the World (Gal. 2:9).

I. Suffering for Christ (Phil. 3:10; 4:14).

J. Supporting Full-Time Servants (Phil. 4:15).

K. Walking in the Light (1 John 1:6–7).

3. **Forbidden Partnership with the Unsaved (2 Cor. 6:14).** This final partnership is one that we are not to have. It is a partnership with unsaved individuals. This idea extends to our business practices and to the concept of whom we choose as friends. However, Scripture is most concerned with an unequal partnership in marriage between a believer and non-believer. It causes problems in every aspect of the family unit. We need to not be anxious to find a marriage partner to the point that we will marry anyone who comes along. God has a plan and that includes having the right person for all believers to marry. It is never an unsaved person. However, if you married your spouse after conversion, and he or she is yet to become a believer, Scripture is very specific that you should stay married. Your church lovingly supports you, and Scripture gives some vital principles specifically for you to live by in this situation (1 Pet. 3:1–6; 1 Cor. 7:12–16).

Conclusion: We have looked at three types of partnerships. We realize that we will never completely understand the relationship between the Godhead but we do know that it exists. We know that we are not to have a partnership with the unsaved world. We can have a relationship but not a partnership. However, we are to have a partnership with fellow believers in the world. That partnership is expressed mainly in the local church.

STATS, STORIES, AND MORE

A Story from Donald Gray Barnhouse
A mother, in one of those delicious moments that make mothers what they are, drew her two-year-old daughter to her and said, "Oh, I love you!" The little girl, very much occupied with the whim of the moment, drew away and said, "Yes, I know." Love was taken for granted.

As early in life as the second year the Word was being illustrated: "even a child is known by his doings . . ." (Prov. 20:11). Tragedy occurs when someone hears the voice of God saying, as He does from Calvary, and as He does from a thousand circumstances of life, "My child, I love you," and is answered with "Yes, I know"—an indifference that shows that His love is not really returned. Most of life's sadness flows from such an attitude. The windows of heaven are opened when we can learn to feel deeply: "We love Him, because He first loved us" (1 John 4:19).[1]

Band of Brothers
In his book about the American Revolution, *Washington's Crossing,* David Hackett Fischer describes the incredible hardships suffered by Washington's forces during the winter of 1776. One of the soldiers was sixteen-year-old John Greenwood who played the fife. "What I suffered on the march cannot be described," he wrote. "They who were with us know best about these things, others cannot believe the tenth part, so I shall say nothing further." What kept the men going? They drew their strength from each other. Greenwood wrote: "The noise of the soldiers coming over and clearing away the ice, the rattling of the cannon wheels on the frozen ground, and the cheerfulness of my fellow-comrades encouraged me beyond expression, and, big coward as I acknowledge myself to be, I felt great pleasure, more than I now do in writing about it."[2]

APPROPRIATE HYMNS AND SONGS

"Called as Partners in Christ's Service," Jane Parker Huber/John Zundel, 1982 Jane Parker Huber (Admin. Westminster John Knox Press).

"Worship the Lord," Fred Koan/Ron Klusmeier, 1974 Hope Publishing Co./ Worship Arts.

"The Family of God," William J. Gaither/Gloria Gaither, 1970 William J. Gaither, Inc. (ARR UBP of Gaither Copyright Management).

"Father God," Jack Hayford, 1973 Rocksmith Music [Mandina/Rocksmith Music (c/o Trust Music Management, Inc.)]

---

[1] Donald Gray Barnhouse, *Let Me Illustrate* (Westwood, NJ: Fleming H. Revell Company, 1967), p. 217.
[2] David Hackett Fischer, *Washington's Crossing* (Oxford: University Press, 2004), pp. 207–208, 220.

FOR THE BULLETIN

Euplius, a Christian in Sicily who was wholly unafraid of persecution, stood outside the governor's office one day shouting, "I am a Christian! I desire to die for the name of Christ." As a result, Euplius was subjected to a series of horrible tortures, then executed on August 12, 304, with his gospels tied around his neck. His last words, repeatedly uttered, were "Thanks be to Thee, O Christ. O Christ, help. It is for Thee that I suffer." ● Today marks the death of writer Nahum Tate in 1715 while in debtor's prison. He is best remembered for the Christmas carol, "While Shepherds Watched Their Flocks." ● When Jabez Bunting was nineteen, he struggled with a life-changing decision, namely his vocation—whether or not to enter the ministry. He took a piece of paper, drew a line down the center (at least figuratively speaking), and set forth the arguments for and against. The "Pros" won, and on August 12, 1798, he preached his first sermon in a cottage in a village called Sodom. He grew to be a powerful leader of the early Methodist movement and the successor to John Wesley. ● America's first missionary, Adoniram Judson, died on this day in 1850. His story is stranger than fiction, and one of the most interesting resources is an old book about the three different women to whom he was married, each a heroine in her own right, entitled *The Three Mrs. Judsons,* by Arabella W. Stuart. ● Today also marks the death, in 1912, of composer William Fischer, who wrote the music to the hymns "Whiter Than Snow," "I Love to Tell the Story," and "The Rock That Is Higher Than I."

Kid's Talk

Gather the children around and tell them: "I have a very important message that everyone in this whole building needs to hear, but I want them to hear it from you, and not over the microphone, but they need someone to personally deliver the message. I need a volunteer." After someone volunteers, "How long do you think it would take for one person to tell everyone here the message? Do you have any other ideas?" Allow them time to suggest that multiple volunteers would be faster. Then tell them, "You know what? Jesus gave us the job to share about Him, not just with everyone here, but with everyone in the world! You came up with a great idea. God doesn't want just one volunteer in one room, He wants all of you to be partners in telling others about Jesus. If every one of you tells your friends about Jesus, think about how many people will hear! Can I ask all of you to volunteer to tell others about Jesus, not just tonight but whenever you get a chance?"

WORSHIP HELPS

Call to Worship
Be exalted, O God, above the heavens; Let Your glory be above all the earth (Ps. 57:5).

Word of Welcome
Isn't it wonderful to be in the presence of the Lord and His people? The Lord created us, not because He needed us in any way, but because He desires fellowship. He created us as social people. When sin entered the world, it broke our fellowship with God, and truly severed our ability to get along with each other. If you're here today, and you've accepted Christ as your Savior and Lord, He has restored you to fellowship with Himself through Jesus Christ, and fellowship with other believers. Christ told His disciples that the world would know Jesus sent them by their love for one another. I want us to do something today that might feel a little uncomfortable, but I think it's important. I'm going to allow a few minutes for you to greet each other. I want the men to greet the men and the women, greet the women. Greet one another with a handshake or a hug, look each other in the eye, smile, and say "I love you brother" or "I love you sister."

Other Appropriate Scripture
- Isaiah 57:15
- 1 Corinthians 13
- 1 John 1:7–9

Additional Sermons and Lesson Ideas

The Peril of Drifting

Date preached:

By Dr. Melvin Worthington

SCRIPTURE: Hebrews 2:1–4

INTRODUCTION: The writer of Hebrews reminds his readers of the danger of neglecting the Word of God.

1. The Reality: Possibility of Drifting. Lot (Gen. 13; 19), Samson (Judg. 13—16), Jonah (Jon. 1), David (2 Sam. 11), and Solomon (1 Kin. 1; 11) serve as examples of individuals who ignored the Word of God.
2. The Ruin: Penalty for Drifting. Drifting results in losing one's *values* (Gen. 19), *vision* (Judg. 16), *virtues* (2 Sam. 11) and *vitality* (1 Kin. 1; 11).
3. The Road: Process of Drifting. The components that contribute to drifting include *ingratitude, inattention, indifference, insensitivity, indulgence, inconsistency,* and the *influence* of one's family, friends, and foes (Matt. 13:1–33).
4. The Remedy—Preventive from Drifting. The remedy includes *diligence, discipline, and discernment.* We need to *heed* the Word of God, *hold* the Word of God, *honor* the Word of God, and *herald* the Word of God.

CONCLUSION: Today, you must make a decision to be a hearer or a doer of God's Word.

The Mark of the Christian

Date preached:

By Rev. Larry Kirk

SCRIPTURE: John 13:31–35

INTRODUCTION: Jesus, just before the end of His earthly ministry, gave the disciples a commandment to be taken very seriously. Let's look at the commandment to love together:

1. This Is the Command of Christ.
   A. A Command Calls for Obedience. Obedience is the outworking of true wisdom (Deut. 10:13; Matt. 7:24–27), it's the evidence of real faith in God (1 John 2:4), and it's the demonstration of authentic love for God (2 John 1:6).
   B. This Is a New Commandment. Love had, of course, been taught before (Lev. 19:18), but Jesus is reasserting it with new force, clarity, and significance.

2. The Command Is to Love One Another. How can the world know we truly follow Christ unless we have this type of love:
   A. Love Involves Commitment (1 Cor. 13:1–8).
   B. Love Is Displayed by Conduct (1 Pet. 2:17).
   C. Love Is Always Caring (1 Pet. 1:22).

CONCLUSION: He who, out of His great compassion for you, loved you, and gave Himself to pay for your sins can pour His love out in your life and through your life!

TECHNIQUES FOR THE PASTOR'S DELIVERY

Impromptu Remarks

In his delightful book, *Public Speaking for Private People*, comedian Art Linkletter advises us to always be ready to give a few impromptu remarks when asked. "The basic principle in speaking off-the-cuff," he wrote, "is that you always try to avoid doing it off-the-cuff. I don't mean you should refuse to speak when asked to—just that you should try to anticipate situations where you may be asked to speak and then prepare ahead of time to give a short talk in case you are called upon."

Linkletter was once invited to a dinner at the White House honoring Britain's Prince Charles. This was during the Nixon Administration, and Linkletter was close friends with the President. At the dinner, he was seated between Bob Hope and the American Ambassador to Great Britain, Jock Whitney.

Before arriving at the White House, Linkletter realized that, being Nixon's friend, he might be called on to give a few spontaneous remarks, so he prepared carefully and selected a few appropriate stories. The dinner came and went, however, and Linkletter wasn't asked to speak.

Afterward on impulse, Linkletter asked his two dinner companions if they, too, had prepared anything to say in the event they were asked. "Are you kidding, Art—I'm always ready," replied Hope. And Ambassador Whitney admitted that he, too, had prepared something "just in case." In fact, Whitney said he had been unable to go to sleep the previous night until he had settled on some suitable remarks in the event he was called to the podium.[1]

Our most powerful communications are often spur-of-the-moment. Just study the sermons in the Bible. Few of them were planned in advance, at least not in the sense that we prepare our sermons. Elijah ran into Ahab and delivered God's message on the spot. Jesus was asked about the Herodian Temple and He extemporized the Olivet Discourse. Peter healed a lame man at

---

[1] Art Linkletter, *Public Speaking for Private People* (Indianapolis/New York: The Bobbs-Merrill Company, Inc., 1980), pp. 158–159.

the Beautiful Gate and a crowd assembled demanding an explanation. Paul saw a pagan altar labeled "To the Unknown God," and it occasioned his spontaneous sermon on Mars Hill.

But it's not as easy as it looks. I seldom feel good about ad-libbing. Recently I was put on the spot to deliver the invocation before a particular gathering, and I later felt I botched the job. Once I was taken by surprise when the chairman of our deacons interrupted an evening worship service to present my wife and me a gift for a pastor's appreciation day, and I later thought of a dozen things I should have said, but didn't.

No wonder entire college courses are devoted to impromptu public speaking. Whole books have appeared on this subject, and it's a category all to itself in the realm of rhetoric and declamation. In seminary, we're reminded that preachers should be ready to preach, pray, or die at a moment's notice.

If you're sitting in seat 34-G on an airplane with no one beside you, you can probably relax, as you're not likely to be called on for a "few words" or a prayer—unless the plane goes down. But in almost every other situation, you're vulnerable. When you walk into any meeting, ask yourself, "What would I say if called on?" If you can think of a good opening line or two, that's a big help. It doesn't have to be funny or clever, just appropriate.

The main thing is keeping your mind and spirit fresh every day. When we speak off the top of our heads, there should be some good material floating on the surface. When we think on our feet, we ought to be standing on some good promises, freshly claimed. The psalmist told us to delight ourselves in the law of the Lord and to meditate on it day and night. We may not have the eloquence of Demosthenes, but we can always stand and say, "Just this morning while reading in Isaiah 40, I noticed something I'd never seen before . . . ."

Or, "Well, this is unexpected; I appreciate your kind words. Your thoughtfulness on my fiftieth birthday means a lot to me. I'm looking at today as a mid-life point, which means I'm planning to celebrate my centennial birthday fifty years from today—

Continued on the next page

and you're all invited! But just last night I was mulling over what the Bible says about the brevity of life in Psalm 90, how we're to number our days and present to the Lord a heart of wisdom. So I ask your prayers that I'll be faithful to do that in the days or years I have left; and I can only hope and pray that the Lord will continue to give me friends as wonderful as all of you."

The Book of Deuteronomy tells us to talk about the Scripture when we sit at home, when we walk along the way, when we rise up, and when we go to bed. So it should always be on our minds. A fresh insight is always better than a stale outline.

It's also helpful to read the newspaper each morning or to make a mental note of one or two stories on your Internet news source. I once read a book entitled *How To Work a Room,* which gave tips on being socially at ease in a room full of strangers. The writer suggested jotting down a couple of interesting items from the newspaper for starting or sustaining a conversation.

If your mind is fresh with an insight from the Scripture and a nugget from the news, you can almost always make conversation with a stranger or give a brief talk to a roomful of people.

Of course, it's always prudent for preachers to have a few favorite outlines, stories, and themes up their sleeves, because sometimes a bit more is called for. If professional comedians keep a few jokes in reserve, and magicians always have a card trick handy, and politicians can give their stump speeches at the drop of a hat, why should we be less prepared?

I'd also advise you to learn the art of praying really fast. Nehemiah, the cupbearer for an ancient Persian monarch, was once asked to make an impromptu speech before the king, and it was a life-or-death occasion. Notice how the Bible describes the exchange: *The king said to me, 'What do you request?' So I prayed to the God of heaven. And I said to the king . . . .*

Had we been there, we probably wouldn't have even realized Nehemiah took the time to pray. It was an invisible, silent, sudden prayer that occurred during the brief pause in the conversation, in the flash of a moment. But God heard and answered that cry—and history was changed.

When you're asked to stand and say a word, learn to pause just long enough to ask God for guidance. It could be that your unplanned utterance will accomplish more for the kingdom than a finely polished, well-scripted sermon.

Finally, smile, relax, speak from your heart, and maintain eye contact. And above all be brief. Impromptu speaking is nothing new for you. When you think about it, it's what we do all day long. Virtually every conversation is impromptu. You don't often use notes or rehearse in advance what you're going to say in your daily chit-chat unless it's a planned conversation with a definite agenda.

Just imagine, then, that you're talking to one person, and be conversational. Relax your hands and look for a way to say a word for the Lord. Remember that Jesus told His followers not to worry in advance when they had to present impromptu speeches before critics. The heavenly Father would give them words to say. We may never stand before enemies seeking our lives for the gospel, but the same heavenly Father can set a watch before our mouths and keep the doors of our lips.

Every good opportunity comes from Him, and we're just to redeem the time, always being ready to give a reason for the hope that is within us.

AUGUST 19, 2007

SUGGESTED SERMON

The Spectrum of Salvation

Date preached:

By Dr. Melvin Worthington

Scripture: Various, especially Romans 1:16
For I am not ashamed of the gospel of Christ, for it is the power of God to salvation for everyone who believes, for the Jew first and also for the Greek.

Introduction: The spectrum of salvation includes justification, sanctification, separation, and glorification. The salvation conveyed in the Scriptures delivers individuals from their past sins, the power of sin and eventually one day from the very presence of sin. The spectrum of salvation includes the following truths:

1. **Salvation's Decision.** Salvation commences with a decision. People are not saved by chance but by choice. Every individual must make an intelligent and deliberate choice to be saved. The basis of one's choice is the composition of the Sovereign. The palmist declares that the entrance of the Word of God gives light. The Psalmist concludes, "The law of the LORD is perfect, converting the soul: the testimony of the LORD is sure, making wise the simple. The statutes of the LORD are right, rejoicing the heart: the commandment of the LORD is pure, enlightening the eyes. The fear of the LORD is clean, enduring forever: the judgments of the LORD are true and righteous altogether. More to be desired are they than gold, yea, than much fine gold: sweeter also than honey and the honeycomb. Moreover by them your servant is warned, and in keeping them there is great reward" (Ps. 19:7–11). The genuine choice to be saved begins with the proper concept of one's self (Eph. 2; Rom. 3). It continues with a burden of sin—a consciousness of sin, followed by a brokenness— a confession of sin, followed by a beseeching—calling on the Savior and concludes with a behavior—the conduct that evidences salvation. Life is made up of choices. Salvation comes as a result of the proper choice rather than by chance.

2. **Salvation's Deliverance.** Salvation delivers one from death (Eph. 2; John 5:24; John 3), darkness (John 3:19–21; 1 John 1:6–7), dominion (Rom. 6—8), disposition (John 3:19–21; Acts 9; Gal. 1), deeds (1 Pet.

4:3, 4; Eph. 2:1–3; Titus 3:3–8; 1 Thess. 1:9; Rom. 6), disease (John 9:23) and disobedience (1 Pet. 1).

3. **Salvation's Difference.** Salvation makes a difference in the lives of those who experience it. It is like passing from death to life, from darkness to light. Salvation results in a changed life (1 Thess. 1:3; 2 Cor. 5:17; 1 Tim. 1). Those who are born of God believe Jesus is the Messiah (1 John 2), doth not commit sin (1 John 3), doeth righteous (1 John 2:29; 3:10), love the brethren (1 John 2:3), overcomes the world (1 John 5:5; James 1:27–28) and keep themselves from the wicked one (1 John 5). Salvation also changes one's love toward the Savior, the saint, the sinner and the Lord's service (1 Thess. 1:3, 9, 10). Salvation causes one to look for the comforting, cleansing and compelling hope—the Second Coming of the Lord Jesus Christ (1 Thess. 1:10). Salvation conforms one to the likeness of Christ (Gal. 4:19; Col. 3:10; 2 Pet. 3:17–18; 2 Pet. 1:5–11). Salvation brings liberty in the place of slavery (Rom. 6; Gal. 5; Rom. 14:1–12). Salvation results in loyalty (2 Tim. 1:12; Eph. 6:13).

4. **Salvation's Demands.** As Christians we are required to glorify God, give our bodies to the Lord, guard our minds, members, motives, morals and means, grow in the grace and knowledge of Christ, glow as lights in this darkened world and go with the gospel.

5. **Salvation's Discernment.** Christians need to discern the times (days), the temptations (dangers), the truth (doctrine), the teachers (disciples), and the testing (discipline).

6. **Salvation's Dividends.** Salvation results in honest living (Acts 6:3), hopeful living (1 Thess. 1:3), holy living (1 Pet. 1:15–16), happy living (John 13:17), helpful living (Rom. 16:3; 2 Cor. 1:11, 24), humble living (Phil. 4; 1 Pet. 5:5–6; James 4:6), and hallowed living.

7. **Salvation's Dangers.** The Christians faces at least three dangers: complacency—unconcern (1 Cor. 9:27), compromise—unfaithfulness (Matt. 24; 2 Tim. 3), and contempt—unbelief (2 Thess. 2; 1 Tim. 4).

Conclusion: People are not saved by chance but by choice. They must choose to receive the Lord Jesus Christ as their Lord and Savior. Have you accepted Christ?

STATS, STORIES, AND MORE

Our Great Savior

There's a little song we sometimes sing around here: "Jesus, name above all names, Beautiful Savior, wonderful Lord . . . ." That song was written by a middle-aged woman from New Zealand who had been studying the subject of the names of Jesus in the Bible. One day she wrote out some of the names on a piece of paper, and she happened to take that paper out to the washhouse so she could mull over it while washing her clothes. Like many New Zealanders, she had a washhouse behind the regular living quarters of her home. Well, while she was washing her clothes, she became aware of the Lord's presence in that washhouse with her, and she began to sing the words, "Jesus, name above all names," and pretty soon she had composed the whole little song right there in that washhouse. She thought to herself, "Well, I'll write it down," and she went to the piano and wrote it out. After finishing, she said, "Lord, is that okay? Is that all right like that?" Sensing the Lord's approval, she went back to her washing, unaware that she had just written a little song that would one day be sung around the world. He is Jesus, name above all names, beautiful Savior, wonderful Lord, Immanuel, God is with us. Even in the washhouse, even in the garage, even in the kitchen, even on the basketball court—we do not have a God who is merely above us; we have a God who is among us and His name is above all names. The Word became flesh and has pitched His tent among us.

APPROPRIATE HYMNS AND SONGS

"Come Just as You Are," Joseph Sabolick, 1993 Maranatha Praise Inc.

"Grace Greater Than Our Sin," Julie H. Johnston/Daniel Brink Towner, Public Domain.

"Salvation Is Here, Joel Houston, 2005 Joel Houston (Hillsong) (Admin. Integrity's Hosanna! Music).

"He Set Me Free," Albert E. Brumley, 1939 Renewed 1967 Stamps Baxter Music (Admin. Brentwood Benson Music Publishing).

"All I Once Held Dear (Knowing You)," Graham Kendrick, 1993 Make Way Music (Admin. Music Services).

FOR THE BULLETIN

One of the greatest—and humblest—leaders of the English Reformation, Thomas Bilney, was burned at the stake on August 19, 1531. He had been converted to the evangelical cause while reading Erasmus' translations of the Pauline letters; afterward he sought to win the great churchman, Hugh Latimer, to Christ, saying, in effect, "Lord, I'm just Little Bilney and I can do little for you, but if I can just reach Latimer, he can do great things." He did reach Latimer, who also was later burned at the stake alongside Nicholas Ridley. ● John Craig was born in Scotland in 1512, studied at the University of St. Andrews, and entered the ministry. While living on the continent, he found a copy of Calvin's *Institutes* and in reading them found himself becoming a Protestant. As a result, he was arrested by agents of the Inquisition, taken prisoner to Rome, and condemned to death at the stake. On the evening of August 19, 1559, while awaiting execution the next day, dramatic news arrived that Pope Paul IV had died. According to custom, the prisons in Rome were thrown open, the prisoners temporarily released. Craig took advantage of the opportunity, escaped to Scotland where he preached Christ and abetted the Reformation until his death many years later at age eighty-eight. ● Today marks the death at age 39, in 1662, of Blaise Pascal, scientist, polemicist and Christian apologist. ● John Bunyan, traveling to London to preach, was caught in a heavy storm and soaked to the skin. On Sunday, August 19, 1688, he was able to preach at the meeting house in Petticoat Lane, Whitechapel, from John 1:13; but it was Bunyan's last sermon. Two days later, he developed pneumonia and shortly afterward passed away. Today also marks the final sermon of Samuel Miller, cofounder of Princeton Theological Seminary who was responsible for training a generation of Presbyterian ministers. His health deteriorated throughout the 1840s, and on Sunday, August 19, 1849, he preached on Hebrews 6:19 at the Dutch Neck Presbyterian Church.

WORSHIP HELPS

Call to Worship
Let all those who seek You rejoice and be glad in You; and let those who love Your salvation say continually, "Let God be magnified" (Ps. 70:4)!

Scripture Reading: Luke 18:18–27
Now a certain ruler asked Him, saying, "Good Teacher, what shall I do to inherit eternal life?" So Jesus said to him, "Why do you call Me good? No one is good but One, that is, God. You know the commandments: 'Do not commit adultery,' 'Do not murder,' 'Do not steal,' 'Do not bear false witness,' 'Honor your father and your mother.'" And he said, "All these things I have kept from my youth." So when Jesus heard these things, He said to him, "You still lack one thing. Sell all that you have and distribute to the poor, and you will have treasure in heaven; and come, follow Me." But when he heard this, he became very sorrowful, for he was very rich. And when Jesus saw that he became very sorrowful, He said, "How hard it is for those who have riches to enter the kingdom of God! For it is easier for a camel to go through the eye of a needle than for a rich man to enter the kingdom of God." And those who heard it said, "Who then can be saved?" But He said, **"The things which are impossible with men are possible with God"** (emphasis added).

Benediction
For if when we were enemies we were reconciled to God through the death of His Son, much more, having been reconciled, we shall be saved by His life. And not only *that,* but we also rejoice in God through our Lord Jesus Christ, through whom we have now received the reconciliation (Rom. 5:10–11).

Additional Sermons and Lesson Ideas

How to Get Out of a Bad Mood

Date preached:

SCRIPTURE: Proverbs 15:13, 15, 30 (NIV)

INTRODUCTION: If you want to be well-liked, esteemed, and sought-after, you must learn to be a cheerful person. Not gushing and bubbly and fizzy, but pleasant, upbeat, optimistic, relaxed, and friendly. Three verses in Proverbs 15 (NIV) give us the secret to acquiring this attitude.

1. Proverbs 15:13 tells us that a happy heart makes a face cheerful. When we cultivate our daily devotions and began each day with the Lord, it strengthens our hearts and others will notice it in our faces.
2. Proverbs 15:15 tells us that a cheerful heart has a continual feast. This is another way of saying, "My cup overflows." It's the same truth we see in Ephesians 1:3 when we're told that God has blessed us with every spiritual blessing in Christ.
3. Proverbs 15:30 tells us that a cheerful look brings joy to the heart. We become carriers of cheer, spreading to others the joy of the Lord in our heart.

CONCLUSION: Martha Washington once said, "I am still determined to be cheerful and happy in whatever situation I may be. . . ." Abraham Lincoln said that a person is about as happy as he makes up his mind to be. Make up your mind to be happy in the Lord.

Put on Love

Date preached:

By Joshua D. Rowe

SCRIPTURE: Colossians 3:12–14 (NIV)

INTRODUCTION: Most of us would never dream of going out of the house without any attention to what we put on. Paul reminds us to pay attention to what we put on, not physically, but spiritually.

1. Recognize That You Are God's Beloved and Holy People (v. 12). As God's people, Paul says to:
    A. Clothe Yourselves with Compassion.
    B. Clothe Yourselves with Kindness.
    C. Clothe Yourselves with Humility.
    D. Clothe Yourselves with Gentleness.
    E. Clothe Yourselves with Patience.
2. Recognize the Lord's Forgiveness (v. 13). We must offer one another the same grace given to us. Specifically, Paul instructs us to:

A. Bear with Each Other.
B. Forgive Grievances Against Each Other.
3. Above All, Put on Love (v. 14). Paul teaches us that love binds together all the virtues of these verses in perfect unity.

CONCLUSION: God has called you as His people, and He wants you to dress the part: not in a physical sense, but what matters more to Him is that you dress yourselves with godly virtues, especially love.

PRAYER FOR THE PASTOR'S CLOSET

Jesus, Thou Divine Companion

Jesus, Thou divine Companion,
By Thy lowly human birth
Thou hast come to join the workers,
Burden bearers of the earth.
Thou, the Carpenter of Nazareth,
Toiling for Thy daily food,
By Thy patience and Thy courage,
Thou hast taught us toil is good.

Every task, however simple,
Sets the soul that does it free;
Every deed of love and kindness
Done to man is done to Thee.
Jesus, Thou divine Companion,
Help us all to do our best;
Bless in our daily labor,
Lead us to the Sabbath rest.
—HENRY JACKSON VAN DYKE (1909)

AUGUST 26, 2007

SUGGESTED SERMON

Life Lessons from a Flawed Hero

By Dr. Woodrow Kroll   *Date preached:*

Scripture: I Kings 3:1–3 and 11:1–6, especially I Kings 11:4 (NIV)
As Solomon grew old, his wives turned his heart after other gods, and his heart was
not fully devoted to the LORD his God as the heart of David his father had been.

Introduction: Alexander the Great conquered the world, yet died at age
33 in a drunken stupor. Hannibal may have crossed the Alps with
elephants, but he had three bushels of gold rings taken off knights he
slaughtered; and he later committed suicide. Julius Caesar conquered
eight hundred cities across Europe and the Middle East, but he was
stabbed by his closest friends. Napoleon was the scourge of Europe,
yet he died in banishment.

Have you noticed that some who leave a strong mark have tragic
lives? Solomon was like that. He was the wisest, wealthiest man who
ever lived; yet there's a tragedy to his life, and we can learn from it.
From my study of his life, it seems to me that Solomon made *three
gigantic mistakes.*

1. **The Mistake of Unholy Alliances (1 Kin. 3:1).** Solomon did what he
   thought he needed to do to solidify his power, but instead of pleasing
   God, he did the opposite. In 1 Kings 1:5, even before he became
   king, his throne was challenged by a half-brother. In 1 Kings 1:7,
   some of his father's allies betrayed him. Solomon's position was
   threatened, and that's why he made an alliance with Egypt. Instead
   of making alliances with the right people in his country, with the
   priests and Levites and leaders in his family, he went to his worst
   enemy. A lot of people do that. Instead of seeking counsel from
   godly people, we go to the world for help. That's why 2 Corinthians
   6 warns about being unequally yoked with unbelievers. We often
   apply that to marriage, but it has to do with *every* area of life, whether
   business or friendship.

2. **The Mistake of Allowing Dark Corners to Remain (1 Kin. 3:2–3).**
   The second mistake Solomon made was in allowing dark corners
   of sin to remain in his life. According to 1 Kings 3:2–3, Solomon

worshiped Jehovah but tolerated incense on the high places. The "high places" were altars on hills around the country devoted to pagan gods, especially the gods of the Canaanites. While Solomon did some wonderful things, he tolerated pagan gods. Blessing comes, not from giving God a corner of our lives; it comes from wholly following Him, giving Him everything. Those dark corners always come back to haunt us.

3. **The Mistake of Allowing the World to Draw Us Away from God (1 Kin. 11:1–4).** Once Solomon became wealthy, his mind drifted from God a bit. In the course of getting everything he wanted, represented by his seven hundred wives, the call of the world drowned out the call of God. See 2 Timothy 4:10 and 1 John 2:15–17. The Bible is clear on this. For you and me as Christians to invest all of our time in *this* world, to invest all of our energy in *this* world, to invest all of our money in *this* world—that isn't just silly, it's stupid! But sometimes the distractions of the world cause us to have a life like Solomon's. He did very well at first. Then he became wealthy, wise, and powerful; and the world became a strong attraction to which he did not summon the energy to resist.

Conclusion: If you and I want to be joyous and fruitful Christians, we can learn from Solomon. We cannot allow these things to go wrong in our lives, because if we do they can spoil our hearts the way they spoiled Solomon's. We must always be aware of how closely we live with God. We can be as wise as Solomon yet still have a foolish life like him if we're not a person after the heart of God. Let me encourage you today to check out, not how wise or wealthy you are, but how closely you're living with God. How intimate are you with God? Are you the person after God's own heart like King David? Or are you a person who has been extremely blessed like King Solomon, yet you haven't handled that blessing very well? Now is the time to change. And that's the good news—God will help you do that in Christ Jesus, His Son.

STATS, STORIES, AND MORE

More from Dr. Kroll
George Barna says that in the evangelical church in America and Canada today, there is much of the world in our churches. We choose to believe only what we want to believe from the Bible; and we choose to believe from the world what we want to believe.

Barna says, "We've made an amalgam religion"—what strikes our fancy! And he's absolutely right! Instead of understanding the Word of God and drawing our strength from the Word of God, we draw our strength from here and from any other place we can find. Solomon did the same thing. That was a mistake. God will accept nothing less than total obedience from us. He certainly would accept nothing less from Solomon. Read Deuteronomy 6:4–5. God never accepts from us a piece of an offering. He never accepts from us a partial sacrifice. That's why Paul says in Romans 12 that we are to totally be sacrificed to Him, to give everything over to Him: to give all of our finances to Him and give all of our children to Him and all of our grandchildren to Him, all of our days to Him and all of our nights to Him—we give it all to Him. He takes care of us because He loves total obedience. Solomon was only partially obedient. He made some mistakes. And making that mistake robs us of the blessing that Solomon lost. This is a man who was extremely wealthy but apparently quite unhappy at the same time because he made many unholy alliances, tolerated sin, and allowed his heart to drift from its pure love for Jesus.

APPROPRIATE HYMNS AND SONGS

"Draw Me Close," Kelly Carpenter, 1994 Mercy/Vineyard Publishing (Admin. Music Services).

"Jesus Draw Me Close," Rick Founds, 1990 Maranatha Praise Inc. (Admin. The Copyright Co.).

"Immortal Invisible," Walter Chalmers Smith/John Robert, Public Domain.

"Everlasting," Rick Founds, 1990 Maranatha Praise Inc. (Admin. The Copyright Co.).

FOR THE BULLETIN

On August 26, 1498, Italian artist Michelangelo was commissioned by Pope Alexander VI to carve the *Pietà*. The sculpture was completed in 1501. ● Johann Heinrich Bullinger, the Swiss Reformer who took over in Zurich after the death of Zwingli, was a tireless preacher, a devoted pastor, a brilliant scholar, and a prolific writer. His hard work eventually left him exhausted and undermined his heath, and he wrote, "I almost sink under the load of business and care, and feel so tired that I would ask the Lord to give me rest if it were not against His will." On his deathbed, on August 26, 1575, he assembled the church leaders of Zurich and preached to them, exhorting them to be pure in their lives and harmonious in their relationships. He closed with a prayer of thanksgiving and a hymn of praise. Then he took each by the hand and with many tears took his leave of them. He died on September 17. ● On August 26, 1708, Ebenezer Erskine wrote, "I offer myself up, soul and body, unto God the Father, Son, and Holy Ghost. I flee for shelter to the blood of Jesus. I will live to him; I will die to him. I take heaven and earth to witness that all I am and all I have are his." He went on to become a popular preacher in eighteenth-century Scotland and the founder of the Scottish Secession Church. ● The first Lutheran synod in America, the Pennsylvania Ministerium, was organized at Philadelphia at Saint Michael's Church on this day in 1748. ● The American Standard Version of the New Testament was first published by Thomas Nelson and Sons on August 26, 1901. It is a literally translated version which is still a gold-standard of excellence for English students of the Bible.

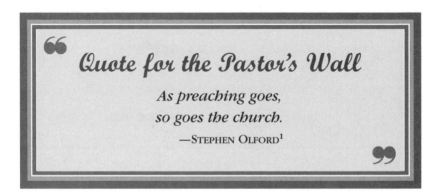

❝

Quote for the Pastor's Wall

*As preaching goes,
so goes the church.*

—STEPHEN OLFORD[1]

❞

---

[1]http://www.olford.org/, accessed March 10, 2006.

WORSHIP HELPS

Call to Worship

I will bow down . . . and will praise your name for your love and your faithfulness, for you have exalted above all things your name and your word (Ps. 138:2 NIV).

An Invitation to Recommitment

In Revelation 2:4, Jesus warned that the Christians in a particular church had drifted away from their first love; they did not love Him as they once did. Could this apply to you and me today? A little later, in Revelation 3:15, He warned believers in another church that they had grown lukewarm, no longer hot and passionate for Him. Could He mean us? Has your love for Christ waned? Has your devotion to Christ weakened? Has your passion for Him faded? How easily the demands and temptations of the world crowd into our hearts, distracting us from wholehearted obedience to Christ. Today Jesus is standing at the door of your heart, knocking, listening, waiting to be restored as the Lord and Master of your life. I'm going to ask you to renew your commitment to Christ. Repent of your sin, and enthrone Him once again in the center of your heart. He allows no rivals. Proclaim Him Lord alone.

Offertory Comments

Someone once said, "Nothing makes a congregation more uncomfortable than these two topics: their neighbors and their pocketbooks," that is, evangelism and tithing. Christ commanded us to preach the gospel to the world (Matt. 28:18–20), and we must be bold about this command. The same holds true with money; Jesus taught more about money than He did about heaven and hell combined! Pastors often feel uneasy in teaching about finances or the discipline of tithing. We know that God will provide, but we also know that He uses you to do so. We know God doesn't need your money, but He wants your heart. Jesus taught that your heart follows your treasure (Matt. 6:21). Today, I ask you to give generously, not because I want your money, but I don't want any one of you to miss out on the blessing that God offers to those who give.

Additional Sermons and Lesson Ideas

A Pattern for Prayer

By Dr. Timothy Beougher

Date preached:

SCRIPTURE: Nehemiah 1:5–11

INTRODUCTION: Abraham Lincoln once asserted, "I have been driven many times to my knees by the overwhelming conviction that I had nowhere else to go. My own wisdom and that of those around me seemed insufficient for the day." For Nehemiah, as it should be for us, it wasn't a last resort, but a first option! Let's look at his example:

1. Acknowledge God's Greatness (v. 5).
   A. His Sovereignty: "Lord God of heaven."
   B. His Holiness: "O great and awesome God."
   C. His Faithfulness: "You who keep Your covenant and mercy with those who love You and observe Your commandments."
2. Confess Your Sinfulness (vv. 6–7).
3. Remember God's Promises (vv. 8–9).
4. Petition God's Help (v. 11).

CONCLUSION: Remember that God is ". . . able to do exceedingly abundantly above all that we ask or think . . ." (Eph. 3:20).

Dream Big, Work Hard, Leave It to God

By Dr. Larry Osborne

Date preached:

SCRIPTURE: Various

INTRODUCTION: Let's look at some passages and applications to keep God in the middle of our dreams and aspirations.

1. It's Okay to Dream Big and Ask for More (1 Chr. 4:9–10; Eph. 3:20–21; James 4:2; Rom. 8:15; 1 Tim. 6:9; Prov. 23:4–5). As we dream big, we should also keep these scriptural principles in mind:
   A. Some Things Need a Soaking in Prayer (Luke 11:1–3; 18:1–8; Matt. 26:36–46; Dan. 6:10).
   B. Character Precedes Blessing (1 Chr. 4:9; Prov. 10:22; 11:18; 20:17; 21:6, 21).
2. Work Hard, and Then Leave It to God (Prov. 21:30–31):
   A. It's Our Job to Prepare the Horse Well (Prov. 12:24; 18:9; 20:4; 2 Thess. 3:7–10; Col. 3:17).
   B. It's God's Job to Decide How the Battle Goes (Prov. 8:13; 16:9; 21:30–31; Josh. 7:1–26; Job 2:8–9; 1 Cor. 4:7).

CONCLUSION: We should always have a balance of powerful prayer as we learn through Jabez, and appropriate attitude adjustment as we learn through Solomon.

William and Marion Veitch
and the Providence of God

William and Marion Veitch, a godly Presbyterian couple, lived with their children in a peaceful home in Scotland in the seventeenth century. William was a preacher, but in those days the Presbyterians were outlawed, and he lived in fear that sooner or later he would be arrested. It happened one night in 1680. Royal Scottish soldiers burst in and dragged William off to prison.

It was all orchestrated by an evil man named Thomas Bell, a vicar in the established church who drank and used profanity and harbored a burning hatred for the Veitchs.

William was taken to Morpeth Prison, leaving Marion at home profoundly troubled. Pouring out her soul to the Lord in prayer, she opened her Bible and drew strength from certain verses, such as "He does all things well," and "Trust in the Lord, and fear not what man can do." Then as soon as she could arrange it, she set off to visit her husband, for it appeared he would be removed to Edinburgh and executed.

Marion's journey took place on a bitterly cold January day. The snow was blinding, and she had to fight the weather on horseback. Night fell, and she trudged on, finally arriving at the prison half-frozen about midnight.

The guards wouldn't let her see William until morning, so Marion sat by the fire and waited. When morning broke, she was allowed to see her husband for only a moment, and only in the presence of guards. Then she was torn away, expecting to never see him again.

Marion went to a friend's house, wept her fill, and opened her Bible. The words of Isaiah 8:12–13 spoke powerfully to her: "... Nor be afraid of their threats, nor be troubled. The LORD of hosts, Him you shall hallow. Let Him be your fear, And let Him be your dread." She rested herself in the Lord and cast her burden on Him.

Meanwhile their archenemy, Vicar Thomas Bell, the one who was responsible for William's arrest, gloated to friends, "Now Veitch will be hanged tomorrow as he deserves." *Continued on the next page*

That evening Thomas Bell called on a friend and the two lingered over the alcohol until about 10 P.M. when he said he must be going. The night was dark and cold, the river was icy and swollen, and his host urged him to wait till morning. But Bell had work to do and victims to prosecute. He rode away warmed by alcohol, but he never reached home. Two days later his dead body was found standing up to his arms in one solid block of ice in the river.

William was soon freed, and the restored couple worked side-by-side until William's death forty years later.

The history of the church and the story of our lives are liberally sprinkled with incidents like that—God's over-ruling, under-girding sovereignty, God's protection, God's provision and His answers to prayer.

In the unfolding of His providence, burdens become blessings, tears lead to triumph, and the redemptive grace of God overcomes the undercurrents of life in the experiences of His children. For them . . .

Ill that God blesses is our good,
And unblest good is ill,
And all is right that seems most wrong
If it be His sweet will.

This is Romans 8:28, lived out in daily experience: All things work together for good to those who love the Lord and are called according to His purposes. Understanding the Sovereignty of God is one of the most liberating experiences a Christian can ever make.

John Calvin once said, "When the light of divine providence has once shone upon a godly man, he is then relieved and set free not only from the extreme anxiety and fear that were pressing him before, but from every care . . . Ignorance of providence is the ultimate misery; the highest blessedness lies in knowing it . . . (It gives) incredible freedom from worry about the future."

No wonder Charles Spurgeon once quipped, "We believe in the providence of God, but we do not believe half enough in it."[2]

---

[2]Excerpted from the editor's book, *Real Stories for the Soul* (Nashville: Thomas Nelson Publishers, 2000), pp. 100–103.

SEPTEMBER 2, 2007

SUGGESTED SERMON

How to Survive a Lion's Attack

By Joshua D. Rowe

Date preached:

Scripture: 1 Peter 5:8–10, especially verse 8
Be sober, be vigilant; because your adversary the devil walks about like a roaring lion, seeking whom he may devour.

Introduction: I have very unpleasant news to start out with today. I must inform you that each and every one of you has your own personal stalker. He walks near you constantly, watching and waiting for the right time; in fact, it's the only thing he ever does. He wants to rip you to shreds as a lion would his prey. Worse than any serial killer or sexual predator, he desires to snuff out not only your earthly life, but your relationship with God and your eternal life. Fortunately, we have a defense laid out for us which involves both our action, and reliance upon God's ultimate protection against the lion's attack, that is, against the devil himself.

1. **Be Sober and Alert (v. 8a).** If you were drunk, how well could you defend yourself? Peter applies this principle with a command to be sober and alert. The word for sober here is well-translated. The recipients of this letter had experienced their share of drunkenness, as Peter pointed out previously (1 Pet. 4:3). The Greek word for drunkenness conveys a "fuzziness" of sight and mind. Our first defense is to see clearly and to mentally realize the battle that is around us daily.

2. **Know Your Adversary: the Lion (v. 8b).** Who is this enemy of ours?

   A. **Our Accuser.** The word translated "adversary" is literally translated "anti-law-one." In other words, Satan is portrayed as both lawless, and an opponent at law. Satan is often referred to as our accuser in Scripture (Job 1:6; Zech. 3:1; Rev. 12:10).

   B. **Our Stalker.** Our text teaches us that Satan, "walks about." Remember the story of Job? In Job 1:6–7, Satan approaches God saying he has been "roaming" back and forth on the earth, and the Lord asks him if he has considered Job to test Him. We have a glimpse into the daily activity of the enemy here: He is very near.

C. **Our Attacker.** Satan is depicted as both a stalking lion, and a devouring lion. Have you ever watched the discovery channel, how a lion ties a napkin around his neck and gently carves his dinner? Of course not! You see graphic images of utter brutality. God, through Peter, wants to paint a vivid picture in our minds of what Satan wishes to do to our relationships, our spiritual lives, our families, and anything else. So what's the plan?

3. **Resist the Enemy Through Faith in Christ and Fellowship of Sufferings (v. 9).** The word translated "resist" means both "to withstand" and "to oppose." How can we have such boldness in the face of a ruthless predator? The verse tells us: ". . . steadfast in the faith, knowing that the same sufferings are experienced by your brotherhood in the world." The ironic truth of spiritual warfare is that we must realize our weakness to harness God's strength. We must continue placing our complete trust in Jesus Christ, and we will be "steadfast," unshakeable! Not only do we have power through faith in Christ, we have encouragement of others all over the world just like us. Do you ever feel attacked and think, "why me?" Guess what, it's not just you! Peter tells us to stand firm, knowing that others all over the world stand with us under the same attack.

4. **Appeal to Your Defender: the God of Grace (v. 10).** We might still be frightened at this text, were it not for verse 10. Peter appeals to the ultimate Defender, as we must likewise do, in whom we place our faith. We are encouraged that:

A. **He Called Us to Eternal Glory Through Jesus Christ (v. 10a).** If we place our trust completely in Christ, we know that we will live with Christ throughout eternity: our enemy is temporary!

B. **Our Suffering Is Temporary (v. 10b).** Peter puts our lives in perspective when he says, ". . . after you have suffered a while." The attacks we face, in view of eternity, are very short-lived.

C. **God Himself Will Work on His Soldiers for Battle (v. 10c).** Peter prays, ". . . may the God of all grace . . . perfect, establish, strengthen, and settle you." Here we have an entire sermon series. Let it suffice to say that God is at work sanctifying us, making us an unshakable, strong force against the enemy.

Conclusion: Be sober and alert, stand firm in the faith, and appeal to the Defender! Even a lion could never shake such a fortress.

STATS, STORIES, AND MORE

Background

The recipients of 1 Peter lived in the northwest corner of Asia Minor, in Roman provinces under Roman rule with mostly pagans. As Jews who were scattered in the Diaspora, their churches were culturally and ethnically mixed with Jews and Gentiles. Some believe it was written very close to A.D. 64 because they place it at the beginning of persecution under Nero. However, the scholarly consensus seems to be somewhere between the dates of A.D. 48 to 64, probably very close to the beginning of this persecution, but before official persecution began. So, the suffering constantly referred to by Peter (see 1 Pet. 1:6; 2:19–21; 3:14–17; 4:12–19; 5:8–10) is probably not official Neronian or Domicletian persecution, but was probably societal conflict and a sort of cultural ostracism. Does this sound familiar? Peter wrote this letter to churches that faced social and cultural opposition from a secular society. Peter could have written this book straight to the churches in our society! This book is unbelievably relevant to our own culture and time.

Why Did Peter Use Imagery of Lions?

Lions were found in Syria, Asia Minor, Greece, Mesopotamia, and even northwest India in antiquity. Besides this, in the mythology of ancient Near Eastern and in the art, lions are commonly found (Assyria, Babylon, Mesopotamia, Canaan, Egypt, and Palestine). The recipients, the majority being Diaspora Jews, would have known scriptural stories and references to lions as well (i.e. Judah as the "lion," Daniel and the lion's den, etc.). The idea of lions in stories or real life was very real to the recipients of the letter.

APPROPRIATE HYMNS AND SONGS

"Blessed Be the Lord My Rock," Alison Nash, 1984 Seam of Gold [div of Christian City Church, Sydney Australia (Admin. Seam of Gold International)].

"Greater Are You," Dennis Jernigan, 1990 Shepherd's Heart Music, Inc. (Admin. Word Music Group).

"Stand Up, Stand Up for Jesus," George Duffield Jr./George J. Webb, Public Domain.

"We Will Overcome," Carol Cymbala, 1988 Word Music, Inc. (Admin. Word Music Group).

"A Mighty Fortress Is Our God," Martin Luther, Public Domain.

FOR THE BULLETIN

Simeon, born about 390 to a shepherd's family in Cilicia, was determined to escape the corruption of the world by living atop a pillar. His first column was six feet high, but soon he built higher ones until his permanent abode towered sixty feet above ground. The tiny perch wouldn't allow for comfort, but a railing kept Simeon from falling while asleep. Simeon lived atop his pole for thirty years like a candle on a candlestick. He died on September 2, 450. ● Today is the birthday, in 1661, of Georg Boehm, Lutheran organist and composer who had the privilege of counting among his pupils young Johann Sebastian Bach. ● The restoration of England's monarchy in 1662 resulted in the Act of Uniformity, removing 2,000 preachers from their pulpits in a single day. Most preached their farewell sermons August 17, 1662. Rev. William Jenkyn secretly continued preaching after the act of uniformity. After the indulgence of 1671, he returned to London where he preached until 1682, when a fresh storm of persecution fell over the evangelical church. Jenkyn was seized by a soldier on September 2, 1684, while spending a day in prayer with some other ministers. He was thrown into Newgate prison where he died on January 18 of the next year. When news reached the palace, a nobleman said to the king, "May it please your majesty, Jenkyn has got his liberty." "Aye!" replied the king, "who gave it to him." The nobleman replied, "A greater than your majesty, the King of kings." ● The United States Treasury Department was established by Congress on September 2, 1879. ● Writer J. R. R. Tolkien died on this day in 1973.

WORSHIP HELPS

Call to Worship

I will love You, O LORD, my strength. The LORD is my rock and my fortress and my deliverer; my God, my strength, in whom I will trust; my shield and the horn of my salvation, my stronghold. I will call upon the LORD, who is worthy to be praised; so shall I be saved from my enemies (2 Sam. 22:2–4).

Scripture Reading Medley

Be sober, be vigilant; because your adversary the devil walks about like a roaring lion, seeking whom he may devour. And I say to you, My friends, do not be afraid of those who kill the body, and after that have no more that they can do. But I will show you whom you should fear: Fear Him who, after He has killed, has power to cast into hell; yes, I say to you, fear Him! Therefore submit to God. Resist the devil and he will flee from you. In this manner, therefore, pray . . . do not lead us into temptation, but deliver us from the evil one. For Yours is the kingdom and the power and the glory forever. Amen (1 Pet. 5:8–10; Luke 12:4–5; James 4:7; Matt. 6:9, 13).

Benediction

But may the God of all grace, who called us to His eternal glory by Christ Jesus, after you have suffered a while, perfect, establish, strengthen, and settle you. To Him be the glory and the dominion forever and ever. Amen (1 Pet. 5:10–11).

Additional Sermons and Lesson Ideas

A Bird's-Eye View of 1 Peter

Date preached:

By Joshua D. Rowe

SCRIPTURE: 1 Peter

INTRODUCTION: Peter wrote this letter to Christians who found themselves as the minority in a secular culture. Taking a look at 1 Peter as a whole gives us some practical guidelines as we strive to live as Christians in a similar setting.

1. Live with Hope (ch. 1). The resurrection of Christ is the central theme of our hope (vv. 3–5).
2. Live as People of God (chs. 2—3). Our lifestyle, as laid out in these chapters, is to serve as an example to the secular society we live in (2:11–17).
3. Live Victorious over Suffering (chs. 4—5). Peter is very clear that if we lead sinful lifestyles we deserve to suffer (4:14–16). He goes on to teach believers how to live victorious lives in the midst of persecution.

CONCLUSION: Now that you've had a bird's eye view, I challenge you to read 1 Peter this week and apply the principles to your life as you live out this week.

Prevailing Prayer

Date preached:

Adapted from an outline by Rosalind Goforth

SCRIPTURE: Various

INTRODUCTION: In her 1921 book, *How I Know God Answers Prayer,* missionary/prayer warrior Rosalind Goforth suggested nine secrets to prevailing prayer.

1. Contrite Humility before God and Forsaking of Sin (2 Chr. 7:14).
2. Seeking God with the Whole Heart (Jer. 29:12–13).
3. Faith in God (Mark 11:23–24).
4. Obedience (1 John 3:22).
5. Dependence on the Holy Spirit (Rom. 8:26).
6. Importunity (Mark 7:24–30 and Luke 11:5–10).
7. Asking in Accordance with God's Will (1 John 5:14).
8. In Christ's Name (John 14:13–14).
9. Willing to Make Amends for Wrongs to Others (Matt. 5:23–24).

CONCLUSION: "As the discerning soul can plainly see, all the conditions mentioned in this list may be included in the one word *Abide.*"

—Rosalind Goforth

SEPTEMBER 9, 2007

SUGGESTED SERMON

Who's to Blame When Towers Fall?

By Dr. Ed Dobson

Date preached:

Scripture: Luke 13:1–8, especially verse 3
Unless you repent you will all likewise perish.

Introduction: This week, the news, ceremonies, and perhaps our own minds will remind us of the terrible tragedy of September 11, 2001. When tragedies strike, who is responsible? Some well-known TV Christian personalities pronounced September 11th as God's judgment on America for their sins. Some people blame governments, some people blame God, some people blame the victims for their sin. So who is to blame? Jesus was once asked a very similar question that will help us sort out this issue.

1. **Background.** This passage is not intended for those whose lives have been broken because of their personal falling towers. This is written to those of us who at a distance observe tragedy, observe falling towers, and wonder, "Why God? Who's to blame? Who's responsible?" The disciples and Jesus were discussing two events:

   A. **A Story of Terrible Personal Suffering (v. 1).** Pilate apparently discovered a plot by the Galilean Zealots, the violently nationalistic Jews, to attack the Roman army or authorities. When these Galileans came to Jerusalem, to the temple to offer their sacrifices, Pilate instructed his soldiers to go into the temple to the altar and kill these Galileans. Their own personal blood mingled with the blood of the animals they brought for sacrifice.

   B. **A Story of Inexplicable Personal Disaster (v. 4).** The next story Jesus brings up as an example: It's about a falling tower. Nobody killed the people in the tower, but the tower simply fell. It had to be a rather large tower by first-century standards, because 18 people were inside. Without warning, without notice, the tower falls and they are killed in the rubble.

2. **Questions Raised by Jesus.**

A. **Were the Victims Worse Sinners (v. 2)?** The essence of Jesus' question suggests that terrible personal suffering, or inexplicable national disaster, can always be traced to personal sin. If you were a first-century Jew, and you heard about the Galileans you would say, "They deserved it. God zapped them, they were terrible sinners." So Jesus raises the question: Do you think these Galileans were worse sinners than all the other Galileans because they died such a terrible death?

B. **Were the Victims Guiltier (v. 4)?** The people in the first century thought that God had this ledger or this scale and when you do something wrong, you become indebted to God, you are guilty before God, and you owe God something. Somehow the people in the tower of Siloam had accumulated such a heavy debt to God, that God had had enough of them.

3. **Jesus' Answer (v. 3).** I love the answer of Jesus, "I tell you, no." However, with Jesus, just about the time you take a "Whew, great answer," He turns right around and gets in your face: "but unless you repent, you will all likewise perish" (v. 3).

A. **We Are All Sinners.** Jesus is saying to the crowds, "You're in the business of making judgment about who's the worse sinner? Who is more indebted to God? Who is guiltier before God?" Jesus said, "I'm here to tell you, 'You're a sinner as well.'"

B. **We All Need to Repent.** What is repentance? It's a change of heart and a change of mind that leads to a change of direction. Paul said being sorry for your sin is not enough (2 Cor. 7:10). It must be a godly sorrow that through the working of the Holy Spirit in your life brings about genuine repentance, a change of heart, a change of mind, a change of direction—turning to the Lord.

C. **We All Need to Repent While We Can (v. 6).** We're the fig tree in this story. The gardener who allows more time for repentance is God, but He's also the One who cuts the tree down when it doesn't bear fruit.

Conclusion: If you've never repented of your sin, turned to Christ, and given your life to Him, you are living somewhere between the second chance and the last chance. The fact that you are here this morning may indicate that God is cultivating the soil of your heart. The Holy

Spirit is plying, touching, convicting, convincing, drawing you to Christ. Jesus is saying, not only are you a sinner, not only do you need to repent, but you need to repent now. While God is kind, while He is long-suffering, while He is patient, while He is the God of the second chance, at some point He will become the God of the last chance. And who knows when the tower will fall on you or fall on me?

STATS, STORIES, AND MORE

In her book, *Appointment Congo,* Virginia Law recounts the missionary experiences she shared with her husband, Burleigh Law, who a missionary pilot martyred in Congo in 1964. Burleigh had come to Christ at age seventeen. He was a junior in high school in the steel-mill town of Weirton, West Virginia, and he attended the local Methodist church with his parents. One day an unimpressive-looking minister named Robert Ling came to town and began pastoring the Methodist church. One of the first things Rev. Ling tried was a Youth Revival. Burleigh wasn't very interested, but he dutifully went and sat on the back row with the other boys. During the altar call on Sunday night, Burleigh went forward and prayed, but returned home with no sense of peace. That night, long after the family was asleep, Burleigh lay in bed thinking, and the next morning he announced to his parents, "I'm not going to school today."

"Not going to school! Why?"

"I've got to go down to see the manager at the lumberyard. I've got a chest of tools to return."

"Tools from the lumberyard? How come?"

Burleigh admitted that he and some buddies had stolen them. Then he admitted he had stolen gas out of the neighbor's car. That morning, he returned the tools, paid the gas, and sought the forgiveness of those he had cheated. That evening, he knelt again at the church altar, asking for forgiveness. This time he left with a sense of peace that never left him.[1]

---

[1]Virginia Law, *Appointment Congo* (Chicago: Rand McNally & Co., 1966), pp. 26–27.

APPROPRIATE HYMNS AND SONGS

"My Life Is in Your Hands," Kirk Franklin, 1996 Lily Mack Music.

"I Will Arise and Go to Jesus," Joseph Hart, Public Domain.

"The Lord Has a Will," Mike Hudson/Barbara Hudson, 1977 Word Music, Inc./Wordspring Music, Inc. (Word Music Group).

"Take My Life," Clint Brown, 1990 Tribe Music Group (Admin. Clint Brown).

FOR THE BULLETIN

September 9, 1747, is the birthday of Thomas Coke, a sophisticated Oxford-educated Welshman who left the Anglican Church in 1777 to become John Wesley's assistant in the new and quickly growing Methodist movement. On this same day in 1784, Coke was consecrated by Wesley to oversee the Methodist work in America. He crossed the Atlantic eighteen times at his own expense, and he died in 1814 while on a missionary voyage to India and was buried at sea. ● On September 9, 1758, an English newspaper editor named Robert Raikes died, leaving the *Gloucester Journal* to his son, also named Robert. It was the latter who used the newspaper as a vehicle for Christian causes that resulted in widespread prison reform and in the advancement of Raikes' Sunday school movement. ● California became the thirty-first state in the union on this day in 1850. ● Today, September 9, 1863, marks the wedding of Ira and Fanny Sankey. As D. L. Moody's song-leader, Sankey became a powerful force in the development of the era of Gospel music. ● Bill Borden of Yale, 25, was ordained on this day, September 9, 1912. He was a young millionaire who offered himself for the China Inland Mission. Upon his acceptance he sailed for Cairo, Egypt, proposing to study Arabic before going on to his work among China's Muslims. In Egypt he contracted cerebrospinal meningitis and died in 1913. He was only 26. This loss of a rich young ruler who had given up all for Christ galvanized many Christians into action. Biographies were written of him. His example inspired a multitude of recruits for mission service. Even his wealth effectively advanced his devoted purposes after he was gone, for in his will he left almost a million dollars to Christian causes.

Call to Worship

The LORD is great in Zion, and He is high above all the peoples. Let them praise Your great and awesome name—He is holy . . . Exalt the LORD our God, and worship at His footstool—He is holy (Ps. 99:2–3, 5).

Invitation to Altar Prayer

An old hymn says, "I must tell Jesus all of my trials; I cannot bear these burdens alone." Today we'd like to invite you to join us at the altar, here at the front of the church, for prayer. The Bible tells us to cast all our cares on Him who cares for us. If you have an illness of body, mind, or soul, we invite you to come for prayer. As you come imagine that you are taking that burden, that illness, that hurt, that problem, and laying it here on this altar, on the footstool of the Almighty. Some problems God alone can solve. Some hurts God alone can heal. With those issues, we have to "let go and let God." Bring your burden to the Lord and leave it here. If you'd like to come and pray privately, you may. If you'd like someone to pray with you, there's someone waiting to do so. Just step out, come, kneel, give Christ your burden, and receive His strength. Cast your burden on the LORD and He shall sustain you. "He shall never permit the righteous to be moved" (Ps. 55:22).

Offertory Comments

I once heard a pastor preach a very direct sermon about tithing. First, he was very clear that his message was directed toward members of the body of Christ and did not want visitors to feel obligated to give. He told his congregation, "Some of you think it's okay to 'tip' Jesus. You reach into your pocket, say to yourself, *I have an extra $20* and throw it in the plate. I want to tell you this morning that Jesus doesn't want a tip; it's your heart He's after. Your checkbook always reflects where your heart is." I thought this sounded quite harsh, but the truth sometimes does. I would encourage you to think seriously about your tithe. Treat it as a discipline and not a demand, as a privilege and not a pain.

Additional Sermons and Lesson Ideas

I Have Seen the Lord

Date preached:

By Rev. Mark Hollis

SCRIPTURE: Isaiah 6:1–8

INTRODUCTION: A little church in our small town reported an apparition on their wall. Some said it was an image of Mary and Jesus. What would we do if we genuinely did see God? Isaiah knew.

1. God's Holiness Illustrated (Is. 6:1–8).
   A. Isaiah Sees the Lord (vv. 1–4).
   B. Isaiah Is Horrified at His Unholiness (v. 5).
   C. Isaiah's Cleansing Is Painful (vv. 6–7).
   D. Isaiah Is Willingly Commissioned (v. 8).

2. God's Holiness Defined.
   A. God's Holiness Makes Him Unique (1 Sam. 2:2).
   B. God's Holiness Is Combined with His Love (Ps. 145:17).
3. My Response to God's Holiness.
   A. I Worship (Ps. 99:5).
   B. I Must Be Holy (1 Pet. 1:15).

CONCLUSION: When we encounter God we are horrified at our unholiness and cry out for cleansing. Our cleansing is a painful process. Once cleansed, God can use us. We respond in worship and holiness.

The Peril of Disbelief

Date preached:

By Dr. Melvin Worthington

SCRIPTURE: Hebrews 3—4

INTRODUCTION: Biblical examples abound regarding the peril of disbelief. It is possible for us to believe the gospel and be saved and yet not believe God can manage our lives. By faith the children of Israel came out of Egypt and yet because of disbelief they refused to go into Canaan.

1. The Comparison (Heb. 3:1–6). The comparison includes *the people addressed* (v. 1) and *the priest analyzed* (vv. 2–6).
2. The Caution (Heb. 3:7–19). The caution includes *the hardened heart* (vv. 7–11) and *the hearkening heart* (vv. 12–19).
3. The Consequences (Heb. 4:1–16). The consequences include *those who are excluded from God's rest* (vv. 1–9) and *those who enter into God's rest* (vv. 10–16).

CONCLUSION: The danger of disbelieving God cannot be underestimated.

SEPTEMBER 16, 2007

SUGGESTED SERMON

The Appeal of Wisdom

Date preached:

By Dr. Al Detter

Scripture: Proverbs 8:1–11; 32–33, especially verse 1
Does not wisdom cry out . . . ?

Introduction: If you could have anything you wished for, what would it be? Most people won't ask for wisdom. Scripture tells us that God appeared to King Solomon and said, "I'll give you one wish. What do you want?" He could have asked for long life, a lot of money, or victory over his enemies (1 Kin. 3:5–13). Solomon instead asked for wisdom. Wisdom is the major theme of the Book of Proverbs. So let's take a look at some truths about wisdom, personified as a woman who calls out to us:

1. **She Tries to Get Our Attention (vv. 1–5).** Wisdom is not shy. She gets out in public places and cries out in a loud voice to get our attention. She stands on the hill by the road we travel, the intersections of our lives and cries out in a loud voice to get our attention. How does wisdom call to us today?

   A. **Wisdom Calls Through People.** God puts people in our lives who know right from wrong, or they know the best from the good. The major voice of wisdom in Proverbs is godly parents, but it could be any number of people in our lives.

   B. **Wisdom Calls Through Conscience.** The conscience operates at every gate and doorway of our lives. It speaks to us about entering or avoiding. Wisdom will say, "It's okay, proceed." Or, "Don't do that. It's the wrong gate."

   C. **Wisdom Calls Through the Scriptures.** The Bible will always guide our steps (Ps. 119:105). It will always tell us what is right and what is wrong. It will always tell us the path of character, integrity, and godly behavior.

   D. **Wisdom Calls Through the Holy Spirit.** When we enter into a personal relationship with God through Jesus Christ, we receive the Spirit of God. When we don't walk by the Spirit, however, we cannot hear His voice.

2. **She Always Speaks the Truth (vv. 6–11).** When wisdom calls, you can't miss her and here is why: verses 6–8 tell us that wisdom is capable only of speaking noble things, right things, truth, and righteousness (the ways of God). She cannot speak wickedness, deception, or perversion. Wisdom will always lift up what is right and repudiate all that is wrong. We have a number of voices in the world that pose as wisdom. I want to identify some of these posers because they are loud voices in our culture.

   A. **The Wisdom of Man.** We live in the age of enlightenment and we think we know the answer to the mysteries of the universe and the best way to live life. God says that His foolishness is wiser than the wisdom of man (1 Cor. 1:20, 25).

   B. **The Acceptability of Sin.** In the Bible, the definition of perversion is "to turn away from what is normal." That begs the question, "What is normal?" The answer, "God establishes what is normal." To depart from what God says is right is to turn away from the normal. We are living in days when what is right is ridiculed and what is wrong is becoming accepted as normal.

   C. **Syncretism.** Syncretism is trying to harmonize opposing beliefs or value systems into an acceptable way of life. In syncretism, Christian people adopt viewpoints, habits, and practices that oppose scriptural teaching. Many of us are formed more by secular and cultural forces than spiritual forces.

3. **She Desperately Wants to Give Us Life's Greatest Blessings (vv. 32–36).** The most blessed people in the world are those who embrace wisdom. They listen to her and heed her instruction (v. 32). Wisdom is to guide every aspect of our lives. Don't think you know better and ignore her. Wisdom's agenda is to bless us. The only way she can bless us is if we watch and wait for her every day, agree with what she says, and do what she tells us to do (v. 34).

Conclusion: In the New Testament, the embodiment of wisdom is Jesus. He is called the wisdom of God (1 Cor. 1:24). Everything said about wisdom in Proverbs is fulfilled in Christ. To come into a personal relationship with Jesus is to find life. To follow His teachings is to find wisdom. For those who do follow Jesus already, will you be among those who are willing to listen to and follow wisdom every day?

STATS, STORIES, AND MORE

More from Dr. Detter

When I was little, my family moved across the street from railroad tracks. Guess what we heard for the first few weeks—the thundering of the trains day and night. After a while, the trains still rolled by, but we didn't hear them anymore. That's often the way it is with wisdom. She shouts to us along the familiar paths we travel every day, but we have become used to her call and it's often hard to hear. Not only this but other voices call out to us.

I can think of two major "big mouths" among many out there twisting the truth and morality of wisdom. The first one is the entertainment industry. It is a lineup of music, TV shows, movies, and the newspaper columnists deceiving us and promoting ungodly lifestyles. What comes out is not the voice of wisdom. It is the voice of a society that has lost its moral compass and is pleasure crazy. The other big mouth is the doctrine of political correctness. It is a doctrine that shuts down the voice of what is right and noble and true in favor of not offending anybody. Today what is noble and true and right is seen as being intolerant and judgmental. Political correctness is not the voice of wisdom.

Our society is losing its foundations. It is making sinful things normal. There are many who are telling us that the gay lifestyle is okay and that same-sex marriages are okay. We are told that it is the right of the mother to kill her unborn child. We are told that it's okay to live together or have sex with people we are not married to if we love them. The majority of people think it's okay to tell a lie if you need to. We can talk about almost every ungodly philosophy and "ism" in the public school but we cannot mention the name of God, Jesus Christ, or the Holy Spirit.

APPROPRIATE HYMNS AND SONGS

"Be Thou My Vision," Eleanor Hull/Mary E. Byrne, Public Domain.

"Immortal Invisible," Walter Chalmers Smith/John Robert, Public Domain.

"O God of Vision," Jane Parker Huber, 1981 Jane Parker Huber (Admin. Westminster John Knox Press).

"His Ways," Dennis Allen/Nan Allen, 1997 Word Music, Inc.

FOR THE BULLETIN

This is the traditional date of St. Francis of Assisi receiving the stigmata, the crucifixion scars of Christ, on Italy's Mt. Albernia, in 1224. ● Today marks the death of an evil man—Tomas de Torquemada, the Inquisitor General of the Spanish Inquisition, who died on September 16, 1498, after torturing thousands of innocent people. As Inquisitor General, Torquemada invented new methods of dreaded tortures, including pulling sufferers apart on the rack, forcing them to drink gallons of water, and burning them alive in green, slow-burning wood. ● As a friend of Israel long before the re-establishment of the Jewish state, Scottish minister Robert Murray McCheyne wrote on September 16, 1840: *I feel deeply persuaded from prophecy, that it will always be difficult to stir up and maintain a warm and holy interest in outcast Israel. The lovers and pleaders of Zion's cause will be always few . . . And is not this one of the very reasons why God will take up their cause. It is sweet encouragement to learn, that though the friends of Zion will probably be few, yet there always will be some who will keep watch over the dust of Jerusalem, and plead the cause of Israel with God and with man . . . Oh, my dear brethren, into whose hearts I trust God is pouring a scriptural love for Israel, what an honor is it for . . . to be made watchmen by God over the ruined walls of Jerusalem . . . that He would fulfill them, and make Jerusalem a blessing to the whole world!* ● Today is the birthday, in 1906, of J. B. Phillips, whose *New Testament in Modern English* was published in 1967.

WORSHIP HELPS

Call to Worship

"Now I will rise," says the LORD; "Now I will be exalted, now I will lift Myself up" (Is. 33:10).

Suggested Scriptures

- 1 Kings 3:5–13
- Psalm 119:105
- Proverbs 3:18, 8:1–11, 8:32–36
- Isaiah 6:20–21
- 1 Corinthians 1:20, 24–25
- 1 Timothy 4:13

Kid's Talk

Ask the children, "If you could ask God for anything in the whole world, what would you ask for?" Allow a few children to answer. Explain or read the story of Solomon from 1 Kings 3:4–15 or 1 Chronicles 1:1–12, where he was allowed to ask God for anything he wanted. Instead of asking to be popular, or to have lots of money, he asked for wisdom! God rewarded him with greater wisdom than anyone ever had, and gave him money and honor too. Explain what wisdom is and that it's more valuable than anything material. End by leading them in a prayer for wisdom.

Additional Sermons and Lesson Ideas

Upside-Down Living (Part 1)
By Dr. Larry Osborne

Date preached:

SCRIPTURE: Matthew 5:1–5

INTRODUCTION: In this passage Jesus describes how life will be radically different for those of us who choose to follow Him. We might as well call it *Upside-Down Living!* Here's what it's like and why those who join the kingdom are so different—and so fortunate. Jesus says, blessed are:

1. The Poor in Spirit (v. 3): Humbled before God. The poor in spirit are fortunate because God only lets this type of person in.
2. Those Who Mourn (v. 4): Those who experience great sorrow in this life. They are fortunate because God will set things straight.
3. The Meek (v. 5): Those who refuse to avenge themselves and instead leave it to God. These are fortunate because God will defend their cause.

CONCLUSION: In a culture that emphasizes health, wealth, pleasures, and a strong will, Jesus teaches us that He expects us to be different!

Upside-Down Living (Part 2)
By Dr. Larry Osborne

Date preached:

SCRIPTURE: Matthew 5:6–12

INTRODUCTION: As Jesus continues His Sermon on the Mount, teaching us to live radically different from the world's standards, He offers these truths:

1. If You Hunger and Thirst for Righteousness (v. 6): You are fortunate because your desire will be satisfied (Matt. 6:33; Eccl.; Phil. 2:13; Rom. 7:15–25).
2. If You Are Merciful (v. 7): You are fortunate because God will show you mercy (James 2:13; Matt. 7:2; 18:23–35; Eccl. 7:21–22).
3. If You Are Pure in Heart (v. 8): You are fortunate because God always judges the heart (1 Sam. 16:7; Jer. 17:9–10; Ps. 51:10; Matt. 15:16–20; Luke 6:45).
4. If You Are a Peacemaker (v. 9): You are fortunate because you are doing God's work (Matt. 5:23; Rom. 12:18; 14:17–19; Rev. 12:10; Eph. 2:18–21; Prov. 17:9).
5. If You Are Persecuted Because of Righteousness (vv. 10–12): You are fortunate because it means your righteousness shows (2 Tim. 3:12; 1 Pet. 4:12–15; Luke 18:29–30).

CONCLUSION: Are you living according to the world's standards or the Word's standards?

Alleine's Alarm

Joseph Alleine was born in 1634, in the village of Devizes Wilthshire, exactly one hundred miles west of London, not far from Bath and just twenty miles from the famous Stonehenge Monuments. Growing up in a Puritan home, he watched his older brother, Edward, whom God was calling to ministry. When Edward died in 1645, still preparing for gospel labor, Joseph was deeply affected and begged his father to let him take Edward's place.

The young man ended up at Oxford, where he studied hard and took his call from God with utmost sincerity. Joseph often neglected his friends for his studies. "It is better they should wonder at my rudeness," he explained, "than that I should lose time; for only a few will notice the rudeness, but many will feel my loss of time." Though barely 21, he was already "infinitely and insatiably greedy for the conversion of souls," devoting every moment to studying, preaching, and evangelizing.

In 1655, Joseph was called to a church in the west of England. He soon married, and his wife, Theodosia, later claimed his only fault was not spending more time with her. "Ah, my dear," he would say, "I know thy soul is safe; but how many that are perishing have I to look after?"

Joseph habitually rose at four in the morning, praying and studying his Bible until eight. His afternoons were spent calling on the unconverted. He kept a list of the inhabitants of each street and knew the condition of each soul. "Give me a Christian that counts his time more precious than gold," he said. At the beginning of the week, he would remark, "Another week is now before us, let us spend this week for God." Each morning he said, "Now let us live this one day well!"

But his time was nonetheless cut short. The restoration of England's monarchy in 1662 resulted in the Act of Uniformity, removing 2,000 preachers from their pulpits in a single day. Most preached their farewell sermons August 17, 1662. Joseph, however, continued preaching. The authorities descended, and

Continued on the next page

CLASSICS FOR THE PASTOR'S LIBRARY—*Continued*

on May 28, 1663, he was thrown into prison. His health soon declined.

"Now we have one day more," he told Theodosia when he was finally released. "Let us live well, work hard for souls, lay up much treasure in heaven this day, for we have but a few to live." He spoke truthfully. He died on November 17, 1668, at age 34.

But he had spent his years well, outliving himself not only in the souls he saved, but in the book he left, a Puritan classic entitled *Alarm to the Unconverted,* and frequently called *Alleine's Alarm.* It is a passionate appeal to the unsaved, begging them to consider and embrace Jesus Christ as personal Savior and Lord. The chapter titles are: Mistakes about Conversion, The Nature of Conversion, The Necessity of Conversion, The Marks of the Unconverted, The Miseries of the Unconverted, Directions to the Unconverted, and The Motives to Conversion.

You can turn to any page in this little book and your eyes will fall on an ardent appeal for Christ. For example:

> Why should not this be the day from which you are able to date your happiness? Why should you venture a day longer in this dangerous and dreadful condition? What if God should this night require your soul . . . ? This is your day . . . ! If you do not make a wise choice now, you are undone forever. What your present choice is, such must be your eternal condition . . . . Now the Holy Spirit is striving with you . . . Now the Lord Jesus stretches wide His arms to receive you. He beseeches you by us. How movingly, how meltingly, how compassionately He calls . . .

This book, first published in 1671, has been the means whereby multitudes of people have discovered the Savior. Perhaps equally important, it has brought home to many of us preachers the urgency of our message. When I read *Alleine's Alarm,* I become alarmed that I'm not more alarmed for the lost. It's a shock to my system, and a shot of holy passion into my bloodstream.

Get to know this purpose-driven Puritan. Find an old copy of his book, let it ignite your zeal for the lost, and heed the call of *Alleine's Alarm.*

SEPTEMBER 23, 2007

I Need Help with My Finances *Date preached:*

Scripture: 1 Timothy 6:3–19, especially verse 6
For godliness with contentment is great gain.

Introduction: Someone once said, "If your output exceeds your income, your upkeep will be your downfall." Low interest rates and easy credit mean that millions of Americans are struggling with loads of personal debt. Some experts say the average amount of personal debt in the United States (excluding mortgages) is nearly $20,000 per family. The typical American family has credit-card debt exceeding $8,000. Add school loans, car loans, and home loans to the mix, and it spells STRESS.

Background: This chapter begins with a warning against false teachers who were in the "ministry" for the sake of money (vv. 3–6). They thought godliness was a means of gain. Paul told Timothy to disassociate from such people. Then Paul shifted gears and warned that covetousness wasn't limited to spurious televangelists. Sometimes all of us are too greedy and money-conscious. His primary point in 1 Timothy 6 is this: Some things in life are truly permanent, and some things are truly passing. The world treats the passing things as permanent, and it treats the permanent things as passing. Christians, on the other hand, regard passing things as passing, and permanent things permanent. The essence of worldliness is when we begin treating passing things as permanent and permanent things as passing. Based on this chapter, I'd like to give you these five questions to ask before making any significant purchase. Suppose you're going to buy a television, a car, a piece of electronics, a new wardrobe, boat, a new tool or toy— anything of significance. Usually our decision to buy is based on whether we have money in our pocket or a piece of plastic in our billfold. Here's a different set of criteria for making those decisions.

1. **Have I Been Bitten by the Buy-It Bug (vv. 6–8)?** Paul recommends godliness with contentment. The word translated *contentment* literally means *self-sufficiency*. This was a favorite word of the Stoics who lived in detachment from externals. The Stoic was the source of his own happiness. The Christian is, in a sense, self-contained, but

instead of finding our sufficiency within ourselves, we find it in our relationship with Christ. His grace is sufficient for us. Self-sufficient people don't have to keep accumulating things to be happy. They carry happiness within themselves. Sometimes we buy things because it makes us feel good. How much better to have your own internal joy that doesn't have to be fueled by the acquisition of things. Paul said, "Having food and clothing, with these we should be content."

2. **What Does This Purchase Say about Me (vv. 9–12)?** Which do I most crave—gold or God? The word "desire" here doesn't just mean we occasionally daydream about having lots of money. It means that the desire to accumulate wealth and possessions becomes the driving force of our lives. In contrast to that, Christians have a different agenda in life, a different set of cravings and desires. Paul goes on: "But you, O man of God, flee these things and pursue righteousness, godliness, faith, love, patience, gentleness. . . .''

3. **Am I Too Engrossed in This Purchase (vv. 13–16)?** In light of the Second Coming of Christ, am I too absorbed in the things I'm accumulating? Notice Paul's emphasis here on the return of Christ. If we're living in the light of His imminent return, that should have an impact on how we value the accumulated possessions of life. See 1 Corinthians 7:29–32.

4. **Am I Enjoying What I Already Have (v. 17)?** There's a wonderful balance in these verses. On the one hand, we're not to be engrossed in the things of this world; on the other hand, we're to be thankful for what God has given us and to enjoy it.

5. **Does This Purchase Diminish My Ability to Give to God's Work (vv. 18–19)?** Why is the most affluent generation of Christians in history only giving about two percent of their income to the Lord? The people described in Haggai 1:3–11 were having cash flow problems because they were spending so much money on themselves they didn't have much left for the great work of their God; as a result His blessing wasn't on their finances.

Conclusion: Don't make purchases lightly or impulsively. We're stewards of the money God has entrusted to us, and we should always ask: "How would Jesus use this money?" Where your treasure is, there will your heart be also. Invest in the permanent, not just in the passing.

STATS, STORIES, AND MORE

Christians don't harbor ambitions of being wealthy in life. We aren't very interested in that. Our goal in life is not the accumulation of wealth. Jesus said, "A man's life does not consist in the abundance of the things he possesses." The writer of Proverbs said (in paraphrase), "Lord, give me neither great poverty nor great wealth. If I have great poverty, I might be tempted to steal; and if I have great wealth, I might be tempted to grow proud."

It's important for us to take care of our families and to meet our obligations in life. But the simpler our lifestyles, the better. If we have food and clothing, let's be content with that.

The great American philosopher, Henry David Thoreau, said in his classic book, *Walden:* "It is desirable that a man . . . live in all respects so compactly and preparedly that, if an enemy take the town, he can, like the old philosopher, walk out the gate empty-handed and without anxiety."

In another place, Thoreau said: "A man is rich in proportion to the number of things which he can afford to let alone."

In another place, Thoreau spoke of an old deacon that he knew. When he died, his possessions were auctioned off; and all the neighbors eagerly gathered together to view them and to bid on them. Thoreau added dryly that the neighbors bought the dead person's trinkets to "carefully transport them to their own garrets and dust holes, to lie there till their estates are settled, when they will start again."

APPROPRIATE HYMNS AND SONGS

"Cry of My Heart," Terry Butler, 1991 Mercy/Vineyard Publishing.

"Great Is Thy Faithfulness," Thomas O. Chisholm/William M. Runyan, 1923 Renewed 1951 Hope Publishing Co.

"Give Thanks," Henry Smith, 1978 Integrity's Hosanna! Music (Integrity Music Inc.).

"God Has Done Great Things," Douglas C. Eltzroth, 1991 Douglas C. Eltzroth.

FOR THE BULLETIN

Today is the birthday, September 23, 1800, of William Holmes McGuffey, language professor, college president, and clergyman. He is best remembered for his six editions of *McGuffey Readers,* which have sold over 120 million copies. ● On the night of September 23, 1846, German astronomer Johann Gottfried Galle discovered the planet Neptune at the Berlin Observatory. The planet, with its diameter four times that of Earth and its eight moons, was named for the Roman god of the sea. ● The Fulton Street Prayer Meeting began on September 23, 1857, in New York City at the instigation of lay-worker Jeremiah C. Lanphier. The meetings sparked the "Third Great Awakening" in which perhaps a million people were converted. ● Richard Armstrong, Presbyterian missionary to Hawaii, died on this day in 1860; and today is the birthday, in 1888, of Gerhard Kittel, the German Lutheran Bible scholar best known for his monumental *Theological Dictionary of the New Testament.* ● Today marks the death of two prominent hymnists: Frances Elizabeth Cox (translator of "Sing Praise to God Who Reigns Above") died on this day in 1897, and John S. Norris (composer of the music for "I Can Hear My Savior Calling") died on this day in 1907. ● On September 23, 1949, President Harry Truman stunned the nation by announcing that the Soviet Union had exploded a nuclear bomb in a successful test, years ahead of what was thought possible by most U.S. officials. ● Television's first color television series began on this day in 1962—"The Jetsons."

Quote for the Pastor's Wall

Footprints of Jesus,
That make the pathway glow;
We will follow the steps of Jesus
Where'er they go.

—MARY B. SLADE, 1871

WORSHIP HELPS

Call to Worship

Be exalted, O God, above the heavens, and Your glory above all the earth (Ps. 108:5).

Exhortation to Prayer

This is an important day in American Christian history, one that reminds us to be diligent in praying for revival. Today is the 150th birthday of the Fulton Street Prayer Meeting, which began on September 23, 1857—exactly 150 years ago today.

In New York City, Jeremiah C. Lanphier, a layman, accepted the call of the North Reformed Dutch Church to begin a full-time program of evangelism. He visited door-to-door, placed posters in boarding houses, and prayed. But the work languished and Lanphier grew discouraged. Lanphier decided to try noontime prayer meetings, announcing the first one for September 23, 1857, at the Old Dutch Church on Fulton Street. When the hour came, Lanphier found himself alone. Finally, one man showed up, then a few others.

But the next week, twenty came. The third week, forty. Soon the building was overflowing. The revival spread to other cities as newspapers spread the story. The revival—sometimes called "The Third Great Awakening"—lasted nearly two years, and between 500,000 and 1,000,000 people were said to have been converted.

Suggested Scriptures

- Matthew 6:2–4; 19–21
- Mark 12:41–43
- Acts 4:32–35
- Hebrews 13:5
- 1 Peter 5:2
- Ephesians 4:28

Additional Sermons and Lesson Ideas

Be of Good Cheer! Your Faith Has Healed You! *Date preached:*

SCRIPTURE: Matthew 11:20–22

INTRODUCTION: According to Eusebius, the "Father of Church History," this woman was a Gentile from Caesarea Philippi, and after she returned home, the city fathers commissioned a statue of her with the Lord Jesus and it stood in front of her house for many years. It commemorated the One who gives us hope.

1. Some Things Can Drain the Life Out of Us. This woman had been losing her life's blood for twelve years, and Leviticus 17:11 says, "The life of the flesh is in the blood." In another sense, things happen to all of us that drain the life right out of us.
2. When We Touch His Hem We Touch Him. In Bible times, a person's clothing represented that person. In touching the hem of His garment, this woman was touching Christ.
3. We Touch Him by Faith. This is a major theme in Matthew's Gospel.
4. Power Goes Out of Him to Heal Us. There are three kinds of healing: Immediate, Gradual, and Ultimate. By His stripes we are healed.
5. Because of This We Can Be of Good Cheer.

CONCLUSION: Do you need to touch the hem of His garment? His healing and cheer can come into your life.

God Our Creator *Date preached:*
By Rev. Mark Hollis

SCRIPTURE: Genesis 2:4–7; 15–25

INTRODUCTION: "I believe in God the Father Almighty, maker of heaven and earth" (The Apostles' Creed).

1. God Has Breathed into Humans His Divine Breath (Gen. 2:4–7).
   A. We Are Infused with the Breath of God.
   B. All Human Life Is to Be Respected.
2. God Has Given Humans a Divine Assignment (Gen. 2:15–17).
   A. God Has Charged Us with Responsibility for His Creation.
   B. We Must Obey Him and Care for His World.
3. God Has Created Us for Relationship (Gen. 2:19–25).
   A. We Are Incomplete Alone.
   B. We Are Completed Through Relationship with God and Others.

CONCLUSION: Human life is sacred and must be honored. We are responsible to be good stewards of God's creation. We are made complete as we live in dynamic and growing relationship with the God of the universe and with one another.

The Pastor's Morning Devotions

An "Interview" with William Law, Author of *A Serious Call to a Devout and Holy Life*[1]

In your classic book, A Serious Call to a Devout and Holy Life, *you advocate that pastors sing during their private morning devotions.*

You need not wonder that I lay so much stress upon singing a psalm at all your devotions, since you see it is to form your spirit to such joy and thankfulness to God as in the highest perfection of a divine and holy life. If anyone would tell you the shortest, surest way to all happiness and perfection, he must tell you to make it a rule to yourself to thank and praise God for everything that happens to you. For it is certain that whatever seeming calamity happens to you, if you thank and praise God for it, you turn it into a blessing. Could you, therefore, work miracles, you could not do more for yourself than by this thankful spirit.

You also advocate using our imaginations during our personal devotions.

Seeing our imaginations have great power over our hearts can mightily affect us with their representations, and it would be of great use to you if, at the beginning of your devotions, you were to imagine to yourself some such representations as might heat and warm your heart into a temper suitable to those prayers that you are then about to offer to God.

Can you give an example?

Imagine to yourself that you saw the heavens open and the glorious choirs of cherubims and seraphims about the throne of God. Imagine that you hear the music of those angelic voices that cease not day and night to sing the glories of Him that is, and was, and

Continued on the next page

---

[1]Law's quotes are excerpted from *A Serious Call to a Devout and Holy Life,* first published in 1728.

CONVERSATIONS IN THE PASTOR'S STUDY—*Continued*

is to come. Help your imagination with such passages of Scripture as Revelation 3:9: "I beheld, and, lo, in heaven a great multitude, which no man could number, of all nations, and kindreds, and people, and tongues, standing before the throne, and before the Lamb." Think upon this till your imagination has carried you above the clouds, till it has placed you amongst the heavenly beings, and made you long to bear a part in their eternal music. If you will but use yourself to this method, and let your imagination dwell upon such representations as these, you will soon find it to be an excellent means of raising the spirit of devotion within you.

You believe in rising early in the morning and praying early in the day, don't you?

I take it for granted that every Christian that is in health is up early in the morning, for it is much more reasonable to suppose a person up early because he is a Christian than because he is a laborer, or a tradesman, or a servant, or has business that wants him. How much is he to be reproached that had rather lie folded up in bed than be raising up his heart to God in acts of praise and adoration? Prayer is the nearest approach to God, and the highest enjoyment of Him that we are capable of in this life. On the other hand, sleep is such a dull, stupid state of existence that even amongst mere animals we despise them most which are most drowsy. He, therefore, that chooses to enlarge the slothful indulgence of sleep rather than be early at his devotions to God chooses the dullest refreshment of the body before the highest, noblest employment of the soul.

SEPTEMBER 30, 2007

Training Yourself for Life

Date preached:

By Rev. Larry Kirk

Scripture: 1 Timothy 4:6–10, especially verse 8
Godliness is profitable for all things, having promise of the life that now is and of that which is to come.

Introduction: Christianity is very unique in that it does not drive us into a stressful attempt to change ourselves so that we can be acceptable to God and others. No. It starts with grace and offers us immediate acceptance, love, and forgiveness through faith in Christ. Christian faith brings together, at the same time, the greatest assurance of love and acceptance and the greatest motivation and empowerment for growth and change. One place you see that is in the passage we're looking at today; it tells us we need certain things *in* our lives to train ourselves *for* life.

1. **We Need the Practical Discipline of Training for Godliness (vv. 6–8).**

    A. **Good Nourishment (vv. 6–7).** Verse 6 teaches us about being nourished in the truths of the faith and it calls these truths the "good doctrine which you have carefully followed." The word "good," in verse 6 is a translation of the Greek word from which we get the word "hygienic" it means, "healthy," or "wholesome." To be nourished, we also must rid ourselves of what is unhealthy: ". . . reject profane and old wives' fables and exercise yourself toward godliness" (v. 7).

    B. **Practical Disciplines (vv. 7–8).** The Greek word translated "exercise" is the word from which we get "gymnasium," and "gymnastics." It describes the kind of training practiced by an athlete who wants to improve performance. You train yourself by diligently practicing the basics. It's possible to train yourself in a bad way. Second Peter 2:14 talks about people who are experts in greed. The Greek there literally says they have been "trained" or "exercised" in greediness. By the way you allow yourself to live, you can be actually training yourself to be selfish, lazy, or prayerless. The truth is, the way you are living your life today is training you for the way you will live your life tomorrow and the day after.

2. We Need the Powerful Dynamic of Hope in God (vv. 8–10).

A. Salvation Comes Through Hope in God (v. 10). Notice: the Scriptures often speak of Christ as our Savior, but here the Scripture says that God is our Savior. We should never think that our redemption or salvation is just the work of Jesus. The Bible reveals that God is a Trinity: Father, Son, and Holy Spirit. Each person in the triune God is fully involved in your salvation. Christ died on the Cross to pay for our sins and rose again to be our Lord and Savior. But the living God, Father, Son, and Holy Spirit, is fully involved in your complete salvation. Salvation does not come through human efforts or discipline. The idea in Scripture is never that you go into spiritual training hoping that through your training you will achieve salvation. Verse 10 says that Christians are people whose hope is in God. God is the Savior for all men. That doesn't mean every one actually receives salvation. At the end of the verse we're told that God's salvation is actually received only by those who believe.

B. Hope in God Empowers You to Train Yourself to Be Godly (v. 8). Hope empowers you because hope isn't just about heaven, or as verse 8 says, "that which is to come." Hope is also about where you find your strength and joy now, in what verse 8 calls "the life that now is." The heart that is hoping in God will be empowered to practice the practical disciplines that lead to a life of godliness.

Conclusion: If you put your hope in God for this life and the life to come and practice those spiritual disciplines that lead to life, your training will be fruitful in this life and in the life to come. That's the promise God gives you here. You can count on it because it is a trustworthy saying, the promise of the living God, the Savior of all men, who has revealed His heart in the saving grace that comes through Jesus Christ. Put your hope in Him and train yourself for life.

STATS, STORIES, AND MORE

More from Rev. Kirk

Today we get all kinds of unhealthy falsehoods and fables served up on television, the Internet, and every other media source. It's very easy in this culture to fill your mind daily with spiritual junk food. Every study I've seen in recent years says that most Americans spend many hours every week in front of computer screens and televisions. And yet, even among Christians few people spend even 15 minutes a day, reading the Bible, praying to God, and nourishing their inner life. The entire Bible could be read in one year in less than 15 minutes a day, but it's rarely done and we suffer a sort of spiritual malnutrition because of it.

Each year major league baseball teams come to Florida for Spring Training. Over the course of several weeks, what do you think these highly paid athletes do? Do they come to Florida to learn about obscure but rarely used baseball strategies? No. They practice fielding, running, batting and conditioning, the basics. Every day they hit, run, and field. Imagine what an army of equipped Christians we would be if we returned to the basics on a daily basis.

A very troubling reality is the growing segment of professed Christians who live self-centered lives, who give less than two percent of their income to the cause of Christ, who rarely share their faith, pray, or read the Bible, who do not resist temptation or handle difficulties well, who refuse to love their enemies, pray for those who hurt them, return good for evil, or refrain from gossip, criticism, and complaining: this is becoming widely accepted as normal Christianity. Today, make a commitment to really train yourself to be a follower of Jesus Christ. Begin practicing some of those basic spiritual disciplines that will help you to be continually growing in your relationship with God.

APPROPRIATE HYMNS AND SONGS

"More Like Jesus," Roger Hodges/Lisa Hilton, 1994 CFN Music (Admin. Music Lifeline).

"I Just Want to Serve You," Bob Stromberg, 1990 Stream Mountain Music (Admin. Stream Mountain Music).

"Take My Life and Let It Be," Frances R. Havergal/Henri A. Cesar Malan, Public Domain.

"In the Light," Charlie Peacock, 1991 Sparrow Song (div. of EMI Christian Music Publishing).

"Lord Be Glorified," Bob Kilpatrick, 1978 Bob Kilpatrick Music (Assigned to Lorenz Publishing—1998).

FOR THE BULLETIN

St. Jerome was born in a little village on the Adriatic Sea around the year A.D. 345. At a young age he went to study in Rome, where he was baptized. After extensive travels, he settled down in Bethlehem, near the sight of the Lord's birth. From the original Hebrew, Aramaic, and Greek, he used his ability with languages to translate the Bible into Latin, the common language of his time. This translation, called the Vulgate, was the authoritative version of the Bible in the western church world for over 1,000 years. He died on this day in A.D. 420. ● Today also marks the death, in 1668, of Stephen Langton, Archbishop of Canterbury, best known for developing the chapter divisions we use today in the Bible. ● Today also marks the death of the great British evangelist, George Whitefield, while on a preaching tour of the American colonies. On Saturday, September 29, 1770, Whitefield rode to Exeter, New Hampshire, where someone, seeing his appearance, told him he was more fit to go to bed than to preach. "It's true," Whitefield replied, then he burst into prayer: "Lord, I am weary *in* thy work, but not *of* it. If I have not yet finished my course, let me speak for Thee once more and come home and die." A crowd assembled and Whitefield stood precariously atop a barrel and preached. Finishing his sermon, he was helped from the barrel to his horse and he continued to Newburyport. That evening a group of friends gathered and asked Whitefield to speak to them. He rose and took a lighted candle, starting up the steps. Turning, he delivered a brief but moving message. When the candle died out, he continued up the stairs and went on to his bed where he died during the night. ● Today is the birthday of Romanian Holocaust survivor Elie Wiesel.

Call to Worship

Praise the LORD, call upon His name; Declare His deeds among the peoples, make mention that His name is exalted. Sing to the LORD, for He has done excellent things; this is known in all the earth. Cry out and shout . . . for great is the Holy One of Israel in your midst" (Is. 12:4–6)!

Reader's Theater or Responsive Reading

Reader 1:   The law of the LORD is perfect, converting the soul.

Reader 2:   The testimony of the LORD is sure, making wise the simple.

Reader 1:   The statutes of the LORD are right, rejoicing the heart.

Reader 2:   The commandment of the LORD is pure, enlightening the eyes.

Reader 1:   Turn away my eyes from looking at worthless things, and revive me in Your way.

Reader 2:   Revive me according to Your word.

Reader 1:   Behold, I long for Your precepts; revive me in Your righteousness.

Both: Let the words of my mouth and the meditation of my heart be acceptable in Your sight, O LORD, my strength and my Redeemer (Ps. 19:7–8; Ps. 119:37, 25, 40; Ps. 19:14).

A Verse from an Old Hymn to Include in Today's Pastoral Prayer

> Incline our hearts with godly fear
> To seek Thy face, Thy Word revere;
> Cause Thou all wrongs, all strife to cease,
> And lead us in the paths of peace.
> —From "Our Fathers' God, To Thee,"
> by BENJAMIN COPELAND, 1905

Additional Sermons and Lesson Ideas

The Peril of Defiance
By Dr. Melvin Worthington

Date preached:

SCRIPTURE: Hebrews 10

INTRODUCTION: The peril of defiance is a distinct possibility. Examples abound in the Scriptures addressing this issue. This solemn warning provides a strong antidote against willful sin.

1. The Shadowy Outline (Heb. 10:1–4): *The representation* (v. 1), *the repetition* (v. 2), *the remembrance* (v. 3), and *the reminder* (v. 4).
2. The Superior Offering (Heb. 10:5–18): *The Sovereign's Will* (vv. 5–10), *the Savior's Work* (vv. 11–14), and *the Spirit's Witness* (vv. 15–18).
3. The Saint's Obligation (Heb. 10:19–25): *The access to the Sovereign* (vv. 19–21) and *the admonition of the Sovereign* (vv. 22–25).
4. The Solemn Observation (Heb. 10:26–31): *The willful sin* (v. 26), *the wrath of the Sovereign* (vv. 27–29), and *the witness of the Scriptures* (vv. 30–31).
5. The Steadfast Overcomer (Heb. 10:32–39): *Their former faithfulness* (vv. 32–34) and *their firm fidelity* (vv. 35–39).

CONCLUSION: Hebrews 10 provides a *pertinent, personal,* and *practical* warning regarding willful sin. The choice is yours.

Heavenly Minded
By Joshua D. Rowe

Date preached:

SCRIPTURE: Colossians 3:1–4

INTRODUCTION: Have you ever heard the phrase, "You're so heavenly minded, you're no earthly good"? Paul teaches us that we must be heavenly minded to be any earthly good!

1. Set Your Heart and Mind on Things Above (vv. 1–3). Paul isn't telling us simply to think of heaven. He's telling us to recognize our union with Christ, who is in heaven! If you have trusted Christ for salvation, you are united with Him. This means:
   A. You Were United with Christ in His Death (v. 3). God counts Christ's death as your death to sin, the payment required (v. 3).
   B. You Are United with Christ in His Resurrection, in His Life (v. 1). Christ is now seated at God's right hand, and your heart and mind should be there with Him.
2. Set Your Eyes Toward Christ's Return (v. 4). If you have been united to Christ through faith, you will be reunited in a physical sense at His return!

CONCLUSION: Paul uses these verses as the foundation for his teaching to the Colossians on how to live the Christian life (Col. 3:5ff.). We should be so heavenly minded that no one can deny our earthly good!

OCTOBER 7, 2007

Dealing with Dishonesty

Date preached:

By Dr. Melvin Worthington

Scripture: Various, especially 2 Corinthians 4:2
We have renounced the hidden things of shame, not walking in craftiness nor handling the word of God deceitfully, but by manifestation of truth commending ourselves to every man's conscience in the sight of God.

Introduction: Corporate communities have been plagued by dishonest people and practices. Company officials have provided dishonest records and reports. The Christian church has been infected by dishonest practices as well. Exaggerated numbers, programs, and promises are forms of dishonesty. Honesty is the hallmark of the Christian church. Above all, honesty and integrity should characterize the Christian.

1. **The Danger Noted.** Paul declared that he had renounced the "hidden things of dishonesty." In order to prevent dishonest behavior one must exercise discernment, determination, and discipline. We can be dishonest in our personal life. Personal honesty and integrity must be guarded at all times. Dishonesty in one's personal life affects the individual, family, and society. It produces criticism, callousness, and cynicism. We can be dishonest in our professional life. Honesty must characterize all of our activities as we participate in the work place. Dishonesty causes division, discouragement, and discontentment in the work place. We can be dishonest in our parental life. Spouses must be honest with each other and with their children. Dishonesty in parental life can devastate families. One reason for the problems which plague the family is dishonesty on the part of family members. Dishonesty is a scourge which plagues society. It must not infiltrate, intimidate, nor influence the church. The Christian church should be characterized by honesty and integrity.

2. **The Directive Needed.** God directs individual honesty. This truth is emphasized by Luke when he says, "But that on the good ground are they, which in an honest and good heart, having heard the word,

keep it, and bring forth fruit with patience" (Luke 8:15). The success of the Word of God is dependent on an honest heart. One of the requirements for deacons in the early church was that they be "of honest report" (Acts 6:3). Those who serve in the various ministries of the church should be characterized by honesty and integrity. Paul reminds the Christians in Corinth that he is praying to God that they be honest when he says, "Now I pray to God that ye do no evil; not that we should appear approved, but that ye should do that which is honest, though we be as reprobates" (2 Cor. 13:7 KJV). God directs institutional honesty. Paul affirms this truth when he says, "Recompense to no man evil for evil. Provide things honest in the sight of all men" (Rom. 12:17). Paul alludes to this truth when he declares, "Avoiding this, that no man should blame us in this abundance which is administered by us: Providing for honest things, not only in the sight of the Lord, but also in the sight of men" (2 Cor. 8:20–21). God directs intellectual honesty. Paul concludes the letter to the Philippians with the following admonition, "Finally, brethren, whatsoever things are true, whatsoever things are honest, whatsoever things are just, whatsoever things are lovely, whatsoever things are of good report; if there be any virtue, and if there be any praise, think on these things" (Phil. 4:8).

3. **The Discernment Nourished.** In order to avoid a life of dishonesty and maintain a life of honesty and integrity the following things must remain in place. There must be the reading of the precepts. Time must be set aside each day for the reading of God's Word. There must be regularity in prayer. Regular time set aside for prayer is essential to a life characterized by honesty and integrity. There must be a renouncing of the practice of dishonesty. We must take a stand against dishonesty and champion honesty and integrity through precept and practice. Maintaining honesty in life requires diligence, discipline, and determination.

Conclusion: Above all the Christian church must be characterized by honesty. We must renounce, rebuke, and reject all forms of dishonesty.

STATS, STORIES, AND MORE

A Kentucky newspaper recently reported on a serious problem in Taylor County, in central Kentucky. Thieves are stealing street signs left and right, creating potential disasters for motorists. Stop signs, road markers, street names, railroad crossings, school zone signs—nothing is off limits to the thieves. Law enforcement officers have tried everything without success. The crimes are punishable with fines and jail time, but the sign-grabbers are hard to catch. They do their work quickly in the darkness of night and drive off. Officials have tried posting the signs higher and bolting them onto posts with reinforced backing, but nothing seems to help. They even have an amnesty program where stolen signs can be dropped off, no questions asked; but that hasn't been successful either. The police chief put his finger on the real issue when he simply told the newspaper: "People should be honest and not take them." That really is the answer to most of society's problems, isn't it? It's the answer to many of our own predicaments too. Try honesty. It's still the best policy.[1]

One day a dapper salesman called on a young grocer named Barney, trying to sell him some canned corn. The salesman's routine was persuasive as he pointed to the beautiful picture of corn on the can's wrapper. Barney took the can, tore off the label, and told the salesman, "My customers don't eat labels. They eat what's inside." Taking the can to the back of the store, he opened it, planning to warm the contents on a small stove he kept for brewing tea. The can was full of hulls. Barney sent the salesman packing without an order, news spread, and Barney's business took off. His name was Barney Kroger's, and it was his insistence on character, quality, and integrity that made his chain of supermarkets a giant in the industry.

APPROPRIATE HYMNS AND SONGS

"Christ in Me," Gary Garcia, 1976 Maranatha Music (Admin. The Copyright Co.).

"Clean Hands Pure Heart," John Slick/Mark Gersmehl, 1986 Paragon Music Corporation (Admin. Brentwood Benson Music Publishing).

"I Want to Be Like Jesus," Handt Hanson, 1991 Changing Church Forum, Inc.

"Purify My Heart," Jeff Nelson, 1993 Maranatha Praise Inc./Heart Service Music, Inc.

"Search Me O God," J. Edwin Orr, Public Domain.

---

[1] "'Honest Would Be the Best Policy" in *The Central Kentucky News-Journal*, editorial page, January 25, 2006.

FOR THE BULLETIN

On October 7, 1518, Martin Luther reached Augsburg for his meeting with Cardinal Cajetan to discuss the Ninety-Five Theses. ● The powerful American Quaker preacher, John Woolman, died on this day in 1722. ● Today is the birthday, in 1810, of Henry Alford, who compiled the first comprehensive English commentary on the Greek New Testament. He's more popularly known, however, as author of the hymn "Come, You Thankful People, Come." ● George Muller, the famous founder of Christian orphanages, married Mary Groves on this day in 1830. In lieu of a honeymoon, the couple set off the next day on a preaching tour. Muller had earlier written: "My purpose had been not to marry at all, but to remain free for traveling about in the service of the Gospel; but after some months I saw, for many reasons, that it was better for me as a young pastor under 25 to be married. The question now was, to whom shall I be united? Miss Groves came before my mind . . . On Aug. 15th, I wrote to her proposing to her to become my wife, and on Aug. 19th, she accepted me. The first thing we did after I was accepted was to fall on our knees and to ask the blessing of the Lord on our intended union." ● Vast crowds gathered in South London on this day in 1857, streaming into the Crystal Palace for a Government-sponsored National Day of Prayer and Humiliation in response to atrocities committed in the Indian Mutiny. The Crystal Palace was three times the length of St. Paul's Cathedral, and over 23,000 people came to hear a patriotic sermon by a 23-year-old speaker named Charles Spurgeon. His text was Micah 6:9: "Hear ye the rod, and who hath appointed it."

WORSHIP HELPS

Call to Worship
And He has exalted the horn of His people, the praise of all His saints . . . a people near to Him. Praise the LORD (Ps. 148:14)!

Offertory Scripture
"Bring all the tithes into the storehouse, that there may be food in My house, and try Me now in this," says the LORD of hosts, "If I will not open for you the windows of heaven and pour out for you such blessing that there will not be room enough to receive it" (Mal. 3:10).

Invitation to Share with the Pastor a Concern
During this time in our worship service, we invite you to share with a pastor (one of our pastors, deacons, altar workers, or staff

members) a concern. There is power in praying with another person. Jesus said, "Again I say to you that if two of you agree on earth concerning anything that they ask, it will be done for them by My Father in heaven. For where two or three are gathered together in My name, I am there in the midst of them" (Matt. 18:19–20). If there is a specific need in your life, someone here is waiting to pray with you about it. If you'd like to frame it in general terms, that's all right. If you need spiritual guidance in your own life, if you need help, if you need encouragement, or if you need God, please come. Come now. Come and kneel. Come and pray. Come and let us join you at your point of need in Christ's stead and in His name.

Hymn Stanzas to Quote During Pastoral Prayer
>Once more we come before our God;
>Once more His blessings ask:
>O may not duty seem a load,
>Nor worship prove a task!
>
>Father, Thy quickening Spirit send
>From Heaven in Jesus' Name,
>To make our waiting minds attend,
>And put our souls in frame.
>
>May we receive the word we hear,
>Each in an honest heart,
>And keep the precious treasure there,
>And never with it part!
>—JOSEPH HART, 1762

Benediction
He has shown you, O man, what is good; and what does the LORD require of you but to do justly, to love mercy, and to walk humbly with your God (Mic. 6:8)?

Additional Sermons and Lesson Ideas

When Someone You Love Sins

Date preached:

SCRIPTURE: Galatians 6:1–5

INTRODUCTION: What happens when someone you know falls into sin? What do you say? How do you handle it? The Bible gives us an excellent outline as a behavior guide in Galatians 6.

1. Take Some Time Away for Personal Inventory to Make Sure Your Own Heart Is Right (v. 1: ". . . you who are spiritual . . .").
2. Seek to Restore (v. 1). This usually involves approaching the person in love and concern.
3. Be Gentle (v. 1).
4. Realize You Are Capable of Falling into Sin, Too (v. 1: ". . . considering yourself lest you also be tempted.").
5. Bear the Other Person's Burdens (v. 2). Keep loving that person and praying for him or her).
6. Remain Humble (v. 3).
7. Realize that You Are Not Ultimately Responsible for the Other Person's Decisions, but for Your Own (vv. 4–5). Sometimes the best thing we can do, having done our best, is leave the other person in the Lord's hands.

CONCLUSION: And remember verse 9: "And let us not grow weary while doing good, for in due season we shall reap if we do not lose heart."

The Unveiling of God

Date preached:

By Rev. Mark Hollis

SCRIPTURE: Various, especially Hebrews 1:1–3

INTRODUCTION: God knows us and wants us to know Him. He has revealed Himself to us through creation, His Word, and Jesus.

1. God Has Revealed Himself to Us Through His Word (Heb. 1:1).
2. God Has Revealed Himself to Us Through Jesus (Heb. 1:2–3). Jesus is:
   A. Heir of All Things (Ps. 2:8).
   B. Creator (Col. 1:16).
   C. God's Glory Revealed (John 1:14).
   D. God Expressed (John 10:30).
   E. Sustainer (Col. 1:17).
   F. Our Purification (1 John 2:2).
   G. Seated at God's Right Hand (Phil. 2:8–11).

CONCLUSION: God has revealed Himself to us through His Son. How will we respond (Matt. 21:33–45)? Will you accept or reject His Son? There are only two choices. Eternity weighs in the balance.

OCTOBER 14, 2007

CLERGY APPRECIATION DAY SUGGESTED SERMON

Work

Date preached:

By Dr. Larry Osborne

Scripture: Various, especially Ephesians 4:28

Let him who stole steal no longer, but rather let him labor, working with his hands what is good, that he may have something to give him who has need.

Introduction: As Christians, it's very easy to skip over our verse for today. It speaks of those who have been stealing. It may have surprised you that this is our verse of study today, or maybe you thought we would apply it to a different category of people. An important concept we must understand today is that Paul wrote this verse to Christians, and thus the verse applies to every one of us today in a very practical way.

1. **Workplace Thievery (Prov. 16:8; 28:6; Ex. 20:15; Titus 2:9–12; Prov. 18:9).** Why would a "committed Christian" steal? Ephesians 4:28 is not referring to robbing banks or breaking into houses. However, the church of Ephesus, just as this church today, had members who were engaging in thievery. Thievery is being dishonest in a transaction.

   A. **Financial Fear.** At times we may feel like we can't make it any other way. So, just now I'm going to be a little dishonest with the IRS or with my boss. The pay is low and the debts are high. Maybe a job is lost and we don't see any other way out but to be financially dishonest in some way (see Prov. 19:22).

   B. **Industry Standards.** Times and situations exist when almost the whole world is dishonest. Do you lie on expense reports? Have you ever taken an extra break because you convinced yourself you've earned it?

   C. **Moral Blind Spots.** The average American doesn't even think about the morality of stealing from a large corporate entity. Have you gotten into a wreck and while you're at the shop, the mechanic offers to add an extra fix to the cost of the repair?

Would you give a second thought to adding as many claims as possible to a worker's compensation report?

2. **Workplace Myths.** Some ideas about work prevalent in our culture, among even us as Christians, are actually myths. Let's look at six specifically:

   A. **Work Is a Necessary Evil (Ex. 20:9–10; Lev. 16:29–30; 2 Thess. 3:10; Prov. 20:21).** How many of us think the best life would be one without work? We must understand two truths. One, *we were made to work.* Even before the Fall of man, in paradise Adam was to work, and God Himself did (Gen. 2:2, 15). Second, *unearned work is dangerous.* All of us have heard stories of lottery winners who became suicidal or even criminal after their winnings: this doesn't happen to all of them, but the principle applies to everyone: it is dangerous (Prov. 20:21).

   B. **There's a Perfect Job Out There Somewhere (Prov. 14:23; 1 Tim. 6:6–8).** How many of us have switched jobs, thinking the next job will be the perfect one? Why does it seem like when you arrive, that the "greener grass" is always just painted concrete? First, *Adam's curse still applies* (Gen. 3:17). From the first sin, work has always been difficult. Second, *contentment comes from within* (Phil. 4:12–13). When we search for the "perfect job," we're implying that something external can make us content.

   C. **Some Christians Are in Full-Time Ministry (2 Cor. 5:20; Dan. 1—6).** The fact is that every job is a ministry assignment (Col. 3:23). We all are in full time ministry. Life and work would be much more exciting if we realized our job is to infiltrate whatever work situation we are involved in!

   D. **Financial Success Is a Sign of God's Approval (1 Tim. 6:5; Job; Ps. 73).** The fact is that money can be a blessing or a curse. The disciples were astonished when Jesus told the "rich young ruler" to give up all his possessions. Why were they surprised? They bought into the myth that we buy into: that wealth is a sign of God's favor, but it's not (Luke 18:18–27).

   E. **God Blesses Us Financially So We Can Get Nicer Stuff (Luke 12:16–21; 1 Tim. 6:17–19; Deut. 24:19–21; 2 Cor. 9:10–11).** The fact is that a fool devours all he has, but a wise man saves and shares (Prov. 21:20; Eph. 4:28).

F. I'll Be Generous When I Hit It Big (Mark 12:41–44; 2 Cor. 8:1–4; Prov. 3:9–10; Luke 16:10–11; Hag. 1:3–11). The fact is: That will never happen if you aren't generous with a little.

Conclusion: Be a man or woman of integrity. If you're stealing in any way, stop. See work as what God meant it to be: an assignment from Him. Live below your means so that you might give back to God and to others in need.

STATS, STORIES, AND MORE

Work or Waste Away
You wouldn't ever dream of locking your car up in the garage for a decade or two. Why? A car is designed to work! If you don't allow it to carry out its function, it will be wasted. God Himself worked for six days and rested on the Sabbath. It's part of who we are, made in the image of God, that we are workers. To deny ourselves of what God designed us to do will mean that we simply become as useless as that car sitting in the garage, wasting away.
—Dr. Larry Osborne

J. C. Penney, who was a devoted Christian and a shrewd business leader, told of an incident that occurred when he was seventeen years old. He had already developed an entrepreneurial flare, and his summer crop of watermelons came ripe just as the county fair opened. Young Jim knew he was doing all right selling his watermelons up and down the main street of his town, but he thought he could make more money outside the gates of the fair. He drove his wagon as close to the main entrance as possible, and people were eager for a slice of his watermelon. Suddenly he felt a firm hand on his shoulder. It was his dad, who said, "Better go home, son. Now."

Jim was bewildered and embarrassed but he went home. When his dad arrived home, he asked the young man, "Do you know why I told you to go home?"

"No, sir," replied Jim.

"Did it mean anything to you that the fair was supported by concessions?"

"No," Jim answered.

His father explained that everyone inside the fair had paid a concession fee, and those vendors were dependent on fair-attendees purchasing their products. Jim protested that he had not gone inside the gates.

"That's just it," replied his father. "Without paying anything toward the support of the fair, you were taking advantage of those who did. Everyone is entitled to earn a living, you and everyone else, but never by taking advantage of others."

It was lessons like that which built bedrock honesty inside the heart of J. C. Penney.[1]

---

[1]Adapted from *What Smart People Do When Dumb Things Happen at Work* by Charles E. Watson (New York: Barnes and Nobel, 1999), pp. 102–103.

APPROPRIATE HYMNS AND SONGS

"We'll Work 'Til Jesus Comes," Elizabeth Mills, Public Domain.

"Work for the Night Is Coming," Annie Coghill/Lowell Mason, Public Domain.

"I Want to Be a Worker," I. Baltzell, Public Domain.

"Is There Anything I Can Do for You?" Dottie Rambo/David Huntsinger,
    1977 Heartwarming Music (Brentwood Benson Music Publishing).

FOR THE BULLETIN

On October 14, 1066, the Battle of Hastings sealed the Norman Conquest of England under the leadership of William the Conqueror who came to be noted for his Christian piety and devotion. ● On this October 14 in 1644, William Penn, American Quaker statesman, was born in London. ● John and Charles Wesley set sail for America on October 14, 1735. John intended to serve as a missionary to Indians, a mission that ended in frustration and failure. It was only afterward, back in London, that the brothers solidified their personal relationship with Christ. It was also on October 14, 1735, that John Wesley began keeping his now-famous Journal. ● Isaac Backus, heir of a family fortune, became a pastor, church-planter, and Baptist evangelist in colonial times, covering over 68,000 miles on horseback. He is best known, however, as a champion of religious liberty. From the beginning of his ministry, Backus fought doggedly for separation of church and state in the American colonies. On October 14, 1774, Backus and his fellow ministers arranged a meeting with the Massachusetts representatives to the Congress and presented a petition requesting full religious liberty. His ideas took root and influenced the American Bill of Rights, granting full religious freedom to Americans. ● Today is the birthday of William G. Fischer, who composed the music to the Gospel hymns, "Whiter Than Snow," "I Love to Tell the Story," and "The Rock That Is Higher Than I." ● The Cuban Missile Crisis began on October 14, 1962, bringing the United States and the Soviet Union to the brink of nuclear conflict.

WORSHIP HELPS

Call to Worship

O LORD, you are my God; I will exalt you and praise your name, for in perfect faithfulness you have done marvelous things, things planned long ago (Is. 25:1 NIV).

Offertory Comments

Have you heard the expression, "Have you been working hard or hardly working?" The sad truth is that most Christians work hard, but hardly tithe. Statistics consistently tell us that the more someone makes, the less percentage he or she tithes. God promises blessings when we trust Him with our finances. I encourage you to give generously and out of love.

Suggested Scriptures

- Leviticus 19:13; 25:6
- Deuteronomy 15:18; 24:14–15, 19–21
- Proverbs 3:9–10; 14:23; 16:8; 18:9; 19:22; 20:21; 21:20
- Haggai 1:3–11
- Matthew 10:9–10
- Mark 12:41–44
- Luke 12:16–21; 16:10–11
- 2 Corinthians 8:1–4; 9:10–11
- Timothy 6:17–19

Benediction

> Sweet Savior, bless us ere we go;
> Thy Word into our minds instill,
> And make our lukewarm hearts to glow
> With lowly love and fervent will.
> —FREDERICK W. FABER

Kid's Talk

Bring three coffee cans and label them: "Savings," "Jesus," and "Me." Bring ten one-dollar bills. Explain that you made some money this week at work, and brought some along to show them a great way to put it to use the way God would want us to. Have them help you count out eight dollars for the "Me" can, and one dollar for the "savings" and one for the "Jesus" can. Encourage them and their parents to make three containers for them. Allow one of the children to put the one dollar from the "Jesus" can in an offering plate.

Additional Sermons and Lesson Ideas

The Last Words of Jesus Christ

Date preached:

SCRIPTURE: Revelation 22:20–21

INTRODUCTION: The hardest sentences for writers are the beginnings and endings of their books. God begins and closes His book magnificently. In this passage, we have:

1. The Last Promise in the Bible: "Surely I am coming quickly." These are the last "red letter" words in the Bible.
2. The Last Prayer in the Bible: "Amen. Even so, come, Lord Jesus." The words "even so" refer back to the adverb "quickly." We are taught to pray, "Yes, Lord, quickly. Come quickly as You have promised."
3. The Last Pronouncement in the Bible: "The grace of our Lord Jesus Christ be with you all. Amen." Until He comes, we need a daily distribution of His manifold grace to enable us through each passing hour.

CONCLUSION: Are you praying and preparing for the quickly coming return of our Lord Jesus?

The Process of Love's Perfection

Date preached:

Based on a Sermon by Dr. W. Graham Scroggie

SCRIPTURE: Philippians 1:9–10

INTRODUCTION: Paul wrote out his prayer for the Philippians, through which we learn both how to appropriately pray for each other, and how central love is in our Christian lives. Paul begins, "And this I pray . . ." (v. 9a):

1. Pray for the Enlargement of Love (v. 9b): ". . . that your love may abound still more and more."
2. Pray for the Enrichment of Love (v. 9c): ". . . in knowledge and all discernment."
3. Pray for the Employment of Love (v. 10): "that you may approve the things that are excellent, that you may be sincere and without offense till the day of Christ."

CONCLUSION: Is your love for the Lord and others evident to all? Are you praying for the enlargement, the enrichment, and employment of love to spread throughout the church?

When You're Worried about a Child

PKs have it rough. They live in a fishbowl, take seriously any word of criticism aimed at their parents, and put up with the unwanted identification of *Oh, you're the pastor's kid*. And then there's the devil to contend with. He knows that one of the best ways to demoralize the pastor is to cause problems in his or her family. Our homes are under more attack than we realize, and nothing is more painful than trying to preach on Sunday morning when your teenage son has been "partying" on Saturday night.

Prodigals are arguably the hardest burden a pastor can bear; yet they aren't hopeless cases. Most prodigals return, and we have weapons at our disposal for pulling down strongholds. The only thing is—it may take some time. If you're anguished now because of a child who has fallen off the wire, here are some things that may help.

First, realize this is a testing time for you as surely as it is for your child. The Lord wants to deepen your faith, develop your endurance, expand your compassion, widen your wisdom, and take you further into the prayer chamber than you've previously been. I was quite shocked when I realized there were problems that I could not solve, despite my best efforts. I had always believed that where there's a will, there's a way. On countless nights, I realized I had to put my child "on hold" and get a grip on myself. When I ran into the stubborn soul of a drifting loved one, I couldn't fix it; I've had to learn to trust the Lord with a new layer of pain and to enter into a new level of joy. One of the great mysteries of the soul is why we grow best in.. well, in manure.

I've known pastors who have wanted to quit because of their children's rebellion. "If I can't manage my own household," we're prone to think, "how can I manage the church of the Lord? I'm disqualified. I'm humiliated. I'm embarrassed. I shouldn't be having this problem."

Ah, yes, but even the Lord had trouble with His kids. As our children become older and begin making their own decisions, we

Continued on the next page

lose a certain amount of control. But what we lose in control, we can gain back in prayer. Stormy Omartian wrote, "When we pray for our children, we are asking God to make His presence a part of their lives and work powerfully in their behalf. That doesn't mean there will always be an immediate response. Sometimes it can take days, weeks, or even years. But our prayers are never lost or meaningless. If we are praying something is happening, whether we see it or not."

So the second rule is: Pray. Remember 1 Samuel 12:23: "Moreover, as for me, far be it from me that I should sin against the Lord in ceasing to pray for you." I've found great comfort in inserting a little word in James 5:16 (NIV): "The prayer of a righteous [parent] is powerful and effective."

Third, don't nag. You can nudge, but there's a big difference between nudging and nagging. I think 1 Peter 3:1 is just as applicable to prodigal children as to prodigal husbands: "Wives, in the same way be submissive to your husbands so that, if any of them do not believe the word, they may be won over without words by the behavior of their wives." I'm not saying that parents should be submissive to their wild kids, but I am suggesting that our conduct and attitude should reflect Christ so magnetically that our kids be drawn back to the Lord "without words."

Fourth, do whatever you can to keep communication open. Avoid arguments whenever possible. Be gentle. Seek to draw out your child, and listen, if possible, without overacting. Proverbs 15:1 is especially true with prodigals—a soft answer turns away wrath.

Fifth, love unconditionally. There may be a time when you have to ask your adult prodigal to move out, and there may be times to lay down the law as it relates to matters under your own roof. But the Bible promises in 1 Corinthians 13:8: "Love never fails."

Sixth, confide in a small circle of friends and learn to lean on their prayers when you're too exhausted to pray yourself.

Seventh, try acting as though God had already answered your prayers. Isn't that a simple definition for faith? Wasn't that Hannah's secret in 1 Samuel 1? After her prayer, she gained assurance from God and her attitude totally changed even though her circumstances were unaltered at that particular moment. Your child needs to see the joy in your life, and sometimes our joy can't come from circumstances; it must come from Jesus Himself.

Eighth, wait, but wait expectantly! "Optimism takes the most hopeful view of matters and expects the best outcome in any circumstances," wrote S. Rutherford McDill, Jr., in his book on this subject. "While the prodigal is busy moving from one misadventure to another, optimism will help the parents discipline themselves to see beyond the mess into the aspirations of the child and focus on those. The prodigal does not necessarily want to be identified with his messes or have his nose rubbed in them. The wise mom and dad look to what the prodigal hopes to accomplish."[1]

Finally, don't underestimate what the Lord can do. We have many forces contending against us for the hearts and lives of our children; but God has promised, "I will contend with those who contend with you, and your children I will save" (Is. 49:25).

I'm counting on that promise.[2]

---

[1] S. Rutherford McDill Jr., *Parenting the Prodigal* (Scottdale, PA, 1996), 41–42.
[2] For more help, see the editor's book, *Moments for Families with Prodigals.*

OCTOBER 21, 2007

When Life Doesn't Seem Fair

Date preached:

By Dr. Timothy Beougher

Scripture: Psalm 73:1–28, especially verse 26
My flesh and my heart fail; but God is the strength of my heart and my portion forever.

Introduction: Our lives often seem filled with sickness, stress, family issues, financial crises, and so much more. Why, then, does it seem others, who don't follow the Lord, have it so much better? Our passage today involves the same question, so turn with me to Psalm 73.

1. **Perspective Begins with God's Revelation (v. 1).** This psalm was written by Asaph. Asaph was a godly man who served as the worship leader in the temple. He was the author of 12 of the 150 psalms. He begins this psalm with an affirmation: "God is good." This truth is based on God's revelation of Himself (cf. Matt. 7:11).

2. **Perspective Is Lost When We Walk by Sight (vv. 2–14).** The problem was this: Even as Asaph was trying to sing that truth, he was struggling with perspective. He had lost his focus of walking by faith and he began to walk by sight. He began to measure life only in terms of what his physical eyes could see.

    A. **We Envy the Wicked (vv. 2–3).** Asaph is not critical of the arrogant. He is not rebuking the wicked. Instead, he is jealous of them! He has decided he wants what they have: "prosperity" which is the word *shalom* in Hebrew, a deep-seated peace. It doesn't seem fair at all! Asaph is judging by only what he can see with his physical eyes.

    B. **We Covet the Fruit of Sin (vv. 4–12).** These verses list the fruit that wicked people seem to reap: they seem physically strong and healthy, they inherit seemingly natural emotional blessings, they are proud, they do whatever pleases them, they mock believers and look down on God, and they seem to be blessed with wealth and an easy lifestyle.

    C. **We Conclude that Obeying God Is Futile (vv. 13–14).** Why live for Jesus when those without Him appear to be doing okay?

Does a godly lifestyle really pay off? When walking by sight it appears at times there is little reward for following God. Asaph was ready to throw in the towel. When we walk by sight, we become confused very easily.

3. **Perspective Is Regained When We Walk by Faith (vv. 15–28).** Human observation creates doubt, but divine revelation restores faith.

   A. **Recalling Our Responsibility to Others (v. 15).** In his struggle, Asaph doesn't trash God in front of others. Deep down he still knows the truth of verse 1, so he doesn't cause others to stumble. The problem is that misery loves company. When we hurt, we want to talk to someone. It is okay to share doubts and struggles, but do it with those more spiritually mature, not with those who are "children."

   B. **Renewing Our Focus on God (vv. 16–17).** Walking by sight doesn't provide the answer; it seems to raise new questions! He got worse! Verse 17 provides the major turning point: "Until I went into the sanctuary of God; then I understood their end." That's why worship is so vital: it helps us regain our perspective! The mysteries of life begin to unravel in the presence of the Majesty.

   C. **Realizing the Destiny of the Wicked (vv. 18–20).** It was in the sanctuary of God that Asaph could see the wicked were really not prospering at all. Instead of envying the things that lost people have, we could focus on what they don't have: salvation. We should be concerned for their eternal predicament.

   D. **Recognizing Our Human Frailty (vv. 21–22).** When consumed by bitterness, Asaph acted like an animal. The term used here describes a grazing animal that lives with his head hunched down, seeing only the ground, and never the sky. When we live for this life only, we are like an animal.

   E. **Rejoicing in God's Blessing on the Righteous (vv. 23–28).** These verses speak of God's presence and His protection (v. 23), His guidance and His glory (v. 24). Asaph realizes God is all he needs (v. 25) and commits to walk with Him no matter what (v. 26). Make that decision now!

Conclusion: When our perspective shifts from our human understanding of the reality of eternity, we won't be able to be quiet. We must speak. We will want to tell of all His deeds. We cannot sit on the good news while people are slipping and sliding into the horrors of hell.

STATS, STORIES, AND MORE

Walk by Faith, Not by Sight

A few years ago the National Transportation Safety Board released its official findings on the plane crash that killed John F. Kennedy, Jr., his wife, and his sister-in-law. The headlines read, "Crash of Kennedy plane blamed on pilot error." What happened is that JFK, Jr. became disoriented while flying and lost control of the plane. He trusted in his feelings instead of relying on the plane's instruments to tell him the truth about what was happening with the plane. A news program interviewed a seasoned pilot who said, "When you become disoriented, it is easy to think you are flying level when in fact you may be in a steep descent. You have to trust your instruments, not your feelings." As I heard that, I thought, *What a parable about life!* When we look at the world around us, it is easy for us to respond and make decisions based on our feelings but our feelings are not trustworthy! We need to follow the sure guide, the Bible, the book that always tells us the truth about our situation and how we are to live.

—Dr. Timothy Beougher

The Puzzle

At professional sporting events, the giant screen on the scoreboard will sometimes display a puzzle. It will begin with the outline of a player's head and then ask, "Who is this player?" People in the crowd begin to shout out names, but initially they are simply wild guesses. Gradually, the puzzle begins to take shape as the features on the player's face begin to fill in. Eventually, everyone in the arena or stadium can see clearly who the player is. That "puzzle game" at sporting events reflects our perspective on life. We may think we have things figured out but we really can't understand until we see the whole picture clearly. Psalm 73 is very similar. Asaph thinks he understands and expresses his constantly-changing conclusions about life being unfair. As he goes through this situation and turns to God, the puzzle becomes clearer and clearer, until finally he comes to a godly understanding.

APPROPRIATE HYMNS AND SONGS

"The Lord Is My Strength," Dennis Jernigan, 1993 Shepherds Heart Music (Word Music Group).

"His Strength Is Perfect," Steven Curtis Chapman/Jerry Salley, 1988 Sparrow Song/Careers BMG Music.

"God Is the Strength of My Heart," Eugene Greco, 1989 Integrity's Hosanna! Music.

"He Knows My Name," Tommy Walker, 1996 Doulos Publishing (Maranatha Music).

"Lord Your Goodness," Reuben Morgan, 1997 Reuben Morgan (Hillsong) (Admin. Integrity Music).

FOR THE BULLETIN

"Bloody" Queen Mary, having already condemned and burned such notable evangelicals as Nicholas Ridley and Hugh Latimer, launched a broadside against Protestant Christians in England on this day in 1555. Over two hundred men, women, and children perished. ● Today is the birthday, in 1808, of Samuel Francis Smith of Boston, Massachusetts, a Baptist pastor and editorial secretary of the American Baptist Missionary Union who is chiefly remembered as the author of the patriotic hymn, "America," which he wrote at age 23 while a student at Andover Seminary. ● Let there be light! Thomas Edison perfects the carbonized cotton filament light bulb on this day in 1879. ● Missionary James Hannington arrived off the African coast in July of 1884 and started inland toward Uganda, unwittingly choosing the most dangerous path and was seized by warriors of the lawless Mwanga tribe. His small diary, crammed with tiny handwriting, is a moving missionary document. It records his capture on October 21, 1885, with these words: "About 20 ruffians set upon us. They violently threw me to the ground. Twice I nearly broke away from them, then grew faint from struggling and was dragged by the legs over the ground, my clothes torn to pieces, wet through, strained in every limb, expecting death." He perished at their hands a few days later. Another missionary martyr in Africa is remembered on this day, Dr. Paul Carlson, medical missionary to Congo. His last message was dated to his wife October 21, 1964: "I know I'm ready to meet my Lord," he said, "but my thoughts for you make this more difficult. I trust that I might be a witness for Christ." He was killed shortly thereafter and his gravestone quotes the Lord's words, "Greater love has no one than this, that he lay down his life for his friends."

WORSHIP HELPS

Call to Worship

Rejoice the soul of Your servant, for to You, O Lord, I lift up my soul. For You, Lord, are good, and ready to forgive, and abundant in mercy to all those who call upon You (Ps. 86:4–5).

Offertory Quote

The tithe is a wonderful goal but a terrible place to stop.

—Bill Hybels

Reader's Theater (May be used as a Responsive Reading)

Reader 1: My soul also is greatly troubled; but You, O LORD—how long? Return, O LORD, deliver me! Oh, save me for Your mercies' sake (Ps. 6:3–4)!

Reader 2: This poor man cried out, and the LORD heard him, and saved him out of all his troubles. The angel of the LORD encamps all around those who fear Him, and delivers them (Ps. 34:6–7).

Reader 1: I am weary with my groaning; all night I make my bed swim; I drench my couch with my tears. My eye wastes away because of grief; it grows old because of all my enemies (Ps. 6:6–7).

Reader 2: Oh, taste and see that the LORD is good; blessed is the man who trusts in Him (Ps. 34:8)!

Reader 1: Depart from me, all you workers of iniquity; for the LORD has heard the voice of my weeping. The LORD has heard my supplication; the LORD will receive my prayer (Ps. 6:8–9).

Reader 2: Therefore we do not lose heart. Even though our outward man is perishing, yet the inward man is being renewed day by day. For our light affliction, which is but for a moment, is working for us a far more exceeding and eternal weight of glory, while we do not look at the things which are seen, but at the things which are not seen. For the things which are seen are temporary, but the things which are not seen are eternal (2 Cor. 4:16–18).

Benediction

> The Lord be with us as we bend
> His blessing to receive;
> His gift of peace upon us send,
> Before His courts we leave.
> —JOHN ELLERTON, *The Lord*
> *Be with Us,* 1870

Additional Sermons and Lesson Ideas

Casting Out Discouragement

Date preached:

SCRIPTURE: Deuteronomy 1:21

INTRODUCTION: Each Christian has a personal ministry, and many people exercise that ministry in the context of a local church. You're a Bible study leader, a visitation worker, a nursery volunteer, a choir member. Beware Satan's greatest tool—discouragement. He wants us to become weary in well-doing. Our greatest weapon is faith in the specific promises God has given that our work for Him is productive. If you feel discouraged remember:

1. The Lord Himself Is with Us (Hag. 2:1–4).
2. His Word Will Not Return Void (Is. 55:10–11).
3. Our Work Is Not in Vain (1 Cor. 15:58).
4. We Will Reap a Harvest if We Don't Give Up (Gal. 6:9).
5. The Results of Our Ministry Outlive Us (Rev. 14:13).

CONCLUSION: We not only walk by faith, we work by faith. Don't give up. God is using you in ways greater than you know.

The Master's Mandate

Date preached:

By Dr. Melvin Worthington

SCRIPTURE: Matthew 28:18–20

INTRODUCTION: Missionary zeal is lagging in many churches. The missionary enterprise is not elective but essential, not optional but an obligation. Any claim to obedience which does not manifest itself in compliance with the *Master's Mandate* is a shaky transaction at best.

1. The Truth Asserted (Matt. 28:18). In this announcement we note the *scope of Christ's power, the source of Christ's power*, and *the sufficiency of Christ's power.*
2. The Task Assigned (Matt. 28:19–20). Christ sets forth the task in which His followers are to be engaged. The task is threefold: *evangelism, education*, and *edification.*
3. The Tender Assurance (Matt. 28:20). Christ's tender assurance includes His *promise* and *presence.*

CONCLUSION: Will you allow those around the world to perish in their sins unwarned, never knowing the way of life? Let's carry out the Master's mandate, the Great Commission, together!

OCTOBER 28, 2007

REFORMATION SUNDAY SUGGESTED SERMON

The Word of Life Revealed

Date preached:

By Rev. Todd M. Kinde

Scripture: 1 John 1:1–4, especially verse 2

The life was manifested, and we have seen, and bear witness, and declare to you that eternal life which was with the Father and was manifested to us.

Introduction: What is Christianity? Who is Jesus Christ? These are questions that we perhaps avoid asking because we are, after all, already Christians or we would not be here, right? This is the concern that John has in writing this little letter. He gives us the purpose of his letter in 5:13. It was written to you who already do believe but need to know assurance of eternal life. In so doing, John answers the questions, "What is a real Christian?" "How can I know that I am a genuine Christian?"

I. **The Revelation of Jesus (vv. 1–2).**

   A. **Human Presence:** The writer of this letter is the disciple John who walked with Jesus and followed Him. John was the youngest of the twelve disciples and would outlive the others. By the time he writes this letter, he is an elderly man some fifty or so years after Jesus died, was buried, rose from the dead, and ascended to heaven. John brings our thoughts back to the beginning of it all, the beginning of the Gospel of Jesus Christ. Jesus was a man. They heard Him teach. They saw Him with their own eyes before and after the Resurrection. They beheld Him and even touched Him. There is no doubt about it, He's alive. In fact, He is the Word of Life!

   B. **Divine Essence:** Of course when we go to the start of John's Gospel we find another beautiful prologue that takes us back not only to the beginning of Jesus' life on earth but to the beginning of time (John 1:1–5). Jesus has a human presence that was experienced by John and the others. But He is more. He is also Divine. He was from the beginning, before the beginning, before time. The Son of God was and has always been. He is The Word of

Life (v. 1) and the Eternal Life (v. 2). The Life that was with the Father (v. 3). Jesus is the Eternal Son of God. Yet, He has not remained in the heavenly places of glory. God has revealed Himself in Jesus Christ to the disciples (v. 2a) and not only to them but to us.

2. **The Witness of the Apostles (vv. 3a, 4a).**

   A. **Spoken Testimony of What Was Heard:** The spoken testimony we receive from the apostle is derived from what he has heard Jesus Himself teach. John heard the teaching of Christ. It is this John who reclined at the table with Jesus at the Last Supper and leaned on Him when Jesus spoke in the Upper Room. This spoken testimony he has passed on to us.

   B. **Written Testimony of What Was Seen:** The written testimony we receive from the apostle is also derived from the personal physical encounter he had with Jesus Christ. The Christian religion has always depended upon written documents of testimony to Christ. Chosen men who wrote by the inspiration of the Holy Spirit produced the Bible as we have it. The original articles are not the machinations of men's imaginations. They are the perfect revelation of God. In this written testimony by the apostles we have the Word of Life, the Eternal Word, the Son of God made manifest to us, right here in the Scriptures in front of us.

3. **The Experience of Believers (vv. 3b, 4b).**

   A. **Fellowship:** Proclamation produces fellowship and the written Scriptures produce joy. The experience of believers is that of communion and joy. This fellowship is not merely in the human dimension but is also with the Father and with the Son (v. 3). It is to share in the Divine Life, the Word of Life, the Eternal Life. The purpose of preaching the gospel is to bring people to know what true life is and to bring them into the fellowship.

   B. **Joy:** Written testimony, the Scripture, produces joy. The progression is like this: proclamation of Christ, sharing of life eternal, and consummated joy. Fellowship with God produces joy complete (Ps. 16:11; John 15:9–12). Why do we not experience this joy? Perhaps part of the answer is in failing to obey and in failing to love (3 John 3–4).

Conclusion: Fullness of joy comes when we see Christ exalted and the Father glorified in the lives of the fellowship. We will know full joy only when we walk in the truth and abide in the fellowship of the Father and the Son.

STATS, STORIES, AND MORE

"Some persons have mere empty titles, which confer but little power and little authority. But the Man-Christ Jesus, while He has many crowns and many titles, has not one tinsel crown or one empty title. While He sits there He sits not there *pro forma;* He does not sit there to have nominal honor done to Him; but He has real honor and real glory. That Man-Christ, who once walked the streets of Jerusalem, now sits in heaven, and angels bow before Him. That Man-Christ, who once hung on Calvary, and there expired in agonies the most acute, now, on His Father's throne exalted sins, and sways the scepter of heaven—nay, devils at His presence tremble, the whole earth owns the sway of His providence, and on His shoulders the pillars of the universe rest. 'He upholdeth all things by the word of His power.' He overruleth all mortal things, making the evil work a good, and the good produce a better, and a better still, in infinite progression. The power of the God-Man Christ is infinite; you cannot tell how great it is. He is 'able to save unto the uttermost them that come unto God by Him.' He is 'able to keep us from falling, and to present us spotless before His presence.' He is able to make 'all things work together for good.' He is 'able to subdue all things unto Himself.' He is able to conquer even death, for He hath the power of death, and He hath the power of Satan, who once had power over death; yea, He is Lord over all things, for His Father hath made Him so. The glorious dignity of our Saviour!
—Rev. Charles Haddon Spurgeon, from his sermon "Christ Exalted," preached on Sunday morning, July 6, 1856

APPROPRIATE HYMNS AND SONGS

"Blessed Assurance," Fanny Crosby/Phoebe P. Knapp, Public Domain.

"I Know Whom I Have Believed," Major Daniel W. Whittle/James McGranahan, Public Domain.

"Be Still," Bryan Harden, 1989 Zion Song Music.

"Forever," Chris Tomlin, 2001 WorshipTogether.com Songs/Six Steps Music (div. of EMI Christian Music Publishing).

FOR THE BULLETIN

According to our best calculations, this is the date, in A.D. 312, that 32-year-old Roman emperor Constantine defeated Maxentius at Milvian Bridge, having seen the sign of the cross in the sky accompanied by the words "By this sign conquer." After the battle, he espoused Christianity, and the persecuted church suddenly found itself the official religion of the Roman Empire. ● Desiderius Erasmus Roterodamus, whose new versions of the Greek New Testament unleashed the Protestant Reformation, was (probably) born on October 28, 1468. ● New England Puritans, wanting to establish a university in New England, established Harvard College on October 28, 1636, in part to avoid the danger of having "an illiterate ministry to the churches." Much of the funding came from the resources of John Harvard. The deaths of many of his family members from the plague left him with large sums and few heirs. When he himself died of disease, he willed half his estate and his entire library to the college, which was named in his honor. ● Colonial missionary John Eliot, Apostle to the Indians, conducted the first Protestant worship service for Native Americans on this day in 1646, preaching to them in their own tongue. ● Today is the birthday, in 1829, of John H. Hopkins, Episcopalian hymnist, and the author of "We Three Kings of Orient Are." ● The Statue of Liberty was dedicated by President Grover Cleveland on October 28, 1886, and celebrated by the first ticker tape parade in the history of New York City. ● Rev. Charles Haddon Spurgeon withdrew from the Baptist Union on October 28, 1887, due to the "Downgrade Controversy."

WORSHIP HELPS

Call to Worship (Prayer)

Lord, we pray with the psalmist, "As the deer pants for the water brooks, so pant our souls for You, O God. Our souls thirst for God, for the living God" (adapted from Ps. 42:1–2). So now in Your mercy grant us Your grace and guidance as we continue to worship, in Jesus' name, Amen.

Word of Welcome

Recognized on this, the last Sunday in October, Reformation day commemorates Martin Luther's posting of his *Ninety-Five Theses* on the door of the Castle Church in Wittenberg, which triggered the movement known as the Protestant Reformation. He, along with others, fought for the ideal known as *Sola Scriptura,* which translated from Latin means "By Scripture Alone." Today our passage from 1 John deals with Jesus Christ, the Word of life. I give you this history so that we might pause and recognize how blessed we are here today. We worship freely, with the Word of God available to every one of us; we worship Christ freely, the living Word of God! Let's praise the Lord together for those who spoke out to reform the church, and allow the Word of God to penetrate our lives in a personal way.

Offertory Prayer

Heavenly Father, You have told us not to worry about our finances, for if You feed the birds of the air and clothe the lilies of the field, You will surely take care of us. I believe You intend to provide for the needs of our people in their individual homes and lives, and I believe You intend to care for our needs as a church. So we thank You in advance, rest in Your Word, and render unto You today our tithes and offerings as an act of faith, love, obedience, and worship, Amen.

Benediction

Holy God who knows us by name, we come to You as Moses did, saying, "If Your Presence does not go with us, do not bring us up from here" (Ex. 33:15). For without Your Presence, our worship and our very existence are in vain. Be always with us, Amen.

Additional Sermons and Lesson Ideas

How to Claim God's Promises for Yourself

Date preached:

SCRIPTURE: Joshua 14:12

INTRODUCTION: There is a promise in Scripture for every circumstance and contingency we face. The basis for our entire life of faith is found in God's promises, and those promises are the secret of the Christian's joy.

1. Claim Them Like Celeb, with Boldness (Josh. 14:9–14).
2. Claim Them Like Abraham, by Faith (Rom. 4:19–22).
3. Claim Them Like David, in Prayer (2 Sam. 7:25–28).

CONCLUSION: "God is not a man, that he should lie . . . Does he promise and not fulfill?" (Num. 23:19 NIV). Not one of all God's good promises can ever fail, and there is a promise today with your name on it. Claim it with boldness, by faith, and in prayer.

Deep Roots

Date preached:

By Dr. Larry Osborne

SCRIPTURE: 1 Timothy 3:6

INTRODUCTION: Paul's instructed Timothy not to place a new convert in leadership, something many churches unfortunately do all too often. Why do we err in this way, and how can we be sure someone is well-rooted and ready for leadership?

1. The Faulty Rationale:
   A. We Mistake Enthusiasm for Maturity (Rom. 10:1–3; Matt. 13:18–23).
   B. We Mistake Spirituality for Maturity (Heb. 5:11–14; Eph. 4:11–15).
   C. We Assume High Profile People Should Be Displayed Not Discipled (1 Tim. 3:6; James 2:1–4).
2. The Tragic Results: Pride and Spiritual Collapse (Prov. 8:13; 11:2; 27:21).
3. What It Takes to Dig to Deep Roots:
   A. Time (Col. 2:6–7; Ex. 23:28–30; Acts 7:23–24).
   B. Trials (James 1:2–4; 1 Pet. 1:5–7; Acts 14:22; Prov. 10:25; 24:10).
   C. Thirst (Prov. 19:27; Phil. 3:13–15).

CONCLUSION: As a church, let's commit to dig deep and commission leaders that will represent Christ well.

SUGGESTED SERMON

I Believe in Jesus

Date preached:

By Rev. Larry Kirk

Scripture: John 1:1–16, especially verse 9
(Jesus) was the true Light which gives light to every man coming into the world.

Introduction: The prologue of John is one of the most well-known passages of the New Testament. Jesus is referred to as the Word, or the *logos* in Greek. For the Greek philosophers the logos was that logical, intelligent, rational force that they believed had to exist behind all of the natural laws they saw at work in the world. For the Jewish theologians it was the outward expression of the invisible God. John was led to apply this word to Christ and fill it with deeper, richer meaning. We learn seven things about this *logos* that we can apply to our lives.

1. **The Word Is Eternal (v. 1).** Go back as far as you want. Imagine it; go back billions of years, trillions of years. He was already there. He comes out of eternity into our world.

2. **The Word Is a Person (v. 2).** Jesus is a being distinct from God and yet one with the Triune God. That power, that reason, which has been present in the world, is a personal being who was with God as verse 2 says, in the beginning.

3. **The Word Is God (vv. 1–2).** You might think that if He was with God, He can't be God, but look at the third statement: "the Word was God" (v. 1). The Word is Himself, fully God. He can be distinguished from the Father, and yet He is one with the Father and equal to the Father. Behind this is the truth of the Trinity. There is one God but that one God exists in three distinct persons. God the Father, God the Son, God the Holy Spirit. These three persons all share the same essence, the attributes, the stuff of God, the spiritual DNA makes God, God. The Father, Son, and Holy Spirit, alone share the essence of God and they share that essence equally. So, the Word was with God and the Word was God.

4. **The Word Is the Creator (v. 3).** Christ Jesus, before His appearance on this earth, made the ocean and the sunrise and the dolphins and the egrets and all that has been created.

5. **The Word Is the Source of Life (v. 4).** Here we have a major theme in the Gospel of John. In John 5:40, Jesus expresses His sorrow that people refuse to come to Him to have life. In John 10:10 He says, "I have come that they may have life . . ."

6. **The Word Is the Source of Light (v. 4).** The life in Jesus Christ is a life that gives spiritual light wherever it is received. Light is a powerful symbol in the Bible. When you walk in the darkness you may stumble over a log, step on a snake, fall off a cliff, or hit your head on a low-hanging branch. Jesus, in coming to earth, turned up the light. In John 8:12 Jesus said, "I am the light of the world . . ."

Application: You have two options in responding to the doctrine taught in this passage:

1. **You May Reject Christ (vv. 10–11).** This is not an indictment of the Jewish race. It's an indictment of the human race. If your response to Christ is to neither recognize Him for who He is, nor receive Him into your life, you have reason to be frightened. You are saying to your Creator, the Light of the World and the Giver of Life, "I don't recognize You and I won't receive You." The Bible says that people who respond to Christ that way will one day face the judgment of God and hear Him say, "You did not recognize or receive Me, now I do not recognize or receive you."

2. **You May Receive Christ (vv. 12–13).** Receiving Christ is not just trying to receive a blessing from Him. It's receiving Him and all that He is. You receive Jesus Christ as your God, your Lord, and your Savior. You believe in His name, the Greek words convey the idea, not just of believing that He existed, but turning to Him and trusting in Him. God wants us, not just to recognize that He came into our world, but to receive Him into our lives.

STATS, STORIES, AND MORE

The True Light

C. S. Lewis was a brilliant Oxford professor who had been an atheist since he was fourteen, but he loved great stories, myths, and children's fables. One day he spent the evening with his friend, J. R. R. Tolkien, author of *The Lord of the Rings*. They talked until 3:00 in the morning. Basically Tolkien asked Lewis: "Why do the stories move you?" Lewis gave a reply, after Tolkien said something to this effect, "The reason you are moved by a story like sleeping beauty is because your soul somehow knows there really is an evil sorcerer who has us under his spell and when you read of the prince who comes and sets her free it's because your soul knows that it really takes a kiss of grace to wake us up and set us free."

Tolkien said these stories are not true, but they reflect a splintered fragment of the true light. The story of Christ is true, and it's the true story that touches the deepest needs of the human heart and changes lives when it is received and believed. Twelve days later, Lewis wrote a friend and said: "I have passed from believing in God to definitely believing in Christ and in Christianity. My long night walk with Tolkien had a great deal to do with it." —Rev. Larry Kirk

APPROPRIATE HYMNS AND SONGS

"Of the Father's Love Begotten," Marcus Aurelius Clemens Prudentius/ John Neale, Public Domain.

"Light of the World," Michael Card, 1981 Mole End Music (Admin. Word Music Group).

"The Light of the World Is Jesus," Philip P. Bliss, Public Domain.

"Shine on Us," Michael W. Smith/Deborah D. Smith, 1996 Milene Music, Inc./Deer Valley Music (Admin. Acuff-Rose Music Publishing).

"All Creatures of Our God and King," St. Francis of Assissi/William H. Draper, Public Domain.

FOR THE BULLETIN

On November 4, 1646, the Massachusetts Bay Colony passed a law making it a capital offense to deny that the Bible was the Word of God. ● On November 4, 1740, a baby was born in Farnham, England, and given the formidable name of Augustus Montague Toplady. By age 12, he was preaching sermons to whomever would listen. At 14, he began writing hymns. At 16, he was soundly converted to Christ while attending a service in a barn. And at 22, he was ordained an Anglican priest. He despised John Wesley's Arminian theology and described him as a prize fighter and chimney sweep. Toplady is best remembered, however, for his hymn, "Rock of Ages, cleft for me, let me hide myself in Thee." ● Today is also the birthday (1771) of another noted hymnist, James Montgomery. Raised by Moravian missionary parents, Montgomery became a noted British journalist who crusaded for humanitarian causes. His hymns include the carol "Angels from the Realms of Glory." ● Frontier Freewill Baptist evangelist David Marks was born on this day in 1805 and called to preach on this day fifteen years later. ● Today's wedding anniversaries: Abraham Lincoln and Mary Todd, in 1842; Missionaries John and Isobel Kuhn in 1929; and U.S. Senate Chaplain Peter Marshall and Catherine Wood in 1936. ● The Chinese Christian leader and writer, Watchman Nee, was born on November 4, 1903, in Swatow, China. He spent his last twenty years in prison where he died at the hands of the Chinese Communists.

WORSHIP HELPS

Call to Worship
You alone are the LORD; You have made heaven, the heaven of heavens, with all their host, the earth and everything on it, the seas and all that is in them, and You preserve them all. The host of heaven worships You (Neh. 9:6).

Scripture Reading Medley on the Name of God
And as for Seth, to him also a son was born; and he named him Enosh. Then men began to call on the name of the LORD . . . Then David said to the Philistine, "You come to me with a sword, with a spear, and with a javelin. But I come to you in the name of the LORD of hosts, the God of the armies of Israel . . . Some trust in chariots, and some in horses; but we will remember the name of the LORD our God. . . . . The LORD will establish you as a holy people to Himself, just as He has sworn

to you, if you keep the commandments of the LORD your God and walk in His ways. Then all peoples of the earth shall see that you are called by the name of the LORD . . . . Silver and gold I do not have, but what I do have I give you: In the name of Jesus Christ of Nazareth, rise up and walk . . . . Praise the name of the LORD. Blessed be the name of the LORD from this time forth and forevermore! From the rising of the sun to its going down the LORD's name is to be praised. The LORD is high above all nations, His glory above the heavens . . . . At the name of Jesus every knee should bow . . . . Blessed be the name of the LORD (Gen. 4:26; 1 Sam. 17:45; Ps. 20:7; Deut. 28:9–10; Acts 3:6; Ps. 113:1–4; Phil. 2:10; Job 1:21).

A Stanza from an Old Hymn to Include in Today's Prayer or Word of Welcome

> All our knowledge, sense and sight
> Lie in deepest darkness shrouded,
> Till Thy Spirit breaks our night
> With the beams of truth unclouded.
> Thou alone to God canst win us;
> Thou must work all good within us.
> —TOBIAS CLAUSNITZER, 1663

Benediction

Search us, O God, and know our hearts; try us, and know our anxieties; and see if there is any wicked way in us, and lead us in the way everlasting (adapted from Ps. 139:23–24).

Additional Sermons and Lesson Ideas

The Ultimate Priest
By Rev. Mark Hollis

Date preached:

SCRIPTURE: Hebrews 10:1–18

INTRODUCTION: Animal sacrifices annually offered could never provide the solution to the problem of sin.

1. Jesus, Our High Priest:
   A. Is the Reality of Which All Others Are the Shadow (vv. 1–4).
   B. Fulfills God's Will (vv. 5–10).
   C. Provided the Only Necessary Sacrifice for Sins (vv. 11–14).
   D. Has Written His Covenant on Our Hearts (vv. 15–18).
      (1) The Law Made Us Aware of Sin.
      (2) Jesus Writes His Law on Our Hearts (vv. 15–16).
      (3) Jesus Is the Only Sacrifice Necessary (vv. 17–18).
2. Since Jesus Is Our High Priest:
   A. Draw Near to God (vv. 19–22).
   B. Hold On to Hope (v. 23).
   C. Spur One Another On (v. 24).
   D. Meet Regularly with the Body of Christ (v. 25).

CONCLUSION: Jesus is our great High Priest. We must draw near to God, hold on to hope, and encourage one another.

The Mother of Mankind
By Dr. Melvin Worthington

Date preached:

SCRIPTURE: Genesis 1—3

INTRODUCTION: God made man and placed him in the Garden of Eden to dress it and keep it. Eve was Adam's counterpart and companion. She was complex, complicated, and complete at the time of her creation.

1. The Special Model (Gen. 2:18–25). *What the Sovereign Discerned* (Gen. 2:18), *What the Sovereign Declared* (Gen. 2:18), and *What the Sovereign Designed* (Gen. 2:19–25) are recorded.
2. The Spouse's Mate (Gen. 1:26–28; 2:18–25; Gen. 3). Adam *needed her, noticed her, named her, nurtured her,* but then *neglected her.*
3. The Serpent's Mischief (Gen. 3:1–7). *The serpent, the strategy, the sin, the sorrow,* and *the summons* are recorded.
4. The Sovereign's Mandate (Gen. 3:12–19). The *cause of the offense, the curse for the offense, the consequences of the offense,* and *the covering for the offense* are dealt with by God Himself.

CONCLUSION: Eve serves as an example of the danger of doubting God's Word, disbelieving God's Word, disregarding God's Word, denying God's Word, and disobeying God's Word.

TECHNIQUES FOR THE PASTOR'S DELIVERY

Deep Breathing

Excerpted from *The Household Guide
or Domestic Cyclopedia:
A Practical Family Physician, Home Remedies
and Home Treatment of All Diseases*

By B. G. Jefferis and L. L. Nichols

Published by J. L. Nichols Company
Limited of Toronto, 1894

Cultivate the habit of breathing through the nose and taking deep breaths. If this habit was universal, there is little doubt that pulmonary affections would be decreased one-half. An English physician calls attention to this fact, that deep and forced respiration will keep the entire body in a glow in the coldest weather, no matter how thinly one may be clad. He was himself half frozen to death one night, and began taking deep breaths and the result was that he was thoroughly comfortable in a few minutes. The deep respiration, he says, stimulates the blood currents by direct muscular action and causes the entire system to become pervaded with the rapidly generated heat.

Lung Strengthener. Long breaths are lung strengtheners, and such exercise has cured severe colds in the lungs, and has been known to do more good than medicine in the early stages, or rather, at the appearance, of consumption. Such precaution and prevention cost nothing and it would be well to adopt the method.

The Art of Breathing. It is perhaps one of the signs of the times, to those alert for indications, that the art of breathing has become more and more a subject of attention. Oculists, as well as physiologists, go deeply into its study in a way hardly touched upon here. Physicians have cured aggravated cases of insomnia by long-drawn regular breaths; fever-stricken patients have been quieted, stubborn forms of indigestion made to disappear. Sea-sickness, too, may be surmounted, and the victim of hypnotic

Continued on the next page

influence taught to withstand the force of any energy directed against him.

Rule of Ascent. In making any ascent, either by stairway or path, the rule is to use one breath for every step. One should breathe through the nostril, not talk, and go systematically to work. The fuller the breath the better.

On the Level. In walking along a level stretch take two steps for every breath. Always begin to exhale or inhale as the same foot touches the ground.

Ridding the Lungs. Inhale as you put the right foot to the ground. Then, as the left touches the ground, exhale naturally, and as the right touches the ground exhale again with an effort, so expelling all the air from the lungs. Then inhale again, now on the left foot, exhale naturally on the right, and with an effort expel the air as the left foot falls. This exercise is kept up for some time, always in this way: left foot, inhale; right foot, exhale; left foot, expel with effort. Again, right foot, inhale; left foot, exhale; right foot, expel with effort. The process of inhaling, therefore, begins with alternate footsteps.

These rules, although simple, have been very beneficial to many.

NOVEMBER 11, 2007

INTERNATIONAL DAY OF PRAYER FOR THE PERSECUTED CHURCH
SUGGESTED SERMON

Cultivating Spiritual Hunger   *Date preached:*

By Dr. Ed Dobson

Scripture: Matthew 5:6
Blessed are those who hunger and thirst for righteousness, for they shall be filled.

Introduction: You'll recall that the Sermon on the Mount was a message given by Jesus to a Jewish audience. It's very Jewish in its context, identifying for us what the kingdom of Jesus would look like on planet earth. The principles of the sermon, specifically the attitudes, have application for each of us today. But when we study the Beatitudes it is very important to take the beatitude and place it in the larger context of biblical teaching. Put on your thinking cap, for we need to see this in the overall context of biblical truth. I want to suggest five thoughts in regard to our verse for today:

1. **We All Hunger and Thirst Spiritually.** That's part of what it means to be a human being. Within each of us (placed there by the Creator God) is a deep sense that there's more to life than the here and now. There's more than the material; there's more than the world as we see it, feel it, touch it, and walk in it. We have a sense of the transcendence of the supernatural (cf. Rom. 1:18–19). Our problem, however: we are spiritually dead (Eph. 2). We often spend undue time and effort filling our lives with "stuff" trying to make us full.

2. **Only God Can Satisfy This Hunger.** Yes, we are born, we are created with a spiritual hunger, but only God can satisfy that hunger. Psalm 107:8 tells us that only God satisfies the inner longings of our spiritual being. We can try all sorts of stuff, cram all sorts of junk into our lives, but they will ultimately be empty without Christ.

3. **We Do not Naturally Turn to God to Fill Us.** You would think that since we were created with a spiritual hunger and that only God can satisfy the hunger, that we would immediately and in the natural course of events turn to God for that satisfaction. The Bible actually states the opposite: "There is none righteous, no not one; there is

none who understands; there is none who seeks after God" (Rom. 3:10–11). Paul says there is nobody who is righteous, not a single person! There is no one who seeks God. All have turned away.

4. **We Desperately Need Righteousness Not of Our Own.** We need something from God that we do not possess on our own: the righteousness of Jesus Christ imputed to my account by faith (see Rom. 3:21). We are all born in sin, we all have turned to our own way. We cannot possibly live good enough to be accepted by God. The wonderful news of the gospel is that, through Jesus Christ, I can be declared as forgiven, as righteous in the sight of a holy, holy God. Happy are those who have been declared righteous by God. Happy and satisfied are those who have been forgiven.

5. **The Righteousness of God Transforms Our Standing Before God and Changes Our Desire for God.** My standing with God is changed when I trust Christ and turn to Him for salvation! There's no more condemnation, no more being an enemy of God (Rom. 5:1). Rather, I have peace with God. God not only changed my standing, He changed my desires, where once I turned from God, now my desire is to love, obey, and serve God (Rom. 6:1).

Conclusion: Jesus says happiness comes to those who are starved and desperately thirsty for righteousness for they are the ones who will eat, drink, and be satisfied. He's saying, number one, that when by faith we believe in Jesus Christ and God forgives all of our sins, that's reason to be happy and to be satisfied. Happy and satisfied are the righteous. Secondly, having received that righteousness God then begins to change our desires and transform our lives. The practical implication to those of us who are followers of Jesus Christ is this: obedience is God's path to happiness and to satisfaction. There's nothing like obedience to the Lord. It brings true happiness and it brings lasting satisfaction.

STATS, STORIES, AND MORE

World Hunger and St. Peter's Fish
Researchers are now suggesting that "St. Peter's Fish," commonly known as Tilapia, may provide part of the answer to world hunger. This fish, which has been cultivated by humans for thousands of years, is a freshwater perch that is ideally suited for large-scale cultivation in many other parts of the world. It's a healthy fish, and an excellent source of protein. Well, in the same way, St. Peter's Message—the message of the church, of the apostles—is ideally suited to meet the spiritual hunger of the world.

God's Grace
Clarence Macartney, a preacher of a bygone era, told the story of two brothers who were convicted of stealing sheep, and, in accordance with the brutal punishment of that day, were branded on the forehead with the letters ST, which stood for "Sheep Thief." One of the brothers, unable to bear the stigma, fled to another area, but he bristled whenever anyone noticed the mark on his forehead. He traveled from place to place until he died at last, full of bitterness. The other brother repented of his misdeed and said to himself, "I can't run away from the fact that I stole sheep. All I can do is to win back the respect of my friends and neighbors." As the years passed, he became a devoted follower of Christ and a respected man in his town. One day a stranger came to town and saw the old man with the letters ST branded on his forehead, and asked one of the townspeople what they meant. The neighborhood man replied, "I don't really know; it all happened so long ago. But I think the letters are an abbreviation for the word 'Saint.'" Yes, that's it! The wonderful grace of God in the believing heart is able to change and transform the odious marking and scarring of sin into a badge of beauty, and the blood of the Lord Jesus makes us His saints.[1]

APPROPRIATE HYMNS AND SONGS

"In the Secret," Andy Park, 1995 Mercy/Vineyard Publishing.

"A Heart After Your Heart," Kenny Synder, 1997 Strong Tower Music.

"Blessed Are Those Who Hunger," Tom Ewing/Jay Stocker, 1994 Tom Ewing/Jay Stocker.

"Hungry," Kathryn Scott, 1999 Vineyard Songs (Admin. Mercy/Vineyard Publishing).

---

[1]Clarence Edward Macartney, *Macartney's Illustrations* (New York: Abingdon-Cokesbury Press, 1945), pp. 304–305.

FOR THE BULLETIN

Two important church councils convened on this day in history. The Fourth Lateran Council opened on this day, November 11, in 1215, one of the chief accomplishments of which was officially confirming the doctrine of transubstantiation. And the Council of Constance ended the long-lasting Western papal schism on this day in 1415. ● Today is the birthday, in 1491, of Martin Bucer, who sought to find compromises between Luther and the Catholics, and between Luther and Zwingli. ● The Mayflower Compact was adopted by the Pilgrims on November 11, 1620; and on this same day 27 years later—November 11, 1647—Massachusetts passed the first compulsory school attendance law in America. ● William Carey, the "Father of Modern Missions," arrived in Calcutta on November 11, 1793. ● Three notable literary figures were born on this day. Russian novelist Fyodor Dostoevsky was born on November 11, 1821; and the Danish theologian and writer, Søren Kierkegaard, was born on November 11, 1855. The twentieth-century writer and apologist, C. S. Lewis, was born on November 11, 1898. ● On the eleventh hour of the eleventh day of the eleventh month of 1918, the Great War ended, and this day—now called Veterans' Day—marks the anniversary of the Armistice which was signed in the Forest of Compiegne by the Allies and the Germans in 1918, ending World War I, after four years of conflict. ● On November 11, 1921, Peter Taylor Forsyth died. He was an English Congregational clergyman and theologian best known for his book, *The Person and Place of Jesus Christ*, published in 1909.

WORSHIP HELPS

Call to Worship
Holy, holy, holy is the LORD of hosts; the whole earth is full of His glory (Is. 6:3)!

Pastoral Prayer
Lord, our God and King, we praise You today for our freedom. We can openly seek after Your righteousness, we can publicly declare our faith to others, and we can worship You freely. Today, Lord, we remember our brothers and sisters around the world who cannot. We ask that You would provide peace to those hostile nations who persecute Your people. We beg for deliverance for Your people, our brothers and sisters, who endure public humiliation, death, torture, rape, or even worse for the sake of Your name and Your gospel. Lord, we ask that

You not allow us to turn a deaf ear to them, but to constantly pray for them earnestly. Give them strength, as You promised to never leave or forsake us. Give them comfort when they do suffer, for You suffered more than anyone could and You promised to bless those who suffer for Your sake. Lord, hear our prayers and awaken us to have the same faith, unshakeable, for it would take but one day for the political or cultural tides to turn, but You O Lord are eternal! Amen.

Offertory Verse
Now concerning the collection for the saints, as I have given orders to the churches of Galatia, so you must do also: On the first day of the week let each one of you lay something aside, storing up as he may prosper (1 Cor. 16:1–2).

Kid's Talk

Gather the children around and ask them about their favorite snacks. Tell them you have two snacks, and you keep them in your pocket. From one pocket, pull out a multigrain bar or an apple or banana or some other simple snack. Explain that it's for your stomach. "My other snack is in this pocket." Pull out a small New Testament. Explain that our souls need nourishment, too, and reading the Bible each day is as important to our inner selves as food and snacks are to our bodies.

Additional Sermons and Lesson Ideas

Esther's Surprise Assignment
By Dr. Larry Osborne

Date preached:

SCRIPTURE: Various, especially the story of Esther

INTRODUCTION: Esther's story teaches us some very important lessons if we want to be used by God.

1. Learn When to Shut Up (Esth. 2:8–10; 20–21; Prov. 11:12; 18:2; 25:15; 29:20).
2. Learn When to Speak Up (Esth. 4:1—5:8; 7:3–6; Mark 8:38; Rom. 1:16–17; 1 Pet. 3:15; 2 Tim. 1:8).
3. Learn How to Serve Humbly (Esth. 2:1–23; 7:3–4; Dan. 1—6; Matt. 20:25–28; 1 Pet. 5:5–6).
4. Watch for God Sightings and Divine Appointments (Esth. 4:14; Gen. 50:20; Prov. 16:4; 1 Cor. 7:17–24).

CONCLUSION: When we submit to the will of God as revealed in Scripture, our humility and service can have immeasurable effects.

How Should We Pray?
By Rev. Larry Kirk

Date preached:

SCRIPTURE: Matthew 6:9–13

INTRODUCTION: We should pray according to the pattern Jesus set for His followers:

1. Pray for God's Perfections to Be Praised (v. 9): "Our Father in heaven, Hallowed be Your name."
2. Pray for God's Purpose (v. 10): "Your kingdom come. Your will be done on earth as it is in heaven."
3. Pray for God's Provision (v. 11): "Give us this day our daily bread."
4. Pray for God's Pardon (v. 12): "And forgive us our debts, as we forgive our debtors."
5. Pray for God's Protection (v. 13): "And do not lead us into temptation, but deliver us from the evil one."

CONCLUSION: We pray not to the idea of a god, but to the God who created us, for to Him alone belongs "the kingdom and the power and the glory forever. Amen" (v. 13).

Raymond Lull

Much of the unreached world today is Islamic, but great inroads are being forged by a new generation of Christian missionary, eager to reach the hearts and minds of Muslims. Increasing numbers of Muslims are coming to Christ, and the gospel is being planted in the hardened soul of many regions of the world. Much of the credit goes to a trailblazer named Raymond Lull (c. 1235–1315).

Lull grew up self-indulged on the island of Majorca off the Spanish coast in the Mediterranean. His father was wealthy and powerful, a friend of the king. Lull, sexually indulgent, slept with many women, even following his marriage and the birth of two children. But one day at age 32, writing some erotic poetry, he was stricken with guilt. He envisioned Christ suffering on the Cross. He was converted.

Majorca was controlled by Muslims, and gradually the young man felt a desire to reach the Islamic world. After providing for his wife and children, Lull gave away the rest of his possessions. He studied extensively for several years, learning the Arabic language and all he could about both Christianity and Islam. With the king's help, he established a school on Majorca for the training of missionaries. He met repeatedly with Popes and Cardinals, trying to persuade them to establish similar schools across Europe for missionary training and language study. He lectured, wrote, and preached extensively. Then he began his actual missionary work at age 55, targeting North Africa.

It began unsteadily. Having announced his departure for Tunis, Lull was joined by well-wishers at the port at Genoa. But he was suddenly overwhelmed by the terror of possible martyrdom. His belongings were unloaded and the ship sailed without him. He quickly recovered and caught the next ship for Tunis. His fears were valid. He found himself in constant danger, living a fugitive's life. He was eventually arrested, deported, and stoned on his way to the boat. But he couldn't stay away, and he made repeated forays into North Africa, always at risk of life and limb. Throughout his 70s and into his 80s, Lull was preaching to Muslims. Finally on June 30, 1314, Lull was seized, dragged out of town, and stoned. He died shortly afterward. But he advanced Christian missions like no one else in his age and paved the way for everyone since with a burden for the Muslims.

NOVEMBER 18, 2007

SUGGESTED SERMON

Wisdom's Protection Plan

Date preached:

By Dr. Al Detter

Scripture: Proverbs 2:11–22, especially v. 11
Discretion will preserve you; understanding will keep you.

Introduction: I'm going to paint two pictures today. The first is a cruise ship in the Caribbean. You're on the open sea. The weather is great. So is the food and entertainment. There's the occasional rough water, the occasional storm, the occasional virus affecting a third of the passengers, but it's basically a fun ride with no real significant threats to safety. The second picture is a cargo ship approaching a harbor noted for hidden reefs and dangerous rocks. There are valuables on the ship along with some good friends. You are navigating safely to harbor but you can't be ignorant of the dangers or it could be deadly. The illusion in the kind of life most of us live is that life is like a cruise ship of fun. We can do pretty much as we wish and not get hurt. The truth is that life is really more like a cargo ship in constant danger. Wisdom reveals the rocks that would otherwise threaten us in the darkness, but it's up to us to steer clear of them. Without wisdom, we won't even see them. In the sea of life there are many dangerous rocks. In this text, we see that wisdom will guard us from two major destructive rocks.

1. **Rock #1: Bad Friends and Their Sinful Behavior (Prov. 2:12–15).** Without discretion and understanding, we won't see this rock. We won't understand who is good for us and who isn't. The function of wisdom is to deliver us from this rock (v. 12). There are people in life who walk in the way of evil (v. 12a). It's not that these people necessarily do the worst of sins, but that they live outside the prescribed path of God for human beings as outlined in His Word. They speak words that ought not to be spoken (v. 12b). Sometimes their language is rotten and vile. Sometimes it is cutting and demeaning. Their words are harmful. When you have wisdom, you realize these aren't your friends. Neither are people who don't live according to Scripture (v. 13). They do what they want to do regard-

less of what the Bible says. When sin no longer bothers a person, it's a sure sign they're on the wrong path (v. 15). They are devious. If you have wisdom, you can see the wrong way. Watch out for false wisdom. False wisdom says that you will be a good influence on bad friends. It doesn't work that way. That's why the apostle Paul says in 1 Corinthians 15:33, "Do not be deceived: 'Evil company corrupts good habits.'"

2. **Rock #2: Immoral Relationships (Prov. 2:16–19).** Immorality is the second huge rock. Without wisdom, the likelihood is high that people are going to crash into it. We live in a sea of dangerous immoral rocks. The function of wisdom is to deliver us from immoral relationships (v. 16). We are cautioned about "the immoral woman" in verse 16. The proper sexual expression is only between two people of the opposite sex who are married to each other. All other sexual activity is strange or immoral. We see a total lack of wisdom in Hollywood. The immoral woman of verse 16 is described as a seductive (v. 16b) and covenant-breaking person (v. 17). She comes on to the man with flattering speech to break the Seventh Commandment. She was formerly married but left her husband. She had a relationship with God but reneged on that as well. She promises a good time but in verses 18–19, we see that her appeal is deadly. Her house bows down to death (v. 18; cf. Prov. 7:27). The road of sexual permissiveness is a one-way street to death (v. 19).

Conclusion: The role of discretion and understanding is to put a warning light by the major destructive rocks of life. Wisdom marks them out and says, "Steer clear of these rocks. Hit them and you can sink your vessel." If you are smart enough to see the warning light and steer clear of the rocks, verses 20–21 say that you will enjoy the blessings of God in your life.

STATS, STORIES, AND MORE

- By the end of 2004, there were 420 million pages of pornography, and it is believed that the majority of these Web sites are owned by fewer than 50 companies (LaRue, Jan. "Obscenity and the First Amendment." Summit on Pornography. Rayburn House Office Building. Room 2322. May 19, 2005).

- The Internet pornography industry generates $12 billion dollars in annual revenue—larger than the combined annual revenues of ABC, NBC, and CBS (Family Safe Media, January 10, 2006, <http://www.familysafemedia.com/pornography_statistics.html>).

- The average age of first exposure to Internet porn is 11 (Family Safe Media, December 15, 2005, <http://www.familysafemedia.com/pornography_statistics.html>).

- The largest group of viewers of Internet porn is children between ages 12 and 17 (Family Safe Media, December 15, 2005, <http://www.familysafemedia.com/pornography_statistics.html>).

- According to comScore Media Metrix, 71.9 million people visited adult sites in August 2005, reaching 42.7 percent of the Internet audience.

- According to comScore Media Metrix, Internet users viewed over 15 billion pages of adult content in August 2005.

- According to comScore Media Metrix, Internet users spent an average of 14.6 minutes per day viewing adult content online.

- More than 32 million unique individuals visited a porn site in Sept. of 2003. Nearly 22.8 million of them were male (71 percent), while 9.4 million adult site visitors were female (29 percent) (Nielsen/Net Ratings, Sept. 2003).

- The cybersex industry generates approximately $1 billion annually and is expected to grow to $5–7 billion over the next 5 years, barring unforeseen change (National Research Council Report, 2002).

- The total porn industry—estimates from $4 billion to $10 billion (National Research Council Report, 2002).

- The two largest individual buyers of bandwidth are U.S. firms in the adult online industry (National Research Council Report, 3–1, 2002).

- 40,000 expired domain names were porn-napped (National Research Council).[1]

---

[1]Statistics from ProtectKids.Com. http://www.protectkids.com/dangers/stats.htm.

APPROPRIATE HYMNS AND SONGS

"Deeper, Deeper," Charles P. Jones, Public Domain.

"I Know Who Holds Tomorrow," Ira Stanphill, 1950 Singspiration Music (Admin. Brentwood Benson Music Publishing).

"God's Power," Larry Mayfield/Elsie Lippy, 1976, 1980 Child Evangelism Fellowship (Admin. The Copyright Co.).

"We've Come to Worship You," Ed Kerr, 1995 Integrity's Hosanna! Music.

"Thank You Lord," Dennis Jernigan, Shepherd's Heart Music (Word Music Group).

FOR THE BULLETIN

Pope Urban II opened the Council of Clermont on November 18, 1095, for the purpose of instigating church reforms and launching the first crusade to liberate the Holy Land from Muslim occupiers. On this same day in 1302, Pope Boniface VIII published his document, "Unam Sanctum," declaring that spiritual power took precedence over temporal power and that submission to the pope was necessary for salvation. ● After years of fund-raising and construction, St. Peter's Basilica was finally consecrated by Pope Urban VIII on November 18, 1626. ● The great German hymnist, Paul Gerhardt, was ordained on November 18, 1851. He labored for much of his life in and around Berlin, serving as preacher, pastor, and hymn writer. Among his greatest hymns is one that says: "Commit whatever grieves thee into the gracious hands / Of Him Who never leaves thee, who Heav'n and earth commands. / who points the clouds their courses, whom winds and waves obey, / He will direct thy footsteps and find for thee a way." ● Today is the birthday, in 1800, of John Nelson Darby of the Plymouth Brethren. It's also the birthday, in 1848, of Russell Kelso Carter, who was a chemistry professor, sheep rancher, minister, author, hymnist, publisher, and medical doctor. He's best known for his hymn "Standing on the Promises" for which he wrote both the words and music. ● Missionary J. Hudson wrote in a letter on November 18, 1857: *Many seem to think I am very poor. This is true enough in one sense, but I thank God it is "as poor, yet making many rich." My God shall supply all my needs; to Him be the glory. I would not, if I could, be otherwise than I am—entirely dependent myself upon the Lord, and used as a channel of help to others.*

WORSHIP HELPS

Call to Worship

Both riches and honor come from You, and You reign over all. In Your hand is power and might; in Your hand it is to make great and to give strength to all. Now therefore, our God, we thank You and praise Your glorious name (1 Chr. 29:12–13).

Testimonies

Today is a good day, if the size and traditions of your church allow it, to ask for some brief testimonies of thanksgiving. The Bible says for the Redeemed of the Lord to "say so," and one of the greatest things we can do with a blessing is to spread it around. Each testimony can begin with the words: "I'm thankful to the Lord today for . . . ." Have ushers with wireless microphones, if necessary, who can go to those who stand to share a word of blessing. The other option is to ask someone in the church to prepare and share a special thanksgiving testimony from the pulpit during the service.

Thanksgiving Scripture Medley

Enter into His gates with thanksgiving, and into His courts with praise. Be thankful to Him, and bless His name. / Oh, give thanks to the LORD! Call upon His name; make known His deeds among the peoples! / Oh, give thanks to the LORD, for He is good! For His mercy endures forever. / I will give You thanks in the great assembly; I will praise You among many people. / We give thanks to You, O God, we give thanks! For Your wondrous works declare that Your name is near. / Open to me the gates of righteousness; I will go through them, and I will praise the LORD. This is the gate of the LORD, through which the righteous shall enter. I will praise You, for You have answered me, and have become my salvation (Ps. 100:4; 1 Chr. 16:8; 34; Ps. 35:18; 75:1; 118:19–21).

Additional Sermons and Lesson Ideas

For the Beauty of the Earth

Date preached:

SCRIPTURE: Genesis 1

INTRODUCTION: As the final brush stroke on the canvas of God's creation, Adam and Eve were drawn into the picture as the recipients of all that had been previously made. Everything in Genesis 1:1–26 was designed for the ones created in verse 27, whom God made in His own image. As heirs of those blessings, we, too, can thank God for:

1. This Planet, So Perfectly Designed to Meet Our Needs (vv. 1–2).
2. The Light, Which Makes Vision Possible (vv. 3–5).
3. The Sky, Beautiful, Full of Life-Sustaining Elements (vv. 6–8).
4. The Soil, Perfectly Designed as Earth's Flooring (vv. 9–10).
5. The Oceans, Awe-Inspiring, Beautiful, Teeming with Life, and Fun (v. 11).
6. The Vegetation, from Tiny Wildflowers to Towering Redwoods (vv. 12–13).
7. The Celestial Heavens: Sun, Moon, and Stars (vv. 13–19).
8. The Animal Life, Strange, Odd, Fully, Frightening, and Companionable (vv. 20–25).

CONCLUSION: This is our Father's world, and to our listening ears, all nature rings and round us sings the music of the spheres. Praise Him as King of Creation!

Thankful Living

Date preached:

By Joshua D. Rowe

SCRIPTURE: Colossians 3:15–17 (NIV, italics added to quotes below for emphasis)

INTRODUCTION: How do you obey the commands of Scripture? Grudgingly? In fear of punishment? Paul gives three of the most incredible and important commands of Scripture about how to live out our daily lives, but in each command he also tells us *how* to obey:

1. "Let the Peace of Christ Rule in Your Hearts . . . And Be *Thankful*" (v. 15).
2. "Let the Word of Christ Dwell in You Richly . . . with *Gratitude* . . ." (v. 16).
3. "And Whatever You Do . . . Do It All in the Name of the Lord Jesus, *Giving Thanks* to God . . ." (v. 17).

CONCLUSION: Are you living peacefully with God and others? Do you allow the word of Christ to penetrate your life daily? Is everything you do worthy to be done in Christ's name? As we carry out these commands of Scripture, let us do so (as Paul constantly reminds us) with thanksgiving.

THANKSGIVING SERMON

How to Have a Great Attitude! *Date preached:*

Scripture: Psalm 100, especially verses 1–2
Make a joyful shout to the LORD, all you lands! Serve the LORD with gladness; Come before His presence with singing.

Introduction: Did you hear about the woman doing her shopping? It was a European village where you go to every shop individually, so she went to the cheese shop for some Swiss cheese for her quiche. Then to the bakery for a baguette. Then to the fruit stand, the vegetable market, and the patisserie. Everywhere she went she frowned, turning up her nose and saying how terrible everyone smelled. After returning home and unpacking her purchases, she discovered that the clerk at the cheese shop had given her limburger cheese instead of Swiss, and the limburger had a very ripe odor. She had been complaining about everyone else when actually she'd been carrying the problem around in her own packages. That's the way it is with our attitudes. Sometimes we think our circumstances stink. We think other people stink. But when we're perpetually unhappy, irritated, depressed, or unpleasant, the real problem may be our own attitudes that we're carrying around inside of ourselves. I've found three different quotes about this.

- The Roman statesman and philosopher, Seneca, said: "A man is as unhappy as he has convinced himself he is."
- Abraham Lincoln reportedly said: "A person is about as happy as they make up their mind to be."
- The Scottish preacher, Robert Murray McCheyne, said: "I feel it my duty to be as happy as the Lord wants me to be."

Let's adopt these words in the middle of the Bible, in the grand old 100th Psalm. It divides into two stanzas that are very similar, but each has its own distinctive theme. The theme of the first stanza is . . . well, I'm going to coin a word here: Gladatude.

1. **Gladatude (Ps. 100:1–3).** Gladatude is having a glad attitude. A hymn says, "When I am sad to Him I go; no other one could cheer

me so. / When I am sad He makes me glad. He's my Friend."
According to this passage, Gladatude is made up of four ingredients.

A. **Shout.** The first ingredient is—Shout: *Make a joyful shout unto the LORD, all you lands.* The psalmist is telling us to let positive, praiseworthy things come from our mouths. Practice the art of praise. The Hebrew word means to shout or to make a noise. It was the word the Hebrews used for the trumpet's call at the beginning of a battle. It was the word used for the shouted call to worship at the beginning of a temple service. It was the word they used for the shout that went up when the king suddenly appeared.

B. **Serve.** The second ingredient to a good attitude is serving. *Serve the LORD with gladness.*

C. **Come.** *Come before His presence with singing.* God created music; and even if we don't have great singing voices, God's music is therapeutic and healing. How many times, when we've been weary and worn, have we found strength in the great songs of the faith?

D. **Know.** *Know that the LORD . . .* If we're going to shout, serve, and come, we must know three things about the Lord. First, He is our God. Second, He is our Maker. Third, He is our Shepherd. Perhaps you remember the story that flashed around the world some time ago regarding the kidnapping of two missionaries in the Philippines. Martin and Gracia Burnham, serving with New Tribes Mission, wanted to celebrate their anniversary at an island resort, but their holiday turned into a nightmare when terrorists burst into the resort and dragged them into the jungle. They spent a year in captivity, faced near starvation, and were caught in the middle of frequent gun battles. In the end, both were shot. Martin was killed, but Gracia lived to tell the story. She said that near the end of their ordeal, Martin said, "You know, Gracia, I don't know why the Lord has allowed this to happen, but today I've been thinking about Psalm 100, how we can serve the Lord with gladness. Just because we're here doesn't mean we can't serve Him with gladness, so let's serve the Lord with gladness." They prayed together, lay down in their hammocks, and the gunfire started. Gracia fell to the ground wounded, and she slid down a steep hill and came to rest beside Martin. He was bleeding from his chest, and he was breathing heavily. He gave one final deep breath, and he was gone. But those words from Psalm 100 never died in Gracia's heart. She said, "The Lord has given me joy. We can have a hard day here at home, but I'm still just dumb enough to be really, really happy. And even when they were dragging me up the hill from Martin and I could see he was white and I could tell he was dead, you know what? I was so happy in my heart that I was getting out of there. I can't explain it, but I don't think I have to feel guilty or deny it."

2. **Gratitude (Ps. 100:4–5).** The last half of the Psalm prescribes the second great attitude we're to cultivate—gratitude. Verses 1–3 tell us to be glad, and verses 4–5 tell us to be grateful. Viennese psychologist Viktor Frankl, who endured the horrors of the Nazi death camps, later wrote that the Nazis took everything from him—his property and possessions, his family and friends, his future and hope, and even the very clothes on his back. In his book, *Man's Search for Meaning,* he said: "Everything can be taken from a man but one thing; the last of the human freedoms—to choose one's attitude in any given set of circumstances." In this passage, the psalmist is telling us to make our way into the tabernacle, to enter through the gates, to walk through the courtyard, to approach the tabernacle in worship, and to do it with an attitude of thanksgiving. Be thankful to Him and bless His name. Thankfulness is the opposite of almost every negative attitude you can think of. What's the opposite of complaining and grumbling? Thanksgiving. What's the opposite of discouragement and depression? Thanksgiving. What's the opposite of anger and anxiety? Thanksgiving. The writer of Psalm 100 lists three reasons to be thankful, and all three have to do with the character of God. First, the Lord is good. Second, His mercy is everlasting (no matter how much we use, there's still an undiminished supply left for us, upon which we can continually draw). The third reason for gratitude is God's truth, which endures to all generations. God will never retire His promises. Heaven and earth may pass away, but His words abide forever. So rejoice today and be glad. Let your face and heart reflect gladatude and gratitude, and make a joyful noise to the Lord, all the earth!

NOVEMBER 25, 2007

SUGGESTED SERMON

A Fresh Look at John 3:16

Date preached:

By Joshua D. Rowe

Scripture: John 3:16

For God so loved the world that He gave His only begotten Son, that whoever believes in Him should not perish but have everlasting life.

Introduction: We see it flashed on posters at sporting events, plastered to bumper stickers. We hear it used to justify all kinds of different theological opinions. Today, let's have a fresh look at John 3:16.

1. **God Loved the World.** What do we mean by this simple phrase? God is the origin of love toward His creation. We did not initiate God's love by our actions or thoughts.

    A. **God.** In John 3:16, God is nominative, He is the source of love (1 John 4:8).

    B. **Loved.** While the verb is aorist, an undefined time of action (appropriate for a timeless God of love), the verb is very strong. God loved, valued, esteemed, manifested generous concern for, and delighted in. This love is not a disenchanted, flighty love, swayed by mood or circumstance as we may see in romantic comedy. His love was pure and directed toward an absolute object, the world, the collective body of His created people.

    C. **The World.** Here we have the recipients of God's love: not only the material, lower world, but the human race. God is the Author, the Originator, and the Source of love toward His creation.

Application: Do you truly embrace and preach God's loving character? His love is the foundation of the gospel!

2. **God Gave the Only-Born Son.** When we read "God *so* loved the world" (italics added), we interpret "so" to mean "so much." In Greek, this word is translated "thus," or, "in this way." This phrase shouldn't be understood as "God loved the world so much that . . ." Rather, we should understand it to say, "God loved the world *in this way . . .*" This places our focus appropriately on the sacrifice of Christ as the

manifestation of God's love, rather than focusing on the intensity of God's love alone.

A. **God.** "He," God, alone acted in history, not because of man's initiative, but because of His love for us.

B. **God Gave.** The word translated "gave" represents an entrusting, a presenting, an offering of a sacrifice.

C. **God Gave the Only-Born Son.** The possessive pronoun "his" is absent in the Greek language. Christ is treated as an entity (as is characteristic of John's writing). Not only this, the describing characteristic of the Son is only-born. This sacrificial language is heavily reminiscent of Genesis 22, of Abraham's offering of Isaac, his only-born son.

Application: We often look to the problems in the world and say, "God can't be loving." We must always remember that the problems exist because of our rebellion against Him. His love is ultimately portrayed to us through the sacrifice of Jesus Christ, the solution to the problems of sin and death in the world!

3. **Whoever Believes in Him Should Not Perish but Have Everlasting Life.** The word "that" connects the idea, answers the question of why God would love the world in a way that required a sacrifice. The answer is incredible:

A. **Whoever Believes.** The phrase, "every one who believes" indicates an all-inclusive invitation, but the participle in the Greek indicates a qualifier of the subject: he or she must believe. The Greek word for believe in and of itself is more than a casual belief in the existence, it's more active: it means to give credit to, to entrust, or commit to the charge or power of.

B. **In Him.** His love manifested through His sacrificial giving of His Son is for each one who believes, not just believes in anything, not just in God or in supernatural things, but "in Him" which refers to the only-born Son. The one who believes must believe in Him.

C. **Should Not Perish.** This verb indicates not a physical death, but a complete and utter destruction.

D. **But Have Everlasting Life.** Just as it sounds, this life has no end. The tense of the verb also seems to suggest an indeterminable time, quite applicable to a life that begins with being "born again" and lasts to all eternity!

Application: Let me speak frankly. Many of us grew up thinking that a mere reciting of John 3:16 and saying, "I believe in Jesus" saves us. We cannot simply mentally believe in Christ, but we must entrust ourselves, giving charge and power completely to Christ. Many use "God so loved . . ." to justify any religion, sin, or lifestyle they choose. We learn here that the only ones who receive eternal life are those who believe in Jesus Christ: all others will perish. Have you entrusted yourself and given control over to Jesus Christ?

STATS, STORIES, AND MORE

No one has loved John 3:16 more than British evangelist Henry Moorhouse (1840–1880). He was born into a Methodist home in Manchester, England, but became a prodigal as a young man. By age 16, he was gambling heavily, leading a gang, dishonest, sly, and sometimes near-suicidal. One day as he walked down the street—he was about twenty—he saw a crowd gathered, and he raced toward it, thinking it was a brawl. It wasn't a fight, but an evangelistic street meeting led by Richard Weaver. One word flew through the air and gripped Moorhouse, and it was the word "Jesus." Moorhouse became a powerful evangelist, though he was small of stature and not a dynamic preacher. In 1867, he had the privilege of meeting the renowned evangelist D. L. Moody, who was touring the British Isles; but Moody wasn't very impressed when Moorhouse offered to come to Chicago and preach for Moody. While Moody was away, Moorhouse showed up and preached every night from John 3:16. When Moody returned the church was experiencing revival, and Moody himself, who attended the last of the meetings, was changed by the emphasis on God's love. "I have never forgotten those nights," Moody later wrote. I have preached a different gospel since, and I have more power with God and man since then."

Moorhouse became known as "the man who moved the man who moved millions." In the last years of his life, Moorhouse preached from a mobile bookstore as he traveled around England and Ireland, distributing literature. Though only in his late thirties, he was failing physically and he passed away on December 28, 1880. Among his final words were these: "If it were the Lord's will to raise me up again, I should like to preach from the text, 'God so loved the world.'" He is buried in the Ardwick Cemetery in Manchester, and John 3:16 is engraved on his tombstone.

(For a fuller account of Moorhouse's impact on D. L. Moody, consult any good Moody biography or do an Internet search for the two men's names. Moody's full description of the event is fascinating, but is too lengthy to reproduce here.)

APPROPRIATE HYMNS AND SONGS

"How Deep the Father's Love for Us," Stuart Townend, 1995 Kingsway's ThankYou Music (Admin. EMI Christian Music Publishing).

"Hallelujah (Your Love Makes Me Sing)," Brenton Brown/Brian Doerksen, 2000 Vineyard Songs (Admin. Music Services).

"You Are My King," Billy James Foote, 1999 WorshipTogether.com Songs (EMI Christian Music Publishing).

"And Can It Be," Charles Wesley/Thomas Campbell, Public Domain.

FOR THE BULLETIN

Today marks the wedding, on November 25, 1520, of Reformation professor Philipp Melanchthon and Katharina Krapp, the daughter of the mayor of Wittenberg. ● November 25, 1697, is the birthday of German hymnist Gerhard Tersteegen. Among his hymns is one that says: "Lo, God is here! let us adore, / And own how dreadful is this place! / Let all within us feel His power, / And silent bow before His face." ● David Brainerd was interviewed and approved by the Scottish Society for the Propagating of Christian Knowledge (SPCK) for missionary service to the New England Indians on November 25, 1742. He labored among Native Americans from the Spring of 1743 until his health failed in 1747. His journal and biography, written by his father-in-law, Jonathan Edwards, is a classic of American spirituality. ● Today marks the deaths of three great hymnists. The "Father of Hymnology," Isaac Watts, died on November 25, 1748. William Bathurst, author of "O For a Faith that Will Not Shrink" died on November 25, 1877. Originally entitled, "The Power of Faith," it was written as William studied Luke 17:5–6, where the disciples asked Jesus, "Lord, increase our faith." And Robert Lowry, American Baptist clergyman, died on this day in 1899. He was a close associate of Fanny Crosby and wrote the music to "Marching to Zion," "All the Way My Savior Leads Me," "I Need Thee Every Hour." He also wrote both the words and music of "Nothing but the Blood of Jesus."

WORSHIP HELPS

Call to Worship

> O worship the King, all glorious above,
> O gratefully sing His power and His love;
> Our Shield and Defender, the Ancient of Days,
> Pavilioned in splendor, and girded with praise.
> —ROBERT GRANT, 1833 (reworded from
> William Kethe's version in the
> Psalter of 1561), *O Worship the King*

Suggested Scriptures

- Numbers 21:4–9
- Psalm 103:1–5
- John 3:1–18
- Romans 3:21–31

**Benediction from an Old Hymn, Suitable
for Closing the Evening Service**

> And now, O Father, from on high
> List (Listen) to our evening prayer,
> Shed o'er our hearts a blissful calm,
> And keep us in Thy care.
> —JANET PATTINSON, 1891

Kid's Talk

Tell the children that you want to teach them something very important about understanding the Bible. Explain that when we read God's Word, we should always be on the lookout for what God does so we can thank Him for it, and what it says we should do so we can obey. Ask someone to recite John 3:16. Enlist the children's help in finding out what God does and what He wants us to do in that verse. Explain: "First, God loved the world. Isn't it wonderful to have parents and friends who love us? It's amazing that God not only created us but loves us too!" Have the volunteer recite the next phrase. Ask the children what this says about God? Continue, "Yes, now we know that God loved us by giving us His Son, Jesus, to pay the price for our sins!" Again, ask the volunteer to recite the final phrase. Ask them what this phrase tells us *we* should do to respond to God's love. Conclude, "Yes, that's right. We need to believe, to trust Jesus with our lives. God loved us by giving us His Son, and we should love Him by believing in Him."

Additional Sermons and Lesson Ideas

Last Days

Date preached:

SCRIPTURE: 2 Timothy 3:1

INTRODUCTION: When Paul referred to "last days" in 2 Timothy, he was thinking of the last days of the ages; but 2 Timothy also represents the last days of Paul himself. It is his last extant letter, written from Rome's infamous Mamertine Prison. How did Paul choose to spend his final months on earth? From the way he opens and closes his letter, we can learn from him to:

1. Stay Duty-Driven for the Lord (1:1–2). Despite the dark, dank atmosphere of prison, Paul penned ministry letters like this one to Timothy. As long as he had breath, he intended to stay active for Christ.
2. Pray (1:3).
3. Reminiscence (1:4–5). Each of us should look back over our days, jot down important items for those who are following us, and thank God for His blessings.
4. Encourage the Younger Generation (1:6–7, and much of the rest of the letter).
5. Anticipate the Future (4:6–8).
6. Study the Word (4:13).
7. Practice the Presence of Jesus (4:17).
8. Praise and Worship the Lord (4:18).

CONCLUSION: Guard against wasted days. These eight activities should be woven into our last days like threads through a tapestry, for the Lord intends to use us until our final moments on earth; then we'll have a new day of eternity in which to serve Him even better.

The Peril of Defection

Date preached:

By Dr. Melvin Worthington

SCRIPTURE: Hebrews 6

INTRODUCTION: The strong, solemn, and specific warning given in this chapter of Hebrews provides us with an antidote to the peril of defection.

1. The Desired Perfection (Heb. 6:1–3). The perfection desired includes, the *exhortation to develop* (v. 1), *the elementary doctrines* (vv. 1–2) and *the enabling Deity* (v. 3).
2. The Described Possibility (Heb. 6:4–8). The possibility described includes, *the denoted position* (vv. 4–5), *the defined danger* (v. 6), and *the distinctive picture* (vv. 7–8).

3. The Declared Perception (vv. 9–12). The declared perception includes, *the confidence revealed* (v. 9), *the conduct reviewed* (v. 10), *the continuance required* (v. 11) and *the counsel reiterated* (v. 12).

4. The Dependable Promise (vv. 13–20). The dependable promise includes *an illustration—Abraham* (vv. 13–15) and *an Immutable—The Almighty* (vv. 16–20).

CONCLUSION: The writer of Hebrews was not interested in arguing doctrine, but with warning those who claim to be the people of God. The truth is simple, despite where you fall on a doctrinal scale, if you turn your back on faith in God, you will face the same wrath and punishment of an unbeliever: hell.

DECEMBER 2, 2007

FIRST SUNDAY OF ADVENT SUGGESTED SERMON

A Greater Than Solomon

Date preached:

By Rev. Charles Haddon Spurgeon

Scripture: Luke 11:31
Indeed a greater than Solomon is here.

Introduction: No mere man would have said this concerning himself unless he had been eaten up with vanity; for Solomon was the ideal of greatness and wisdom. Any person really greater than Solomon would be the last to claim such preeminence. For men to compare themselves with another is not wise, and Christ was wise; it is not humble, and Christ was humble. If our Savior said He was greater than Solomon, we must fully believe it and proclaim it.

1. **Points of Likeness.** When the Savior gives us a comparison, it is proof a likeness was intended by the Holy Spirit as a type of Christ.

   A. **In Wisdom.** Solomon intermeddled with all knowledge and was master in all sciences. He was a naturalist, engineer, and architect. He understood government. God gave him wisdom like the sand of the sea. Yes, but our Savior knows infinitely more. He will teach you all you need to know, for all wisdom is in Him. Our Savior knows things past, present, and future. The secrets of God are with Him. Solomon might have wisdom, but he could not be wisdom to others; Christ Jesus is that to the full. In the universal knowledge stored up in Him there is enough for your guidance and instruction even to the end of life.

   B. **In Wealth.** Solomon had great treasure. He made gold to be as stones, so rich did he become. He had multitudes of servants. But, oh, when you consider the wealth of Solomon, what poor stuff it is compared with the riches treasured up in Christ. He was stripped even to the last rag; He possessed no wealth but of sorrow and sympathy. Yet He had the power to make many rich, and therefore must be rich Himself. Will not the Holy Spirit teach you the art of appropriating the Lord Jesus and all He is and has? Go to Him to be enriched.

C. In Peace. Solomon was *the prince of peace.* His name signifies peace. His father was a great warrior, but Solomon had not to carry on war. No trumpet of invader was heard in the land. Ah, but a greater than Solomon is here; for Solomon could not give his subjects peace of mind, he could not bestow rest of heart, he could not ease their burden of guilt. But that Man of Sorrows is greater than Solomon in His peace-giving power. Come and trust Him, then shall your peace be as a river, and your righteousness like the waves of the sea. Am I addressing one of God's people who is sorely troubled? Brother or sister, do not think you must wait a week or two before you can recover peace. You can become restful in a moment, for He is our peace. There is no peace like the peace Jesus gives; it is like a river, deep, profound, renewed, ever flowing, overflowing, increasing, and widening into an ocean.

D. In Great Works. Solomon built the temple. He erected palaces, fortifications, and aqueducts to bring streams from the mountains to the various towns. Yet a greater than Solomon is here, for Christ has brought living water from the throne of God right down to thirsty men, being Himself the eternal aqueduct. Christ has built fortresses behind which His children stand secure against the wrath of hell. He has founded a wondrous temple, His church, of which His people are the living stones, fashioned, polished, rendered beautiful—a temple which God Himself shall inhabit, of which Christ is architect and builder, foundation and chief cornerstone.

E. In Dominion. The kingdom of the Jews extended from the river of Egypt right across the wilderness to the Persian Gulf. We can scarcely tell how far Solomon's dominions reached. Our Lord Jesus Christ at this moment has dominion over all. The feet that were nailed to the tree are set upon the necks of His enemies. The hands that bore the nails at this moment hold the scepter of all worlds: Jesus is King of kings, and Lord of lords! Hallelujah! As surely as God lives, unto Him shall every man bow the knee, and every tongue shall confess that Jesus Christ is Lord, to the glory of God the Father.

Conclusion: You have heard the report; now, like the Queen of Sheba, go and see for yourself. Get to Christ, as to His dominion, come under His sway and own His scepter. Go and trust your King; love your King; praise your King; delight in your King. Let us delight in His love; and we shall surely say, "A greater than Solomon is here."

STATS, STORIES, AND MORE

Some years ago I was away from this place for a little rest, and I was thinking to myself, "Now, I wonder whether I really respond to the power of the gospel as I should like to do? I will go and hear a sermon and see." I would like to sit down with you, in the pews sometimes and hear somebody else preach—not everybody, mark you, for when I hear a good many I want to be doing it myself. I get tired of them if they do not glow and burn. But that morning I thought I would drop into a place of worship such as there might be in the little town. A poor, plain man, a countryman, began preaching about Jesus Christ. He praised my Master in very humble language, but he praised Him most sincerely. Oh, but the tears began to flow. I soon laid the dust all round me where I sat, and I thought, *"Bless the Lord! I do love Him." It only wants somebody else to play the harp instead of me, and my soul is ready to dance to the heavenly tune. Only let the music be Christ's sweet, dear, precious name, and my heart leaps at the sound. Oh, my brethren, sound out the praises of Jesus Christ! Sound out that precious name! There is none like it under heaven to stir my heart. I hope you can all say the same. I know you can if you love Him; for all renewed hearts are enamored of the sweet Lord Jesus. "A greater than Solomon is here."*   —Rev. Charles Haddon Spurgeon

APPROPRIATE HYMNS AND SONGS

"Joyful, Joyful We Adore Thee," Henry Van Dyke/Ludwig van Beethoven, Public Domain.

"Sing to the King," Billy James Foote/Charles Silverster Horne, 2003 WorshipTogether.com Songs/Six steps Music (EMI Christian Music Publishing).

"Shout to the Lord," Darlene Zschech, 1993 Darlene Zschech (Hillsong) (Integrity Music Inc.).

"O Little Town of Bethlehem," Phillips Brooks/Lewis H. Redner, Public Domain.

"The First Noel," Public Domain.

FOR THE BULLETIN

After the great London Fire of 1666, the famous architect, Christopher Wren, was commissioned to design and rebuild fifty of the city's churches. His most ambitious project was St. Paul's Cathedral, which was the fourth successive church building to sit on that site since A.D. 604. The dedication of the building and first service at St. Paul's was on December 2, 1697. The building has survived to this day as a London landmark, although it was struck by a bomb and damaged during the Blitz on October 9, 1940. ● President James Monroe articulated the "Monroe Doctrine" in an address to Congress on December 2, 1823. ● Today is the birthday of two notable nineteenth-century British missionaries. Mary Slessor, in 1848, who became a pioneer missionary from Aberdeen, Scotland to Calabar, West Africa; and C. T. Studd in 1860, Britain's star cricketer who left fame and fortune to become a missionary to China. ● Frances Ridley Havergal, 36, read a booklet titled "All For Jesus," which stressed the importance of making Christ King of every corner and cubicle of one's life. That prompted Frances to make a fresh, complete consecration of her life to God. Years later her sister asked her about it, and she replied: *Yes, it was on Advent Sunday, December 2, 1873, I first saw clearly the blessedness of true consecration. I saw it as a flash of electric light. There must be full surrender before there can be full blessedness.* Shortly afterward she wrote her "Consecration Hymn," the song that became her life's theme: "Take my life and let it be, consecrated, Lord, to Thee . . ."

WORSHIP HELPS

Call to Worship

Sing to Him, sing psalms to Him; talk of all His wondrous works! Glory in His holy name; let the hearts of those rejoice who seek the LORD! Seek the LORD and His strength; seek His face evermore (1 Chr. 16:9–11)!

Learn a "New" Christmas Carol

One of the most beautiful hymns ever written is "Of the Father's Love Begotten." The words were written in Latin by Aurilius Clemens Prudentius, who was born in northern Spain in A.D. 348, not long after Christianity was legalized in the Roman Empire. At age fifty-seven, Prudentius retired from government service and entered a monastery where he devoted himself exclusively to worship and writing. Today we have nearly four hundred poems from his hand and he has been called "the prince of early Christian poets." The musical setting for "Of the Father's Love Begotten" is a probing score called *Divinum Mysterium,* composed nearly a thousand years ago.

Advent Scripture Reading

For unto us a Child is born, unto us a Son is given; and the government will be upon His shoulder. And His name will be called Wonderful, Counselor, Mighty God, Everlasting Father, Prince of Peace. Of the increase of His government and peace there will be no end, upon the throne of David and over His kingdom, to order it and establish it with judgment and justice from that time forward, even forever. The zeal of the Lord of hosts will perform this (Is. 9:6–8).

Benediction

Who is wise? Let him understand these things. Who is prudent? Let him know them. For the ways of the LORD are right; the righteous walk in them, but transgressors stumble in them (Hos. 14:9).

Additional Sermons and Lesson Ideas

A Special Name
Date preached:

SCRIPTURE: 1 John 1:1

INTRODUCTION: Sometimes when we love someone we coin a new name for them, a personal one used only by us. John, "the disciple whom Jesus loved," coined a new name for Jesus, a theological one, used only by Him in Scripture. Jesus is the *logos*—the Word, God's ultimate communication to humans. John used this term as a title for Christ five times in three books, telling us five different things about Christ:

1. The Deity of the Logos (John 1:1): The Word is God Himself.
2. The Humanity of the Logos (John 1:14): The Word became flesh.
3. The Accessibility of the Logos (1 John 1:1): The Word was the manifestation of God among us, and John touched Him, saw Him, handled Him, and testifies about Him.
4. The Activity of the Logos (1 John 5:7): The Word is the Second Person of the Trinity who makes known to us and testifies to the truth.
5. The Eternity of the Logos (Rev. 19:13): The Word is coming again to usher in eternity.

CONCLUSION: The Logos was John's special word for Christ, and Christ is God's special Word for you and me.

The Master's Men
Date preached:

By Dr. Melvin Worthington

SCRIPTURE: Various

INTRODUCTION: The deplorable conditions which exist in our homes, communities, churches, and country can be traced to the reluctance of men to fulfill their responsibilities.

1. No Men. There are frequently no men to do the work (Judg. 6; 1 Sam. 17; John 5). Where are the men who will contribute their *time, talent, tithe,* and *testimony* to the work of God?
2. New Men. God is looking for new men—men whose character, conduct, and career have been changed (2 Cor. 5). Such new men are characterized by consistency in their *attitudes, actions,* and *allegiance.*
3. Needy Men. The Master's men have seen the Lord of Hosts (Is. 6). Isaiah not only saw the *person* of the Lord, but he sensed His *presence.*
4. Now Men. Now is the time when men in the church need to acknowledge their role, accept their responsibility and act readily (cf. 1 Tim. 2:8).

CONCLUSION: Where there is no man, will you be the Master's man and set the proper example for others to emulate?

DECEMBER 9, 2007

SECOND SUNDAY OF ADVENT   SUGGESTED SERMON

He's My Son Too!

Date preached:

By Dr. Robert Norris

Scripture: Matthew 1:18–25, especially verse 24
Then . . . Joseph did as the angel of the Lord commanded him . . .

Introduction: When we enter the Advent season, we often focus on the divine Christchild, which is obviously central. However, we shouldn't miss the interaction of the divine with very human character. Today, we will focus on Joseph. The Scripture records several things about Joseph that give to us a picture of the man and of his character.

1. **Joseph's Character.**

    A. **Nobility.** Joseph was "a son of David." The Scripture is very deliberative about the fact that the heritage and lineage of Joseph were important. In the genealogy of Matthew, when it says of Joseph that he was "of the house and lineage of David," the Scripture does not only mean that he was descended from David, but that he was directly related to the royal blood line of the house of David. This had a double implication in the Gospel record of the birth of Jesus. It was he who was able to give Jesus the legitimate use of the title, "Son of David." In fact in the New Testament that title is reserved only for Jesus, with the single exception of Joseph. At the same time, because he was related to the royal line, Joseph was required to travel to the family city of Bethlehem to be registered.

    B. **Righteousness (v. 19).** Verse 19 tells us Joseph was a "just man." This powerful statement says a great deal about the character of the man. It meant that he was devout. The phrase is used to describe an "observant Jew." He was not only morally upright; he was a man who kept the law of God. But it also meant that he had a respect and awe for God's plan of salvation. We see that in his dealing with Mary, he was not prepared to subject her to any public ridicule. Much less was he prepared to see her possibly tried and stoned for "adultery." Joseph was a man who was open to the things of God. Indeed there is one school of thought that has Joseph belonging to a Jewish group called the "Anwim" or "poor ones," men and women who were devout and committed to living a life of holiness and obedience to the law; Mary, Elizabeth, and Zechariah were thought to be a part of the Anwim as well.

2. **Joseph's Crisis (Matt. 1:18).** Matthew speaks of Mary being "betrothed" to Joseph. This introduces a concept that is foreign to our culture and will require some explanation. Betrothal was like our engagement, except it was binding. It was viewed as the first part of marriage, though the couple still lived with their respective families. The betrothed could be called the "wife" of her fiancé, and the man could be called the girl's "husband" (e.g., Joel 1:8; Matt. 1:19). A betrothed woman could be punished as an adulteress, whereas the punishment of an un-betrothed woman was different (Deut. 22:23, 24, 28–29). The second part of marriage was when the man brought his betrothed to his home. We are specifically told that Mary and Joseph had not yet "come together." That she was "found to be with child" prior to this second part would be a serious offense, one which could have been punished by death, though this was not typically done in the first century.

   A. **God's Intervention (vv. 20–23).** The angel tells Joseph not to be afraid to take Mary as his wife. Mary, he says, is still a virgin; the child within her is the result of the miraculous work of the Holy Spirit, and He will be the Savior of His people in fulfillment of Isaiah 7:14, Jesus, Immanuel, God with us.

   B. **Joseph's Reaction (vv. 24–25).** How does Joseph respond to this extraordinary dream and stunning message? He responds with immediate obedience. That is, he took her home. They lived together from that point on as husband and wife, with one qualification, that he kept her a virgin until she gave birth to Jesus. This, too, reveals his character.

Conclusion: Joseph is one of the most human characters of the story of the nativity. He was the man who suffered such great pain as he thought he must lose the woman who was pledged to be his, and he in his struggling forced her away from him. Yet he is the one appointed by God who, like Job, finds that in the will of God there is both deep satisfaction and personal peace. He reminds us that those longed for desires of our hearts are to be found nowhere else.

STATS, STORIES, AND MORE

Not long after Pope John XXIII was elevated to the papacy, he did something quite unexpected. He got into this car with the apparent intention of driving to the Vatican Gardens, but instead the driver swung around suddenly, pulled out of the motorcade, sped around St. Peter's Square, and disappeared into the Roman traffic without the benefit of an escort. Vatican officials were frantic, as were the civil authorities of Rome. Almost instantly, the entire Italian government was in a state of high alert, and the whole country was about to shift into crisis mode. What had happened to the Pope? As it turned out, he had just decided that he wanted to see an old friend. Word had reached him that this friend, who lived in a home for old and retired Catholic priests, needed to see him; but the old man had not asked for an audience because how could a humble priest request the time of the Holy Father? While the Italian police searched frantically for him, Pope John was sitting serenely in a rocking chair in a nursing home, surrounded by twenty-two old priests, having a lively time of gossiping away the afternoon. This story reminds us of that remarkable day when the Lord of Glory stunned the angels of heaven by taking an unexpected turn and making the most startling trip in human history. Jesus suddenly left the divine motorcade, as it were, to descend to the depths of this earth to spend time with the humble likes of you and me.

APPROPRIATE HYMNS AND SONGS

"What Child Is This?," William Chatterton Dix, Public Domain.

"Angels We Have Heard on High," James Chadwick/Edward Shippen Barnes, Public Domain.

"Born Is the King," Beverly Darnall/Michael W. Smith, 1994 Word Music Inc./Milene Music, Inc.

"Angels from the Realms of Glory," James Montgomery/Henry T. Smart, Public Domain.

FOR THE BULLETIN

When Ulrich Zwingli, Swiss Reformer and pastor in Zurich, was killed on the battlefield of Kappel, one man stood ready to take his place in Zurich. On December 9, 1531, Heinrich Bullinger succeeded Zwingli in the Great Church and assumed the leadership of the Reformation in German-speaking Switzerland. ● Today is the birthday, in 1608, of John Milton, English poet, theologian, and hymnist. He is best known for his classic *Paradise Lost,* but his hymns are classics, too, including the lovely "Let Us with a Gladsome Mind," which he reportedly wrote when he was only fifteen: "Let us, with a gladsome mind, Praise the Lord, for He is kind. / For His mercies aye endure, ever faithful, ever sure." ● On December 9, 1840, the famous Scottish missionary and explorer, David Livingstone, started on his first journey to Africa, sponsored by the London Missionary Society. ● Today is the birthday of the Christmas card. On December 9, 1843, the first Christmas cards were created in England, designed like post cards and sold for a shilling each. ● Today is the birthday, in 1863, of Dr. G. Campbell Morgan, British Bible expositor, pastor, and writer, in Gloucestershire, England. ● December 9, 1893 marks the death of George Job Elvey, the church composer who wrote "Diademata," the music to which we sing "Crown Him with Many Crowns," and St. George's Windsor ("Come, Ye Thankful People, Come"). ● Today marks the funeral, in 1878, of Uncle John Vassar, famous preacher and personal evangelist. His family had gathered around him and his last words were "Farewell . . . farewell . . . Hallelujah!"

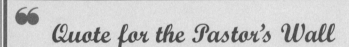

" Quote for the Pastor's Wall

One more day's work for Jesus,
One less of life for me!
But Heav'n is nearer,
and Christ is clearer
Than yesterday, to me.
—ANNA B. WARNER, 1869
"

Call to Worship

Come let us adore Him, O come let us adore Him, O come let us adore Him, Christ the Lord!

Advent Scripture Reading

Now the birth of Jesus Christ was as follows: After His mother Mary was betrothed to Joseph, before they came together, she was found with child of the Holy Spirit. Then Joseph her husband, being a just man, and not wanting to make her a public example, was minded to put her away secretly. But while he thought about these things, behold, an angel of the Lord appeared to him in a dream, saying, "Joseph, son of David, do not be afraid to take to you Mary your wife, for that which is conceived in her is of the Holy Spirit. And she will bring forth a Son, and you shall call His name JESUS, for He will save His people from their sins." So all this was done that it might be fulfilled which was spoken by the Lord through the prophet, saying: Behold, the virgin shall be with child, and bear a Son, and they shall call His name Immanuel," which is translated, "God with us." Then Joseph, being aroused from sleep, did as the angel of the Lord commanded him and took to him his wife, and did not know her till she had brought forth her firstborn Son. And he called His name JESUS (Matt. 1:18–25).

Offertory Comments

As our minds are filled with Christmas joy and giving, I hope we remember the most precious gift in history. God gave His only Son to us. We often visit the story of the wise men who came to see the Christchild bearing gifts of gold, frankincense, and myrrh. In all of your holiday giving, I hope you will remember that the most important gift given on the first Christmas was Christ Himself. Secondly, I hope we all remember that in recognition of that, the wise men brought their gifts to set before Jesus in honor, thanksgiving, and recognition of Him. What gifts have you decided to give this season? I truly hope you've kept the focus on giving to Jesus.

Additional Sermons and Lesson Ideas

Mary's Blessing in Bethlehem
Date preached:
By Dr. Larry Osborne

SCRIPTURE: Luke 1—2; Matthew 1—2

INTRODUCTION: What would you expect? If angels came to you saying you were to be the mother or earthly father of His Son, how would you expect it to happen? We can learn much about humility from God's dealings with Mary, Joseph, and the birth of Christ.

    1. Mary's Great Assignment and Promise (Luke 1:26–55).
    2. Some Likely Assumptions. We would, and perhaps Mary did, assume that financial security, good reputation, and a stable family life would accompany birthing the Christ.
    3. Some Surprising Realities:
        A. Financially: Poverty (Luke 2:22–24; Lev. 12:7–8).
        B. Reputation: Ridicule (Matt. 1:18–20; Luke 3:23; John 1:45–46).
        C. Family Life: Difficult (Matt. 2:13–23; 23:26–27; Luke 2:1–7, 41–50; John 19:25–27).

CONCLUSION: We should realize that God's favor does not mean life will always be easy for us. However, if we submit to His will through difficulty and tragedy, we play major roles in His work on earth, and we will receive just reward in His kingdom.

Life Lessons for Your Own Journey
Date preached:
By Dr. Larry Osborne

SCRIPTURE: Various

INTRODUCTION: Mary and Joseph had grave difficulties throughout life, including the incredible stress that came as they journeyed to Bethlehem. As we travel on our own journeys throughout life, what do we know about the hardships and blessings we will face?

    1. Hardship (Luke 9:23–24; Acts 14:21–22; 1 Pet. 4:12–19).
    2. Confusion (Is. 55:8–9; Heb. 11:6; Prov. 3:5–6).
    3. Protection (1 Cor. 10:13; 1 Thess. 3:3; Ps. 34:15–19; Rom. 8:35–39).
    4. Provision (Phil. 4:19; 2 Pet. 1:3–4; Eph. 1:17–20; Ps. 23:4–5; Luke 10:17–20).
    5. Purpose (Jer. 29:11; John 10:10; Eph. 2:10; Rom. 8:28).

CONCLUSION: The Lord who guided Mary and Joseph through that difficult experience of bearing the Christchild, He will also guide us through trials and bring us to ultimate glory for His sake.

DECEMBER 16, 2007

THIRD SUNDAY OF ADVENT   SUGGESTED SERMON

You CAN Miss It!

Date preached:

By Dr. Timothy Beougher

Scripture: Luke 2:4–7; Matthew 2:1–12, especially Luke 2:7
There was no room for them in the inn.

Introduction: Have you ever had anyone give you directions and then add the words, "you can't miss it!"? How many of us have heard this only to completely miss it? It is possible to miss something, even with it right in front of you! Did you know most people miss Christmas every year? That may sound like a ridiculous statement, particularly in America, where holiday advertisements deluge us focusing on December 25th. Yet arguably many people who participate in Christmas celebrations are oblivious to the true reality of what it is they are celebrating. They participate in many activities, but they miss the main event: Jesus Christ.

1. **We Get Sidetracked by Other Things (Luke 2:4–7).** Scripture doesn't specifically mention him, but that night in Bethlehem, an innkeeper made a decision. Standing before him was a man and his pregnant wife. He turned them away saying he had no room for them. And in so doing he missed Christmas. He was occupied with other things and simply didn't have time to try to help them. Perhaps he could have asked a guest if he would consider giving up his room for a pregnant woman. Or he could have even given up his own living quarters for Mary and Joseph. He was sidetracked with other things.

Application: *Affirm that Nothing Is More Important than Seeking Christ.* Contrast the innkeeper with the individuals who did celebrate the first Christmas! The shepherds were busy as well; they were occupied in other things, but they were willing to lay aside even good things so they might go and participate in the wondrous celebration of Christ's birth. Make sure you make room for Christ this year. Don't become sidetracked with other things, even good things, so that you miss the "main event" of Christmas.

2. **We Are Scared of What We Might Lose (Matt. 2:1–3).** This passage introduces us to another individual who missed the first Christmas:

King Herod. Unlike the innkeeper, he wasn't ignorant; he was well-informed concerning the birth of Christ. He had all the facts at his disposal. Verse 3 tells us this "disturbed" Herod. He didn't like this talk about someone who had been born "King of the Jews." He didn't want any competition for his throne. If the innkeeper's problem was being sidetracked with other things, Herod's problem was that he was scared of what he might lose. Herod wasn't from a Jewish background. His father had done some favors for Rome and in return the Herod family was given the right to rule Judea, which was under Roman occupation. Herod fancied himself the "King of the Jews." So you see why he panicked when he heard of one who had been born as "King of the Jews." His supremacy was being challenged.

Application: *Acknowledge God Is the Giver, Not a Receiver.* You say, Okay, I can see why King Herod missed Christmas. But what does that have to do with me? Herod missed Christmas because he wanted to be king. He wasn't about to let someone else rule over him. He saw Jesus as a threat to him, and so he missed Christmas. If we believe that becoming a Christian and following God's ways means we lose too much, we will be fearful about it.

3. **We Become Satisfied with Intellectual Knowledge (Matt. 2:4–6).** The religious leaders missed the first Christmas. Why? Not because of ignorance. The chief priest and scribes (or teachers) of the law knew exactly where Christ was to be born. When asked a theological question, "where will the Christ be born?" they knew the right answer. They knew the Bible very well, well enough to quote Micah 5:2, which prophesied hundreds of years in advance that the Messiah would be born in Bethlehem. They knew the right answers, yet they missed Christmas. Here were the experts in Bible knowledge, the ones who knew the right answers, and yet they didn't even bother to walk the few miles from Jerusalem to Bethlehem to see for themselves that the Messiah had indeed been born.

Application: *Act on What We Know to Be True.* There is no better time than Christmas to trust Him as your Lord and Savior if you've never done that before. And if you are a follower of Christ, there is no better time to recommit to live the way He wants you to. Let's act on what we know to be true and make this the best Christmas ever for us and for our families.

STATS, STORIES, AND MORE

Missing the Main Event

There's an old story about a country boy who wanted more than anything to see the circus. When the circus came to a nearby town, the boy emptied his piggy bank of his hard-earned money and headed in to see his first circus. He returned home that afternoon with all his money. His father asked, "What happened? Didn't you go to the circus?" "O, yes," said the boy. "The trucks full of animals came right down the street and I got to see it all and it didn't cost me a thing. Nobody ever asked for my money." The father said, "You didn't see the circus at all! You just saw the parade! You only got a glimpse of it! You missed the main event!"

Missing the Bus

I read a humorous story about a man who went into the bus station in Athens, Georgia, to buy a ticket to Greenville, South Carolina. The ticket clerk told him that the bus would be a little late. While he was waiting, he thought he'd walk around the station. He spotted a machine that had a sign that read: "For 25 cents, I will tell you your name, your age, your hometown, and other interesting information."

The man was sure it was a scam, but his curiosity got the best of him and he put a quarter in the machine. A card came out of the slot which read: "Your name is Bill Jones. You are 35 years old. You live in Athens, Georgia. You are waiting for a bus to Greenville. The bus is delayed."

The man was dumbfounded. How could the machine possibly know that? He quickly put in another quarter. The card read: "As I told you before, your name is Bill Jones. You are 35 years old. You live in Athens, Georgia and you are still waiting for a bus to Greenville. The bus is delayed a little longer."

The man decided he would try to stump the machine. So he ran across the street to a toy store and bought a pair of those Groucho Marx glasses with the thick eyebrows and mustache. He also bought a wig and a cane. Then he hobbled back to the station.

He approached the machine and inserted a quarter. Out came the card and it read: "Well, it's you again. Your name is still Bill Jones. You are still 35 years old. You still live in Athens, Georgia and you still want to go to Greenville, South Carolina. But the problem is that while you weren't paying attention, you missed your bus!"

APPROPRIATE HYMNS AND SONGS

"Joy to the World" Isaac Watts/George Frederick Handel, Public Domain.

"Amen," Ken Bible/Tom Fettke, 1997 Pilot Point Music (Admin. The Copyright Co.).

"Away in a Manger," Martin Luther/John Thomas McFarland/Murray, Public Domain.

"O Come, O Come Emmanuel," John M. Neale/Henry S. Coffin/Thom Helmore, Public Domain.

"He Came All This way," Mark Condon, 2004 Bridge Building Music Inc. (div. of Brentwood Benson Music Publishing).

FOR THE BULLETIN

Martin Luther's coworker and secretary, Caspar Cruciger the Elder, died on December 16, 1548. He was pastor of the Castle Church in Wittenberg and served as secretary to Luther for several years, aiding him in the translation of the Bible. ● Today is the birthday of one of history's greatest orators, revivalists, evangelists, and preachers—George Whitefield, who was born in Gloucester, England, on December 16, 1714. As he preached in the open air throughout the countryside and made repeated trips to America, he held crowds of thousands in suspense of his every word. His key message: "You must be born again!" ● Today is also the birthday, in 1786, of the German church musician, Konrad Kocher, who wrote the music to our hymn, "For the Beauty of the Earth." ● On December 16, 1811, the Mississippi River flowed backward. This is the date of the great series of earthquakes that rocked the eastern half of America, raising and lowering parts of the Mississippi by 15 feet and creating Reelfoot Lake in Tennessee. Church bells as far away as Philadelphia rang from the tremors. Methodist preacher Peter Cartwright, one of America's most colorful itinerant evangelists, recorded several earthquake experiences in his autobiography, saying: *This earthquake struck terror to thousands of people, and under the mighty panic hundreds and thousands crowded to and joined the different churches. [One woman went running through the streets, crying],* "My Jesus is coming in the clouds of heaven . . . I must go and meet him . . . Hallelujah! Jesus is coming, and I am ready. Hallelujah! Amen." *And on she went, shouting and clapping her hands, with the empty pail on her head.*

WORSHIP HELPS

Call to Worship
O come, O come, Emmanuel, and ransom captive Israel, that mourns in lonely exile here until the Son of God appear. Rejoice! Rejoice! Emmanuel has come to thee, O Israel.[1]

Advent Scripture Reading
And it happened, when Elizabeth heard the greeting of Mary, that the babe leaped in her womb; and Elizabeth was filled with the Holy Spirit. Then she spoke out with a loud voice and said, "Blessed are you among women, and blessed is the fruit of your womb! But why is this granted to me, that the mother of my Lord should come to me? For indeed, as soon as the voice of your greeting sounded in my ears, the babe leaped in my womb for joy. Blessed is she who believed, for there will be a fulfillment of those things which were told her from the Lord" (Luke 1:41–45).

Word of Welcome
As we reflect on the birth of our Lord Jesus Christ, we often remember the story of Mary and Joseph, how they were trudging along to Bethlehem on their difficult journey. Mary was due any day now. It turned out that on the way to Bethlehem for the mandated census, Mary went into labor. We envision their cold journey with no friends or family around to help them. We imagine a grumpy innkeeper turning them away, leaving them the choice of only a manger for a birthing room. Despite their hardship, the Christchild was born. I hope every one of you was greeted as you came in to the warmth of this house today, for here the Christchild is welcome and so are all who wish to worship Him.

A Stanza from an Old Christmas Hymn to Use in the Pastoral Prayer or Word of Welcome
> The happy Christmas comes once more,
> The heavenly Guest is at the door,
> The blessèd words the shepherds thrill,
> The joyous tidings, "Peace, good will."
> —From an 1810 Danish hymn
> by NIKOLAI GRUNDTVIG

---

[1] Adapted from John M. Neale's Translation of the 12th Century Latin "Veni, veni Emanuel." Translation recorded in the form of the 1851 Mediaeval hymn "O Come, O Come Emmanuel."

Additional Sermons and Lesson Ideas

The Three Gifts
Date preached:

SCRIPTURE: Matthew 2:9–12; Romans 5:1–5

INTRODUCTION: As we prepare for Christmas, we notice some gifts at the cradle of the Christchild. Three are for Him—gold, frankincense, and myrrh. But on the other side of the cradle are three other gifts, His to us. There is an exchange of gifts at Christmas. He gives:

1. A Life That Is Forgiven (Rom. 5:1). We are justified by faith and have peace with God.
2. A Life That Is Forever (Rom. 5:2). We rejoice in hope of the glory of God. "Hope" here is a reference to the return of Christ and our life in glory with Him.
3. A Life That Is Fortified (Rom. 5:3–5). We persevere in tribulations, strengthened by His love which is shed abroad in our hearts by His Spirit.

CONCLUSION: Receive Christ's gifts. He came all the way from heaven to give them to you.

Christ Is Christmas
Date preached:

By Dr. Melvin Worthington

SCRIPTURE: Various, especially Matthew 1 and John 1

INTRODUCTION: What is Christmas? Santa Claus and reindeer? Brilliant tinsel trees and trips to visit family and friends? Gifts, gatherings, and giving? Christmas is a time when we should recognize, remember, and reflect on the coming of Jesus Christ into the world.

1. The Significant Time. Christ's coming was prophesied (Gen. 3:15; 1 Pet. 1:18–20). Christ's coming was prefigured throughout the Old Testament's servants and sacrificial system. Christ's coming was proclaimed by the angels (Luke 2).
2. The Significant Truths. Reflecting on Christmas involves considering the significant truths of Christmas such as: the *Person* who came (John 1:1–4; Matt. 1:23), the *Purpose* for which He came (John 14:6; Rom. 3; 5), the *Place* to which He came (Phil. 2; Luke 2), and the *People* to whom He came (Rom. 5).
3. The Significant Task. Christmas provides an ideal time to *share* the gospel, *show* the gospel, and to *support* the gospel.

CONCLUSION: The meaning and message of Christmas is an incredible missionary story that needs to be told.

DECEMBER 23, 2007

FOURTH SUNDAY OF ADVENT   SUGGESTED SERMON

Prepare the Way . . . with Receptivity!

By Rev. Todd M. Kinde

Date preached:

Scripture: Luke 2:8–20, especially verse 14
Glory to God in the highest . . .

Introduction: There are two scenes in the Christmas Eve story: one in the field and one at the manger. The first scene in the field records a heavenly visitation of angels in proclamation and praise (2:10–14). The second scene at the manger records an earthly response also of proclamation and praise (2:17–18, 20). This is the pattern for the follower of Jesus today. The heavenly activity is the reality to which we aspire and so we pattern ourselves after it. And so it is that we often pray, "may it be 'on earth as it is in heaven.'"

1. **The Shepherds.** The shepherds were, I imagine, greatly surprised by the angelic visitation. The angel's message was quite simple, "A Savior is born, it is good news of great joy for all peoples, and you will find Him wrapped in cloths and lying in a feeding trough." Their response was to go quickly to look for this wonder (v. 16). Once the shepherds found the Savior they received Him in the same way that the angel had appeared to them and in a manner that we, too, can follow.

   A. **Proclaim:** They proclaim the good news of great joy to all who would hear (v. 17). It is like our little Christmas song that tells us to, "Go tell it on the mountain, over the hills and everywhere. Go tell it on the mountain that Jesus Christ is born." The word "angel" simply means "messenger." As the shepherds heard the message from the angels so they themselves became messengers of the good news that night. You and I are also to be messengers of the good news as we receive Jesus with great joy.

   B. **Praise:** The essence of this good news and the cause for great joy comes in the praise of the heavenly host (v. 14)—peace, peace with God! You mean to say that after all my failures, all my disappointments with others and even with God Himself, after all my running away, and mean thoughts about Him, I can be at peace with Him? Yes! He has made a way for us to know His favor and grace. And this is cause to praise Him. To ascribe the glory that is His alone as the sovereign Creator, Savior, and Recreator. The angels praise God in verse 14. The shepherds praise God in verse 20. You and I are to praise God tonight for the coming of His Eternal Son to save us and to make peace for us with God.

2. **Mary.** Well, this is only chapter 2 of a story that Luke writes with 24 chapters. Mary gets another bitter taste of the future in verse 35, "a sword will pierce through your own soul also." "Also?" "He will die?" Yes, the conclusion is this, Jesus came to make peace for us with God by dying for sinners. He was raised up to life the third day as evidence that God the Father is pleased and has had mercy on us (Luke 24:25–26, 46–48). This Christmas, treasure up this truth pondering it in your heart. We all deserve a lump of coal in our stockings. But Jesus has taken the coal and replaced it with this treasure. Receive His gift.

Ponder: How does Mary receive all this about the baby she bore and now holds in her care? She "treasured up all these things pondering them in her heart" (v. 19). Just think of what has happened. She is in a place not her own home; she has given birth to a son that was conceived by miracle through the Holy Spirit; angels have visited; shepherds have visited; the people around are in wonder; this little baby is called Christ, Savior, Lord; and He will bring God's peace and favor to us! How!? How can this be!? What does this all mean!?

Conclusion: How can we receive the gift of God to us in the coming of His Eternal Son to earth? Proclaim the good news of great joy for all peoples. Praise God for His mercy and peace extended to us in Christ. Ponder the purpose of His coming to die for sinners and make peace for us with God.

STATS, STORIES, AND MORE

During World War II, General Dwight Eisenhower was in Europe, directing the planning for the D-Day Invasion. It was during intense moments of preparation that word came of the death of his father. What do you do at such a moment? It was impossible for Eisenhower to leave his command. He couldn't possibly return home, nor was it possible for him to take time off to grieve and process his sorrow. But, as he wrote in his book, it also was not possible to go ahead with business-as-usual. What did he do? He sent everyone out of his office and he set aside thirty minutes to think about his dad, to write out his thoughts in a diary, and to just put down his feeling on paper. After half an hour, he forced himself to get back to work; but he left his office early that evening to spend some more time in the evening thinking about his dad and putting his feelings to paper. That's all he could do. But as we think of Christmas this year, think of this. If General Eisenhower, in the midst of planning for the invasion of Europe, could shut the door and spend half an hour thinking about the death of his earthly father, should we not find a way of shutting the door, opening our Bibles, and thinking about the birth of our earthly Savior? Sometimes we need to take time to ponder these things in our hearts, as Mary did. During this Christmas season, take the time to sit at your desk in the soft glow of a single lamp, reading through the Christmas story, contemplating and praising and worshiping God.

- Elizabeth, learning of Christmas, was filled with the Holy Spirit and cried out with a loud voice.
- Mary said: *My soul magnifies the Lord.*
- Zacharias said: *Blessed be the Lord God of Israel.*
- The angels said: *Glory to God in the highest.*
- The shepherds returned glorying and praising God.
- Simeon held the Child in his arms and blessed God.
- Anna gave thanks to the Lord and spoke of Him.

APPROPRIATE HYMNS AND SONGS

"Glory to God," Mark Condon, 2004 Bridge Building Music Inc. (div. of Brentwood Benson Music Publishing).

"Silent Night," Joseph Mohr/Franz Gruber/ ohn Free Young, Public Domain.

"Hark the Herald Angels Sing," Charles Wesley/Felix Mendelssohn, Public Domain.

"I Heard the Bells on Christmas Day," Henry W. Longfellow/Jean Baptiste Calkin, Public Domain.

FOR THE BULLETIN

St. Philip, popular leader of the Russian church in the mid-1500s, was critical of Ivan the Terrible for the latter's treatment of peasants. On one occasion, when the Tsar was attending mass, Philip spoke openly against him. As a result, Philip was arrested, bound in chains, and shuttled from one prison to another for months before finally being murdered in his cell on December 23, 1569. ● On December 23, 1685, John Bunyan, author of *Pilgrim's Progress,* wrote out his last testament in his own hand. It began, "To all people to whom this present writing shall come, I, John Bunyan of the parish of St. Cuthberts, in the town of Bedford, brazier, send greetings . . . ." The document was to insure that should he be arrested or martyred for his faith, his possessions would be properly allocated. Having completed the document, he hid it. It was so well hidden that his wife Elizabeth was never able to find it; and Bunyan's last testament wasn't discovered until 150 years after his death when his house was being demolished. He had hidden it between the bricks of the chimney. ● Today is the birthday (1841) of the British evangelical pastor and writer, Handley C. G. Moule, Anglican theologian. He once said, "There is no situation so chaotic that God cannot from that situation, create something that is surpassingly good. He did it at the creation. He did it at the cross. He is doing it today." ● Today marks the death of pastor and evangelist, J. Wilber Chapman, who passed away on December 23, 1918. His last message had been on December 15 at the First Presbyterian Church of Jamaica, New York, on the subject "Christ, Our Only Hope."

Kid's Talk

Ask the children if they have heard the story of the wise men who came to give gifts to Jesus. Take a minute to give them an overview of the Advent, focusing on the wise men's sacrifice to Jesus. Ask them if they would like to give Jesus a gift this Christmas. Tell them that Jesus taught that whoever does kind things to the least of His created people does them ultimately to Him (Matt. 25:39–41). Encourage them to pick one gift they receive this Christmas, whether it's something small from their stocking or socks or whatever they choose, and tell their parents that's their Jesus gift. Collect these gifts the following week to distribute to the poorer children of your community. You might have a follow-up Kid's Talk with some pictures or letters from the recipients.

WORSHIP HELPS

Call to Worship
My soul magnifies the Lord, and my spirit has rejoiced in God my Savior . . . for He who is mighty has done great things for me, and holy is His name (Luke 1:46–47, 49).

Advent Reading from Luke 2 of the King James Version
And it came to pass in those days, that there went out a decree from Caesar Augustus that all the world should be taxed. (And this taxing was first made when Cyrenius was governor of Syria.) And all went to be taxed, every one into his own city. And Joseph also went up from Galilee, out of the city of Nazareth, into Judaea, unto the city of David, which is called Bethlehem; (because he was of the house and lineage of David:) To be taxed with Mary his espoused wife, being great with child. And so it was, that, while they were there, the days were accomplished that she should be delivered. And she brought forth her firstborn son, and wrapped him in swaddling clothes, and laid him in a manger; because there was no room for them in the inn.

Offertory Comments
Can you think of any gift, any earthly possession, any sacrifice equal to God's giving His own Son? Yet, at Christmas time we tend to focus on giving and receiving gifts to our families and friends to the neglect of giving tithes and offerings to God. I'm not trying to make anyone feel guilty or obligated, for God doesn't desire obligatory gifts any more than we do. I do urge you, however, to resist the tide of our time. Don't get so caught up in gifting others that you forget to give to the Christ of Christmas.

Additional Sermons and Lesson Ideas

The Joy and Music of Christmas
Date preached:
By Dr. David Jeremiah

SCRIPTURE: Various

INTRODUCTION: Agnosticism doesn't have any Gloria, atheists have no carols, but Christianity is filled with music and Christmas is a time of singing. In Luke, there are six different songs almost back to back, by Elizabeth, Mary, Zacharias, Simeon, Gabriel, and the angelic hosts. There is music at Christmas because:

1. The Old Testament Prophecies Have Been Fulfilled. See Luke 2:25ff.
2. The Problem of Sin Has Been Resolved. See Luke 1:68ff.
3. The Pain of the Lowly and Forgotten Has Been Remembered. See Luke 1:46ff. Christmas is God clothing common people, even the poorest of peasants, with dignity and honor.
4. The Possibility of Peace Is Renewed in Our Hearts. See Luke 2:8ff.
5. The Purpose of Life Is Illustrated in the Songs of the Nativity. Throughout these songs is a note of glory and praise to the Father.
6. The Predictions of Christ's Second Coming Are Secure.

CONCLUSION: In 1744, Charles Wesley wrote a Christmas hymn that is seldom sung, but it incorporates most of the prophecies and the thoughts I have shared with you: Come, Thou long-expected Jesus, born to set Thy people free . . .

And the Word Was God
Date preached:

SCRIPTURE: John 1:1

INTRODUCTION: Matthew tells us about the birth of Christ from Joseph's perspective. Mark skips the Christmas story. Luke gives it from Mary's perspective. And John tells us about the birth of Christ from the heavenly Father's viewpoint, which begins with the identity of Christ Himself. He is the "Word"—God's ultimate communication to this planet.

1. Christ's Pre-existence. "In the beginning was the Word." The life of Jesus Christ did not begin with His birth in Bethlehem. Jesus is eternal in the heavens, the ancient of days, without father or mother, without beginning or ending.
2. Christ's Co-Existence. "And the Word was with God." John was alluding here to the doctrine of the Trinity. Jesus is co-equal with the Father and Spirit.
3. Christ's Divine Existence. "And the Word was God." This is one of John's great themes—Jesus was and is very God of very God.

CONCLUSION: Jesus Christ is God Himself, the Master. Our lives should revolve around Him, we should keep our eyes continually on Him, we should leap to do His bidding, and we should bring our crowns and trophies and lay them at His feet.

DECEMBER 31, 2007

The Danger of Finishing Badly

By Rev. Peter Grainger   *Date preached:*

Scripture: 1 Kings 3, 10:23—11:13, especially 11:11
Because you have done this, and have not kept My covenant and My statutes, which I have commanded you, I will surely tear the kingdom away from you and give it to your servant.

Introduction: News bulletins which report on marathons usually show two pictures: the beginning of the race with the huge mass of runners "taking off" and the end of the race with the winners breaking the tape at the finish. What we fail to see is the important part of the race: the middle. Many of those who started so well and so cheerfully struggle to keep going. Some limp home long after the first runners have finished and gone home. Others fail to finish at all. I want to look at a striking and sad example from the Bible of someone who started well but finished badly. That person was one of Israel's greatest kings: Solomon.

I. **Divine Favors (1 Kin, 3:5–10).** Right at the beginning of his reign, the Lord met with Solomon in a dream and the Lord granted him a remarkable favor. Wisely Solomon asked for wisdom (1 Kin. 3:10). Because of this wise choice, the Lord not only granted Solomon wisdom but also wealth beyond that of any other king, which gave to Solomon an international fame far beyond Israel's borders. No one could have a better start in life and more God-given privileges, gifts, and possessions than Solomon. Yet none of it prevented him from ending his reign in disaster and incurring the Lord's anger and condemnation and judgment. Indeed, it was because of all these privileges that the Lord judged Solomon all the more severely and held him accountable.

Application: If you are a Christian, you are the privileged recipient of divine favors. God has shown His love and grace to you, blessing you with every spiritual blessing in Christ (Eph. 1:3). But none of these things in themselves will ensure our future prosperity as a church or that as individuals we will finish the course well. The story of Solomon and the subsequent history of Israel is a solemn warning against any such complacency.

2. **Divided Loyalties (1 Kin. 11:1–13).** After describing the glory of Solomon in chapter 10, the writer of 1 Kings begins the next chapter with a note of contrast: "King Solomon loved many foreign women" (1 Kin. 11:1). The ensuing verses describe the huge number of wives and concubines that Solomon acquired. While polygamy is not specifically condemned in the Law of Moses, it is rarely practiced and almost always leads to disaster—illustrated not least by the lives of the patriarchs—the consequences of which we still live with even today. Most of these women were chosen from royal families of other nations so as to forge political alliances. While Solomon's reign did enjoy peace, this decision was utterly condemned by the Lord for religious (and not racial) reasons. Verse 4 tells "his wives turned his heart after other gods . . ." Solomon had a heart problem.

Application: Do you have a heart problem that's affecting your running? The best remedy is to start with a healthy heart and keep it that way. And a healthy heart is always and can only be one that is fully devoted to the Lord your God. The first and great commandment is to love Him with all your heart and soul and mind and strength. And any other love which dilutes that love or even displaces it will affect your running and lead to spiritual disaster.

3. **Disastrous Consequences (1 Kin. 11:9–13).** To all outward appearances, Solomon's policy seemed to work well as evidenced by Israel's increasing influence in the region. Everything in Solomon's life and kingdom seemed to be fine. Everyone in Israel was very happy—except for one person, the only person whose opinion really counted in the final analysis. The Lord became angry with Solomon. The Lord diagnosed his heart-problem and the consequence was that Solomon's glorious reign would be followed by disaster (v. 11).

Application: Each one of us is fully accountable to the Lord for the choices we make, who we love and His commands that we either keep or disobey. Every day and every choice we make affects our future and whether we will finish well or badly. Old age will usually reveal the truth, how you have been running, and the real state of your heart. May we continue the race faithfully, and finish this year the way we want to finish the race of life: in obedience to our Saviour, Jesus Christ.

STATS, STORIES, AND MORE

When the Olympic Games were held in St. Louis in 1904, there was an unusual entry in the Marathon. A small Cuban mail carrier named Felix Caracal announced one day to his fellow postal workers he was going to travel to the States and win the Marathon for Cuba. He was without money or backing, yet he quit his job and began begging on the streets of Havana, seeking traveling funds. Somehow he collected enough money, took a boat to New Orleans, and promptly lost his money in a dice game. He hitched rides to St. Louis where he arrived hungry and in rags. Members of the American team befriended him and gave him some food and a place to sleep. He had no running clothes and no running shoes, only heavy street shoes. Nevertheless, he cut off his pants above the knees and there he was at the starting line, street shoes and all. It was a sweltering day; the heat and humidity were oppressive. One by one, many of the other runners collapsed. Felix, however, being from Cuba, thought nothing of the blistering conditions. With only two miles to go, Felix had a huge lead. He was running alongside an orchard and he spotted some apples and stopped to eat some of them. They were green, and soon he was stricken with severe stomach cramps. He lost the lead, though he did come in fourth, doubled-over with pain. Of the thirty-one starters that day, only fourteen finished, and Felix was fourth among them.

APPROPRIATE HYMNS AND SONGS

"Another Year Is Dawning," Frances R. Havergal/Samuel Wesley, Public Domain.

"All for Jesus" Mary Dagworthy James, Public Domain.

"Be the One," Al Denson/Don Koch/Dave Clark, 1990 John T. Benson Publishing Co. (Admin. Brentwood Benson Music).

"Come, Christians, Join to Sing," Christian Henry Bateman, Public Domain.

FOR THE BULLETIN

December 30, 1678, marks the birth and baptism of William Croft, the English church musician and organist who composed the hymn tune entitled St. Anne ("O God, Our Help in Ages Past"). ● One of America's greatest preachers, Charles Finney, who had been a drunken lawyer in New York before his conversion, was licensed to preach on December 30, 1823, by the St. Lawrence presbytery of New York. ● President Rutherford B. Hayes and his wife Lucy were married on this day in 1852. Being devout Methodists, they began each day with prayer and they also organized Sunday evening worship services at the White House. Lucy brought to Washington a college degree (she was the first President's wife to have one), a gift for hospitality, and an open commitment to Jesus Christ. But she didn't bring any alcohol. Official Washington was shocked by her banning of alcoholic beverages from the Executive Mansion, and the First Lady is known as "Lemonade Lucy" to this day. Mrs. Hayes died eight years after leaving the White House. Her husband lived four more years before dying on January 17, 1893, his last words being, "I know I am going where Lucy is." ● In Shantung Province in Japan, rioters in the Boxer Rebellion captured a 24-year-old English missionary named Sidney Brooks who was working with Propagation of the Gospel in Foreign Parts. He was returning from vacation on December 30, 1899. He was tortured for hours before being killed, becoming the first Boxer martyr.

WORSHIP HELPS

Call to Worship
Make a joyful shout to God, all the earth! Sing out the honor of His name; make His praise glorious. Say to God, "How awesome are Your works! Through the greatness of Your power Your enemies shall submit themselves to You. All the earth shall worship You and sing praises to You; they shall sing praises to Your name." Selah. Come and see the works of God; He is awesome in His doing toward the sons of men (Ps. 66:1–5).

Offertory Prayer
Lord, as we gather in Your presence, in this house of worship and prayer, we cannot help but recognize Your goodness to us. Like the psalmist, each day we ". . . taste and see that the LORD is good . . ." (Ps. 34:8). In view of Your mercy and Your provision,
Continued on the next page

especially the ultimate sacrifice of Jesus Christ on the Cross of Calvary, we willingly give to You our tithes and offerings. We ask that You bless it for Your sake and for ours, in Jesus' name we pray, Amen.

An Old Hymn for the Last Day of the Year
"The Year If Gone, Without Recall" is the quaint title of an anonymous Latin hymn from the early 1700s, which was translated into English in the 1800s by British hymnist Francis Pott.

> The year is gone, beyond recall,
> With all its hopes and fears,
> With all its bright and gladdening smiles,
> With all its mourners' tears.
>
> Thy thankful people praise Thee, Lord,
> For countless gifts received;
> And pray for grace to keep the faith
> Which saints of old believed.
>
> O Father, let Thy watchful eye
> Still look on us in love,
> That we may praise Thee, year by year,
> With angel hosts above.
>
> All glory to the Father be,
> All glory to the Son,
> All glory, Holy Ghost, to Thee,
> While endless ages run.

Benediction
Now may the God of peace who brought up our Lord Jesus from the dead, that great Shepherd of the sheep, through the blood of the everlasting covenant, make you complete in every good work to do His will, working in you what is well pleasing in His sight, through Jesus Christ, to whom be glory forever and ever. Amen (Heb. 13:20–21).

Additional Sermons and Lesson Ideas

The Holy Spirit: God's Great Provision

Date preached:

Rosalind Goforth, Adapted from her 1921 book,
How I Know God Answers Prayer

SCRIPTURE: Various

INTRODUCTION: God knew our frailty, that our hearts are desperately wicked. He therefore made kingly provision so rich, so sufficient, so exceedingly abundant, that as we study it we feel we have tapped a mine of wealth too deep to fathom. God's greatest provision is the gift of His own Being in the Person of the Holy Spirit. Here are some of the things the Holy Spirit does for us:

1. He Begets Us into the Family of God (John 3:6).
2. He Seals or Marks Us as God's (Eph. 1:13).
3. He Dwells in Us (1 Cor. 3:16).
4. He Unites Us to Christ (1 Cor. 12:13, 27).
5. He Changes Us into the Likeness of Christ (2 Cor. 3:18).
6. He Helps Us in Prayer (Rom. 8:26).
7. He Comforts (John 14:16).
8. He Guides (Rom. 8:14).
9. He Strengthens Us with Power (Eph. 3:16).
10. He Is the Source of Fruitfulness (John 7:38, 39).

CONCLUSION: As we end this year, let us commit ourselves this coming year, not only to physical exercise, but to keeping in step with the Spirit (Gal. 5:25).

Focus on Finishing

Date preached:

By Dr. Melvin Worthington

SCRIPTURE: 2 Timothy 4:7–8

INTRODUCTION: To finish well one must recognize and respond to the conflict. The Christian life is an unavoidable conflict—a pitched battle (2 Tim. 4:7). Here we learn how to win, and finish well:

1. Run the Course—Aggressively Follow the Course (1 Tim. 4:7). The Christian life is rightly compared to a hotly contested race (Heb. 12:1–2; 1 Cor. 9:24). Aggressively running the course requires *discernment, discipline,* and *determination.*
2. Rely on the Compass—Abide by the Compass (1 Tim. 4:7). Paul unashamedly declared that he had "kept the faith." That is, he defended the doctrine of the faith, upholding and maintaining it in and by his ministry. The compass (the Word of God) gave him *instruction, insight,* and *inspiration.*
3. Rejoice in the Crown—Anticipate the Crown (1 Tim. 4:8). Paul anticipated the crown of righteousness which awaited him at the conclusion of the race. Anticipation of the crown contributed to *his faithfulness, his focus,* and *his fidelity.*

CONCLUSION: To finish well, we must wage a constant battle against sin, the world, the flesh and the devil, and win victory by the power of the Lord Jesus Christ.

WEDDING SERMON
Wedding: A Garden Enclosed

Dear friends, we have gathered here today with hearts of joy and love for these two persons, _____ and _____, who are being united this hour in the bonds of Christian marriage. Even in this age of innovation and experimentation, no one has yet discovered a richer relationship than the biblical institution of marriage; and in our age of liberation when restraints are rejected and holiness is belittled, there is still nothing as winsome or as wonderful as a godly home.

The Lord speaks of this throughout His Word, and the words "home," "family," and "marriage" occur a combined total of over four hundred times in the Bible. Marriage is God's invention, His ordained institution for our welfare and for the advancement of the human race; and Scripture upholds the splendor and sanctity of marriage, home, and family as something precious in God's eyes.

In the very middle of the Bible, however, is an oft-ignored book totally devoted to this subject, picturing marriage with vivid images and opening with the surprising words: "Let him kiss me with the kisses of his mouth—for your love is better than wine."

This book, which follows the books of Proverbs and Ecclesiastes in our Bibles, is called the Song of Songs, or sometimes the Song of Solomon or the Canticles. I'd like to read a few passages from this book today, just to remind us of the way marriage *should* be. The writer of Song of Songs said:

> He brought me to the banqueting house,
> And his banner over me was love . . .
>
> My beloved spoke, and said to me:
> "Rise up, my love, my fair one,
> and come away.
> For lo, the winter is past,

The rain is over and gone.
The flowers appear on the earth;
The time of singing has come,
And the voice of the turtledove is heard in our land.

My beloved is mine, and I am his . . .

Come, my beloved,
Let us go forth to the field;
Let us lodge in the villages.
Let us get up early to the vineyards;
Let us see if the vine has budded,
Whether the grape blossoms are open,
And the pomegranates are in bloom.
There I will give you my love.

Many waters cannot quench love,
Nor can the floods drown it.

Notice how this book pictures marriage in terms of a secret garden, a private park of flowing fountains, fragrant flowers, and aromatic spices. It says:

A garden enclosed
Is my sister, my spouse,
A spring shut up,
A fountain sealed.
Your plants are an orchard of pomegranates
With pleasant fruits,
Fragrant henna with spikenard,
Spikenard and saffron,
Calamus and cinnamon,
With all trees of frankincense,
Myrrh and aloes,
With all the chief spices—
A fountain of gardens,
A well of living waters,
And streams from Lebanon.

That's a very lovely picture, and an accurate one, for marriage is a beautiful and fruitful garden, enclosed by the stone hedge of faithfulness and through which the winds of the Holy Spirit blow. It enriches our lives with perpetual bouquets of blessings.

But there's one thing omitted in the Song of Solomon—and that's what I'd like to talk for a moment about. Behind the weeping willows and the rambling roses, in the corner of the garden built against the back wall almost hidden from sight, is an all-important tool shed.

If you've ever done outdoor work, you know that plants and fountains require constant maintenance, flower beds must be cultivated, and fruitful vines must be pruned. Gardens must be planned and planted, weeded and watered, talked to and tended, harrowed and harvested. A beautiful garden is well worth the effort, but *effort* it is; and there are three important tools of the trade.

The first is *Discipline*. In a few minutes, the two of you will pledge to leave all others and to cleave only and always to the person you love today. That means you must maintain constant vigilance of anything that would arouse the suspicions or fears of the other. You must live above reproach. You must avoid friendships that may draw you into a relationship closer in any way than the one you are forming today. You must build a stone hedge of holiness that cannot be breached, even as the Bible says in 2 Corinthians 7:1: "Therefore, having these promises, beloved, let us cleanse ourselves from all filthiness of the flesh and spirit, perfecting holiness in the fear of God."

The second tool is *Dialogue*. Most marriages fail because the partners gradually stop communicating. They become too busy, too bored, or too bitter. It's not always easy to be a good conversationalist or to open up when we'd rather shut down. But talking together and praying together are the two greatest ways of building up, edifying, cheering, encouraging, affirming, and drawing near to the person you are today taking as your life's partner.

The third tool is the simple practice of *Dating*. Even with all our modern research, most marital experts still point to one practice as more important than all other for longevity in marriage. Couples who play together stay together. I want to encourage you to maintain a date night all the weeks of your lives, and plan periodic "get-aways" all the years of your marriage. It sounds counter-intuitive, but it's true—we all have to work hard to enjoy being together. It takes effort to make a marriage seem effortless, just as a beautiful garden takes a lot of muscle grease and manpower. But by guarding your time with each other and building an exclusive friendship with frequent dates and periodic "get-aways," you will be sowing the seeds of joy in your home.

So today, ladies and gentlemen, we are planting a garden, and in a few years it will either be a fragrant, aromatic garden of grace like the one in the Song of Songs that brings forth its fruit in season, or it will become a neglected patch of heartache and sorrow. I know it will be the former, because I know the caliber and capabilities of the two who stand before us today and for whom we are praying with love and joy in our hearts. And I believe the Lord Himself will send the needed showers of blessings even as He has promised to bring the increase and to make us fruitful for His glory.

If you, then, _____ and _____, are prepared to join one another in this abiding relationship, will you please join hands and repeat after me.

(To man): I love you, _____, and today I take you as my wedded wife, pledging and promising with all my heart, before God, to love you, to cherish you, to care for you and to serve you as your faithful and steadfast husband all the days of our lives on earth.

(To woman): I love you, _____, and today I take you as my wedded husband, pledging and promising with all my heart, before God, to love you, to cherish you, to care for you, and to serve you as your faithful and steadfast wife all the days of our lives on earth.

WEDDING SERMON

Wedding: A Promise-Anchored Home

Dear friends, we have gathered today in the sight of our heavenly Father and our earthly friends to unite in Christian marriage these two, _____ and _____, who, in a few moments, will be affirming their vows and pledging their promised love to one another. A promise is a sacred thing. It is a stated declaration of what we intend to do or, in some cases, of what we intend to refrain from doing. It is a pledge that will be ratified by our future conduct and will expose our true character.

Promises are priceless and they are precious. They are the anchor that holds us steady in turbulent times. They form the basis for trusting one another, and the foundation for our faith in God.

There are three people present today and making promises today. _____ and _____ are going to exchange their vows one to the other, but the most remarkable person in this room is unseen; for the everlasting God is here, present in the very place, observant, participating, and offering this couple the vows of His eternal Word.

We have a God who has given us a Bible full of promises for all the concerns and contingencies of life. It's hard to calculate how many promises are actually contained in the Word of God. One man reportedly took a year-and-a-half to read through the Bible, noting all the promises the Lord offers us, and he came up with over 7,000 of them.

We can't review all 7,000 today; but a handful of them are fitting for this holy hour, and I want to remind us of them as a way of recommending to us the importance of establishing a divinely anchored marriage and a promise-based home.

The apostle Peter, in his second epistle, said that our Lord's "divine power has given us everything we need for life and godliness through our knowledge of him who called us by his own glory and goodness.

Through these he has given us his very great and precious promises, so that through them (we) may participate in the divine nature and escape the corruption in the world caused by evil desires" (2 Pet. 1:3–4 NIV).

Numbers 23:19 says, "Does (God) speak and then not act? Does he promise and not fulfill?" (NIV) The Book of 1 Kings, in chapter 8 and verse 56 says, "Praise be to the LORD, who has given rest to his people . . . Not one word has failed of all the good promises he gave" (NIV).

The promise-anchored home is one in which we realize that our own human resources cannot create happiness in a home or sustain the momentum needed in marriage. We need a supply of grace found only in the reservoir of Scripture. We need specific promises from God for each passing moment, hour, day, and year. We need a lifeline from God for a lifetime of living. We need a pledge from our Lord for every crisis, a comforting word for every heartache, a guiding word for every decision, and a patient word for every provocation.

So we must search out those promises that meet every current need, even as God has sworn on the basis of His own honor to care for His children. He has promised good to His people.

For example, the Lord gives us general promises of blessings. Psalm 84:11 says, "For the LORD God is a sun and shield; the LORD will give grace and glory; no good thing will He withhold from those who walk uprightly." Psalm 23 says, "Surely goodness and mercy shall follow me all the days of my life." And Romans 8:32 says, "He who did not spare His own Son, but delivered Him up for us all, how shall He not with Him also freely give us all things?"

Then there are His specific blessings for our physical and financial needs. Jesus Himself said, "Do not worry, saying, 'What shall we eat?' or 'What shall we drink?' or 'What shall we wear?' For after all these things the Gentiles seek. For your heavenly Father knows that you need all these things. But seek first the kingdom of God and His righteousness, and all these things shall be added to you" (Matt. 6:31–33).

Third, the Lord promises to meet all our spiritual and emotional needs. Psalm 29:11 says, "The LORD will give strength to His people; the LORD will bless His people with peace."

Fourth, the Lord promises to guide us. Psalm 37:23 says, "The steps of a good man are ordered by the LORD, and He delights in his way."

Next, God promises to deliver us from trouble. Psalm 34:19 says, "A righteous (person) may have many troubles, but the LORD delivers him from them all" (NIV).

The Lord also promises to hear and answer our earnest prayers. Jesus said in the Upper Room Discourse, "If you abide in Me, and My words abide in you, you will ask what you desire, and it will be done for you."

The Lord even promises His constant forgiveness for all our faults and failures. In Isaiah 43:25, He declared, "I, even I, am He who blots out your transgressions for My own sake; and I will not remember your sins."

One of God's most precious promises is that of eternal life through Jesus Christ, for God even swears to deliver us from death. Jesus Himself avowed in John 11:25, "I am the resurrection and the life. He who believes in Me, though he may die, he shall live. And whoever lives and believes in Me shall never die."

Perhaps the greatest of all God's promises is that all-encompassing word in Romans 8:28 that all things will providentially work out for the good to those who love God and are called according to His purpose.

The promise I'd like to close with, however, isn't as well-known; yet it is an apt word for this hour. In His Word, the Lord promises to bless our Christ-centered homes in ways we can never fully imagine or appreciate. There's a wonderful little verse hidden away in the Book of Proverbs, and I commend it to you as a foundation for your home. Found in Proverbs 3:33, it simply says: "The LORD . . . blesses the home of the righteous" (NIV).

The Lord blesses the home of the righteous. The subject of the sentence is the Lord. He's the source and instigator of the promise. The verb is that all-pervasive word "bless" which encapsulates all the good things that God has ever or will ever lavish on those He loves. And the object of His blessing is the home of those found righteous in Christ. The Lord blesses the home of the righteousness.

May He bless your home. May He bless you and keep you and make
His face to shine upon you and give you peace—as He has promised.

Now I would ask you, _____ and _____,
to join hands for the exchanging of your vows.

_____ (man), will you repeat after me: As I take you,
_____, to be my wedded wife, I promise to love and
to cherish you always, to forsake all others for you, and to faithfully
serve you as we together serve our Lord Jesus Christ all the days of our
lives.

_____ (woman), will you repeat after me: As I take you,
_____, to be my wedded husband, I promise to love
and to cherish you always, to forsake all others for you, and to faithfully
serve you as we together serve our Lord Jesus Christ all the days of our
lives.

Then you are each given to the other as husband and wife in the permanent bonds of holy matrimony, to have and to hold, to love and to
cherish, in both weal and woe, in sickness and in health, in poverty
and wealth as long as you both shall live.

FUNERAL SERMON

Departures and Arrivals

Today we have gathered in memory of _____.

Personal Comments

Scripture: 2 Timothy 4:6: "The time of my departure is at hand."

Introduction: There are two sides to death when a Christian passes from this life. There is *this* side and *that* side. From this side, our brother (sister) is going. From that side, he (she) is coming. Our earthly perspective at this moment is the view from the point of departure. Paul referred to that in 2 Timothy 4:6 when he spoke of his departure, a word he used for his approaching death. Now, when something departs, it doesn't cease to exist. Sometimes in traveling overseas, the loud speaker instructs us to go to the departures lounge. It means the plane is about to take off, and we need to get to the gate. If you take a cruise, you will be instructed to go to the port of departure. That word implies travel, a trip, a transport. But if there is a departure, there must also be an arrival. When I take a trip by automobile, I kiss my spouse goodbye, drive to my destination, and I'm welcomed there by those I'm meeting. Our dear friend has departed, which means we're looking at the scene from the leaving-side; but if we could only see him (her) at the arrival side. Well, the Bible does give us some information, and on the authority of God's Word, I can describe to you three different welcomes he (she) is receiving.

1. **When Christians Arrive, They Are Welcomed by Angels.** In fact, the Bible teaches that angels are the conductors that transport us to our heavenly home. In Luke 16:22, Jesus said something very interesting about the death of the beggar Lazarus. In this life, Lazarus was disdained as riffraff. The dogs licked his sores, and he ate the garbage tossed away by others. But Lazarus loved the Lord, and when he died Jesus said he was "carried by the angels" to heaven (Luke 16:22). This is one of the most comforting verses in the Bible

about the process of dying. It means we'll never have to worry about making our way across the great divide. The angels will sweep us up, carry us through the skies, and deposit us safely at home. I believe angels gather around the bedside of dying saints to guard and transport their souls as they slip the bonds of earth and wing their flight to healthier climes.

2. **When Christians Arrive, They Are Welcomed by Christ.** Just as we can't wait to see Jesus, He can't wait to see us. When godly Stephen was being stoned to death for his faith, we read in Acts 7:56 that he "gazed into heaven and saw the glory of God, and Jesus standing at the right hand of God." Elsewhere in the New Testament, we read of Jesus being seated at the right hand of God. But as Stephen prepares to make the journey across the vale, Jesus stands to welcome Him.

3. **When Christians Arrive, They Are Welcomed by Friends from All the Ages.** In the passage in Luke 16 about Lazarus, we read that the angels carried him to "Abraham's bosom." That is, this poverty-lashed beggar suddenly found himself walking alongside Abraham and enjoying fellowship with the greatest hero of Jewish history. Another favorite Bible story tells us of the meeting Jesus enjoyed with Elijah and Moses atop the Mount of Transfiguration. Fellowship with the redeemed of all the ages is a heavenly reality. And that truth is reinforced by that wonderful passage about the Rapture and resurrection at the end of 1 Thessalonians 4. In this text, Paul told his friends not to grieve beyond measure for those who have fallen asleep in Jesus. Notice those two precious words in 1 Thessalonians 4:17: "with them." We will be raised and will be "with" one another. And then the words, "And thus we shall always be with the Lord." The old hymn says, "Friends will be there I have known long ago. Joy like a river around me will flow."

Conclusion: There are tears in our eyes today only because we're looking at our friend from the "departure" terminal rather than the "arrivals" lounge. But the Lord has given us the privilege and the responsibility of seeing things from a different perspective. He has given us glimpses into heaven. He has given us promises in His Word. And that makes all the difference. May the Lord comfort us with these words today.

FUNERAL SERMON

Suitable for the Death of a Child, Baby, or Pre-born Infant

Scripture: Matthew 18:14: "Even so it is not the will of your Father who is in heaven that one of these little ones should perish."

Introduction: I don't know how many little caskets I've buried through the years, or how many grieving parents I've tried to comfort. These things are very hard, among the hardest we face. I've never adjusted to it, and I know that we're in the presence today of a level of pain almost beyond bearing. But I do know this. I represent the God of all Comfort, and I have a book whose message is sufficient, even for times like this. The Bible says about Jesus Christ, that He does all things well. The Bible also promises that all things work together for good to those who love the Lord. Those two great truths, the first about the person of Christ and the second about the providence of God, apply to our hearts today. The Bible assures us that children go to heaven to be with the Lord. The Lord loves children and isn't willing for any of them to perish. Not one of them will be lost. Let me show you three Scriptures on this.

1. **"I Shall Go to Him"** (2 Sam. 12:16–23). When David said in verse 23: "I shall go to him, but he shall not return to me," he understood that he would see his baby again in heaven, that the child had gone to be with the Lord. His grief was great, but his joy came from anticipating the coming reunion.

2. **"She Is Not Dead But Sleeping"** (Mark 5:21–43). The mourners at the funeral of this little girl were wailing in grief, but that wasn't Jesus' perspective when He arrived on the scene. Christ looked at the little form lying there and said three remarkable things:

    A. **She is not dead!** Those words are for every mom, dad, or grandparent who has lost a little one. This child that miscarried, this child that was stillborn, this child that was aborted, this child that died of SIDS, this child who perished in the natural disaster—these children are not dead. This is Bible-speak. This is Jesus-talk.

B. . . . **but sleeping.** This little body is resting, and his (her) soul is with Jesus.

C. **Talitha, cumi . . . Little girl, I say to you, arise.** The miracle of this little girl's resurrection was a token of what He is going to do when He comes again, and the dead in Christ are raised first.

3. **It Is Well with the Child (2 Kin. 4:8–37).** In this passage, a woman's son dies, and in her grief she goes to see the prophet Elisha who asks her if all is well with her family and with her son. Before telling him specifically what had happened, she made a remarkable observation: "It is well." There is something about those words that have comforted thousands of heartbroken parents. It is well with the child.

Conclusion: Our earthly lifespan is brief at best, and very shortly we'll all be together in the Lord forever if we know Him as our Savior. We shall be with this child again. He (or she) is not dead, but sleeping. It is well with the child, for the Lord Jesus isn't willing that any of these little ones should perish. Wherefore comfort you yourselves with these words.

FUNERAL SERMON
The Mercy of God

Suitable for the Funeral of an Unbeliever

Today we have gathered in memory of _____.

Personal Comments

_____

Scripture: Psalm 136

_____

Introduction: The Bible teaches that God's ways are not our ways, and His thoughts are not our thoughts. "For as the heavens are higher than the earth, so are My ways higher than your ways, and My thoughts than your thoughts" (Is. 55:8–9). God's wisdom is infinite, and He possesses total knowledge. Our knowledge is faulty and limited, and I cannot tell you today about our friend's spiritual condition or eternal destination. But I can tell you several things that I know to be true on the basis of the Word of God.

1. **God Is a God of Mercy.** The word "mercy" occurs in the Bible 359 times—that's almost one time for every day of the year. There is one chapter in the Bible in which the word mercy occurs 26 times, almost one time for every day of the month. It's Psalm 136, which contains 26 verses, every one of which ends with the phrase, "For His mercy endures forever." Let me read some it for you: *O give thanks to the Lord, for He is good! For His mercy endures forever. Oh, give thanks to the God of gods! For His mercy endures forever. Oh, give thanks to the Lord of lords! For His mercy endures forever. To Him who alone does great wonders, for His mercy endures forever . . . .* (Read as much of this Psalm as you would like.) By the time we read through this Psalm in its entirety, we almost begin to feel tired of saying that one sentence over and over, until it dawns on us that we must never grow tired of the mercy of God. We can never hear about it too often or think about it too much. We need that mercy every day and every hour, and His mercy endures forever. So when I am tempted to feel troubled

as I do today, I just let that verse cycle over and over in my mind: *For His mercy endures forever.* It is of infinite comfort to us.

2. **Christ Is a Christ of Compassion.** The second thing we know is that Christ is a Christ of compassion. Listen to these Scriptures from the Gospels: *When He saw the multitudes, He was moved with compassion for them . . . . Jesus called His disciples to Himself and said, "I have compassion on the multitude . . . ." When the Lord saw her, He had compassion on her and said to her, "Do not weep . . . ." So Jesus stood still and called them, and said, "What do you want Me to do for you?" They said to Him, "Lord, that our eyes may be opened." So Jesus had compassion and touched their eyes . . . . Now a leper came to Him, imploring Him . . . Then Jesus, moved with compassion, stretched out His hand and touched him, and said to him, "I am willing; be cleansed"* (Matt. 9:36; Matt. 15:32; Luke 7:13; Matt. 20:32–34; Mark 1:40–41). There are many mysteries in life, but there are two great certainties—God's mercy and Christ's compassion. We must never underestimate our Lord.

3. **We Are Responsible for Our Own Souls.** But there is a third truth we can know, and I would be remiss if I neglected it. We are responsible for our own souls. We can't be responsible for the souls of others, but we do have a charge from God for ourselves. The Bible warns us not to neglect so great a salvation as Christ provided (Heb. 2:3). The entire teaching of Scripture is found in this. God created us, but we disobeyed His laws, violated His character, and rebelled against His authority in our lives. Because of our sinfulness, death fell upon the human race. But God Himself, in mercy and compassion, became the perfect sacrificial offering known as Jesus Christ, who died on Calvary's Cross in our stead, shedding His blood for our sins. He rose from the grave to give us forgiveness and eternal life. And He bids us come and follow Him. The Book of Romans teaches that all of us have sinned and have fallen short of the glory of God (Rom. 3:23). The wages of sin is death, but the gift of God is eternal life (Rom. 6:23), for God demonstrated His love toward us in that while we were yet sinners, Christ died for us (Rom. 5:8). And Romans 10 says: "If you confess with your mouth the Lord Jesus and believe in your heart that God has raised Him from the dead, you will be saved. For with the heart one believes

unto righteousness, and with the mouth confession is made unto salvation . . . For whoever calls on the name of the LORD shall be saved" (Rom. 10:9–10, 13). I wonder if someone here is willing to call on the Lord today.

Conclusion: Life is short and uncertain, as we've been reminded today, but God is a God of mercy and Christ is a Christ of compassion. We are responsible for our own decisions to follow the Lord Jesus, and perhaps today He is calling you to confess Him as Lord and believe in your heart that God has raised Him from the dead.

FUNERAL SERMON

Appropriate for an Unexpectedly Tragic Situation

Today we have come in honor and memory of _____.

Personal Comments

Scripture: John 13:7: What I am doing you do not understand now, but you will know after this.

Introduction: Our hearts are full of "Whys" today, for the taking of our brother (sister) seems so untimely and senseless. Friends and family are here, and there is so much love in this room. We're in the presence of praying people, and in the very presence of the Lord Himself who can comfort us, even in times like this. My habit throughout life is to seek comfort in the Word of God, and when I turn to the Bible today, I'm strengthened by three observations having to do with the past, the future, and the present.

1. **In the Past, We Find That Even the Heroes of Scripture Asked the Question "WHY?"** The writer of Psalm 42 prayed, "Why have You forgotten me?" (v. 9). Joshua cried, "Alas, Lord GOD, why have You brought this people over the Jordan at all—to deliver us into the hand of the Amorites?" (Josh. 7:7). In Judges 21:3, the Israelites cried, "O LORD God of Israel, why has this come to pass?" Job asked many "Why" questions, such as: "Why have You set me as Your target?" (Job 7:20). King David cried out to God, saying, "Why are You so far from helping me?" (Ps. 22:1). The people of Jeremiah's day asked, "Why does the LORD our God do all these things to us?" (Jer. 5:19); and Jeremiah himself prayed, "Why is my pain perpetual and my wound incurable?" (Jer. 15:18). Even our Lord Jesus Christ shouted into the darkness of Calvary's sky, saying, "My God, My God, why have You forsaken Me?" (Matt. 27:46). These saints of old had the same questions we have, and yet they didn't always receive immediate answers. It's not that the question "Why?" is

unanswerable. God possesses total knowledge, He has infinite wisdom, and He knows the answer to every question—even the hardest. But sometimes the answers take time to develop to where we can see them, like the pictures in an old photographer's darkroom. That leads me to my second observation from the Bible.

2. **In the Future, Our Questions Will All Be Answered.** The apostle Paul wrote in 1 Corinthians 13:12, "For now we see in a mirror, dimly, but then face to face. Now I know in part, but then I shall know just as I also am known." One day we'll have the capacity to understand, and we'll have all the answers we need. One of the most comforting things Jesus ever said was in John 13:7: "What I am doing you do not understand now, but you will know after this." Evangelist Vance Havner wrote in one of his books, "God marks across some of our days, 'Will Explain Later.'" The Bible speaks of a day for God's children when "God will wipe every tear from their eyes; there shall be no more death, nor sorrow, nor crying. There shall be no more pain" (Rev. 21:4). And, I might add, no more unanswered questions and no more "Whys?"

3. **In the Present, We Simply Have to Trust Him.** But we aren't living in the past anymore, and we aren't yet in the future. How do we cope today, and where do we turn? In the present, we simply have to trust Him. Someone observed that Christians don't live by explanations; they live by promises. Mark 3:37 assures us that Jesus does all things well, and Romans 8:28 promises that all things work together for good to those who know God and who are called according to His promise. We may not know *Why*, but we know *Who*. We have to turn our eyes upon Jesus and look full in His wonderful Word. We have to look unto Jesus, the Author and Finisher of our faith. That was the only answer given to Job, who lost his wealth, his health, and his seven children in a series of unparalleled disasters. His friends tried to comfort him, and they failed. He himself tried to reason through his problems, but found no conclusions. Then the Lord appeared to him out of a whirlwind, reminded him of who had made the cosmos, and said, in effect, "You've got to respect and fear and trust Me, even with these tragedies." And when Job did that, God worked it all for good in his life. The Bible says, "Trust in the LORD with all your heart and lean not on your own understanding. In all your ways acknowledge Him, and He shall direct your paths" (Prov. 3:5–6).

Conclusion: Maxwell Cornelius was born and raised in Pennsylvania where he became a brick mason. One day in an accident his leg was broken, and the doctors determined that it would have to be amputated. After the surgery, Cornelius was unable to continue his profession in the construction business, so he enrolled in college and the Lord called him into the ministry. Because of his wife's failing health, he moved to California where the weather was good for her, and there he built a large Presbyterian Church. But when an economic depression swept through the area, he was left with tremendous financial obligations— not only his own but those of the church as well. No sooner had he emerged from those difficulties, then his wife passed away. He preached the funeral himself, and he ended his remarks with a poem he had written, which later became a hymn, well-known in its day. The words say:

> *Not now, but in the coming years,*
> *It may be in the better land,*
> *We'll read the meaning of our tears,*
> *And there, some time, we'll understand.*

> *Then trust in God through all the days;*
> *Fear not, for He doth hold thy hand;*
> *Though dark thy way, still sing and praise,*
> *Some time, some time we'll understand.*

> *We'll catch the broken thread again,*
> *And finish what we here began;*
> *Heav'n will the mysteries explain,*
> *And then, ah then, we'll understand.*

> *We'll know why clouds instead of sun*
> *Were over many a cherished plan;*
> *Why song has ceased when scarce begun;*
> *'Tis there, some time, we'll understand.*

> *God knows the way, He holds the key,*
> *He guides us with unerring hand;*
> *Some time with tearless eyes we'll see;*
> *Yes, there, up there, we'll understand.*

Special Services Registry

The forms on the following pages are designed to be duplicated and used repeatedly as needed. Most copy machines will allow you to enlarge them to fill a full page if desired.

Sermons Preached

Date	Text	Title/Subject

Sermons Preached

Date	Text	Title/Subject

Sermons Preached

Date	Text	Title/Subject

Sermons Preached

Date	Text	Title/Subject

Sermons Preached

Date	Text	Title/Subject

Sermons Preached

Date	Text	Title/Subject

Sermons Preached

Date	Text	Title/Subject

Marriages Log

Date	Bride	Groom

Marriages Log

Date	Bride	Groom

Funerals Log

Date	Name of Deceased	Scripture Used

Funerals Log

Date	Name of Deceased	Scripture Used

Baptisms/Confirmations

Date	Name	Notes

Baptisms/Confirmations

Date	Name	Notes

Baby Dedication Registration

Infant's Name: _____

Significance of Given Names: _____

Date of Birth: _____

_____

Siblings: _____

_____

_____

_____

Maternal Grandparents: _____

Paternal Grandparents: _____

Life Verse: _____

Date of Dedication: _____

Baby Dedication Registration

Infant's Name: _____

Significance of Given Names: _____

Date of Birth: _____

_____

Siblings: _____

_____

_____

_____

Maternal Grandparents: _____

Paternal Grandparents: _____

Life Verse: _____

Date of Dedication: _____

Wedding Registration

Date of Wedding: _____

Location of Wedding: _____

Bride: _____

      Religious Affiliation: _____

      Bride's Parents: _____

Groom: _____

      Religious Affiliation: _____

      Groom's Parents: _____

Ceremony to Be Planned by Minister: _____ By Couple: _____

Other Minister(s) Assisting: _____

Maid/Matron of Honor: _____

Best Man: _____

Wedding Planner: _____

Date of Rehearsal: _____

Reception Open to All Wedding Guests: _____ By Invitation Only: _____

Location of Reception: _____

Wedding Photos to Be Taken: _____ During Ceremony

                         _____ After Ceremony

Other: _____

Date of Counseling: _____

Date of Registration: _____

Wedding Registration

Date of Wedding: _____

Location of Wedding: _____

Bride: _____

    Religious Affiliation: _____

    Bride's Parents: _____

Groom: _____

    Religious Affiliation: _____

    Groom's Parents: _____

Ceremony to Be Planned by Minister: _____ By Couple: _____

Other Minister(s) Assisting: _____

Maid/Matron of Honor: _____

Best Man: _____

Wedding Planner: _____

Date of Rehearsal: _____

Reception Open to All Wedding Guests: _____ By Invitation Only: _____

Location of Reception: _____

Wedding Photos to Be Taken: _____ During Ceremony

                             _____ After Ceremony

Other: _____

Date of Counseling: _____

Date of Registration: _____

Funeral Registration

Name of Deceased: _____

Age: _____

Religious Affiliation: _____

Survivors: _____

    Spouse: _____

    Parents: _____

    Children: _____

    Siblings: _____

    Grandchildren: _____

Date of Death: _____

Time and Place of Visitation: _____

Date of Funeral or Memorial Service: _____

Funeral Home Responsible: _____

Location of Funeral or Memorial Service: _____

Scripture Used: _____ Hymns Used: _____

Eulogy by: _____

Other Minister(s) Assisting: _____

Pallbearers: _____

_____

Date of Interment: _____ Place of Interment: _____

Graveside Service: _____   No _____

Funeral Registration

Name of Deceased: _____

Age: _____

Religious Affiliation: _____

Survivors: _____

    Spouse: _____

    Parents: _____

    Children: _____

    Siblings: _____

    Grandchildren: _____

Date of Death: _____

Time and Place of Visitation: _____

Date of Funeral or Memorial Service: _____

Funeral Home Responsible: _____

Location of Funeral or Memorial Service: _____

Scripture Used: _____ Hymns Used: _____

Eulogy by: _____

Other Minister(s) Assisting: _____

Pallbearers: _____

_____

Date of Interment: _____ Place of Interment: _____

Graveside Service: _____ No _____

Indices

Subject Index

Abortion, 22–24

Adversity, 91, 117, 126–128, 131, 153–155, 196–198, 326–328

Alleine, Joseph, 295–296

Anger, 16–18

Anxiety, 31–33, 41–42, 61–63

Attitude, 80, 267, 360–362

Backsliding, 21, 212–214, 256

Baptism, 181

Bible, 232

Brengle, Samuel Logan, 61–63, 96, 224–226

Bowles, Charles, 98–99

Christmas, 370–395

Clarke, Samuel, 40–43

Communion, 70–71

Cross, 69, 120–122

Deception/Dishonesty, 134–136, 311–313

Decision Making, 69

Discipleship, 187–189

Discouragement, 332

Easter, 106–111

Faith, 77, 82, 105, 131, 192, 196–198, 328

Father's Day, 187–192

Fear, 111

Fear of God, 25–27, 309

Forgiveness, God's, 34–36

Forgiving Others, 36

Foxe, John, 132–133

Funerals, 408–417

Generosity, 64

Gilmour, James, 46

Giving, 6, 29, 68, 96, 116, 157, 209, 222, 244, 287, 320–321, 392

Gospel, 13, 210, 223, 363–365

Grace, 349

Guidance, 205–207

Holiness, 61–63, 168, 217, 288

Holy Spirit, 39, 49, 163–165, 168, 399

Hospitality, 158, 198

Hymn Story, 110, 231

Jesus Christ, 53–55, 97, 245, 264, 268, 333–335, 339–341, 370–372, 375

Joy, 78–80, 179–181, 360–362

Judgment, 233–235, 238

Kindness, 64–66

Law, William, 303–304

Linkletter, Art, 258–261

Love, 256, 267, 322

Lull, Raymond, 353

Marriage, 44–46, 49, 59, 72–74, 174, 227–229, 400–407

Memory Techniques, 50–52

Mercy, 53–55

Missions, 118–119, 332, 353

Money, 297–299

Mother's Day, 144–146, 149, 344

Names of God, 21

New Year's Day, 2–7, 192

Newton, John, 185–186

Obedience, 217

Offering—see Giving

Palm Sunday, 100–102, 105

Parenting, 144–146

Patriotism, 160–162

Peace, 106–108

Penney, J. C., 319

Pentecost, 163–165

Persecution, 132–133, 275–276, 347–348

Prayer, 91, 232, 245, 274, 282, 301, 303–304, 352

Prayer, Answered, 42–43, 46, 106, 108

Preaching Techniques, 50–52, 175–178, 202–204, 258–261, 345–346

Prodigals, 316, 323–325

Promises, God's, 40–43, 149, 210–211, 338, 404–407

Prudentius, Aurelius Clemens, 14–15

Sanctity of Life, 22–24, 302

Satan, 92–94, 134, 277–279

Sexual Purity, 150–152, 354–356

Sickness, 83–85, 153

Sin, 212–214

Singles, 44–46, 49

Spiritual Warfare, 39

Stillness, 82

Thanksgiving, 359, 360–362

Tithing – see Giving

Tongue, 240–242

Trapp, Rosemarie, 246–250

Troubles and Trials – see Adversity

Vacations, 193–195

Veitch, William and Marion, 275–276

Weddings, 400–407

Wisdom, 25–27, 354–355

Work Ethic, 317–319

Worship, 82, 86–88

Wrath of God, 55

Scripture Index

Genesis 1, 359

Genesis 1—3, 30, 344

Genesis 2:4–25, 302

Genesis 4:1–8, 125

Genesis 4:1–24, 59–60

Genesis 24:1–27, 44–45

Genesis 24:26–67, 205–206

Genesis 25—48, 184

Exodus 40:43—Lev. 1:1, 218

Leviticus 1:1, 218–220

Leviticus 14, 77

Leviticus 19:33–34, 158–159

Deuteronomy 1:21, 332

Deuteronomy 4:27–31, 126–127

Joshua 14:12, 338

1 Samuel 25, 59

1 Kings 3, 394–395

1 Kings 3:1–3, 269–270

1 Kings 10:23—11:13, 394–395

1 Kings 11:4, 269–270

1 Chronicles 4:8–9, 174

Nehemiah 1:5–11, 274

Esther 2:1–23, 352

Esther 2:8–21, 352

Esther 4:14, 352

Job 19:1–29, 8–9

Psalm 27, 149

Psalm 46, 82

Psalm 62, 30

Psalm 62:8, 232

Psalm 73:1–28, 326–328

Psalm 84, 78–79

Psalm 100, 360–362

Psalm 101, 217

Psalm 103:3, 214

Psalm 106, 192

Psalm 119:38, 149

Psalm 136, 412–414

Psalm 139:14, 22–23

Proverbs 1:1–7, 25–26

Proverbs 2:6–11, 69

Proverbs 2:11–22, 354–355

Proverbs 3:1–8, 25–26

Proverbs 3:27–30, 64–65

Proverbs 8:1–33, 289–290

Proverbs 15:13–30, 267

Proverbs 16:9, 184

Isaiah 6:1–8, 288

Isaiah 26:13, 139–140

Isaiah 46:8–13, 70–71

Isaiah 60:16, 21

Amos 8:1–14, 233–234

Amos 8:8–14, 238

Matthew 1, 387

Matthew 1—2, 381

Matthew 1:18–25, 376–377

Matthew 2:1–12, 382–383

Matthew 2:9–12, 387

Matthew 5:1–12, 294

Matthew 5:6, 347–348

Matthew 6:9–13, 352

Matthew 11:20–22, 302

Matthew 11:28–30, 125

Matthew 18:14, 410

Matthew 21:1–11, 105

Matthew 26:17–25, 100–101

Matthew 27:4—28:2, 238

Matthew 28:1–15, 111

Matthew 28:16–20, 118–119, 332

Luke 1—2, 381

Luke 2:4–7, 382–383

Luke 2:8–20, 388–389

Luke 11:31, 370–371

Luke 13:1–8, 283–285

Luke 17:14, 77
Luke 18:9–14, 91
Luke 19:1–10, 169–171
Luke 23:34, 34–36
Luke 24:36–49, 106–107
John 1, 387
John 1:1, 393
John 1:1–16, 339–341
John 3:5–8, 49
John 3:16, 13, 363–365
John 4:19–24, 86–88
John 11:1–27, 196–198
John 13:7, 415–417
John 13:31–35, 256–257
John 15:1–11, 112–114, 117
John 15:11, 179–180
John 16:13, 168
John 19:28, 238
John 20, 110
Romans 1:16, 262–263
Romans 5:1–5, 387
Romans 6:23, 212–213
Romans 8:18–39, 131
Romans 8:28, 153–155
1 Corinthians 1:18–25, 69
1 Corinthians 1:18—2:5, 120–122
1 Corinthians 3, 158
1 Corinthians 6:1–9, 139
1 Corinthians 7:1–9, 49
1 Corinthians 7:10–16, 174
2 Corinthians 4:2, 311–312
2 Corinthians 11:14, 92
Galatians 5:17–18, 201
Galatians 5:22–23, 179–180
Galatians 6:1–5, 316
Ephesians 4:26–27, 16–17
Ephesians 4:28, 317–319
Ephesians 4:29, 240–241
Ephesians 5:3–14, 150–152

Ephesians 5:15–20, 163–165
Ephesians 5:25–29, 72–73
Philippians 1:9–10, 322
Colossians 1:15–16, 97
Colossians 1:17–20, 97–98
Colossians 2:6–7, 187–188
Colossians 3:1–4, 310
Colossians 3:12–14, 267–268
Colossians 3:15–17, 359
Colossians 3:17, 13
Colossians 3:19, 72
1 Timothy 3:6, 338
1 Timothy 4:6–10, 305–306
1 Timothy 6:3–19, 297–298
2 Timothy 1:1–7, 144–145
2 Timothy 1:7–14, 77
2 Timothy 2:8–9, 160–162
2 Timothy 3:1, 368
2 Timothy 4:6, 408–409
2 Timothy 4:7–8, 399
Titus 1:1–3, 201
Hebrews 1:1–3, 316
Hebrews 2:1–4, 256
Hebrews 2:17—3:1, 53–54
Hebrews 3, 288
Hebrews 4, 288
Hebrews 4:14, 245
Hebrews 6, 368–369
Hebrews 10, 310
Hebrews 10:1–18, 344
Hebrews 11, 7
Hebrews 11:4, 125
Hebrews 11:23–29, 192
Hebrews 12:1–3, 2–3
James 5:19–20, 21
1 Peter 1, 282
1 Peter 1:7, 105
1 Peter 3:1–7, 227–228
1 Peter 3:7, 72

1 Peter 5:8–10, 277–278

2 Peter 1:3–4, 210–211

1 John 1:1, 375

1 John 1:1–4, 333–335

1 John 1:1–8, 251–252

1 John 2:3–11, 217

1 John 2:21, 134–135

Revelation 22:20–21, 322